LOST VIRGINIA

LOST VIRGINIA

VANISHED ARCHITECTURE OF THE OLD DOMINION

BRYAN CLARK GREEN

CALDER LOTH

WILLIAM M. S. RASMUSSEN

HOWELL PRESS

Charlottesville, Virginia

Generous financial support for the exhibition and catalogue
Lost Virginia *has been provided by Nancy C. Baird.*

Designed by Carolyn Weary Brandt

Library of Congress Cataloging-in-Publication Data

Green, Bryan Clark, 1967-
    Lost Virginia : vanished architecture of the Old Dominion / Bryan Clark Green, Calder
Loth, William M.S. Rasmussen.
        p. cm.
    Published to coincide with a spring 2001 exhibition at the Virginia Historical Society featuring the images from the book.
    Includes bibliographical references and index.
    ISBN 1-57427-127-X (hc)
        1. Lost architecture--Virginia. I. Loth, Calder, 1943- II. Rasmussen, William M. S.
(William Meade Stith), 1946- III. Virginia Historical Society. IV. Title.

    NA730.V8 G74 2001
    720'.9755--dc21

                                                                2001016987

Printed in China

10 09 08 07 06 05 04 03 02 01   10 9 8 7 6 5 4 3 2 1

Published by Howell Press, Inc.
1713-2D Allied Lane
Charlottesville, VA 22903
(804) 977-4006
http://www.howellpress.com

CONTENTS

This volume and the exhibition that it documents are products of a collaborative effort undertaken by the Virginia Historical Society and its immediate neighbor, the Virginia Department of Historic Resources (DHR). As a private institution that collects, preserves, and interprets historical records and artifacts, the Society presents in its museum galleries a program of changing exhibitions; this book was created to serve as the catalogue for one such show, *Lost Virginia: Vanished Architecture of the Old Dominion*, which runs 27 January through 20 May 2001. The Virginia Department of Historic Resources, a state agency, is charged with promoting the preservation of buildings and sites that have historic significance or are closely related to the values upon which the commonwealth and nation were founded. One effective tool used by the DHR to raise public awareness of the commonwealth's architectural legacy is its register book, which identifies and celebrates some eighteen hundred surviving historic resources. The *Lost Virginia* exhibition and book complement *The Virginia Landmarks Register* by identifying that part of the state's legacy that has vanished and by pointing out the vulnerability of architecture. *Lost Virginia* reminds us of the awesome responsibility to preserve significant buildings and sites, an obligation that we all share.

The Virginia Historical Society and the Virginia Department of Historic Resources routinely collaborate to promote the appreciation of history. The DHR displays a portion of its extraordinary archaeological collection in the society's permanent exhibition *The Story of Virginia*. The DHR will soon open its own exhibition gallery within the Society's museum. In the *Lost Virginia* project both institutions have contributed the expertise of their staffs and have pooled the resources of their libraries and photograph collections. We thank the curators and authors of *Lost Virginia*, William M. S. Rasmussen and Bryan Clark Green at the society and Calder Loth at DHR, for conceiving and putting together so important an exhibition and catalogue. This subject has long needed treatment. Books about the lost architecture of other regions, such as New York City and London, have existed for decades; *Lost Virginia* is the first comprehensive look at the buildings that have vanished from the landscape of the commonwealth.

Because it has engaged the skills of thirty-five contributors,

Lost Virginia stands as evidence of the Society's role as "The Center for Virginia History." The exhibition's curators have reached far beyond the walls of the complex that houses the Society and DHR to engage prominent architectural historians throughout the commonwealth to research and write entries for this volume. The list of contributors to this book carries the names of scholars resident in Roanoke, Lexington, Danville, Charlottesville, Orange County, Alexandria, Washington, DC, Richmond, Petersburg, Williamsburg, and Norfolk-Portsmouth. *Lost Virginia* is an ambitious project that succeeds through the efforts of many.

Virginia's important history is a legacy to be shared with all Americans. Here the English settlement of the continent began. Here many of the founding fathers lived and eight presidents were born. Here the first Africans set foot in English America. Here Civil War campaigns were fought. The compilation of images and accounts in *Lost Virginia* provides readers with a unique window into that past. As the authors demonstrate, when we review the lost architecture of the commonwealth we are better informed about those who came before us; we find new evidence of what has been achieved in the region and of how life was lived here. The pages that follow show remarkable buildings, including handsome colonial mansions, imposing classical courthouses, towering steepled churches, giant flour mills, and extravagant urban and resort hotels, as well as humble cottages and outbuildings. These structures are part of our cultural heritage, and they should not be forgotten.

While one-third of the buildings pictured in this book were lost to fire, some three-fifths were intentionally demolished. Following the establishment in 1966 of the Virginia Historic Landmarks Commission, which in 1989 became the Virginia Department of Historic Resources, the losses caused by demolition have lessened dramatically, though not entirely. We hope that the *Lost Virginia* exhibition and book will contribute to the public will to preserve the best parts of our architectural environment so that future generations can learn the past from actual historic buildings rather than from photographs of what is vanished.

Charles F. Bryan, Jr.
Director
Virginia Historical Society

H. Alexander Wise, Jr.
Director
Virginia Department of Historic Resources

ACKNOWLEDGMENTS

This project is first and foremost a collaborative effort. Without the assistance of thirty-two scholars who contributed entries (and whose names are listed on pages xxiv–xxv), this volume would have given less substantial treatment to the subject of Virginia's lost architecture. We thank these colleagues for their major contributions. We also want to acknowledge our debt to the many historians and preservationists who laid the foundations on which this project is built, and we thank many other individuals who contributed advice and encouragement.

The *Lost Virginia* project is one that two of the principal authors have discussed for more than a few years. In 1998, when Bryan Green joined the staff of the Virginia Historical Society, this ambitious undertaking came within reach. Serious research for the exhibition and book began when Dr. James Kelly at the Society encouraged us to proceed; Jim deserves the credit for moving us from talk to action.

Others at the Virginia Historical Society have earned our thanks. Dr. Nelson D. Lankford edited this book. E. Lee Shepard, Robert F. Strohm, Frances Pollard, Janet Schwarz, and Christa LaPrade shared their knowledge of relevant manuscripts and books in the Society's collection. In the Reading Room, Tom Illmenensee and Michelle McClintick pulled many books for us. Ron Jennings photographed many of the images in this book, making the most of originals that were faded and indistinct. Dale Kostelny and Drew Gladwell installed the exhibition. Christine O'Malley, a graduate student at the University of Virginia, was the first intern to work on this project, when it was still an idea taking shape. She was followed by Virginia Commonwealth University work-study student Lisa Huber and museum assistant Stephanie Jacobe; Stephanie began as a volunteer on the project and provided invaluable assistance in organizing the many files and photographs that accrued. We especially thank the Society's director, Charles F. Bryan, Jr., for his unwavering support of this project and his confidence in us.

At the Virginia Department of Historic Resources, we thank Director H. Alexander Wise, Jr., for his equally unswerving commitment to *Lost Virginia.* Kathleen Kilpatrick, Deputy Director, also provided needed support. Suzanne Durham and Harry Hubbard, the department's archivists, provided research assistance.

We also have been aided by staff at other institutions. We particularly want to thank Barnabas B. Baker, a volunteer at Portsmouth Public Library; Chandler Battaile of Richmond; Jennifer Bean and her colleagues Gen Pelot and Martha Rowe at the Museum of Early Southern Decorative Arts in Winston-Salem, North Carolina; Shirley Belkowitz, Temple Beth Ahabah, Richmond; Charles Brownell, Virginia Commonwealth University; Louise Brownell, registrar at the Maryland Historical Society; Al Chambers, architectural historian in Washington, DC, and expert on Lynchburg architecture; Mike Cobb, curator of Hampton City Museums; David Coffey, Virginia Military Institute; Brian Conley, Fairfax County Public Library; Charles Cooper, Virginia Beach; Patty Cooke, Louisa County Historical Society; Sam Daniel, Prints and Photographs Division, Library of Congress; Jim Epstein, Drawings and Archives, Avery Architectural and Fine Arts Library, Columbia University; Cathy Grosfills, Visual Resources Department, John D. Rockefeller Library, Colonial Williamsburg Foundation; Elizabeth M. Gushee and Audrey C. Johnson, Picture Collection, Library of Virginia; Brenda Gwynn, Director, Smyth County Museum; Peggy Haile, city historian, Norfolk; Mary Ruffin Hanbury, Virginia Department of Historic Resources; Julian Davis Hudson, Director, Prestwould Foundation; Delos Hughes, Washington and Lee University; Tamara Kennelly, University Library Special Collections, Virginia Tech; Lisa McCowan, Special Collections Assistant, Leyburn Library, Washington and Lee University; Henry McGill, Richmond, for photographs from his personal collection; Stephen Mansfield, Virginia Wesleyan College; William Martin, Director of the Valentine Museum, for making the Cook Collection of photographs available to us; T. Michael Miller, Research Historian, Office of Historic Alexandria; Pauline Page, microphotographer, University of Virginia; Isabelle Parker, Collections Department, Mount Vernon; Jim Palmer, archivist, Arlington Historical Society; John and Margaret Peters of Richmond; Donald Pfanz, National Park Service, Fredericksburg; Susan Pillow, Jones Memorial Library, Lynchburg; Dennis J. Pogue, Director of Restoration, Mount Vernon; Selden Richardson, Library of Virginia; Teresa Roane, Director of Library and Photographic Services at the Valentine Museum, for her knowledge of Virginia photography and great generosity in sharing it; Jeff

Rodgers, Virginia Department of Transportation; Jeanne Solensky, Downs Collection, Winterthur Museum; Suzanne Savery, Petersburg Museum; Katherine Smith, librarian-curator, Edgar Allan Poe Museum, Richmond; Katie Smith, Bath County Historical Society; Jennifer Tolpa, Massachusetts Historical Society; Dulaney Ward, City of Petersburg; Regina West, Special Collections Department, Alderman Library, University of Virginia; Richard Guy Wilson and K. Edward Lay, University of Virginia; Mrs. Calvin P. Wright, Alleghany Historical Society; Mrs. Wesley Wright, Valentine Museum trustee; and Jack Zehmer, Virginia Department of Historic Resources.

At Howell Press, we wish to thank Ross Howell for his interest in this book and Carolyn Brandt for her design of it.

Bryan Clark Green
Calder Loth
William M. S. Rasmussen

Architecture is a measure of human aspiration and achievement. But if buildings are to be read in that fashion, those that are now lost must be considered along with those that still stand; only then do we see the full landscape of a region. Literally hundreds of Virginia buildings of architectural or historical importance and interest are now lost. Many have been demolished, some have been replaced by larger, more functional structures, and a number have burned. Some even were abandoned and lost to neglect as populations and needs have shifted. The consequence is that significant evidence of history in Virginia has vanished from the Earth, and perhaps inevitably, this evidence has been at least partly forgotten. Although exhibitions and publications about the lost architecture of other regions have appeared, no effort has previously been made to document and reconstruct the appearance of the Virginia landscape of earlier times, when the nation's destiny and history often were intimately tied to this setting. *Lost Virginia* seeks to recover, at least in a gallery setting and on paper, this lost architectural heritage by presenting a sampling of it grouped in categories of domestic, civic, religious, and commercial buildings. While this evidence may appeal as nostalgia, its greater value is to revise incomplete views about architecture in Virginia and in turn about patterns of life in the region.

Significant Buildings That Are Lost

The lost buildings examined in this study are either significant themselves or representative of significant architectural trends that developed in the commonwealth following the first English settlement. The losses have been great, as is illustrated by the sheer quantity of photographs in this book. To magnify the point, it is perhaps helpful here to offer an overview of several dozen key buildings that are lost.

We can start by looking at some of the earliest buildings in the Virginia colony that aspired to sophisticated design. It is remarkable that we know as much about them as we do, because they vanished long ago. Green Spring, the rambling mansion built in James City County in the mid-1600s by the governor, Sir William Berkeley, was certainly exceptional for its time and place. Conceived at least in part to set a cultural ex-

Figure 1. The Capitol in Williamsburg, detail of the *Bodleian Plate*, a copperplate engraving, ca. 1732–47, formerly owned by the Bodleian Library, Oxford. (Colonial Williamsburg Foundation)

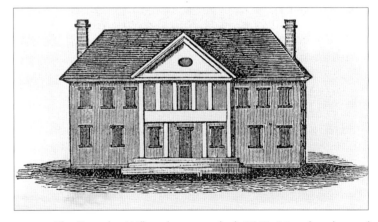

Figure 2. The Capitol in Williamsburg, as rebuilt 1749–56 and as depicted in Henry Howe, *Historical Collections of Virginia*, 1845. (Virginia Historical Society)

ample for Virginians to emulate, it disappeared not long after B. Henry Latrobe sketched it in 1796 and thereby left us a record. Fairfield, an unusually large and elaborate mansion in Gloucester County built by Lewis Burwell in the 1690s, was lost to fire in 1899. Lancaster County's Corotoman, which burned in 1729, was the home of the wealthiest Virginian of his era, Robert "King" Carter. Also gone is the H-shaped Williamsburg Capitol of 1699–1705 (fig. 1, burned 1747), which was conceived to be an impressive edifice in the Anglo-Dutch tradition of town halls, guildhalls, and market houses of England. It was rebuilt after the

1747 fire with a portico (fig. 2), only to burn again in 1832. Thomas Jefferson was critical of the Doric and Ionic details of this second capitol but considered it "the most pleasing piece of architecture we have."[1] (The first building was reconstructed from 1928 to 1934 by the Colonial Williamsburg Foundation.[2]) The colonial governor's residence in the new capital, built from 1706 to 1721, was so grand for early Virginia that contemporaries referred to it as a "palace." (It burned in 1781 and, like the Capitol, has been reconstructed.) Germanna, built in Orange County in the 1720s by retired governor Alexander Spotswood and burned in the 1740s, was called by William Byrd II an "Enchanted Castle." From the written record and the fieldwork of archaeologists, it is known to have been a massive brick and stone dwelling, two stories high and eighty feet long, elegantly furnished, and one of the largest and finest residences constructed in the central Virginia Piedmont during the entire century.

Virginia's famed Georgian mansions—the ones that are still standing—are appreciated by modern tourists, and for more than a century they have inspired Colonial Revival architects nationwide. These, however, are but part of a larger group that was built in this style in the colony. Rosewell, erected in Gloucester County circa 1721–41, was the grandest and most lavishly designed house in the Virginia colony and one of the largest structures built in colonial America. Belvoir (ca. 1735), residence of the English-born Lord Fairfax, who gave his name to the county in which it sat, was significant for its differences; the floor plan of the house was more English than colonial, and the rooms were filled with fine English furniture and fabrics. Cleve (ca. 1746) in King George County and Peckatone (ca. 1750) in Westmoreland County were imposing and sophisticated early Georgian designs, similar in both plan and elevation to extant Carter's Grove in James City County. Nomini Hall (ca. 1772) in Westmoreland County was large; the house and its support buildings were a measure of gentry aspirations in the colony and of the extraordinary wealth of the owner, Robert Carter III. A host of smaller, brick Georgian buildings, such as Bull Hill (mid-18th century) in Hopewell, are also presented in this study as accomplished designs that warrant remembering. Mannsfield (ca. 1770s) in Spotsylvania County was a classic example of the five-part Palladian mansion that epitomized mid-Georgian design in America; it is forgotten today because it was shelled into ruins during the Civil War, and only dim photographs of the broken walls record its appearance. Ravensworth (ca. 1796) in Fairfax County, which perpetuated mid-Georgian principles of design beyond the colonial period, should be val-ued in the same way.

As many as three hundred Anglican churches may have been erected in Virginia during colonial times, because the Anglican Church was the government-established religion. All but some fifty of those buildings are now gone; most vanished in the years following the 1784 act disestablishing the Anglican Church. An example like Eastern Shore Chapel in Virginia Beach (1755) proves that these could be significant because of the quality of their understated Georgian design.

As to lost 19th-century Virginia buildings as important as the 18th-century ones just cited, the numbers are comparable. For example, Barboursville (1817–22) in Orange County was the home of a governor, James Barbour, and was designed, at least in its basics, by Thomas Jefferson; it was built by several of the president's workmen. Kinloch (1847–48) in Essex County was a Greek Revival structure of remarkable refinement designed by an accomplished urban architect, Robert Cary Long, Jr., of Baltimore. The Lodge (or Elk Hill, 1851–52) in Amelia County was a Tudor-Stuart manor house; it was the design of New York architect A. J. Davis. Mount Erin (or Cameron Castle, ca. 1815 and later) in Petersburg can be cited as a second representative of what was a group of adventuresome and exotic 19th-century designs; buildings of this type were easily forgotten once they were lost and when Victorian styles went out of taste. End-of-the-century mansions of extravagant size, like Nydrie (1889) in Albemarle County, a kind of Scottish baronial castle with fifty rooms, and Mount Athos (1899–1900) in Orange County, a summer home that was furnished in florid Gilded Age taste, were highly successful designs.

A list of lost 19th-century civic architecture that holds exceptional importance would start with B. Henry Latrobe's Virginia State Penitentiary (1797–1806) in Richmond, a building that made a significant statement about rationalized and humanitarian penology and about how design should express the character or nature of a building. Thomas Jefferson's Rotunda (1817 and later) was the centerpiece of the University of Virginia, a complex that even today is ranked among the most accomplished schemes for an academic community. Stanford White rebuilt the Rotunda after the great fire of 1895 that gutted it, yet White's interior was removed between 1973 and 1976 for a reconstruction of Jefferson's design; the original fabric of both great architects is now gone. Other early buildings that stood as important evidence of how classical architecture was adapted to civic uses in new ways in a new republic were Robert Mills's Richmond City Hall (1816–18), his Alexandria Courthouse (1838), and his Annex to the Rotunda at the University of Virginia (1850–53). It is remarkable that the early mental hospital, Eastern Lunatic Asylum (expanded in the middle decades of the 19th century) in Williamsburg, is little known today, because its campus displayed both classical and medieval-style buildings worthy of note. The first public institution in America created solely for the care of the mentally ill, the asylum—like Latrobe's penitentiary—was a beacon of enlightened humanitarianism. As to 19th-century religious structures that are lost, a surprising number of churches and synagogues of distinction are gone. Two important Classical Revival examples are Thomas U. Walter's Second Baptist Church in Richmond (1840–42) and Levi Swain's Christ Episcopal Church in Norfolk (1828), both abandoned by their congregations and later demolished.

The list of lost 19th-century commercial buildings of special importance includes the giant flour mills of Richmond; these were highly visible evidence of the industrialization of the 1850s that was radically changing the traditional image of the Old South as a rural plantation society frozen in time. The Gallego, Haxall, and Dunlop mills signaled progress and were among the largest structures then standing in America. Also almost forgotten today are significant hotels, such as the Union (1817), which introduced to Richmond high-style Classical Revival architecture, and the city's Exchange Hotel (1840–41), designed by the nation's leading architect in the genre, Isaiah Rogers, and celebrated as one of the great buildings of its time. Some of the Victorian resorts, like the Allegheny Hotel (1890–91) in Goshen, were more than ordinary examples of the romantic eclectic architecture of the period that was inspired by European traditions; these resorts were as impressive as any built in America and typically were the work of out-of-state designers.

Charles Dickens visited the Exchange Hotel, and Edgar Allan Poe gave a public reading there of his poem "The Raven." Such anecdotes tell about the prominence of that hotel. Other lost Virginia buildings warrant re-creation, on paper, less for their architectural merit than because important historical figures lived in them or significant episodes of history unfolded within their walls. Those episodes are tied to important American history, particularly that of the Revolutionary era, the early Republic, and the Civil War. George Washington's remarkable multisided barn at Mount Vernon (ca. 1795), a building of his own design, is lost (it has been reconstructed, but on a different site). So is Martha Washington's childhood residence in New Kent County, Chestnut Grove (ca. 1735–50), and in the same county the first White House (before 1709), where she married

the future president. Only three birthplaces of Virginia's eight presidents remain standing: Berkeley (William Henry Harrison), Greenway (John Tyler), and the Woodrow Wilson Birthplace. Of the five presidential birthplaces that have disappeared, at least the appearance of one, that of James Monroe, is known, through a contemporary print; the fifth president of the United States was born in 1758 in a modest wood-frame house in Westmoreland County. Patrick Henry's birthplace of Studley (early 18th century, Hanover County) and his homes of Salisbury (ca. 1763, Chesterfield County) and Red Hill (late 18th century, Charlotte County) are gone. (Red Hill has been reconstructed.) Little remains standing at Menokin (ca. 1768–78, Richmond County), the plantation of a signer of the Declaration of Independence, Francis Lightfoot Lee. Gone is the original, small frame house (ca. 1810) at the tract in Charlotte County from which John Randolph of Roanoke took his name. The *Southern Literary Messenger* Building (1813) in Richmond, where Edgar Allan Poe served as editor from 1835 to 1837, was long ago taken down. Oakland (1812), the family plantation in Hanover County of the Virginia author and diplomat Thomas Nelson Page, burned. Richmond's Libby Prison, which became notorious during the Civil War because it housed some thirty thousand Union prisoners in a dirty and unhealthful environment, was later carted off to Chicago to serve as a visitor attraction, only to be demolished there. The Appomattox County Courthouse (1846) is gone; this was closed on Palm Sunday 1865, when Robert E. Lee surrendered to Ulysses S. Grant inside Wilmer McLean's farmhouse across the street, thereby ending the Civil War. The Richmond residence of renowned Union spy Elizabeth Van Lew (Adams–Van Lew house, 1802 to ca. 1836) inspired no local preservation movement to save it. Buildings closely associated with African-American history have been allowed to disappear. One was the Alexandria Slave Pens (ca. 1828), a site of suffering for thousands of slaves who passed through the place on their way to the deep South. Another was the St. Luke Penny Savings Bank (1909) in Richmond, which stood for more than half a century as an example of African-American progress because it was financed, designed, built, and operated by African-Americans. Also there was Richmond's True Reformers Hall (1891–95), the meeting place of an organization that endorsed African-American self-reliance and that W. E. B. DuBois called "probably the most remarkable Negro Society in the Country."

A number of buildings in Virginia that were designed by major American architects are lost. The group by Thomas Jefferson includes not only the Rotunda (1817–26) at the Uni-

Figure 3. Jamestown in the early 20th century. (Virginia Historical Society)

versity of Virginia but also the Anatomical Theatre (1826–27) there, the only building designed for the University by the Sage of Monticello but not built during his lifetime. In addition to the Orange County plantation house of Governor James Barbour called Barboursville, Jefferson's domestic work included (the first) Edgehill (ca. 1798), the Albemarle County home of his daughter Martha Randolph. His Buckingham and Botetourt County courthouses are lost. Jefferson advised on the design of the now lost Moldavia (begun 1798, Richmond), where Edgar Allan Poe lived briefly as a teenager. Master builders who were trained by the third US president erected Jeffersonian structures, such as Christ Episcopal Church (1824–26) and the Carr house (ca. 1830), both in Charlottesville, that are gone. Already mentioned are buildings in Richmond, Alexandria, and Charlottesville by Robert Mills, who studied architecture with Latrobe and Jefferson and later became a kind of "court architect" to the Andrew Jackson administration. Elk Hill also has been mentioned, as an important design by A. J. Davis, the nation's premier practitioner of mid-century romantic styles; his Williamson house (1852), part of the Gothic complex at Virginia Military Institute, is also gone. In addition to the Exchange Hotel in Richmond, Isaiah Rogers also was the architect of the classical jewel there that was the Exchange Bank (1841), which was lost in the city's evacuation fire of 1865. Ammi B. Young, the first supervising architect for the Treasury Department, produced the Alexandria Post Office and Customhouse (1856–58). A young John McArthur, Jr., of Philadelphia, later the designer of the landmark city hall there, conceived

First Presbyterian (1852–53), a richly ornamented church overlooking Richmond's Capitol Square that contemporaries described as Byzantine in style. To mention one final familiar name, Frank Lloyd Wright designed the long-vanished Larkin Company Pavilion (1906–7) for the Jamestown Tercentennial, which was held in Norfolk.

Towns have disappeared from the Virginia landscape. The first to be lost was America's first permanent English settlement. Jamestown was a sprawling village that was hastily and inconsistently built (fig. 3). Most of the buildings there were small and simple one-and-a-half-story structures that burned when Nathaniel Bacon's followers set fire to the town in 1676. Too little is known today about the architecture of Jamestown because the landscape was scavenged at an early date, without the care that would have been given by today's archaeologists. As to later towns that disappeared because of economic failure, any number could be cited here. One was Warren, in Albemarle County; it developed around Mount Warren (ca. 1780), the home of Wilson Cary Nicholas, and Nicholas's facilities for shipping wheat. Today only a few houses remain.

Whole blocks of cities have disappeared as communities have evolved. For example, the McKee block (19th century, fig. 4) in Charlottesville, part of the area around Court Square that once was a primary commercial district, held at different times a wide variety of stores and shops. These included dry goods stores, a hatter's shop, a post office, a tailor shop, a hotel, a jewelry store, a grocery, a bank, and a printing shop. One of the buildings was a frame house moved to the site from the nearby

Figure 4. The McKee block in Charlottesville, before 1921. (Special Collections Department, University Archives, University of Virginia Library)

Figure 5. Church Street, between Eighth and Tenth Streets, Lynchburg, 1885. (National Archives)

Figure 6. East Market, Norfolk, 1870s. (Valentine Museum)

town of Milton. The entire block was razed before 1921 to create a park for an equestrian statue of Thomas Jonathan "Stonewall" Jackson.[3] A block in Lynchburg that is lost is Church Street between Eighth and Tenth Streets, recorded in an 1885 photograph that was taken to show construction progress on the United States Court House and Post Office, whose foundation appears in the foreground (fig. 5). Across well-named Church Street, from left to right, were the Methodist Protestant Church (1829), with its modest steeple, the Greek Revival First Baptist Church (1850s), and the Gothic Revival Second Presbyterian Church (1851–52). Mason's Hall (1846–48) stood be-

tween the Baptist and Presbyterian churches. All are now gone, the last casualty being Mason's Hall, which burned in 1999 in a conflagration that also destroyed a letter George Washington had written to the fraternity soon after it organized in 1793.

Figure 7. 1200 block of East Broad Street, Richmond, site of the Medical College of Virginia; Monumental Church is visible at far right. (Valentine Museum)

The Court House and Post Office, barely begun in 1885, was replaced by a new building on the same site in 1909.[4] Innumerable blocks in Norfolk have been lost, none more picturesque than those around East Market (fig. 6), which emerged as early as the 1680s. With the end of ferry service to Berkeley and Portsmouth in the 1950s, activity slowed there; the whole area was redeveloped in the 1960s.[5]

Entire blocks, such as the 1200 block of East Broad Street (fig. 7), are gone from the landscape of Richmond, which initially was a city of houses and churches, as well as of businesses at the waterfront. Early Richmonders, if they could come back today, would little recognize the downtown area, now a clutter of concrete office buildings and shops around a few surviving churches. The single greatest destructive force in the history of Richmond's cityscape was the evacuation fire of April 1865, which created a large burned district that was immediately recorded by such Union photographers as Andrew Russell (fig. 8). As mentioned above, among the losses were Isaiah Rogers's Exchange Bank. Others lost in the fire and reconstructed in this study are the Gallego complex of flour mills, the Italianate

Kent, Paine and Company Headquarters (ca. 1858), and one church, United Presbyterian at Franklin and Eighth Streets. The last was rebuilt with contributions from across the nation as Grace Street Presbyterian Church (1872). To cite one loss in the rebuilt, postwar city, the Second Empire buildings at Eighth and Main Streets in Richmond, which were known collectively as the Pace Office Block (fig. 9), were gutted by fire circa 1900.[6]

How Virginia Buildings Have Been Lost

"It is sad to see an ancient abode of so much refinement, elegance, and hospitality swept away," wrote a reporter for the Lynchburg *Daily Virginian* in 1876 about the burning of Mount Athos (ca. 1800) in Campbell County. No doubt the same sentiments were expressed when Barboursville was destroyed by fire in 1884 on Christmas Day. When a building was not intentionally removed, fire generally was what destroyed it. Fully one-third of the examples surveyed in this book, some six dozen buildings, were burned. Half of those losses occurred in

Figure 8. Richmond in April 1865, as photographed by Andrew J. Russell. (Virginia Historical Society)

Figure 9. Pace Office Block, Richmond, early 20th century. (Valentine Museum)

the early 20th century, when heating and electrical systems were increasingly available and less than reliable; perhaps poor heating as well as primitive wiring systems contributed to the upsurge of fires at that time.

In 1729 the destruction of Corotoman was reported in the *Maryland Gazette* as follows: "The fine large house of Col. Carter on Rappahannock was also burnt lately. [The other was Mount Pleasant, Thomas Lee's house.] The particulars of this loss we cannot give you but we are informed that it is very great." The fire at Corotoman is representative of most in that we have no record as to what precisely caused it. Most early fires probably originated in chimneys that were either poorly designed or in disrepair. The historian Robert Lancaster would blame such a catastrophe on "a mouse and a match," as he did the loss in 1900 of Oakland (built after 1788) in Cumberland County. But in some instances we know more. In 1975, Caserta (ca. 1840, Northampton County) was struck by lightning and burned to the ground only five years after it had been listed on the Virginia Landmarks Register and the National Register of Historic Places. In 1990, Fort Rhodes (built after ca. 1770, Page County) also was struck by lightning and burned. How many earlier houses, one wonders, were so lost? At least one type of building was particularly susceptible to fire; this was the gristmill, because of the volatility of flour dust. The large mills in Richmond owned by the Gallego, Haxall, and Dunlop companies burned repeatedly during the 19th century. Byrd Mill (1740, Louisa County) had somehow survived nearly two and a half centuries of continuous operation when it burned in 1968. An occasional building has been destroyed by arson, such as the 1886 Pace Memorial Methodist Church in Richmond, in 1966, and Sea View (ca. 1762) in Accomack County, in 1974.

Fire was a frequent threat in early Virginia. The Ambler house in Jamestown survived one fire in 1862 only to be destroyed by a second blaze thirty-three years later. The buildings at Eastern Lunatic Asylum fell victim to fires in 1876, 1885, and 1902. When the Surry County courthouse (1907) burned in 1922, it became the fourth courthouse there lost to fire. The Mecklenburg Hotel and Sanitorium (1903, Chase City) operated for only six years before the principal building was lost to flames. Fires remain a threat to buildings in the modern era. The Peacock Ballroom (1906) in Virginia Beach burned in 1955. Most recently, in the summer of 2000, Thomas U. Walter's Greek Revival Presbyterian Church in Lexington (1845) was gutted by fire, a casualty of workmen using heat for paint removal.

In a few exceptional instances, such fires were not catastrophic, at least to some of the parties involved. Liberty Hall (1793) in Lexington was insured in 1802 for $3,333.34. This was a timely move, for in January 1803 the roof caught fire, and as the *Richmond Recorder* reported, "the flames had got to such an extent that all exertions to extinguish them proved fruitless."[7] The fire of 1895 that consumed Thomas Jefferson's University of Virginia Rotunda and Robert Mills's Annex to it began in the latter building; it reportedly originated from a spark in the electric line to a trolley car. The Annex was never a popular architectural work, but the loss of the Rotunda was a catastrophe.

Generally, the losses caused by fire were great. For example, in 1901 a large complex at the Homestead (ca. 1848, 1890s, Bath County) was leveled by fire. In 1909, when Grove Hill (ca. 1800–1804, Botetourt County) burned, the Roanoke Valley lost its best early mansion. In 1926 Ravensworth (ca. 1796–1800) housed many of the Washington-Custis family portraits that had descended to George Washington Parke Custis; seventeen of those were lost when fire leveled the house. In 1933 a blaze at Dover (1845, Goochland County) destroyed one of the more sumptuous, classical interiors of the period.

More Virginia buildings have been lost to demolition than fire. Some three-fifths of the examples surveyed in our study, more than 120 buildings, were demolished; nine-tenths of that group were removed in the 20th century. Nearly as many were razed in the third quarter of the 20th century as were taken down in the first fifty years. In more recent decades, however, preservation efforts have slowed the destruction.

The buildings were demolished for various reasons. Many houses were razed when neighborhoods shifted in composition from residential to commercial. Any number of examples could be cited here. The town of Waynesboro was laid out in a linear fashion, with houses like that of the Withrow family (ca. 1826) on the front edges of lots; by 1955 the area had become predominantly commercial, and the Withrow House was demolished to make way for a five-and-dime. Rose Hall (1830) would have been Waynesboro's foremost heritage site had it not been removed in 1963 to make room for what is now an aging shopping center. In 1982, as Harrisonburg's commercial downtown expanded into formerly residential areas, the site of the Morrison house (1824) was given to parking spaces for a local seed company. About 1961 the site of the Shelton-Burton house (1884) in Danville became a parking lot for a bank that had been built in a changed neighborhood. In Richmond, the Alexander McRae house was advertised for sale in 1820 as ideally located for any "genteel family," yet almost immediately it became instead a business location. The Ludlam-Anderson house (1844) was demolished in 1893 so that the Jefferson Hotel could be built.

It followed that when neighborhoods lost much of their residential base, churches more often than not relocated with their congregations, and the old houses of worship were often demolished. An example is Richmond's St. James's Episcopal Church (1837–40), which even was incorporated with the provision that if the congregation moved, the building had to be demolished rather than sold for commercial use. St. James's congregation relocated not only to a more residential neighborhood but also to a larger building; the original structure no longer met the needs of the church.

Buildings often were demolished when they were outgrown. Besides the first St. James's, innumerable examples of churches and synagogues could be cited here, such as First Baptist Church in Charlottesville, which was housed in successively larger buildings in 1833, 1852, 1904, and the 1970s. Courthouses also were frequent victims; these had to be replaced when they no longer were large enough to handle the courts' business. To mention but one example, the Arlington County courthouse (1898) expanded into wings in 1929 and 1950, then was demolished and rebuilt in 1959, only to be demolished and rebuilt a second time in 1997. Hotels in 19th-century Virginia routinely were taken down. Those structures became outmoded after relatively short usage, when such amenities as plumbing, lighting, and heating were dramatically and frequently upgraded. In Richmond, the Union Hotel (1817) was superseded by the Exchange Hotel (1840–41), which in turn was superseded by the Jefferson Hotel (1895); only the last has escaped demolition. Among the other types of commercial and civic buildings that were demolished when they proved obsolete were train stations, such as Union Station (1890) in Lynchburg, school buildings, such as the Anatomical Theatre (1826–27) at the University of Virginia, and bridges, such as the Springwood Truss Bridge (1884) in Botetourt County, which was replaced by a concrete structure.

Buildings were demolished when the properties on which they stood were developed for new uses. In 1850 the route of the new Richmond and Danville Railroad was projected through the center of the 1792 Amelia County courthouse, forcing its demolition. Land development, however, has been largely a modern problem. Ossian Hall (1783) was actually burned in 1959 by the Fairfax County Fire Department as a training exercise, but the burning was a way of demolishing a building that stood in the way of a housing complex that had

developed around it. Garst Log House (ca. 1800) in Roanoke County was taken down in the 1970s to make room for a similar development. In the 1960s Maplewood (ca. 1873) in Fairfax County lost part of its property to the Capital Beltway and the cloverleaf serving Tyson's Corner; the house was then demolished to make way for an industrial park. Mindless and massive urban renewal programs of the modern era have destroyed such properties as the Crawford House Hotel (1835) in Portsmouth and Norfolk's Christ Episcopal Church (1828) and Monticello Hotel (1896–98). Conversely, insufficient development also has resulted in the demolition of buildings, including a group of land boom hotels erected around 1890 but little needed after the Panic of 1893. To cite one example, the Rockbridge Hotel (1889–92) in Glasgow was sold soon after completion for a small fraction of what it had cost to build; it was used only as a storage barn for hay until it was demolished.

Buildings have been demolished when their styles seemed old-fashioned. Victorian designs in particular have suffered from changing tastes, whereby such structures as the wooden, Queen Anne–style Massie House (1899), which stood in a neighborhood of antebellum brick buildings in Lynchburg, and the Second Empire–style Mount Sharon (1888–90) in Orange County were pulled down because they seemed less than attractive to 20th-century eyes. Hayes Hall (1888) was the architectural centerpiece of Virginia College and Virginia Seminary in Lynchburg, but after standing for a century this large and imposing structure, also in the Second Empire style, failed to inspire efforts sufficient to save it. The romantic eclectic post offices in Danville (1883) and Roanoke (1893) seemed outmoded almost immediately following their completion; they were demolished because the 1893 World's Columbian Exposition in Chicago initiated a classical revival in architecture that rejected different ideals, particularly for civic commissions.

Some buildings were lost to the forces of nature and time. Storms or flooding demolished or contributed to the destruction of mills and houses, such as Drummond's Mill (before 1843) in Accomack County, Towles Point (after 1711) in Lancaster County, and the Tebbs house (ca. 1762) in Dumfries. Other buildings developed structural problems that necessitated demolition. Black Heath (ca. 1790) in Chesterfield County was undermined by coal shafts dug too near its foundations. The removal of bearing walls from the Bowers house (1828–29) in Petersburg made the building too dangerously unstable for restoration. The aging bricks of Eastern Shore Chapel (1755) were found to be unusable when the encroachment of Oceana Naval Air Station forced the removal and attempted rebuilding of that structure. The collapse of an upper floor in Thomas Jefferson's Capitol in 1870 generated so much hysteria that the Richmond City Hall of 1816–18 by Robert Mills was demolished in 1874 out of fear that it too might be structurally unsound.

Finally, and ironically, a few buildings were demolished in the name of preservation. The creation of Colonial Williamsburg in the early 20th century caused the demolition of Spencer's Hotel (ca. 1840) on Duke of Gloucester Street. Belle Farm (ca. 1775–80) in Gloucester County was taken down for reconstruction in Colonial Williamsburg, a rebuilding that never happened. After the interiors of Cherry Grove (before 1737) in Northampton County were stripped for preservation in a museum, the house fell into ruin.

Recent Historic Preservation in Virginia

The years following World War II took an especially heavy toll on Virginia's architectural resources. Economic prosperity and the need for new housing to accommodate postwar population growth put significant pressure on historic buildings and neighborhoods. The notion of "progress" made it fashionable to clear away landmarks for new development. Moreover, civic leaders and businessmen then had little notion that historic resources actually help maintain a community's good image and can be economic as well as cultural resources. The upshot is that Virginia's cities, towns, and countryside saw countless traditional scenes swept away. Also, changing tastes resulted in architectural prejudice that led ultimately to demolitions. Fanciful Victorian houses were pulled down largely because people simply thought them ugly.

Perhaps the greatest loss of Virginia's architectural legacy and indeed that of the whole nation came from the well-intended but highly misguided federal program called "urban renewal," which was put into full force in the early 1960s. Through this self-inflicted process, American cities suffered nearly as much destruction of historic fabric as did much of the European landscape during World War II. Most of the historic core of Norfolk was swept away by the Norfolk Redevelopment and Housing Authority in the 1960s with little or no record preserved of the port's architecturally rich, albeit deteriorated, neighborhoods. Tragically, it eventually became all too clear that it was far easier to tear down than to replace; much of Norfolk's cleared area remained an empty field for nearly forty years.

The city of Alexandria, which in 1960 had one of the nation's most intact early cityscapes, amazingly inflicted urban renewal on itself as well, wiping out half a dozen blocks of

18th- and 19th-century buildings to make way for bland new construction in the city's heart. Most of Richmond's east Jackson Ward, a residential neighborhood that was gently developed during the 19th century and is a nationally important African-American district, was removed in the 1960s for a coliseum project. Sections of the destroyed area still remain parking lots today. Portsmouth was more mindful of its distinctive Olde Towne Historic District but took down nearby blocks of urban housing that today would be seen as prime candidates for rehabilitation. As with Norfolk, much of the demolition area is still empty space.

The nation's insatiable desire to add highways has also resulted in the devouring of historic fabric, to say nothing of the cultural landscape. Begun in the 1950s, the Interstate Highway program was a much-needed undertaking, but it was particularly brutal in its early stages. Interstate 81 in the Shenandoah Valley was planned with little or no concern for historic preservation and wiped away numerous early farmsteads. Planners of urban expressways were no less blind to the cultural resources in their paths. Richmond lost most of its downtown canal system to an expressway that also sliced through the Oregon Hill neighborhood. The interstate highway that runs north of downtown Richmond split Jackson Ward, the same district that lost entire blocks of real estate to the city's coliseum project.

Concerns over the destruction wrought by such federal programs led in 1966 to the passage of the National Preservation Act, which established the National Register of Historic Places. The act set up a system of review of those federally funded or authorized programs that endangered historic buildings and districts; the act encouraged alternative actions. At the same time the Commonwealth of Virginia accepted a leadership role in the preservation of its irreplaceable legacy of historic properties. In 1966 the General Assembly passed the Virginia Historic Landmarks Commission Act, which established the Virginia Landmarks Register as the state's official roster of properties worthy of preservation. Both the state and federal programs have since carried out their mission of encouraging the preservation of historic places through a variety of incentives.

In Virginia, one of the most creative programs established in 1966 was the Preservation Easement program, which encouraged owners of privately held historic landmarks to forego development and subdivision rights and to impose strict architectural controls. To date, the commonwealth, through the Virginia Department of Historic Resources, holds preservation easements on nearly three hundred historic properties throughout the state. Thus, such privately owned landmarks as

Figure 10. Unidentified colonial ruin, Elizabeth City County (now Hampton). (Virginia Historical Society)

Westover, Berkeley, Mount Airy, Sabine Hall, Tuckahoe, and many others have been legally removed from harm's way in perpetuity.

Perhaps the most enlightened federal program encouraging historic preservation was the Tax Reform Act of 1976, which provided generous tax credits for projects that rehabilitate historic buildings. The effect of this program was to make rehabilitation cost-effective and thus preferable in many cases to demolition and replacement. Since passage of the act, several hundred million dollars' worth of rehabilitation activity has been certified in Virginia.

Because many other programs and examples of success could be cited, it finally may be safe to say that through the leadership of the state and federal governments, working in concert with local and regional private preservation organizations, the widespread erosion of historic resources has been significantly curtailed. Inevitably, interesting and important historic buildings and structures still will be lost, either through the pressures of growth or by such natural disasters as fires and floods. It is hoped, however, that Virginians, along with all other Americans, have come to value historic buildings and to recognize that such structures, both grand and simple, both famous and typical, are community assets and a means of establishing a sense of time and place.

Buildings Lost and Found

Lost Virginia locates more than three hundred buildings of note that once stood in the commonwealth. Many other important structures, however, are beyond visual recovery, because either they never were sketched or they were gone before the era of photography; sadly, we will never have tangible images for a number of categories of Virginia buildings. For instance, few 17th-century buildings remain, and the appearance of the majority of the dwellings and churches of Virginia's first century of settlement was never recorded. We known remarkably little about Jamestown. We have no image of the early fabric of Hampton, the oldest continuously English-speaking community in the Western Hemisphere; only pictures of its Civil War ruins exist. We will never know much about the appearance of the streets of colonial Norfolk. Then there are the innumerable colonial seats named in documents but little described there, such as the Randolph family properties in central Virginia and the early Fitzhugh family houses in Stafford and King George Counties, all lost long ago (these are mentioned in passing on the following pages, in the entries on Chatsworth and Boscobel). We have no surviving complex of colonial-period slave quarters and only the scantiest record of their appearance. One can but guess at the solemn splendor of the Shenandoah

Figure 11. Log house, Prince William County. (Historic American Buildings Survey, Library of Congress)

Valley's many antebellum barns, virtually all of which were destroyed during the Civil War by Union forces under Gen. Philip Sheridan. We will never know the appearance of much of Richmond in the years before the evacuation fire. Long is the list of buildings that were distinguished for their history, and perhaps for their design as well, but for which there is no image. At the same time, photographs survive of structures of which virtually no history is known, or at least has yet to be discovered. For example, the colonial ruin that was photographed in the no-longer-extant county of Elizabeth City (fig. 10) defies identification. Vernacular buildings can be particularly problematic. For instance, the history of a log house in Prince William County (fig. 11) examined half a century ago by the Historic American Buildings Survey remains unknown today.

The lost architecture of Virginia is a legacy with which time and man have not dealt gently. Only a sampling of it can be resurrected in these pages.

Notes on the Photographs

The photographs and other illustrations presented in this book vary in quality. Dim or hazy images are used by necessity, when no other illustration of a significant building survives. In contrast, some of the photographs, such as those from the Cook Collection of the Valentine Museum, have high artistic merit; those glass plates were made by skilled, professional artists. The photographers working for the Historic American Buildings Survey in the early and mid–20th century also were sensitive to aesthetics, but they were guided by a different agenda: to record buildings and architectural elements with maximum clarity. Less interesting aesthetically are photographs from other collections, such as the ones commissioned (and in some cases made) by Robert A. Lancaster, Jr., for his *Historic Virginia Homes and Churches* (1915), and by Mary Wingfield Scott for her *Houses of Old Richmond* (1941) and *Old Richmond Neighborhoods* (1950).

In many cases, however, these photographs—the only known images of lost buildings of significance—are invaluable. Lancaster's book, one of the first comprehensive overviews of Virginia's architectural heritage, has proven to be an especially important source. Not only are a number of the structures that he illustrated now gone, but Lancaster's information on buildings and the genealogical data that he gathered about owners also facilitated research through insurance records, family papers, and early county and town histories.

Also indispensable to *Lost Virginia* are innumerable family-owned photographs donated by individuals and families to such institutions as the Virginia Historical Society. Knitted into a large collection, these images present a mosaic of information about the Virginia landscape that is compelling and otherwise unavailable. Many of these photographs are simple snapshots, but the information that they record often is found nowhere else.

Sources of Photographs

Photographs have been borrowed principally from the collections of the Virginia Historical Society, the Valentine Museum, the Library of Congress, the Colonial Williamsburg Foundation, the Library of Virginia, and the Virginia Department of Historic Resources. The many other regional and local collections that contributed images are listed in the credit lines that appear with each of the entries. In all, photographs were gathered from some twenty-nine institutions and twenty-eight early publications.

Criteria for Inclusion

This book can be only a sampling of the hundreds, if not thousands, of buildings of architectural interest that the commonwealth has lost. As explained above, a number of those buildings cannot be resurrected because they were never photographed, sketched, or even described. Of the structures presented here, most were selected because of their architectural or historical importance. Others were chosen to represent types, such as stores, bridges, taverns, domestic dependencies, and log dwellings. We have also pursued a geographical balance among the entries. Where lost buildings have already been well covered in other publications, as with the architecture of Colonial Williamsburg and the buildings of early Richmond, we limited our selections in order to focus instead on the little-known and undocumented architectural wealth of the mid– and late 19th century, a period that produced some exceptionally fine architecture in Virginia. In looking for buildings unique to the region, we also tended to emphasize pre-20th-century works, using the rationale that a 1910 bungalow in Waynesboro is often not very far removed from a 1910 bungalow in a midwestern town. Furthermore, many of the photographs of lost 20th-century buildings have not yet made their way to institutional repositories, making the more recent losses difficult to quantify.

The three hundred plus buildings pictured in this book form a group that suggests the importance, quality, variety, and geographical extent of the lost architectural legacy. The following pages will introduce readers to many of the most significant examples of lost Virginia architecture.

EDITORIAL NOTES

All sources consulted in the writing of entries are cited at the rear of the catalogue, each under the name of the appropriate entry. These paragraphs of bibliographical information form the section titled "Bibliographical Notes"; this section serves in place of a single massive bibliography. Frequently cited sources and the abbreviations used to identify them in the "Bibliographical Notes" are listed at the beginning of that section. Within the section, entries are grouped into the four major divisions of the book—i.e., "Domestic Architecture," "Civic Architecture," "Religious Architecture," and "Commercial Architecture." Within each of those four units, entries are listed in alphabetical order. A building that carries an owner's full name is alphabetized according to the last name (e.g., sources consulted for the Miles Bott house appear within the unit entitled "Domestic Architecture" and under "Bott, Miles"). Exceptions are occasions when structures are strung together to form group entries (e.g., covered bridges, early retail stores, and taverns), which are listed in the notes under the first word of the entry (e.g., the entry "covered bridges" is found in the unit "Civic Architecture").

CONTRIBUTING AUTHORS

Thirty-five authors contributed to this volume. The majority of the entries were written by the three principal authors (Green, Loth, and Rasmussen). Entries written by the remaining thirty-two authors are identified by the authors' initials. In those few instances where entries were jointly written by one of the three principal authors and another contributing author, the initials of both appear.

ALM	Ann L. Miller, Virginia Department of Transportation Research Council, Charlottesville, Virginia
ASM	Ann Smart Martin, Chipstone Professor of American Decorative Arts, Department of Art History, University of Wisconsin-Madison, Madison, Wisconsin
BCG	Bryan Clark Green, Associate Curator for Prints and Photographs, Virginia Historical Society
CCL	Calder C. Loth, Senior Architectural Historian, Virginia Department of Historic Resources
CEB	Charles E. Brownell, Professor of Art History, Virginia Commonwealth University, Richmond, Virginia
DCW	Dale C. Wheary, Director of Historical Collections and Programs, Maymont Foundation, Richmond, Virginia
DRT	Donald R. Traser, Historian, Richmond, Virginia
EAC	Edward A. Chappell, Architectural Historian, Director of Architectural Research, Colonial Williamsburg Foundation, Williamsburg, Virginia
EJS, Jr.	Edwin J. Slipek, Jr., Architecture Critic, *Style Weekly*, Richmond, Virginia
GRG	Gary Grant, Historian, Danville, Virginia

JGZ, Jr.   John G. "Jack" Zehmer, Jr., Architectural Historian, Capital Region Office, Virginia Department of Historic Resources, Petersburg, Virginia

JMH   James Murray Howard, Curator and Architect for the Academical Village, University of Virginia, Charlottesville, Virginia

JOP   John O. Peters, Writer and Architectural Photographer, Richmond, Virginia

JS   John Salmon, Historian, Virginia Department of Historic Resources

KEL   K. Edward Lay, Cary D. Langhorne Professor Emeritus of Architecture, School of Architecture, University of Virginia, Charlottesville, Virginia

KGS   Kathryn Gettings Smith, City of Alexandria, Department of Planning & Zoning, Alexandria, Virginia

KLJ   Karri L. Jurgens, Architectural Historian, Richmond, Virginia

LC   Laura Carr, Architectural Historian, Richmond, Virginia

MB   Michael Bourne, Architectural Historian, Architectural Research Department, Colonial Williamsburg Foundation, Williamsburg, Virginia

MBR   Muriel B. Rogers, Assistant Curator for Virginia House, Virginia Historical Society

MM   Michael McDonough, Architectural Historian, Scottsville, Virginia

MRH   Mary Ruffin Hanbury, Architectural Historian, Portsmouth Regional Office, Virginia Department of Historic Resources, Portsmouth, Virginia

MTP   Margaret T. Peters, Historian and Program Manager, Virginia Department of Historic Resources

PHS   Pamela H. Simpson, Professor of Art History, Washington and Lee University, Lexington, Virginia

RB   Ray Bonis, Assistant Archivist, James Branch Cabell Library, Virginia Commonwealth University, Richmond, Virginia

RDW, Jr.   R. Dulaney Ward, Jr., Planning Consultant, City of Petersburg, Petersburg, Virginia

RGW   Richard Guy Wilson, Commonwealth Professor and Chair, Department of Architectural History, University of Virginia, Charlottesville, Virginia

SAC, Jr.   S. Allen Chambers, Jr., Architectural Historian, Lynchburg, Virginia, and Washington, DC

SATJ   Stephanie A. T. Jacobe, M.A. Candidate, Architectural History, Virginia Commonwealth University; Museum Assistant, Virginia Historical Society

SR   Selden Richardson, Archivist for Architectural Records, Library of Virginia, Richmond, Virginia

SSB   Shirley Showers Belkowitz, Director, Beth Ahabah Museum and Archives, Richmond, Virginia

THR   Tom H. Ray, Cataloging Coordinator, Library of Virginia, Richmond, Virginia

TTP, Jr.   Thomas Tyler Potterfield, Jr., Historic Preservation Planner, City of Richmond, Richmond, Virginia

WLW   W. L. Whitwell, Architectural Historian, Roanoke, Virginia

WMSR   William M. S. Rasmussen, Curator of Art, Virginia Historical Society

LOG HOUSE, New River vicinity, Giles County
Built probably early 19th century; demolished probably early 20th century

From the late 17th century through the early 19th century, log construction was commonly employed by Southerners for a variety of building types because the technique was effective and wood was abundant. Walls and chimneys were built by stacking round logs, hewn logs, sawn planks, or poles on top of one another; then, for stability, those ends that lapped at the corners were notched. Log structures varied in quality from sturdy plank dwellings (such as the Brock Farm Quarters, q.v.) to less-permanent, crudely built cabins.

This log dogtrot, a type so named because two units are linked by an open passageway, was constructed of logs hewn on two sides and fitted together at the corners by means of carved-out V-notching. The interstices between the logs were chinked and daubed, and the chimneys were constructed of masonry, an indication that this building was intended to be permanent. No information is available about the interior, but it must have been dark, as only two glazed openings pierced the visible long elevation, and one of those openings was in the loft above the passageway. A third small opening may have been present in the visible short wall, but the photograph is not clear. The house is surrounded by a series of Virginia, or snake, fences. Unpeeled logs are piled in the foreground, logs of the sort that would have been split into rails to maintain the fences.

Hundreds of dogtrots and related log structures once dotted the landscape of western Virginia. (Photograph: Virginia Historical Society)

CHAPTER I

Lost Domestic Architecture

The lost Virginia houses pictured in the following pages contribute to our understanding of past lifestyles and aspirations. Many of the buildings also are significant for their design quality. Some are important because specific historical episodes are associated with them. Most are early structures that inform about the appearance of the Virginia landscape before rural populations shifted and urban neighborhoods changed.

Domestic architecture in Virginia is surveyed here in a roughly chronological order. Illustrated as it is by lost examples, this is admittedly an unusual overview. The information that emerges is as illuminating as it is diverse. For instance, while we discover grand colonial mansions that were noteworthy accomplishments of design and construction, we find that some of the wealthiest men of that era, such as Peter Randolph of Chatsworth (before 1751, Henrico County), chose not to build extravagant brick houses. Even Lord Fairfax settled for a non-monumental homestead at Greenway Court (before 1760) in Clarke County. Or we notice how the Eastern Shore was more densely populated during the colonial period than was the mainland, because the soil's remarkable fertility meant that relatively compact landholdings could be productive plantations; the consequence was that many dignified houses, like Cherry Grove (before 1737) in Northampton County, were built there. Or we are reminded that sophistication and quality of design were hardly limited to what are today's largest cities but instead were found in many portions of the state. The town house of William Bowers (1828–29) is evidence of the urbanity of 19th-century Petersburg and the superb quality of architecture there; Grove Hill (ca. 1800–1804) in remote Botetourt County rivaled the best city architecture of the period. Or we discern patterns of influence. For example, these lost buildings demonstrate time and again that the two-story piazza invented by George Washington for Mount Vernon was a popular motif; it reappeared at a number of Classical Revival town houses, such as the Adams–Van Lew residence (1802 and ca. 1836) in Richmond.

Enough houses from 19th-century Richmond are gathered here to demonstrate how urban landscapes can change dramatically in appearance. We find that early Richmond little resembled the city that it is today. The Harvie-Gamble house (ca. 1797), perched above the James River, was a cosmopolitan neoclassical design. The Greek Revival Ludlam-Anderson house (1844) was stately. So too was the Hayes-McCance house (enlarged 1832–34); a stream, lake, cottage, and bear pit were included in its remarkable garden. Unusual types of houses also brought variety to the city's landscape: the Alexander McRae house (1804–9) and Moldavia (begun 1798) both were "bowed," or polygonal, rather than rectangular.

Important buildings of an entirely different nature are included in this section. Houses such as Fort Rhodes (ca. 1770–80) in Page County, with its Germanic spatial arrangements, and the Garst log house (ca. 1800) in Roanoke County, the two parts of which were connected by a dogtrot, remind the reader of vernacular traditions.

Design periods come into sharper focus in the following pages, where missing pieces are provided for assembly into the overall picture of the Virginia landscape. We find little-known Georgian buildings, such as Tar Bay (ca. 1746, Prince George County), Sea View (ca. 1762, Accomack County), and Belvidere (before 1757); the last was said by an English traveler in 1759 to be "as romantic and elegant as anything I have ever seen." We find important Jeffersonian and Federal-style houses, such as Barboursville (1817–22, Orange County) and Grove Hill. We find superb expressions of the Greek Revival, including Dover (1845, Goochland County) and Kinloch (1847–48, Essex County). We find significant houses designed in 19th-century romantic styles. Lost Gothic residences include A. J. Davis's Williamson house (1852) at Virginia Military Institute and William A. Pratt's folly in Richmond, which was called Pratt's Castle (1853). Italianate villas include Sabot Hill (ca. 1851, Goochland County) and the David Bryce Payne house (ca. 1860, Lynchburg). Second Empire houses include Hawfield (1881) and Mount Sharon (1888–90), both in Orange County. Queen Anne–style houses include Roseland Manor (1886–7, Hampton), Westbrook (1888–92, Richmond vicinity), and Mount Athos (1899–1900, Orange County). We find Nydrie

(1889, Albemarle County), a Scottish baronial castle. Such impressive piles sadly were among the most vulnerable of Virginian and indeed American house types. Years later, younger generations had little love or need for such extravagant works, which required costly staffs to maintain. To cite a final example, that of classicism, which returned to Virginia in the 20th century, we discover the Whitmell S. Forbes house, one of the grandest "Southern Colonial" mansions built in Richmond and another extravaganza for which a succeeding generation had little use.

It must be remembered, however, that the examples presented in this volume are only a sampling of the hundreds, if not thousands, of interesting domestic buildings lost over the years. Nonetheless, those shown help fill some of the many holes in Virginia's rich architectural tapestry. The recovery, at least on paper, of these domestic designs furthers our understanding of architectural style and architectural accomplishment in Virginia.

GREEN SPRING HOUSE, near the junction of Virginia state routes 5 and 614, Colonial National Historical Park, James City County
Old Manor House built ca. 1645–53, demolished by 1781; Mansion House built ca. 1659–1660s, demolished 1796–97

Seventeenth-century Chesapeake building was dominated by perishable post-hole construction rooted in the Stone Age. Amid such structures, controversial governor and pioneering agriculturist Sir William Berkeley erected the first of the mansions of Virginia. Like many later builders of great Virginia houses, Berkeley created his dwelling by degrees. He began by gradually constructing the building known in the 20th century as the Old Manor House; later, he joined this structure to a second one, the so-called Mansion House, which was extended with a rear ell at an unknown date. The plantation was occupied by the forces of Berkeley's adversary Nathaniel Bacon in 1676 and passed to the Ludwell family after Berkeley died in 1677. The Old Manor House had disappeared by 1781, when the property was the site of the Battle of Greenspring Farm, and the much-altered Mansion House had fallen into decay by the 1790s. In 1796 and 1797, the architect B. Henry Latrobe recorded the Mansion House, pictured here, and made designs both for renovating it and replacing it for William Ludwell Lee. Lee instead replaced the mansion with a non-Latrobe house that burned in the 19th century. Today, the only historic structure that survives above ground on the site is a ruined outbuilding.

The story of Berkeley's Tudor-Stuart structures remains largely undecipherable. It is nonetheless clear that the development of Green Spring House was a major episode in the modification of European architectural customs in response to the New World. The most evident example is the long southern porch, which was in place on the Mansion House not later than 1683 and which Latrobe recorded in a later metamorphosis. No element has played a more definitive role in the history of American architecture than porches in all their various functions (sheltering an entry or interiors from the weather, making a building more dignified, creating an outdoor living space, providing a vantage point for looking at a building's setting) and under all their various names (piazza, portico, galerie, stoep, veranda, umbrage, breezeway, deck). The Mansion House's porches forecast the great development of long porches on Virginia houses, from Corotoman (ca. 1720, q.v.) through Mount Vernon after Washington's second rebuilding (1774 ff.) and countless later Virginia dwellings.
At an unknown date, the Mansion House acquired a court bordered by serpentine brick walls, running partly over the Old Manor House foundation. Undulating walls came to North America in the 18th century from Britain, where they are called serpentine, crinkle-crankle, crinkum-crankum, or ribbon walls. In their most familiar form, these structures are perishable because they are thin partitions of brick or other materials stiffened by their own regular undulations rather than by piers. Green Spring had two important but little-studied variations on the serpentine plan: pillars to reinforce the brickwork and a bold, bell-shaped curvature. When George Washington redesigned Mount Vernon for the second time, he made extensive but little-noticed use of serpentine walling, including a surviving or reconstructed forecourt wall on much the same plan as that at Green Spring. (Image: Maryland Historical Society)
CEB

FAIRFIELD, White Marsh vicinity,
Gloucester County
Built ca. 1692, ca. 1694, and later; burned ca.
1899

Two of the brashest houses known from early Virginia overlooked Carter's Creek on the north bank of the York River. Both Fairfield and Rosewell (q.v.) burned—Fairfield circa 1899—and only Rosewell now has substantial ruins above ground.

Fortunately, six or seven pre-fire photographs make Fairfield one of the better-known large masonry houses built before double-pile edifices began to take center stage in the Chesapeake region. Like William Berkeley's second house at Green Spring (q.v.) and Robert Carter's Corotoman (q.v.), Lewis Burwell's Fairfield had a series of spaces placed end-to-end in a shallow rectangular block. Two chimneys pierced the ridge, both with pairs of diagonally set stacks joined at the caps. A broader wing with a high single story extended forward from one end, boldly elaborated by three taller, diagonally set stacks above a chimney slab rising through a roof hip. This larger chimney more overtly resembled the upper parts of those at Bacon's Castle (1665) and 17th-century English examples, which can be read as simplifications of the more elaborate, fetishized chimney flues of grand 16th-century edifices. But the Fairfield chimneys also have 18th-century parallels in Virginia (at Winona in Northampton County) and Maryland (at the Reward, 1750, Somerset County)

Precisely how the building was planned is harder to discern, though it is claimed that the narrow gable held an iron tie plate inscribed *L.A.B. 1692*, and a brick plaque once visible on the larger chimney is said to have been dated 1694. It seems most likely that the main block between the smaller chimneys began with a two-room, hall-chamber plan and that old descriptions of a large entertaining room in the wing are correct, though it may also have contained a smaller, unheated room at the rear. In short, the house may have begun with two detached sections, one private and the other public, reminiscent of René de Durand's familiar remark in the 1680s that Virginians "whatever their rank . . . build only two rooms with some closets on the ground floor, & two rooms in the attic above; but they build several like this, according to their means."

This interpretation assumes that the central section was an addition built sometime after 1694. Both the character of the windows and the placement of openings suggest some rearrangement of fenestration in the 18th and early 19th centuries.

The use of three stacks on the wing suggests that a cooking fireplace and thus a kitchen occupied the cellar and that one of the other cellar rooms contained vaulted storage space. (Photograph: Virginia Historical Society)
EAC

RINGFIELD, Yorktown vicinity,
York County
Built ca. 1698, burned 1920

The burning of Ringfield on 14 December 1920 deprived Virginia of a key example of early colonial gentry architecture. The tall two-story structure, with its massive T-shaped chimneys, could easily have been mistaken for a prosperous English farmhouse of the same period. The house was likely built by Joseph Ring, a prominent York County planter and public official, sometime before he wrote his will in 1698. The property passed through various hands over the subsequent century and a half until Julius Helm purchased it in 1886. In 1918, Gustave Helm, Jr., sold Ringfield to Mr. and Mrs. D. L. Flory. It probably was the Florys who altered the house by replacing its early, narrow dormers with the wide Colonial Revival ones shown in this photograph. The Colonial Revival front-door surround was also part of the remodeling. The beautiful glazed-header Flemish bond was left untouched. The sash windows shown may have replaced earlier ones, but if Ringfield was indeed built in the late 17th century, it undoubtedly originally would have had leaded casements. The earliest photographs of the house, however, show sliding sashes. Regrettably, no record of Ringfield's interior appearance survives.

The Florys kept the property for only two years, selling it to the US government in 1920 for twenty-seven thousand dollars. It then became part of what is now the Yorktown Naval Weapons Station and briefly served as the residence of the first inspector for ordnance. Ringfield was vacated several months later and soon destroyed by fire. Whether the fire was accidental was not recorded. (Photograph: Colonial Williamsburg Foundation)

MALVERN HILL, Varina vicinity, Henrico County
Built late 17th century; burned 1905

This remarkably early structure was first a frame house with a brick chimney. Around that east chimney, the house was later rebuilt in brick, either in the late 17th or early 18th century. The chimney stood until circa 1980; it was one of the commonwealth's finest examples of early diaper brickwork (glazed headers in a diamond pattern). Malvern Hill was cruciform in plan, a rare and significant brick example of that type. Not only did the addition of front and rear porches enhance privacy and provide a place for the stairs, but the cruciform plan transformed the simple hall-parlor structure into a building that seemed considerably larger and more imposing than it actually was.

The first house at Malvern Hill was built by Thomas Cocke (1639–97), a burgess. The property remained in the Cocke family until the late 18th century, when it was purchased by Robert Nelson, brother of Thomas Nelson of Yorktown. Its location, east of Richmond on a steep slope overlooking the James River valley, brought troops to the site during three wars. Lafayette is said to have camped there during the Revolution, as did Virginia forces during the War of 1812. In 1862 Malvern Hill was in the thick of a fierce Civil War battle that took its name from the property. Today the site is owned by the National Park Service. The ruins have been pilfered; only one corner of the house remains. (Photograph: Valentine Museum)

ROLLESTON, Virginia Beach (formerly Princess Anne County)
Built ca. 1700; burned by 1900

This interesting colonial dwelling was built by descendants of William Moseley, a Dutch immigrant. It is better known for its association with Henry Wise, Virginia governor from 1856 to 1860, who purchased the estate from his brother John. During the political upheaval prior to the Civil War, the recently retired Wise was a celebrity and active in local Democratic politics. He was appointed a brigadier general in the Confederate Army in 1861. In 1862, when Union forces occupied the region, Rolleston was used by the American Missionary Association as a school for African-Americans, then as a home for displaced former slaves liberated by the Union forces, and finally as a regional headquarters and school for the Freedmen's Bureau. Although Wise did regain title to the property, he never returned to live there. The house burned sometime in the late 19th century. (Photograph: Virginia Historical Society)
MRH

COROTOMAN, Weems vicinity, Lancaster County
Built ca. 1700–1720s; burned 1729

Corotoman was the seat of the wealthiest Virginia planter of his generation, Robert "King" Carter (1663–1732), owner of forty-four plantations and one thousand slaves. The great brick house that he erected is known today only by its foundations.

The appearance of Carter's mansion was long the subject of fascination and speculation. An archaeological excavation of the site, undertaken by the Virginia Department of Historic Resources in 1978, revealed evidence that was hardly disappointing. The house must have been imposing; at ninety feet, the foundations are remarkably long. Corotoman was a single-pile structure, but a gallery carried its width to forty feet. The gallery ran the length of the river front, projecting at the center and ends. The house was at least one and a half stories tall over a high basement, but there may have been two full stories, as at Fairfield (q.v.) and Green Spring (q.v.), seats of similar scale and pretension. The plan provided three major rooms, plus large English "closets" that encased the end chimneys. The center hall was paved with polished white marble imported from England, and marble and delft tiles decorated two of the hearths. Other excavated fragments suggest that the façade was enriched with applied pilasters and door pediments of stone and brick. The *Maryland Gazette* for 4 February 1729 recorded that "the fine large house of Col. Carter on Rappahannock was . . . burnt lately. . . . The particulars of this loss we cannot give you but we are informed that it is very great."

A wooden ancillary dwelling at Corotoman survived long enough to be photographed as a ruin prior to its total destruction around 1930. This smaller building is recorded in Carter's 1732 will and was later referred to as the Spinsters' House. It probably served as a dependency and possibly predated the mansion. Archaeologists posit that it was the dwelling of John Carter, either the father or older brother of King Carter, and was constructed about 1680. If so, this hall-parlor structure was more substantial than most; it was not a post-hole house but built on a brick foundation. As in the best post-hole structures, the walls were lined with mortar produced from oyster shells.

In the spring of 2000 the three-acre Corotoman site was purchased by the Association for the Preservation of Virginia Antiquities. (Photograph: Virginia Department of Historic Resources)

MORATTICO HALL, southern Richmond County, at the confluence of Lancaster Creek (formerly Morattico Creek) and the Rappahannock River Built ca. 1720–30; demolished ca. 1927

Morattico Hall stood on a narrow point of land, called Hale's Point, at the southern tip of Richmond County. Charles Grymes II constructed it around 1721, when he became a justice for Richmond County. The one-thousand-acre tract had been patented to his grandfather in 1661. Grymes later became a sheriff and burgess. His wife, Frances Jennings, was the daughter of Edmund Jennings, one-time president of the Virginia Council and acting governor in the years 1706–10.

The full complexity of Morattico Hall's building history will probably never be known due to the erosion that caused part of the house to fall into the Rappahannock River around 1927. Charles W. Selden, president of the

American Furniture and Fixture Co. in Richmond, purchased the property about that time and demolished the remainder of the house after removing its woodwork. The woodwork was installed in a new house built on the property.

A painted overmantel panel and two smaller painted panels formerly in the house were acquired in 1928 by Henry Francis duPont and displayed at his home, Winterthur, near Wilmington, Delaware. Ten years later, additional paneled woodwork, removed from the new house, was acquired for the expanding Winterthur Museum. The Flock Room and Morattico Hall, a re-creation installed at the museum in 1939 and 1940 by Thomas T. Waterman, were created from the paneling after a thorough examination of the material and the photograph shown here.

This photograph depicts a one-and-a-half-story brick dwelling with a side passage plan and an attached lower addition. The original entry door was replaced in the mid–19th century with a new door, transom, and sidelights. The windows appear to have remained intact. A T-plan chimney and the placement of the dormers in relation to the cornice suggest a double-pile arrangement similar to the Somers house in Northampton County and St. Richard's Manor in St. Mary's County, Maryland.

If the house was built two rooms deep, as this photograph suggests, it would have been a substantial dwelling for the period (at Grymes's death, there were sixteen beds in the house). As reconstructed at Winterthur, Morattico's Flock Room is one of the most impressive rooms from an early-18th-century Virginia house, as was befitting a rising political leader of Richmond County. Upon his death in 1743, Grymes owned about two thousand acres of land; the house, a storehouse, and a mill, along with sixty-eight slaves, were on the plantation. The property passed to Grymes's daughter Lucy and her husband, Henry Lee, who sold it in 1767. (Photograph: Historic American Buildings Survey, Library of Congress)
MB

MATTISSIPPI (STURGIS HOUSE),
Occohannock Creek, Northampton County
Built ca. 1700–1715; abandoned ca. 1950

Although Col. Thomas Johnson mentioned "Mattasippy Neck where I now live" in his will of 1658, the brick hall-parlor house pictured here almost certainly postdates his lifetime. It was probably built by his son Obedience or his grandson of the same name, who inherited the property in 1709. Whichever the case, Mattissippi was old; until 1950 it was one of the oldest standing structures on the Eastern Shore.

Mattissippi's form and size were not unusual in the early Virginia landscape, but its masonry construction was. Handsome brickwork with glazed headers distinguished the building and set it apart from the many earthfast hall-parlor houses in the colony. The placement of doors and windows at Mattissippi was determined as much by function and expense as by aesthetics. On the principal façade, which fronted the water, separate exterior doors provided access to the hall (to the left in the photograph) and to the smaller second room, which with its large fireplace served as a kitchen. The hall was lit by a window on each front; the kitchen by only one window. Closets in three corners and a stair in the fourth (in the hall) flanked the end chimneys. Above were two chambers. This attempt at "permanent" architecture with decorative detailing was an ambitious undertaking for its time and place.

Mattissippi is the Indian name for the Johnson property, a tract close to the Chesapeake Bay. Francis Sturgis owned the land from 1869 until he sold it in 1899, when nonresident ownership began and led to the eventual loss of the house. (Photograph: Historic American Buildings Survey, Library of Congress)

BEWDLEY, on the Rappahannock River, Lancaster County
Built early 18th century; burned 1917

Bewdley, a commodious frame plantation house, was one of Virginia's more unusual colonial structures. Its four end chimneys, serving the four corner rooms, gave minaret-like vertical accents to the house. Between each pair stood an exterior doorway. Such an arrangement alone would have made Bewdley noteworthy. Even more out of the ordinary, however, were the two tiers of dormers, which allowed room for two attic stories instead of one. Bewdley burned in 1917; its one surviving chimney was incorporated into the 1930s facsimile of the house. With Bewdley's loss, Wolftrap Farm in Isle of Wight County is perhaps the only remaining early Virginia house with a double tier of dormers. (Photograph: Valentine Museum)

UNIDENTIFIED HOUSE,
Gloucester County
Built 18th century; survived into the early 20th century

The builder of this Gloucester County residence developed an alternative to the hall-parlor house by rotating the roof ninety degrees from the norm. The ground floor was little changed, in that there were still two rooms and a stair. But the second floor, with several large windows, was better lit. Plus, a small third-floor room, also lit, fit under such a highly pitched roof. The design was inventive, while the crisp lines and simple geometry gave the house visual appeal. (Photograph: Library of Congress)

PENDLETON HOUSE (EDMUNDSBURY),
Bowling Green vicinity,
Caroline County
Built early 18th century; burned 1931

Revolutionary patriot and jurist Edmund Pendleton, born in Caroline County in 1721, made this unusual house his principal residence for much of his life. The structure was distinctive for its center chimney, a form rarely seen on colonial Virginia plantation dwellings. Close examination of the photograph, however, shows a seam in the center of the façade, indicating that the house evolved to this form and may originally have been a single-cell dwelling with an exterior end chimney. If that is the case, the right side was probably the original section and would thus have had a façade with a center entrance flanked by windows. Other distinctive features were the shed dormers and the rough boarding (or logs?) sheltered by the porch. Edmund Pendleton served as a delegate to the Continental Congress. He was also chairman of the Virginia Committee of Safety from 1775 to 1776, president of the convention that ratified the United States constitution, and the first president of the Virginia Supreme Court of Appeals. He died in 1803 and was buried at Edmundsbury, but in 1903 his body was moved to Bruton Parish Church in Williamsburg. Regrettably, Caroline County lost the residence of its most famous son when the house was destroyed by fire in 1931. (Photograph: Virginia Historical Society)

EASTWOOD, London Bridge vicinity, Virginia Beach
Built first quarter 18th century; demolished shortly after 1940

Eastwood was the countryseat of William Aichison, a prominent Loyalist merchant residing in Norfolk. The Norfolk fire of 1 January 1775 was begun when Virginia troops ignited one of seven town houses that the hated Aichison owned in that prosperous seaport. By the time the house was ablaze, Aichison's slaves had already joined Lord Dunmore's British troops, propelled by the governor's promise of freedom for any slave who joined him. Aichison fled to Eastwood, but wherever he went—and the list includes Princess Anne County, Northampton County, and Pasquotank County, North Carolina—committees of safety treated him as a suspect and made it clear that he was not welcome. The aged and ailing Aichison did not live through the year.

Eastwood was a visually engaging example of Virginia's colonial vernacular. The three-bay house was laid up in glazed-header Flemish bond with interior end chimneys. The windows had nine-over-nine lights on the ground floor and six-over-six in the shed dormers above. As was typical of such small early manor houses, it had a hall-parlor plan, with the front door entering into the larger of the two rooms. In this larger room the closed-string, turned-baluster stair ascended to the second floor. Both fireplaces on the ground floor were large, measuring five by seven feet, and were finished with finely carved rolled mouldings and a pulvinated frieze. Both mantels were removed and erected in nearby modern dwellings, and the stair is now in the collection of the Winterthur Museum. Upon investigating the structure in 1940, architectural historian Thomas T. Waterman described its condition as "ruinous." (Photograph: Historic American Buildings Survey, Library of Congress)

TOWLES POINT, Bertrand vicinity, juncture of Rappahannock and Corotoman Rivers, Lancaster County
Built after 1711; abandoned ca. 1920

Situated on a commanding point of land close to the Chesapeake Bay, Towles Point was notable for both its ownership by one family for more than two hundred years and its English vernacular features, which in the 17th century had been adapted on Virginia's Eastern Shore.

Henry Towles, Jr. (d. 1734), whose father had emigrated from Liverpool, moved to the mainland from Accomack County in 1711 and built Towles Point soon thereafter, in a style that he or his housewright remembered. The one-and-a-half-story, brick-ended house had a catslide roof. This gable type, by change of pitch, served to extend a two-room plan to double-pile by sheltering small rooms (or cells) added to the rear. The end chimneys of Towles Point were massive, exterior, and pyramidal. The roof was steeply pitched. The openings were unevenly spaced. These features are all found on the Eastern Shore; one example is Locust Grove (ca. 1710–25) in Northampton County. The chimney treatment, steep gable roof, and asymmetrical elevation can be traced to postmedieval cottages of England's West Country and Highlands.

Early houses like Towles Point, low to the ground and half brick/half wood, mark the transition in the colony to permanent architecture. In plan they were transitional to the double-pile, cross-passage house. Photographs taken in the 1930s record the interior stairs at Towles Point running upward in what probably was a cross passage, perhaps wide only at the front of the building as at Locust Grove. In the photograph shown here, the stairs are to the right of the entrance, breaking the fenestration. To the left, lit by two windows, was probably the parlor or best room. Above was a chamber to either side of the stairs; each had its own fireplace. Eugene Bradbury, who examined Towles Point in 1933 for the Historic American Buildings Survey, believed that the house initially had four tall chimneys, so that all six rooms were heated. The brickwork shows evidence of extensive repairs. This suggests that the unusual storage pents, sandwiched between chimneys on both ends, were later additions. A storm circa 1920 that severely damaged the house and caused its abandonment by Baltimore lawyer Howard Towles was but the last in a series of natural disasters that in the course of two centuries threatened its vulnerable fabric. (Photograph: Historic American Buildings Survey, Library of Congress)

BARN ELMS, Hartfield vicinity, Middlesex County
Begun ca. 1718; burned 1932

Barn Elms was begun by Col. Edmund Berkeley, whose will of 1718 refers to "the house I am now building" and its need to be "secured with a good roof." This "house" actually was the two buildings shown here, although in the 18th century both were only one and a half stories tall. The colonel's intention was that Barn Elms "be finished by [his] son," also named Edmund, who presumably did so during the next decade.

The Barn Elms complex was described in some detail by Carter Burwell Berkeley, the great-grandson of the first Edmund, who advertised the 1,140-acre plantation for sale in 1806 as "surpassed in goodness of quality by few estates in the county." There was "a spacious Dwelling House consisting of two buildings of brick . . . connected by a covered way" (the covered way was removed in the 19th century). Both buildings apparently had center-passage plans. In the smaller structure there were two rooms to each side off the passage; in the larger, "a very spacious" room for entertaining filled one side. The complex also contained "a kitchen and laundry of brick, . . . with two rooms below stairs, on each [and one room above] . . . about 30 feet by 20." There was a wooden dairy, a smokehouse, a brick stable, a carriage house "42 feet by 20 . . . with a hip'd roof that affords a spacious upper apartment," an icehouse, a barn, and "a very spacious falling garden . . . on which much care and attention have been bestowed." In the 1830s Barn Elms was purchased by Paulin Blackburn, who after the Civil War used bricks from several of the outbuildings to raise the two principal buildings to two stories.

The arrangement of one-and-a-half-story structures at Barn Elms seems peculiar to modern eyes but actually followed precedent in the region. In 1686 a French traveler to Virginia, René de Durand, noted that "Whatever their rank, & I know not why, they build only two rooms with some closets on the ground floor, & two rooms in the attic above; but they build several like this, according to their means." In 1705 Robert Beverley added that Virginians had "extent enough of ground to build upon; and now and then they are visited by high winds, which would incommode a towring fabrick." Hewick, the brick, 18th-century Robinson family house that still stands near the Barn Elms site in Middlesex County, followed this same regional pattern. That plantation had multiple buildings, and the main house also was one and a half stories high initially, until the 19th century (1849), when it was raised to two full stories. (Photograph: Virginia Historical Society)

ROSEWELL, White Marsh vicinity, Gloucester County
Built ca. 1721–41; burned 1916

The largest and most lavishly designed house in colonial Virginia, and one of the grandest built in early America, Rosewell rose three stories over a raised basement on a prominent site off the York River at Carter's Creek. There, in the wilds of the Virginia rural landscape dotted primarily with wooden earthfast cottages, the house must have been an extraordinary sight.

Construction was begun by Mann Page I, a son-in-law of wealthy Robert "King" Carter, after an earlier frame house had been destroyed by fire in 1721. Page chose not simply to match in extravagance the new Governor's Palace in nearby Williamsburg but instead dared even to better that structure; Rosewell was one story taller, almost twenty feet longer (seventy-one feet), and had two cupolas instead of one. Because this project was so ambitious for its time and place, Rosewell almost was a folly. In 1730, at the death of the builder, the house remained incomplete, and in 1741 the builder's son, Mann Page II, was still paying construction debts. A pair of connecting units that would have linked the house to its two north dependencies apparently was planned but never built. Those dependencies were large, each the length of a sizable house, sixty by twenty-four feet. A huge stable (one hundred by twenty-four feet) and a circular icehouse, both of brick, were constructed.

Surprisingly, given its location, Rosewell resembled a fashionable English town house in a number of ways: the masonry keystones, apron window panels, compass-head stair windows, and crowning brick parapet all were features of a specific Queen Anne house type developed in London when fire-prevention ordinances of 1707 and 1709 abolished wooden cornices. Thus it may have been designed by an English architect; if not, the talented workmen who built it and unquestionably were trained in England may have remembered the house type well enough to lay out its plan and elevations on their own. The brickwork that they crafted is considered the finest produced in all the American colonies. The walls were Flemish bond embellished with molded, carved, and rubbed brick, random glazed headers, and stone windowsills. The door frames and parapet cap were of a type sufficiently in vogue in London to appear in William Salmon's *Palladio Londinensis* (1734). As for the interior, the hall was paved with black and white marble imported from England. For decades, architectural historians have regarded the stair as the most richly embellished of all American examples. It was six feet wide, with spiral balusters and newels carved with Corinthian capitals, vines, leaves, and flowers. The brackets carried scrolled consoles feathered with acanthus leaves. The fascia board at the top of the run was carved with leafage, flowers, and rosettes.

The third owner of Rosewell was hard pressed to keep the plantation profitable and its buildings in order. This was John Page, the son of Mann Page II, a friend of Thomas Jefferson and later (from 1802 to 1805) governor of Virginia. In 1771 he was forced to address the deteriorating fabric of the house: "As [it] is very much out of repair, I have engaged a man to put it in saving condition next Spring." Following Page's death in 1808 Rosewell was largely abandoned for the next thirty years, until Page's widow died and the plantation changed hands. In 1815 an insurance policy noted its "bad repair"; English visitors in the 1830s or '40s recorded that "rats had eaten holes in the panelling [*sic*], plaster was falling, the roof was leaking, windows were broken, and there had been other destruction by vandals. The yard was badly overgrown and many of the shade trees [were] dead."

Around 1840, owner Thomas Booth sealed Rosewell from the destructive elements, but the significant alterations that he made detracted from the original character of the house. Booth removed the marble from the floor of the hall, resashed the house, replaced the entrance doors, stripped the walnut and mahogany paneling and mantels from the interior walls, removed the original lead covering from the roof, along with the parapets and cupolas, changed the roof from a deck-on-hip to a low hip, added pediments to the end pavilions, and cut down the avenue of cedar trees leading to the mansion. The house was owned by the Greaves family when it burned in 1916.

Rosewell today is an impressive ruin. In 1935 a bill passed by Congress authorized the incorporation of Carter's Grove, Greenspring, and Rosewell into the new Colonial National Historic Park centered at Yorktown, but only the Greenspring site was purchased. In 1979 the Greaves family donated the ruins and a small tract of land to the Gloucester Historical Society. The Rosewell Foundation was then established to manage the site. It has since stabilized the ruins and constructed a visitor's center and museum on the grounds. (Photograph: Valentine Museum)

GERMANNA, northeastern Orange County
Built 1720s; burned ca. 1740s

Germanna, the plantation residence of Lt. Gov. Alexander Spotswood, was built in what is now northeastern Orange County, overlooking the Rapidan River. Construction apparently took place in the mid-1720s, although the house may have incorporated elements relating to Fort Germanna (established 1714). After his removal from office in 1722, Spotswood retired to Germanna, from which he managed holdings that included considerable portions of modern-day Orange, Culpeper, and Spotsylvania Counties. After a sojourn in England to defend his land acquisitions, Spotswood returned to Virginia. He and his family were in residence at Germanna by 1732, when a visiting William Byrd II left a brief description mentioning a spacious house, which he dubbed an "Enchanted Castle" and which included a reception area "elegantly set off with pier glasses" and furnished with a tea table and china, as well as the intrusions of "a brace of tame deer [that] ran familiarly about the house." The Germanna residence apparently burned shortly after Spotswood's death in 1740 and was never rebuilt, although a later house was built near the ruins by the Gordon family and stood until the mid–20th century. Archaeological excavations of the Spotswood house, undertaken during the 1980s and 1990s, yielded evidence of an elaborate Georgian mansion, two stories high and built of brick, with carved stone elements and a slate roof. The center block measured approximately eighty by thirty-five feet; a columned or arcaded portico apparently added an additional ten feet to the river side. Wings or dependencies flanked the main block, and a forecourt framed by additional dependencies extended from the front of the house. One of the earliest documented dwellings in the region, Germanna was also one of the largest and finest colonial residences ever built in Virginia. Spotswood's inventory contains an extensive list of elaborate furniture and decorative elements (most of the personal property must have been removed from the house before it burned, since many items also appear on the inventory of his son John in the 1750s). With its terraced gardens and plantation complex, located on what was then the frontier, Germanna must have been an impressive sight. (Photograph: Virginia Department of Historic Resources)
ALM

BELVOIR, Fort Belvoir, Fairfax County
Built after 1735; burned 1783

Belvoir was the Fairfax family seat that was the immediate neighbor of George Washington's Mount Vernon estate. The mansion there was owned by Thomas, sixth Baron Fairfax of Cameron, a peer of the realm who forfeited his ancestral home of Leeds Castle in England to set up residence in the American colonies. He came to Virginia in 1735 to administer the Northern Neck proprietary that he had inherited; this was a five-million-acre tract of land between the Rappahannock and Potomac Rivers, which stretched westward to their headwaters. It had been awarded in 1649 by the future King Charles II. To help with the rent and sale of these lands, Fairfax enlisted the aid of a cousin, William, who preceded him to Virginia, supervised the construction of Belvoir, and became master of the house in the 1750s, when Lord Fairfax relocated to Greenway Court (q.v.).

The exact appearance of Belvoir is unknown, but much can be deduced from surviving records. It was a large Georgian mansion with four rooms and a wide entrance lobby on the first floor, five rooms on the second, and a piazza or porch on one short side of the house. Its floor plan differed from the usual center-passage type erected by many native-born Virginians. This house probably influenced George Washington's ideas about how he would alter Mount Vernon in more ways than can be determined today.

The furnishings at Belvoir were extraordinary. In addition to the fine case pieces and chairs that were found in other Virginia mansions, the house had highly expensive mirrors, large carpets, and seemingly countless yards of fine fabrics to serve as draperies and to cover furniture. More money was spent on textiles than anything else. For instance, the dressing chamber, with its sixty-seven yards of blue damask fabric "in the neatest manner," must have rivaled many such rooms of the nobility in London.

Today the site is incorporated into Fort Belvoir, a major US Army installation, and may be visited. (Photograph: Virginia Historical Society)

CHESTNUT GROVE, on the Pamunkey River, courthouse vicinity, New Kent County
Built ca. 1735–50; burned 1926

Chestnut Grove is remembered as the house where Martha Dandridge, the future Martha Washington, spent her youth prior to her marriage there in 1750 to Daniel Parke Custis. A tasteful and imposing two-story wooden structure with hipped roof and end chimneys, Chestnut Grove was actually smaller than it seemed; its plan was single-pile. This was perhaps as grand a dwelling as could be realized by Martha's father, John Dandridge, who sat to have his portrait painted before he emigrated from London in 1715, arriving in the colony as a young man with aristocratic ambitions but little cash in hand. He worked his way up in the county militia to the rank of colonel and served as clerk of the New Kent court for twenty-six years, until his death in 1756. Around 1730 Dandridge purchased the Chestnut Grove property; at some point he accumulated the means to start construction there. In 1768, when Dandridge's son Bartholomew advertised the plantation for sale, the house was described as having three rooms and a passage on each floor; the five-hundred-acre property was said to have "all the necessary out-houses, with a good orchard." The unoccupied house burned when it was opened for fall cleaning in 1926. (Photograph: Valentine Museum)

CHERRY GROVE, Eastville vicinity, Northampton County
Built before 1737; destroyed 1971

Cherry Grove was situated on or near the site of the earliest settlement on the Eastern Shore, which was made by Thomas Savage in the 17th century. Savage selected a tract midway up the peninsula, along the Chesapeake Bay. Cherry Grove probably was built by his son, Nathaniel Littleton Savage, who died in 1737. It was a one-room-deep, center-passage structure covered by a gambrel roof, which allowed spacious upper rooms; this type was more common in colonial Virginia than is generally recognized. The woodwork was of exceptional quality. The entrance doors were unique, having panels with a St. Andrew's cross pattern on the exterior and diagonal battens on the inside face. The staircase was enclosed and its passage paneled. The parlor was elaborately wainscoted, as was the chamber above it. In 1971 the Cherry Grove woodwork was sold; it is now displayed in the Museum of Early Southern Decorative Arts in Winston-Salem, North Carolina. Its removal by careless workmen destroyed the fabric of the house, an act condemned by H. Chandlee Forman in his book *The Virginia Eastern Shore and Its British Origins*. (Photographs: Collection of the Museum of Early Southern Decorative Arts)

DRYSDALE GLEBE, Newtown vicinity, King and Queen County
Built 1745; burned 1954

This simple structure was remarkably elegant on account of its fine brickwork, laid in Flemish bond with glazed headers and rubbed brick trim at the openings and corners. The brickwork survived in superb condition prior to the conflagration that destroyed it. In structure and detailing, the glebe house recalled the colonial Anglican churches of the county, particularly Upper Church in Stratton Major Parish, which still stands. That building is of similar size and shape, with almost identical brickwork that shows off the artistry of the colonial mason.

As with the county's churches, window placement at Drysdale glebe was regular but guided as much by function as aesthetics, and thereby not entirely symmetrical. The plan, however, was pure geometry: the house measured fifty by twenty feet, with a ten-foot cross passage (a double square) that separated square rooms (twenty by twenty feet in size). The staircase, with square newel posts and turned balusters, repeated the theme of simplicity and elegance. By 1762, with the creation of new counties and the redrawing of boundary lines, Drysdale glebe was poorly positioned for its resident minister to serve his parishioners. The property was subsequently sold into private hands. (Photograph: Library of Congress)

CLEVE, near Dogue, King George County
Built ca. 1746; burned 1800 and 1917

A Northern Neck plantation that stretched along the Rappahannock River, Cleve was the seat of Charles Carter, son of Robert "King" Carter of Corotoman (q.v.). A fire in 1800 destroyed the interior after only a half-century of use but left the brick and stone walls standing. A second fire in 1917 caused the demolition of the rebuilt structure except for a small section of one corner and the basement, on which a third residence was later constructed. Photographs and notes taken shortly before the second fire provide valuable information about the exterior. New brickwork visible in the two gable ends suggests that Cleve was originally built with a hipped roof, as were most of the Georgian mansions in the colony. Stone quoins, bold rusticated stonework around door and window openings on the two principal façades, and a molded stone watertable stood in dramatic contrast to the darker brick walls. Two high and square brick chimneys were silhouetted against the sky. This imposing exterior, inspired by English designs of the type published by architect James Gibbs, was evidence of the Carter family's sophisticated tastes.

Cleve's plan is known from the surviving foundations and from photographs of the exterior. It was a variation of the plan of nearby Marmion, also in King George County. At Carter's Grove (built 1749–55) in James City County, this plan was further enlarged and refined. With this house type, a seven-bay façade was the principal front, which generally faced the river; a five-bay elevation was given to the land side. On the interior, the entrance on the seven-bay façade opened to a broad three-bay entrance hall, centered on a narrower stair hall. Nearly square rooms flanked both halls. Cleve shared with Carter's Grove the placement of servants' lobbies at each end of the land-side rooms. Carter's Grove was built for Carter Burwell, nephew of the builder of Cleve. (Photograph: Virginia Historical Society)
MM

TAR BAY, Hopewell vicinity, Prince George County
Built ca. 1746; burned ca. 1965

Nearly forgotten, Tar Bay's colonial mansion is now a ruin dramatically sited overlooking the bend of the James River of the same name. Although the loss of the county's records inhibits documentation of the construction date, it is believed that the house was erected in 1746 for Daniel Colley but was not fully finished at that time. The chimneys had exterior fireplace openings, filled in, for possible future additions that were never built. A distinctive and unusual feature was the extension from the river front, giving the house a T-shaped floor plan. Often such a projection contained the staircase; this one did not. In other aspects, Tar Bay was a conventional example of high-style Virginia Georgian architecture. Its five-bay façade with paired windows was covered by a hipped roof with a modillion cornice. The brickwork was laid up in standard Flemish bond with gauged-brick jack arches. Exceptional was the absence of a belt course, a feature normally found on two-story brick colonial mansions.

The property was owned by the Colleys into the early 19th century and then passed through the Cocke family to the Ruffin family. The Ruffin family was using it as a summer home when it burned around 1965. (Photographs: Virginia Department of Historic Resources)

JAMES MONROE BIRTHPLACE, Colonial Beach vicinity, Westmoreland County
Built ca. 1750; dismantled ca. 1850

Only three birthplaces of Virginia's eight presidents remain standing: Berkeley (William Henry Harrison), Greenway (John Tyler), and the Woodrow Wilson Birthplace. Of the five presidential birthplaces that have disappeared the appearance of only one, that of James Monroe, is known through a contemporary image. Monroe, fifth president of the United States, was born in 1758 in a modest wood-frame house on Virginia's Northern Neck, less than ten miles from George Washington's birthplace. Archaeological investigation of the site undertaken in 1976 revealed the foundation of a fifty-seven-by-eighteen-foot structure, which conforms to the print pictured here of the Monroe family house published in Robert Sears's *A Pictorial History of the American Revolution* (1845). Monroe's father, Spence Monroe, was a carpenter and joiner. The house, which may have been built by Spence Monroe, was a simple vernacular structure typical of the scores of rustic dwellings that dotted Virginia's colonial landscape but have since all but disappeared. James Monroe lived here until 1774, when he enrolled in the College of William and Mary. He later inherited the property but sold it in 1781. The house eventually was abandoned and finally dismantled circa 1850. The site, now marked by a stone obelisk, is preserved in a county-owned park. (Image: Virginia Historical Society)

TEDINGTON, Sandy Point, Charles City County
Built ca. 1750; burned 1928

A bookplate bearing the names of William Lightfoot (1724–64) and Tedington, along with the date 1750, establish the early history of this house. William Lightfoot built Tedington (later misspelled and known as Tettington) on a tract along the James River acquired by his grandfather Philip Lightfoot, who arrived in the colony (in Gloucester County) as early as 1671; the grandfather is buried at the Tedington tract, where a magnificent colonial family tomb remains. William's father, also named Philip Lightfoot (1689–1748), was a wealthy merchant of Yorktown and member of the powerful governor's Council. William Lightfoot never inherited the family mansion in Yorktown; it remained the home of his mother, who outlived him.

Tedington is named for Britain's Teddington, near Twickenham in Richmond-upon-Thames, west of London. No doubt William Lightfoot knew the London Teddington when studying abroad. There, full-length, life-size portraits of him and his younger brother Francis (who died before 1748) were painted, with both sitters in court dress; those canvases, along with portraits of William's wife, Mildred Howell (as a child), and others of her family, hung at Tedington. Fine English silver was said to have been housed there as well. Displays of family portraiture were not uncommon in Charles City County at this date; the collections at Tedington, Chatsworth (q.v.), Shirley, and Wilton followed the example set by William Byrd II at Westover. The wainscoting at Tedington was appropriately grand. Not every wall of every room was paneled, as at Wilton, but the handsome treatment of the stairs and the parlor was of similar design and quality.

On the exterior, Tedington resembled Toma Hund (also Charles City County and lost); both were long, gambrel-roofed structures. Like Chatsworth (q.v.) and Shirley, both featured a two-level portico, a motif introduced at midcentury at the second Capitol in Williamsburg. The double portico probably made its first appearance in Charles City County as an addition on one of the now lost houses. (Photograph: Virginia Historical Society)

BULL HILL (MITCHELLS), Mansion Drive, Hopewell
Built mid–18th century; burned 1925

A classic example of Virginia's colonial Georgian architecture, Bull Hill, which stood on a promontory overlooking the Appomattox River valley, is all but forgotten today. Its construction date is uncertain. It is said that Col. Alexander Bolling, grandson of the pioneer Robert Bolling, was born here in 1722, but that birth must predate this building. During the Revolutionary War, in May 1782, Lord Cornwallis spent a night in the house while on his march through Prince George County and eventually to Yorktown. Legend has it that Cornwallis's discussion of his plans to capture Lafayette were overheard by young Susanna Bolling, who crept through a secret passage, crossed the Appomattox, and warned the French nobleman. Like its downstream neighbor Weston Manor, Bull Hill was occupied by Federal troops in the final months of the Civil War, as shown in this 1865 photograph. The plantation served by the house eventually was incorporated into the city of Hopewell. The house was gutted by fire in 1925 and its bricks used in a Tudor Revival dwelling erected on the site, the focal point of Hopewell's Mansion Hills development.

This 1865 photograph shows the house having all the attributes of a high-style, mid–18th century mansion, including Flemish-bond brickwork, gauged-brick belt course, modillion cornice, and hipped roof. Tall windows with what appear to be original nine-over-nine sash mark the carefully proportioned five-bay façade. Except for the later front porch, the house in 1865 appeared essentially unchanged. The similarity of the house to Tar Bay (q.v.), also a Prince George County dwelling, suggests the possibility of a common master builder. (Photograph: Library of Congress. This photograph was long misidentified as Upper Gisborough, a house that formerly stood in Washington, DC. The photograph was published under the name of Upper Gisborough in *Capital Losses*, by James M. Goode [Smithsonian Institution Press, 1979], p. 4.)

THE GLEBE, vicinity of Saluda and Urbanna, Middlesex County
Built 1750–57; burned 1913

In 1667 the vestry of Christ Church in Middlesex County voted to construct a glebe house for the parish minister. That structure was unsubstantial, however, and had to be replaced in 1695. By 1728 the second glebe was so deteriorated that its resident, Bartholomew Yates, judged it no longer habitable; repairs kept it standing for an additional two decades. In 1750 the vestry voted to build a two-story brick house, pictured here, fifty by thirty feet, with a cellar but without dormers. Stephen Johnson won the bid to construct the house, but he turned the project over to undertaker Mourning Richards. In 1766 a sizable garden on the site (708 feet in perimeter) was enclosed. The glebe was sold into private hands in 1814 and named Huntington plantation.

The 1750 glebe house was notably different from its predecessors but akin, architecturally, to the handsome churches of the parish, two of which, Christ Church and the Lower Chapel, still stand. It was an imposing Georgian dwelling built with glazed-header Flemish bond brickwork. The floor plan was typical of the period for large Virginia houses: two rooms were placed on both sides of a center passage, on both floors. Unusual was the additional small room set off to the side, probably intended as a library or study appropriate for a minister. The porch and window shutters pictured here were added in the 19th century. (Photograph: Virginia Historical Society)

EAST HILL (BOLLINGBROOK), on Bolling's Hill between Jefferson and Madison Streets, and between Bank and Franklin Streets, Petersburg
Built ca. 1750–75; eastern building burned 1855, western building demolished 1925

In 1706 the second Robert Bolling purchased the land that his family was to call Bollingbrook from Richard Jones. During the course of the 18th century, the Bollings constructed at least four dwellings on the brow of the hill known as Bolling's Hill, two on East Hill and two on West Hill. The two dwellings on East Hill composed the main group; both are shown in the engraving pictured here. An 1829 insurance policy confirms that they were seventy-two feet apart; apparently the Bollings intended to construct a larger building in the center. The main block of both buildings was a center-passage, five-bay unit of one story over a high English basement. Both buildings had side wings, but the eastern building also had a chamber wing extending from the south elevation.

It was from the East Hill buildings on 25 April 1781 that Mary Marshall Tabb Bolling watched the Battle of Petersburg, which resulted in the orderly withdrawal across the Pocahontas Bridge of the Virginians under Baron von Steuben and Peter Muhlenberg in the face of a British attack—a battle in which her young son Robert was a participant. It was from this house on the next day that she watched the British burn the shipping in the harbor and all of the tobacco in her inspection warehouses—the Bollings owned five of the seven official tobacco inspections at the Falls of the Appomattox, a leading center of the North American tobacco trade. It was here that she entertained William Phillips, Benedict Arnold, and Lord Cornwallis during their occupation of Petersburg in April and May of 1781, herself confined to the chamber wing. Here Phillips died. Here Arnold saw the end of his military career, when he was displaced by the arrival of Cornwallis. Here Cornwallis gathered the third-largest British army of the Revolution, only to lead them off to ignominy at Yorktown.

In 1783 young Robert Bolling, Jr., lived at West Hill (q.v.), even after his mother's death. The East Hill dwellings were occupied by various parties, including his sister Mariana and his son Robert Buckner Bolling. In 1855 the eastern dwelling, the structure that Robert Buckner Bolling referred to as Bollingbrook, burned. The western building was demolished around 1925. (Engraving: Benson Lossing, *Field Book of the Revolution*, 1850)
RDW, Jr.

PECKATONE, on the Potomac River, Sandy Point vicinity, Westmoreland County
Built ca. 1750; burned 1886

Peckatone was one of the grand Georgian mansions of colonial Virginia, akin in size and design to Carter's Grove and Cleve (q.v.). The house is little remembered today. The only record of its appearance is this hazy photograph of the gutted ruin; no descriptions or drawings are known. No clues to its floor plan remain at the site; the brick ruins were removed more than a half-century ago for use in the restoration of Stratford. Was the seven-bay façade that is shown here repeated on the north front, or was that elevation five bays across as at Carter's Grove and Cleve? Was the entry a hall that was wider and set forward from the stairs, as at Carter's Grove and Cleve? All we can answer is that the pairing of windows close to the entrance suggests that they lit a hall broader than the simpler center passage common to many Virginia houses.

From the evidence in this photograph of subtleties in proportioning and detailing, Peckatone may have been one of Virginia's better-designed 18th-century works. The chimneys were so tall as to offer a bold verticality that served to check the horizontal sweep of seven bays. The windows, taller on the lower level, were positioned to establish both regularity and even a sense of motion; they were tastefully framed with both rubbed brick and stone flat arches and sills, an elegant touch that was not overstated. The façade was at the same time both instantly impressive yet engaging to the lingering eye. Only one dependency is known to have been built at Peckatone; this two-story, three-bay, gable-roofed brick structure may date to a later period.

The name Peckatone reportedly honored an Indian chief of the region. The tract had been owned by the Corbin family since the mid–17th century. Gawin Corbin built the mansion; he willed it to his wife, Hannah, provided that she never remarry. Hannah Corbin's papers (at the Virginia Historical Society) prove the widow capable on her own as a plantation manager; she lived unmarried with her husband's former doctor. Martha, the daughter of Gawin and Hannah Corbin, became notorious on her maturity as a tyrant to her overseers and slaves; local legend described her demise in a hurricane that swept away not only the mistress of Peckatone but her coach and coachmen as well. (Photograph: Thomas Tileston Waterman, *The Mansions of Virginia, 1706–1776*, copyright © 1946 by the University of North Carolina Press, renewed 1974 by Janet R. Hale. Used by permission of the publisher.)

AMBLER HOUSE, Jamestown
Built mid–18th century; burned 1862 and 1895

The Ambler family owned a large portion of Jamestown Island; accordingly the Ambler house was the largest residence built there. Severely damaged by an 1862 fire, the house was rebuilt only to be gutted by a second fire, in 1895, leaving only a ruin. Old photographs and archaeological investigation, however, permit a partial reconstruction of the house. It would have had a hipped roof initially. With a thirty-eight-by-fifty-four-foot footprint and solid brick construction, the Ambler house was a small version of the Governor's Palace (forty-eight by fifty-four feet) in nearby Williamsburg. The symmetrical and carefully proportioned five-bay façades of both residences identify these as examples of the early classic house type that was imported to the colony from England beginning in the late 17th

century. In a departure from English precedent, the Ambler house was given a wide central passage—thirteen feet—that by midcentury was not infrequently seen in Virginia. The passage was sufficiently wide to serve as a habitable space, popular during warm weather because of its cross-ventilation. The stabilized ruins are today part of the Jamestown National Historic Site. (Photographs: Virginia Historical Society)
MM

CHATSWORTH, Tree Hill vicinity, Henrico County
Built before 1751; burned ca. 1915

Chatsworth was a Randolph property. There were many in the colony, where the family was large, influential, and even renowned. "You must be prepared to hear the name Randolph frequently," noted a French traveler to Virginia in the 1780s, the marquis de Chastellux, who recognized the clan as "one of the most numerous and wealthiest" of the colony's "first families." When writing *Moby Dick* in 1851, Herman Melville cited the Randolphs as the quintessential "old established family in the land," the ultimate contrast to those families whose sons were forced into the perilous profession of whaling.

The dynasty was founded in 1680 by William Randolph I, who established a plantation at Turkey Island below the falls of the James River. One of his sons, John Randolph, was even knighted. Third generation Randolph brothers and cousins so dominated the machinations of colonial politics that their solidarity annoyed Lt. Gov. Robert Dinwiddie and challenged his authority. The colonial Randolphs established a dozen plantations along the James River. Much of the architecture they erected is of interest because the family controlled tens of thousands of acres, a significant portion of the settled Virginia landscape.

The house at Turkey Island was renovated or perhaps entirely rebuilt around 1770 by Ryland Randolph, a grandson of the builder. It was destroyed during the Civil War, but early-19th-century accounts describe a two-story brick house with wings of one story, roofed with a large dome. Also lost are significant houses of the second generation of Randolphs. Curles, the nearby home of Richard Randolph, was a two-story, single-pile wooden structure, twenty-five by ninety-five feet. Less is known about Dungeness, the Goochland County home of Isham Randolph, because it burned before 1800.

Houses of the third generation of the family have fared better. William Randolph III built Wilton, which was moved to Richmond in 1933 by the Colonial Dames. Its original site is close to Turkey Island. A cousin, also named William Randolph, extended his father Thomas's Tuckahoe (Goochland County) into an H-plan type. Peyton Randolph expanded the Williamsburg house of his father, Sir John Randolph. Peyton's brother John built a town house there later called Tazewell Hall, which also survives, although altered after two moves.

Peter Randolph (1717–64) built Chatsworth, not far from both Turkey Island and the original site of Wilton. He was the brother of William Randolph III and a man of significant accomplishments. A preeminent landowner and slaveholder who owned some twenty thousand acres and 250 slaves, Peter Randolph was equally successful with his public career. Not only a burgess, he was also appointed in 1749 surveyor-general of the customs for the Southern District of America and was made a member of the governor's Council. By that date he probably had built his mansion; the seat appears on the 1751 Fry-Jefferson map of Virginia.

Chatsworth was an impressive Georgian structure. If it predated Wilton (ca. 1750–53), which the core of the house resembled, it may have been the most fashionable of the Randolph houses at the time it was erected. A later traveler, J. F. D. Smyth, described it as "a very good house with an agreeable perspective." Peter Randolph's executor called him "a most expensive Man in every Article of Life." Unlike his brothers and cousins, who settled for John Wollaston's moderate-sized canvases, he commissioned from the painter extravagant three-quarter-length portraits of himself and his wife to hang at Chatsworth; his intent apparently was to match the handsome canvases at neighboring Westover. The unusual double portico at Chatsworth is oddly proportioned and almost certainly was not original to the house. (Photograph: Valentine Museum)

BOSCOBEL, Fredericksburg vicinity, Stafford County
Built ca. 1752; burned 1915

The colonial history of Stafford and King George Counties is inseparable from that of the Fitzhugh family, whose Virginia founder, William Fitzhugh (1651–1701), settled in the region in the late 17th century. On a wilderness frontier, he and his descendants became patrons of architecture, silver, and portrait painting. The first Fitzhugh built Eagle's Nest, describing it as not "an ordinary Virginia house" (not a post-hole building), but a "very good" framed structure with brick chimneys and thirteen rooms, several of which were hung with tapestries. A part of that building is possibly incorporated within the current Eagle's Nest that occupies the site. William Fitzhugh III constructed Chatham, a larger building, which survives. Also standing is Marmion, built by Maj. John Fitzhugh, the fifth son of the first William.

Lost Fitzhugh residences of note are Bedford, the home of Henry, the second son of the dynasty founder; Bellair, built by Henry's third son, John; and Boscobel, the residence of Henry's second son, Thomas (1725–68). Little is known about Bedford and Bellair, which are of interest because each housed a sizable collection of family portraits. Boscobel's owner celebrated his family heritage in a different manner, by copying the two hundred letters of his grandfather William Fitzhugh I. The replica letter book is marked with the word "Boscobel" on its back cover.

Boscobel was situated on a ridge between the Potomac and Rappahannock Rivers; appealing views, enjoyed from its porches, extended both north and south. Like Eagle's Nest, this was a frame house of traditional Virginia form. Robert Lancaster, who visited the house shortly before it burned, described the architecture as "after the order of a roomy cottage." Only forty by twenty-seven feet in plan, the house nonetheless had seven rooms on the first floor and four on the second; a half-dozen were given large fireplaces. A cast-iron fireback in one was stamped *T. F. 1752*, an indication that the building that survived into the 20th century was the original colonial structure. Insurance policies of 1803, 1805, and 1816 document wooden dependencies (a seventeen-by-twenty-four-foot kitchen and a sixteen-by-twenty-eight-foot "dwelling house") that defined a forecourt. (Photograph: Valentine Museum)

OLD STONE FORT, Middle Marsh Brook, Middletown vicinity, Frederick County
Built 1755, expanded ca. 1800; demolished after 1941

The so-called Old Fort was a two-story structure built of native stone and covered with a gable roof; the front and rear elevations were six bays in length. Originally, however, the house was only one and a half stories in height and two bays long; it was expanded about 1800 into an I-house. Such an alteration followed a common practice among German-speaking farmers of the Shenandoah Valley who with time became increasingly Anglicized.

Popular myth holds that this building served as some sort of a fort early in its life; the appellation, however, has less to do with any military or defensive function and more to do with British-American misreadings of the solid nature of these Valley Rhenish houses. Among the evidence offered as explanations of the supposed defensive function of this structure are, in addition to its general stocky, solid appearance, the presence in the basement of a small splayed opening at shoulder height said to have been a rifle hole. To further add to speculation, in the center of this opening was a branched, wrought-iron swivel that was said to have been a rifle loop. In reality, the "rifle loop" was simply a wrought-iron grate used to secure the opening (itself already narrowed to deter both thieves and animals from entering). German-speaking farmers in the Valley tended to unite work, living, and storage areas, and as the basement was used for the preparation and storage of foodstuffs (of prime interest to both thieves and animals), it was a part of the house in need of securing. Also, in the foundation of the chimney was a pool formed by a spring. An overflow carried the water across the floor in a rill and through the entire length of the house to the south end. This was commonly explained as an arrangement so that drinking water would be available during times when refuge was sought in the house. In reality, the water was there because the basement functioned as a kitchen. This followed the Valley Rhenish inclination to unite work and living functions, functions that in a British-American farm would have been spread among the main house and several ancillary buildings.

In plan, the first floor was divided by a sheathed longitudinal partition, forming a large east room. The western room was further divided by a cross-partition into two small, square, unheated rooms. It would appear that this building initially was a *Flurküchenhaus*, or hall-kitchen house. With that plan, a front (and often rear) door led into a narrow kitchen room, or *Küche*, which is served by a large cooking fireplace. This room was the cooking and primary living space and corresponded to the British-American hall. A wider room called a *Stube* was located on the opposite side of the chimney and was used for more formal gatherings (corresponding to the British-American parlor). Perhaps the most dramatic alteration to the plan, made circa 1800, was the removal of the central chimney and its replacement with two exterior chimney stacks, typically fitted out with cast-iron Franklin stoves. As a result, the house as photographed resembled the British-American double-pile, side-passage house more strongly that it revealed its Rhenish origins. (Photograph: Historic American Buildings Survey, Library of Congress)

BELVIDERE, in block bounded by Pine, China, Belvidere, and Spring Streets, Oregon Hill, Richmond
Built before 1757, with later additions; burned 1854

One of the great English contributions to modern life is the ability to look at the countryside as if it were a series of compositions like those found in paintings. In the 18th century, this Picturesque point of view began to reshape Virginians' perceptions of their own terrain, and viewers had started to react to the beauty of the falls of the James River by the middle of the century. One historic response to the locale was the property called Belvidere. The very name of the estate is an 18th-century British spelling of *belvedere*, meaning a building commanding a fine view and taken from the Italian for "a fair sight."

Belvidere occupied part of the extensive lands that William Byrd I accumulated in the 17th century. These holdings were inherited by William Byrd II, the founder of Richmond, in 1704 and then by William Byrd III in 1744. Whether or not an earlier dwelling had stood where the villa was constructed, by 1757 Elizabeth Hill Carter Byrd, William Byrd III's estranged wife, was living on the site, and the estate was called Belvidere. The two-story wooden dwelling was apparently a single-pile house. In 1759, the Rev. Andrew Burnaby, an English traveler, noted that "colonel Byrd has a small place called Belvedere, . . . as romantic and elegant as anything I have ever seen," because of its views of the "most picturesque and beautiful cascade" in the middle of "a prodigious extent of wilderness." The new love of irregular nature may not have affected the layout of the Belvidere gardens, however. On the river side, the grounds were laid out as a series of terraces, the treatment that apparently dominated 18th-century gardening in the Chesapeake region.

The house at Belvidere was the home of a succession of prominent Virginians. After the disintegration of William Byrd III's fortune and just before his suicide at Westover in 1777, the property left his family for good. George Washington's nephew Bushrod Washington owned Belvidere from 1795 through 1798, until his appointment to the United States Supreme Court. The Washingtons entertained their friend B. Henry Latrobe at Belvidere, and Latrobe, enchanted by the scenery, drew five identifiable landscapes on the property, one of which is pictured here.

By the time of the Washingtons' occupancy, the original part of the house at Belvidere had become the center section of a dwelling with paired wings to the east and west and a portico to the north. In the courtyard on the north stood a pair of outbuildings, an office at the east, and what was intended to be a kitchen at the west. The Belvidere portico, with its rectangular pillars, overhanging eaves, and pronounced brackets, could have been one of the economical exercises in the square Tuscan order that interested 18th-century Virginians, and it may have had a familial relationship to the Tuscan order that George Washington used for the piazza and quadrants at Mount Vernon in his rebuilding of 1774 through 1787. The upper level of the Belvidere porch might have served as an outdoor room. Significantly, the porch did not stand on the south façade, facing the sun and the river view, but on the north, enjoying the coolest exposure and looking down an avenue that led to the road from Richmond to Westham. This portico was an early member of a tribe of tiered Richmond porches, often with square pillars but varying in purpose and form, that thrived at least into the 20th century.

In 1798 the Washingtons sold Belvidere to the civic leader and real estate speculator Col. John Harvie, Jr. Harvie had just commissioned a Latrobe house (q.v.) in view of Belvidere but sold the new building to Robert Gamble and lived at Belvidere until his death in 1807. In 1814 Harvie's widow sold Belvidere to another Latrobe patron, Benjamin J. Harris, who had built a house called Clifton (q.v.). Harris, a wealthy tobacco and cotton manufacturer, preserved and probably enlarged the Belvidere mansion and its dependencies but cut most of the estate up into a residential subdivision called Belvidera.

As of the early 19th century, Belvidere had acquired an array of outbuildings, including a greenhouse. By no later than mid-1817, the grounds had extensive serpentine walling with regular undulations, like Jefferson's later serpentine walls at the University of Virginia. No doubt the source of the Belvidere walling was Britain, where these so-called crinkle-crankle, crinkum-crankum, or ribbon walls developed as a standard possibility for gardens during the 18th and 19th centuries.

Harris lost his fortune by speculating in what would become the Fan District. Industrial development along the James and its canal, together with the nearness of the expanding penitentiary (q.v.), doomed the villa at Belvidere in the 1830s, and the house had been a rental property for two decades when a fire destroyed it in 1854. An antebellum tenant house from Belvidere still exists at 307 South Cherry Street. Vestiges of the terraced gardens remain visible between Holly Street and the CSX train tracks. The vistas from the site are lost, but in the views from Hollywood Cemetery, which occupies part of the former Belvidere tract, the beauty of the James, one of Richmond's greatest treasures, is preserved. (Image: Maryland Historical Society)
CEB

GREENWAY COURT,
White Post vicinity, Clarke County
Built before 1760; abandoned ca. 1830

Greenway Court was the residence of Thomas, sixth Baron Fairfax of Cameron, after he vacated Belvoir (q.v.), leaving it to the care of his cousin William Fairfax. At Greenway Court, in what was then the backwoods, Lord Fairfax was better positioned to administer the rent and sale of his five-million-acre inheritance, the Northern Neck proprietary. He changed to frontier garb and became a recluse. Historians believe that this immensely wealthy figure was a misogynist as well.

Greenway Court is first mentioned in documentary

records in 1760. At that date the house apparently was sixty feet long and included a banquet hall. Two later owners built lateral additions of twenty feet each, so that 19th-century visitors described a long structure. The best account was written by novelist John Pendleton Kennedy, who in 1853 was there with Washington Irving, author of a monumental biography of George Washington; Fairfax had employed Washington as a surveyor. Kennedy described the house as built of stone and stuccoed, "still standing, though very much broken down and decayed." It was "nearly one hundred feet in length, with a heavy, beetling porch, of which the floor [was] guarded by close panel-work instead of railing. It [had] dormer windows in the roof, two belfries. . . . There [were] earthenware vessels . . . for martens or swallows to make their nests in, built in each chimney—three in each" and "double rooms through the front." Apparently the structure was single-pile but exceptionally deep. Irving and Kennedy were told that Fairfax used this building for "the entertainment of his guests," while he himself lived nearby in a "small cabin of the simplest structure, made of clapboards, . . . and not above twenty feet square." The cabin was one of several outbuildings almost randomly placed around the "large grass-plot or court" from which the complex derived its name. Only the foundations of its chimney were visible in 1853. Kennedy made note also of a carriage house and a limestone land office ("in which Lord Fairfax transacted his business") that had been "left without any apparent effort at repair, to moulder away under the hand of time." Nonetheless, the small land office has survived to this day, as has a porter's lodge and a plank "powder house." (Image: Virginia Historical Society)

WEST HILL, on Bolling's Hill just west of Adams Street and north of Tabb Street, Petersburg
Built ca. 1760–80; demolished 1950

West Hill was a large, five-bay frame dwelling, sixty by twenty-eight feet, that rose a story and a half above a high English basement. It evidently had been expanded in both directions from an earlier three-bay house. It stood on the brow of Bolling's Hill, looking directly down on the Pocahontas Bridge, the main route across the Appomattox River.

At the close of the American Revolution, young Robert Bolling, Jr., was living at West Hill, while his widowed mother continued to make East Hill (q.v.) her home. In 1783 he laid out forty-six lots north of Bolling's Hill in a development that he called Bollingbrook, which immediately became the most valuable real estate in the community. The young Bolling made it more valuable still by giving the town land for both a farmer's market and a courthouse complex. (The courthouse acre, being just downhill from West Hill, has grown and swallowed up the West Hill property—the site of the house and its dependencies is now occupied by court buildings and the police department.) Then, between 1809 and 1813, Bolling laid out hundreds of lots in the area south of Bolling's Hill, creating the neighborhoods known today as Poplar Lawn, Bunker Hill, and Delectable Heights. He remained at West Hill until circa 1823, when he completed construction of Centre Hill (still extant), a dwelling on a far grander scale than anything Petersburg had seen before. After Bolling moved out of West Hill, the house began a slow decline that did not abate until its demolition in 1950. (Photograph: Virginia Historical Society) RDW, Jr.

SEA VIEW, Locustville vicinity, Accomack County
Built ca. 1762; burned 1974

The extraordinarily fertile soil of Virginia's Eastern Shore enabled a relatively compact landholding to be a productive plantation. As a result, the region was more thickly populated during the colonial period than was the mainland, and a relatively large quantity of 18th-century dwellings were built there. Many of these houses survived well into the 20th century, but by the 1950s a number of them stood abandoned. Their rescue has been inhibited by the reluctance of farmers there to sell any part of their holdings. A noteworthy example of the Shore's many deserted landmarks was Sea View, a refined Georgian dwelling erected by James Henry soon after 1762. The house was situated on a lonely site near the shore of Burtons Bay, on the Atlantic side of the peninsula. The two-story brick structure was set off by its gauged-brick jack arches, gauged belt course, and modillion cornice. Although much of the woodwork had been removed before 1960, the handsome Georgian stair, some paneled wainscoting, and paneled doors remained until vandals burned the house in 1974. Only portions of the walls survived the fire. (Photographs: Virginia Department of Historic Resources)

TEBBS HOUSE, Dumfries,
Prince William County
Built ca. 1762; destroyed by storm
1933

The town of Dumfries was founded in 1759 by wealthy planters and merchants, including George Mason of Gunston Hall, John Tayloe II of Mount Airy, and the now all-but-forgotten Maj. Fouchee Tebbs, who owned the brick Georgian mansion pictured here. An equally imposing colonial house, Williams' Ordinary, which still stands in Dumfries, was probably built by the same masons, because the two buildings share the uncommon features of coursed stonework at the basement level, header bond brickwork, stone window lintels, stone quoins, and a low hipped roof. An early wood structure in Dumfries that survived into the 20th century was the Merchent house (q.v.). The town is little remembered in the context of colonial architecture because its anticipated growth was cut short following the silting of

its harbor, the relocation of the county seat to Brentsville, and a catastrophic fire in 1833.

The Tebbs house was an impressive exercise in Georgian design, if a peculiar one. The gradation of window heights was well handled, as were the full cornice and the interior woodwork of the "great room," which ran the depth of the house, south of the passage. Less successful were other features, notably the center doorway with an archivolt too small for the pilasters that supported it, the absence of stone lintels on the side windows, and the placement of chimney and stairs (one flue had to bend to reach its stack, while the principal stairs gave no entry to one of the upper rooms). While these oddities hint at inexperience of the builders, two construction features suggest that they were not native to the colony. Header bond brickwork was rare in early America except in Annapolis; it was popular for finer-quality 18th-century buildings in England. The great room of the Tebbs house was framed with north-south girders enforced above and below with smaller, perpendicular joists; this system was rarely seen in Virginia but known in England and called there a carcase floor. (Photograph: Historic American Buildings Survey, Library of Congress)

SALISBURY, site of present
Salisbury Country Club,
Chesterfield County
Built ca. 1763; burned 1923

Salisbury is famous as one of several houses lived in successively by Patrick Henry; he resided there from 1784 to 1786, his final term as governor. Henry rented Salisbury from Thomas Mann Randolph, who in 1777 had purchased the property from Abraham Sallé, its likely builder.

The only image of Salisbury is the photograph shown here, which was published early in the 20th century by Robert Lancaster. He described the setting as seemingly "lonely and remote by reason of the deep woods" nearby. Lancaster found the rooms "big, bright, [and] airy," even though the structure was

relatively small. The rooms were well lit because transoms expanded the height of the windows; precedent for this unusual feature is found not in English but in French architecture, which was known to Huguenots resident in Chesterfield County. The plan was double-pile, with asymmetrical chimneys; a visitor to the house remembered two passages perpendicular to one another. A hipped roof with dormers and several porches gave the house distinction, even a slight sense of grandeur.

In the mid–19th century Salisbury was owned by Gen. Edward Johnson, a veteran of the Mexican and Civil Wars. The original Salisbury tract is now occupied by a modern development that carries the same name. (Photograph: Robert Lancaster, *Virginia Homes and Churches,* 1915)

MENOKIN, Warsaw vicinity, Richmond County
Built ca. 1768–78; fell into ruins ca. 1965–90

Named for the thousand-acre tract on which it stood, Menokin was historically important as the residence of Francis Lightfoot Lee, a signer of the Declaration of Independence. The house also held architectural distinction. Only three bays wide and forty-three feet long, it was but two-thirds the length of many Virginia mansions of the period. Nonetheless, Menokin was a remarkably monumental structure, as were its flanking dependencies, due to the simple geometry and bold stonework of the façades. The house is of further interest as one of few buildings from early America for which a detailed original plan and elevation survive (at the Virginia Historical Society).

Francis Lightfoot Lee apparently had little to do with the architecture of Menokin, which is tied more closely to his wife, Rebecca, and her father, John Tayloe II of neighboring Mount Airy. Use of the plantation was a wedding gift in 1769 from the father to the daughter. In 1771 one of the structures on the property was sufficiently completed for the couple to move in; two years later Tayloe guaranteed that "the buildings [of Menokin would be] finished at the expense of my estate," and in 1778, the year before his death, he deeded to Rebecca "all that tract . . . of 'Menokin'" and those who worked it ("twenty negro Slave[s] . . . together with their Increase" of the past nine years). Menokin is explicable only in the context of John Tayloe and Mount Airy. Not only was the plantation carved from his land holdings, but the mansion's unusual façade was almost certainly derived from the elevations of the two principal Mount Airy dependencies that it closely resembles. Some of the workmen in the employ of joiner-architect William Buckland, who received payments from Tayloe to finish the interiors of Mount Airy from 1761 through 1763, probably built Menokin; Buckland is also mentioned in Tayloe's account book in 1768. Buckland or one of his craftsmen may have produced the architectural drawing of Menokin. If the almost cubic form of the main house, the squat proportions of the fenestration, and the double belt course (not on the drawing) recall Scottish and English examples of the period, perhaps the draftsman and the workmen were immigrants inclined to refine Menokin along the lines of Old World models that they could remember.

At the deaths of Rebecca and Francis Lightfoot Lee in 1797 without heirs, Menokin passed to a Lee nephew but remained in the family for only that additional generation. At some undetermined date the house was stuccoed—as had been planned initially–and a crude porch was constructed. In the 1940s the house was abandoned; in the 1960s its woodwork was removed to prevent its being looted and eventually placed in the care of the Association for the Preservation of Virginia Antiquities. (The paneling of the principal room is currently on extended loan to the Virginia Historical Society.) Menokin is now largely collapsed, but two corners and the chimneys are intact. The site and the now stabilized ruins are owned by the Menokin Foundation, established in 1995 to preserve them and possibly reconstruct the complex. (Photograph: Virginia Historical Society)

DAIRY, YORK COUNTY POOR FARM, Grafton vicinity, York County
Built mid– to late 18th century; demolished 1970s

Dairies, ventilated buildings for the storage of milk, butter, and cheese, were once a common and essential feature of Virginia's rural landscape. The best examples were designed both to have visual appeal and to keep dairy products cool. Most were ten or twelve feet square with plastered walls, deep eaves, paved floors, and long openings just beneath the eaves for ventilation. Frequently the openings were filled with decorative slats to keep out birds and other animals. This example, a twelve-by-twelve-foot frame structure, was built on the grounds of the York County Poor Farm, a working farm for indigents sponsored by the county.

The dairy shown here was long a familiar landmark to motorists traveling along US Highway 17 between Yorktown and Newport News. The photograph was taken in the 1930s by the Historic American Buildings Survey (HABS), which had as its mission the documentation of examples of early American architecture whose preservation was threatened. One of the HABS architects (possibly Charles Peterson, a founder of HABS) is shown standing against the dairy for scale. By the 1970s the dairy was fast deteriorating and was serving as a backboard for a basketball hoop. It and an adjacent cluster of early structures, which together formed what was known as the Virginia Poor Farm Group, soon vanished in the wake of Highway 17's strip development. (Photograph: Historic American Buildings Survey, Library of Congress)

FORT RHODES, Luray vicinity, Page County
Built ca. 1770–80; burned 1990

Fort Rhodes, until struck by lightning and burned in 1990, graphically illustrated the evolution of Rhenish-American houses in the 18th and 19th centuries. German-speaking farmers quickly abandoned traditional village arrangements in favor of isolated farmsteads when settling in southeastern Pennsylvania, western Maryland, and the Shenandoah Valley. By the third quarter of the 18th century, Swiss Mennonites in what is now Page County were building detached, internal-chimney farmhouses reflecting some of the spatial arrangements of the Rhenish *Ernhauser*.

Fort Rhodes (one of several nondefensive houses to assume the appellation *Fort*) was among the largest. John Rhodes (sometimes spelled Rodes) built it around 1770, on the site of a house built by his grandfather, who had been killed there by Indians in 1764, at the time of Pontiac's Rebellion. The hewn-log walls of the second house stood two stories above a large stone-vaulted work cellar, which contained a spring. The spring served for preparation and storage of food as well as providing water that was pulled up to the main floor through a hole in the vault. A chief characteristic of Rhenish-American houses was the incorporation of work and storage space within the body of the building. Indeed, the principal doorway led directly into the landowner's kitchen, and it was through this space that people generally entered the *Stube*, or dining/entertaining room. At Rhodes, however, there also appears always to have been a roughly centered exterior doorway opening directly into the *Stube*. An off-center chimney provided an oversized fireplace for the kitchen and a means of fueling an iron stove in the *Stube*.

Subsequent owner-occupants altered this and other old houses standing so obviously outside the mainstream of British-American building. Most dramatically, sometime during the years 1820–40, Fort Rhodes's remodelers removed the internal chimney and replaced it with two smaller exterior stacks, each serving two fireplaces, the first-floor ones fitted with Shenandoah Valley–made cast-iron Franklin stoves. They likewise removed cooking to a detached kitchen. The old house thus came to both appear and function much like contemporary double-pile, side-passage houses of predominantly British-American origin. The fenestration changed too, from low, horizontal windows cut through a minimum of wall logs to less archaic six-over-six and nine-over-six sash windows. The interior was further altered by plastering the log walls, and hiding the previously exposed floor joists on the main level. (Photograph: Virginia Department of Historic Resources)
EAC

MANNSFIELD, east of Fredericksburg, Spotsylvania County
Built ca. 1770s; destroyed by shelling 1863

In the 1790s the English traveler Isaac Weld journeyed through northern Tidewater Virginia, where he met gentlemen he described as well educated and living "in a style, which approaches nearer to that of English country gentlemen, than what is to be met with any where else on the continent." Among them was Mann Page III (1749–1803), the builder of Mannsfield, who had been raised in the manners of the English gentry at Rosewell (q.v.), as had his wife, Mary Tayloe, at Mount Airy. Like Rosewell and Mount Airy, Mannsfield was one of the largest and most formal of the mansions built in colonial Virginia. This symbol of Old Dominion culture was obliterated by artillery fire during the Civil War.

Mann Page III graduated from the College of William and Mary in 1768. Beginning in 1772, he served Spotsylvania County as a burgess, a delegate to the Continental Congress, and a delegate to the Virginia General Assembly. He married in 1776. Page, whose mother also was a Tayloe, provided his wife and cousin a house very much like the structure in which she had grown up. Stylistically, Mannsfield was of a type known in the colonies from printed sources like James Gibbs's *Book of Architecture* that had been published in England early in the century, beginning when Lord Burlington revived Palladian ideas. But the house was just as closely tied to its Virginia neighbor, Mount Airy.

Mannsfield incorporated so many design elements from the Tayloe house one wonders whether craftsmen engaged at Mount Airy worked also for Page. Was John Tayloe II involved in the design process at three houses, his own Mount Airy, his daughter Rebecca's Menokin (q.v.), and his daughter Mary's Mannsfield? Mount Airy, begun circa 1754, is distinguished as the first house in America to achieve Palladio's plan for an expansive five-part "villa." It is a showpiece of Mid-Georgian features: each long façade has a central pavilion and pediment to give emphasis to the center, and the house is flanked by quadrant passageways leading to a pair of advanced dependencies. Those features were repeated at Mannsfield. The stone walls at Mannsfield were dressed with quoins and framed window openings, as at Mount Airy. The measurements of the main house at Mannsfield, sixty-nine by fifty-one feet, were almost exactly those of Mount Airy. The flanking dependencies at Mannsfield had the same central chimney, and thus the same appearance, as the ones at Mount Airy. (These were a laundry and kitchen, according to an 1806 insurance policy. They were long, 45 by 28 1/2 feet, and in that respect more like the ones at Rosewell.) The floor plan of Mannsfield, unearthed when the house site was excavated in 1934, was akin to that at Mount Airy: there was a sizable center hall (albeit one with stairs), and chimneys were placed on inner walls. The hall was supported by earth, possibly to carry a marble floor, as was reportedly installed at both Mount Airy and Rosewell.

By the late colonial period Palladian ideas seemed dated to B. Henry Latrobe, who visited Mannsfield in 1796: "Mr. Page's house is built of Stone of a good but coarse grit in the style of the Country Gentlemen's houses in England of 50 Years ago." "It is a tolerably good house," he wrote, "but the taste is indifferent." To Page, however, and to the later Georgian revivalists, the style seemed both appropriate for rural Virginia and timeless. (Photograph: Virginia Historical Society)

NOMINI HALL, near Montross, Westmoreland County
Built ca. 1772; burned 1850

Named for a nearby creek that empties into the Potomac River, Nomini Hall was significant because of its ambitious scale and its association with one of colonial Virginia's leading families. The immense size of both the house and its support buildings reflected the extraordinary wealth of its owner.

Robert Carter III (1728–94) led a perplexing life. He was the grandson and namesake of powerful Robert "King" Carter, but both his father and grandfather died in 1732, when the boy was only four years old. The father had established a seat at Nomini circa 1729 but had little time to develop it. Soon the son gained a stepfather, John Lewis, and an adopted home, Warner Hall, in Gloucester County. At age nine, the young Carter was placed by uncles at the College of William and Mary. At twenty-one, he searched for four years in London for an environment in which so wealthy a Virginia heir might belong. According to cousin John Page, the future governor, the experience left Carter "inconceivably illiterate, and also corrupted and vicious." In 1758, at age thirty, Carter was appointed to the governor's Council; for the next decade he lived in Williamsburg. Abruptly, in 1772, he retired to Nomini Hall, but in the end he rejected the plantation lifestyle as well. Eventually he abandoned his political life, converted to the Baptist faith, and freed his nearly five hundred slaves. He retreated to Baltimore, the family home of his wife, Frances Ann Tasker, and became a Swedenborgian disciple. Nomini Hall was willed to his heirs.

Robert Carter III altered substantially whatever house had been erected at Nomini by his father. The Palladian windows that are shown in the 19th-century sketch illustrated here would have been exceptional before midcentury and prove the point. To judge from his orders to merchants in England in 1772 and 1773 for such items as carpets, plate with the family crest, and an organ, he developed Nomini Hall at that time. The appearance of the new house is known only from the sketch and from a lengthy description written in 1774 by Philip Fithian, tutor to the Carter family.

Fithian described a "Great-House" even longer and deeper than the norm for a Georgian mansion in the colony; Nomini Hall measured seventy-six by forty-four feet. The plan was ordinary in one respect: there were "4 Rooms on a Floor." Below were "a dining Room where we usually sit ["parlor" was the term more often used for such a room]; the second is a dining Room for the Children; the third is Mr. Carter's study; & the fourth is a Ball-Room 30 Feet long." "Above stairs" were rooms for "Mr. & Mrs. Carter," for their daughters, and "the other 2 for occasional Company." Atypical, and now a matter of speculation, was the arrangement of the passage(s) and stairs, because what was apparently the south elevation is pictured with not only Palladian windows but also two doors. Fithian described a porch in front of the doors ("a beautiful Jutt . . . 18 ft. long & 8 Feet deep from the wall, which is supported by 3 tall pillars"); it had been removed by the time of the sketch. He called the other long front of the house "the most beautiful," because of its "Row of 7 Windows" and "large Portico in the middle" (probably one story, given the date of this account). The entire house was "now perfectly white." The new covering of stucco, the five chimney stacks ("2 of these serve only for ornaments"), the peculiar structure of the roof as sketched, and the orientation of the approach road to the narrow east façade all raise the possibility that the house of Robert Carter II was incorporated into the mansion of the son, creating a unique structure.

A schoolhouse, stable, coach house, and washhouse stood "at equal Distance [100 yards] from each corner" of the main house. All were substantial in size, forty-five by twenty-seven feet long. The schoolhouse and washhouse both had a pair of bedchambers on the upper floor. The stable and coach house, located to the west, were "higher pitched to be convenient for holding Hay & Fodder." These were not visible from the house, which had no windows on its west elevation. Other dependencies on the western perimeter of this landscaped "Square" were a kitchen, bake house, dairy, storehouse, "& several other small Houses." These "form[ed] a little handsome Street." The land on the opposite side, to the east, was laid out as a garden, with walks, a terrace, and a bowling green. Beyond was a three-hundred-yard-long roadway lined with "2 Rows of tall, flourishing, beautiful Poplars." These must have been planted by Robert Carter II; they alone survive at the site today. (Image: Virginia Historical Society)

BELLE FARM,
Gloucester County
Built ca. 1775–80; taken down
1930

Belle Farm was a casualty of the evolving conception of Williamsburg's restoration in the 1920s and '30s. The initial conceiver, Rev. W. A. R. Goodwin, benefactor John D. Rockefeller, Jr., and the architectural firm Perry, Shaw and Hepburn struggled as early as 1928 with the problem of how to replace missing buildings that would flesh out their portrait of the 18th-century capital. It was clear from the beginning that the principal public buildings would be reconstructed, but what of the missing houses and shops?

Initially the planners embraced schemes for moving early houses from less central parts of Williamsburg and from the Virginia countryside. Two rural houses were recorded, demolished, and their finish material moved to town. Ultimately the museum's thinkers rejected the assembled-village model and chose to re-create as explicitly as possible the particular buildings whose outlines survived in the ground and archives.

Belle Farm was dismantled in 1930 for rebuilding, possibly on Palace Green. Its remains were relegated to a warehouse until 1952, when architect Ernest M. Frank designed a house to contain them in suburban Williamsburg. The woodwork was removed about 1991 and installed in a new house near Tappahannock.

When first visited by the Williamsburg architects in 1928, Belle Farm stood in a circa 1775–1800 condition. The front expressed the era's fascination with geometric shapes by stretching a broad, overhanging gable roof across a two-story, central-passage block. The lower front rooms were joined to a third reception-quality space beyond a stair passage in a rear ell, which was picturesquely covered by a gambrel or mansard roof. Two design drawings found on boards in the house portray an arched opening and a mantel with overmantel; both drawings had been used when developing woodwork for the front spaces of the original house. (Photograph: Colonial Williamsburg Foundation)
EAC

MOUNT WARREN,
Warren, Albemarle County
Built ca. 1780; burned 1926

Mount Warren was the home of Wilson Cary Nicholas, governor of Virginia from 1814 to 1816. Nicholas was born in 1761 in Williamsburg and attended the College of William and Mary, where he studied law under George Wythe, as had Thomas Jefferson. During the Revolutionary War he married Margaret Smith of Baltimore and built his home on property along the James River that had been patented by his grandfather Dr. George Nicholas in 1729. The town of Warren grew up, beginning circa 1793, around facilities for shipping wheat used by the younger Nicholas.

Mount Warren was an H-plan complex consisting of a twenty-by-forty-foot, one-story frame house connected by a twenty-by-twenty-foot hyphen to a forty-by-forty-foot, two-story frame dwelling with three classical porticoes.

The 19th century saw many houses built in Warren, along with a tavern, gristmill, warehouse, distillery, blacksmith shop, and ferry. Today only a few houses remain. (Photograph: Prints Collection, Special Collections Department, University Archives, University of Virginia Library)
KEL

RED HILL,
Brookneal vicinity,
Charlotte County
Built late 18th century;
burned 1919

Patrick Henry,
"orator of the Revolu-
tion," assembled this
remote Charlotte
County plantation
through successive
purchases of alluvial
bottomlands and un-
dulating countryside,
making it his final
home. There he built a
modest frame dwell-
ing with a complement
of outbuildings, includ-
ing his law office. This
house (seen in the pho-
tograph at the far right) was later incorporated into a larger structure (the two-story building at the center of the photograph), all of which was destroyed
by fire in 1919. The property remained in the ownership of Henry family descendants until 1944, when it was purchased by the Patrick Henry Memorial
Foundation, which has since developed the property as a museum. The original Red Hill has been reconstructed. Also on the property are Henry's law office outbuilding, which survived the fire, and the graves of Henry and his wife. (Photograph: Valentine Museum)

OSSIAN HALL,
Annandale vicinity, Fairfax
County
Built 1783; burned 1959

Named for an imaginary
Gaelic warrior and bard of the
third century, Ossian, whose
fictional exploits were highly
popularized in Scotland in
1763 as if they were real,
Ossian Hall was essentially a
replica of Mount Vernon, at
least in the use of a giant piazza across the entire back of
the house. As an early copy of
its neighbor, Ossian Hall was
important as unmistakable evidence of George Washington's
influence on American architecture.

The plantation was part of
the same Fitzhugh family tract
from which Ravensworth (q.v.)
was carved. Henry Fitzhugh, a
cousin of William Fitzhugh of Ravensworth, inherited the land on which his son Nicholas would build Ossian Hall. The house was later sold, in 1804, to
David Stuart, a physician, statesman, and friend of George Washington's; he married Eleanor Custis, the widow of John Parke Custis, the son of Martha
Washington. After living for some fifteen years at Hope Park, twenty miles distant, the Stuarts longed to move closer to Mount Vernon and Eleanor's children, who lived nearby. The giant piazza at Ossian Hall may have been original to the house, or it may have been added by the Stuarts.

Ossian Hall was the residence of Sen. Joseph L. Bristow from 1918 until his death in 1944. It was then sold by his heirs to a developer who subdivided
the large tract into small homesites. The house had had no resident owner for fifteen years when vandals stripped its hardware and much of the original
paneling. Accordingly, no one could object effectively in 1959, when Ossian Hall was deliberately burned by the Fairfax County Fire Department as a
training exercise. Annandale Fire Co. #23 then reportedly carried as its emblem on fire trucks an image of Ossian Hall. (Photograph: Historic American
Buildings Survey, Library of Congress)

CORBIN HALL (CHINCOTEAGUE FARM),
Horntown vicinity, Accomack County
Built 1787; burned 2000

Until it was gutted by fire on 14 February 2000, Corbin Hall was perhaps the most academic example of Georgian architecture on Virginia's Eastern Shore. The interior was noted for its woodwork, including a fully paneled parlor and a stately Georgian stair. A dominant feature of the interior was the stair-hall arch, which was framed by fluted pilasters set on pedestals. One of the region's few two-story brick plantation dwellings, the house was built for George Corbin on land purchased by his father in 1745. The construction date of 1787 is assumed from two inscribed bricks. The house was sited at the top of a series of earth terraces to command a sweeping view of Chincoteague Bay. The fire, believed to have been caused by an electrical fault, left only the finely crafted brick walls. Although the current owner is considering rebuilding within the shell, Corbin Hall's outstanding 18th-century joinery is irreplaceable. (Photograph: Virginia Department of Historic Resources)

BLACK HEATH, Midlothian vicinity, Chesterfield County
Built ca. 1790; demolished 1920s

Named for the coal deposits on the property and the Heth family that owned this estate, Black Heath was a two-story, hipped-roof, brick mansion, six bays wide, that at an early date was extended by unmatched wings with gambrel and gable roofs. This union of three colonial roof types, all outdated by 1790, may seem an odd visual mix until it is remembered that Westover, as it was restored during the Colonial Revival period, displays the same inventory of roof designs. Among the dependencies was a circular brick dovecote.

Black Heath was built by Capt. Henry Heth (d. 1821), a veteran of both the American Revolution and the War of 1812. He married in 1787. In 1792 Heth commenced coal mining operations that soon were among the most productive in the new nation. The empty coal pits, however, proved to be problematic. In 1809 Heth consulted B. Henry Latrobe regarding the pumping of water from them. A century later the house was abandoned and subsequently pulled down following the collapse of coal shafts nearby. (Photograph: Virginia Historical Society)

EXETER, Leesburg vicinity, Loudoun County
Built 1790s; burned 1980

Erected for Dr. Wilson Cary Selden in the 1790s, the main house at Exeter was the nucleus of one of the largest complexes of plantation buildings in the region. The house, an amalgam of Federal-derived forms and motifs, blended several roof types into a seven-part plan. The structure featured a two-level Doric portico, pedimented dormers with intersecting tracery, richly detailed mantels, and other interior trim of fine workmanship. Exeter stood neglected for many years until it was destroyed by fire in 1980. The site has been consumed by one of the vast housing developments on the northern edge of Leesburg. (Photograph: Valentine Museum)

(SECOND) VIEWMONT (FRY HOUSE), Carter's Bridge vicinity, Albemarle County
Built ca. 1790s; burned 1939

The house pictured is the second of three built on the same foundations and incorporating the same ramped, gable-end chimneys. The first Viewmont, which may have closely resembled the structure shown here, was the residence of Col. Joshua Fry. Born in England and educated at Oxford, Fry became a professor of mathematics at the College of William and Mary about 1720. In 1751, while living at Viewmont and active as a surveyor, Fry, with Peter Jefferson, produced a definitive map of Virginia. Three years later Fry was given command of the Virginia Regiment, an army newly formed on the eve of the French and Indian War. En route to his command, he fell from his horse and died of his injuries. The authority over the regiment then passed to young George Washington, whose actions soon initiated a world war involving France and England.

The first Viewmont may have been constructed

as early as 1737, the year Fry's eldest son, John, was born. The house passed out of the Fry family in 1786, when it was purchased by Gov. Edmund Randolph. It burned before 1800. As rebuilt, the house was double-pile with a center passage.

Viewmont later passed into the possession of the Moon family; Charlotte "Lottie" Digges Moon became famous as a Baptist missionary to China from 1873 until her death in 1912. When Viewmont was again destroyed by fire, a third house was built on the site, in 1941, by architect Charles Baker. (Photograph: Virginia Historical Society)

SPRING HILL (PRISON HILL), Tabb Street between Market and Union Streets, Petersburg
Built 1790s; demolished ca. 1920

In 1784, when Petersburg was chartered and given its own government and courts, young Sarah Newsum, through her mother as she was not yet of age, presented the town with two acres on the slope south of Brick House Run for its town buildings. The foundations of a jail had been completed on "Prison Hill" when Sarah, the heiress of Peter Jones of Folly Castle, married in 1786 the dashing Revolutionary War officer Erasmus Gill. Gill inflamed the town's common council by inserting himself into the process, trying to get a better deal than his bride had offered, and the council, outraged, accepted the offer of Robert Bolling of a much smaller parcel. In 1799, the merchant Robert Moore purchased the Prison Hill property, which, when he died in 1804, he left to his son Archibald. It is difficult to judge by the land books just when the house there was built, but it appears that Moore either bought the house already in place or constructed it in 1799.

Spring Hill enjoyed a commanding situation on a hill above the valley of Brick House Run. Shown in the upper right, the frame house was distinguished by fine porticoes at both ends of the center passage, a balustrade that carried the plane of the walls above the projecting roof line, and four tall external chimneys that gave a liveliness to the otherwise very formal house. The northern portico was obviously intended for sitting and taking in the spectacular view of the valley and town beyond. In 1849, the two-acre Spring Hill property was subdivided into nineteen lots. Spring Hill was soon surrounded by buildings ranging from an armory to fine dwellings. As the 20th century opened, the street was losing its residential character, and the house succumbed circa 1920 to a commercial enterprise. (Image: detail of Henry Robinson, "View of Market Street," watercolor, city of Petersburg)
RDW, Jr.

BROCK FARM QUARTERS,
state route 615, Nimo vicinity,
Virginia Beach
Built ca. 1793; damaged in 1933, derelict
by 1939, subsequently lost

Brock Farm Quarters displayed plank construction, a labor-intensive technique akin to log cabin construction that took advantage of the abundance of wood in early Virginia. Large sawn planks or logs were laid horizontally and notched at the corners; these planks formed the thickness of the walls. Unlike other types of log construction, the planks were close fitting and required no fill between them. Considerable labor, however, was required to saw the wood into the two- to six-inch-wide, close-fitting planks. Because of its solidity, plank construction was used for buildings that required security, such as storehouses, smokehouses, and prisons. The technique was not uncommon throughout the South in the 18th and 19th centuries, even in the older, settled areas of the Chesapeake region.

Brock Farm Quarters was a one-story structure with a loft in its gable roof. All walls were constructed of plank approximately three inches thick. The planks were dovetailed together. These rested on a Flemish bond brick foundation wall. Apparently there was never a framed floor; the earth of the single room within was tamped to a firm, even surface. Architectural historian Thomas T. Waterman examined the structure in 1939 and concluded that it was constructed without the use of any iron whatsoever. There were no nails in the sidewalls, and the original shingles appear to have been pegged into place. The door in the middle of the south front was hung on wood hinges; the wood pintles remained in place and were similar to those found at a smokehouse on Lansdown Road, near Fredericksburg. On the north side, the original window opening was simply cut through the plank, without any framing or sash. By the time Brock Farm was photographed, the entire west wall had been removed. No evidence of a chimney survived. A 19th-century addition obscured the east end of the structure.

The roof of Brock Farm Quarters was damaged by a pair of hurricanes that swept through the region in August and September 1933. When the structure was examined in 1939, the roof had not been repaired. (Photograph: Historic American Buildings Survey, Library of Congress)

MOUNT VERNON BARN,
Mount Vernon vicinity, Fairfax County
Built ca. 1795; abandoned late 19th century

This remarkable sixteen-sided barn was built on George Washington's Dogue Run tract, one of the president's five farms. It stood for a century. It was impressive evidence of Washington's abilities as an innovative farmer and an amateur architect. The barn provided a place for wheat to be threshed indoors, where it remained not only dry but also secure from pilferers. Within the circumference of the walls, horses were paraded in a circular path, treading on the wheat to separate the straw from the grain, which fell through the floorboards of the second story and was collected below. The near-circular shape of the barn was cost-effective in that it gave maximum square footage with a minimum quantity of building materials, but the carpentry was complex and thus made such a structure expensive.

A sketch in Washington's hand of the plan of the barn is on a sheet that contains as well

calculations of how many bricks were needed to build a large rectangular barn on the president's River Farm. The multisided barn had probably proved too expensive and too difficult a construction project to repeat. It is possible that Washington intended to experiment with different types of barn designs, weighing how each functioned against its cost.

The Mount Vernon Ladies' Association erected a replica of the sixteen-sided barn in the 1990s, although not on the original site. (Photograph: Mount Vernon Ladies' Association)

RAVENSWORTH, Springfield vicinity, Fairfax County
Built ca. 1796–1800; burned 1926

An expansive and impressive Palladian house, Ravensworth displayed the classic elements of the Mid-Georgian style: it was a five-part structure, the center of which was given emphasis by a projecting central pavilion with pediment, Palladian window, and even a bull's-eye window, a favorite motif of James Gibbs, whose *Book of Architecture* (London, 1728) helped to disseminate the style. Mid-Georgian design was introduced in Virginia around 1750; the fact that it was outdated by the end of the century seems to have mattered little to builders at plantations like Mannsfield (q.v.) and Ravensworth. A two-level piazza that stretched across the rear of the center section of this wooden house may or may not have been an original feature. The piazza was likely inspired by that on nearby Mount Vernon.

Ravensworth had been a Fitzhugh family property since late in the 17th century, when William Fitzhugh I acquired the 21,996-acre tract and rented it to French Huguenot refugees. The name, which was taken from the baronial seat of Ravensworth in England, was given to the land by Fitzhugh's descendants a generation after his death. None of the family had built there until William Fitzhugh III, of Chatham, near Fredericksburg, relocated, possibly to be near both the new national capital and George Washington. Fitzhugh's name appears in Washington's correspondence as early as 1785, when he made a gift of deer for the Mount Vernon deer park; in the later 1790s he dined at the general's with increasing frequency along with his daughter Mary Lee, who would soon marry Washington's step-grandson, George Washington Parke Custis. In 1796 Fitzhugh advertised Chatham for sale and moved to a town house in Alexandria while he built the new mansion at Ravensworth.

The Custises raised a daughter, Mary Randolph Custis, who married her childhood playmate and distant cousin Robert E. Lee. Ravensworth was left in trust to Mrs. Lee, thus the plantation came to be remembered primarily as a Lee residence. Two of the Lees' sons, George Washington Custis Lee and William Henry Fitzhugh (Rooney) Lee, eventually lived there. Earlier, Robert E. Lee's mother had died there. Many of the Washington family portraits that descended to George Washington Parke Custis hung at one time at Ravensworth. Seventeen of the paintings were lost in the fire that leveled the house. The handsome brick stable at Ravensworth, with recessed pillars and arches, survived the 1926 fire. In 1957 the Lee family sold the property to developers. The stable was demolished in 1960. (Photograph: Historic American Buildings Survey, Library of Congress)

HARVIE-GAMBLE HOUSE (THE WHITE HOUSE, GRAY CASTLE), Gamble's Hill, Richmond
Begun ca. 1797; demolished late 1880s

B. Henry Latrobe, the English-trained founder of the American architectural profession, lived in Virginia from 1796 to 1798. Around 1797, he designed a commodious suburban villa on a hill overlooking the James River for the Richmond civic leader and real estate speculator Col. John Harvie, Jr. The site had a panoramic view, and the Harvies apparently sculpted the hillside into a grand terraced garden. However, they seized an opportunity to buy a nearby mansion called Belvidere (q.v.) and sold the Latrobe house to Robert Gamble, who probably finished the building. After passing through other hands, the house served as McGuire's University School from 1876 to 1888 and was razed not long after the school moved out. The headquarters of Ethyl Corporation now occupy the site.

For the Harvies Latrobe aimed at creating the latest and best in cosmopolitan neoclassical design. He employed his standard system of passive solar principles in orienting the house so that the main rooms would gather warmth from their southern exposure, and he planned the north, east, and west sides for protection against winter winds and hot summer light. He furthermore used a kind of triple window (a "Wyatt window") and a bow in the south-facing rooms to make the most of the panorama along the James. In his drawings he adorned the façades with a combination of Greek Doric porches and the boldly projecting cornice of a Tuscan order at the eaves. These primitivizing orders would have been up-to-the-minute abroad.

In early Richmond, a competition was taking place among bow window and porch types, particularly in connection with designing houses so as to make the most of views of the James. In this contest, Latrobe's Harvie-Gamble project offered the English idea of a central bow on the garden façade, a front portico, and a somewhat contrived disposition of side porches and hyphens linked to pavilions. This planning was part of Latrobe's British background, but he well knew that such arrangements suited life and taste in Virginia.

Nonetheless, in his inexperience, Latrobe overreached himself. In places the planning in his drawings for the Harvies is forced, and because of an excessive variety of motifs, the façades in his elevations are not coherent. Latrobe's later design for the Harris house known as Clifton (q.v.) amounted to his own critique of the Harvie project.

Certain ideas that Latrobe entered into the local architectural contest via the Harvie design were overwhelmed at once. The wings were not executed, and by 1802 a miscellany of porches and outbuildings served the house instead. The Harvies and their unknown builder simplified the plan of the dwelling and probably eliminated all of Latrobe's avant-garde detailing. Still, Latrobe's conception had an influence on Richmond domestic architecture. His informal disciple Alexander Parris designed the Wickham house (1811–13, Richmond; now part of the Valentine Museum) as the most important direct derivative of the Harvie-Gamble house. In imitating Latrobe's central, south-facing bow, however, Parris introduced Richmonders to an improvement based on precedent by Charles Bulfinch of Boston, a porch stretching in front of the bow and sheltering the whole length of the south façade from the summer sun. By 1852, in a piquant episode in the local contest of architectural elements, a porch of this Bulfinch/Parris type had materialized along the south face of the Harvie-Gamble house. (Image: Robert Lancaster, *Virginia Homes and Churches*, 1915)
CEB, KLJ

CONRAD HOUSE,
12 North Cameron Street, Winchester
Built ca. 1797; demolished 1970

Formerly standing directly across Cameron Street from Winchester City Hall, the Conrad house was a proud and prominent landmark in the heart of the city. The two-story Federal mansion helped define the community's historic image. During the Civil War, Winchester citizens flocked to the dwelling's roof deck to watch the battles being waged in the surrounding countryside. In 1959 the property was purchased by the city as a potential site for a new city office building and parking lot. For the next ten years a debate ensued over the merits of a parking lot versus the preservation of the house. By the end of the decade, the debate had become widespread, attracting the concern of

the National Trust for Historic Preservation and the Virginia Historic Landmarks Commission. Despite the pleas of citizens that the Conrad house was an irreplaceable asset, city fathers remained adamant if not obdurate in their stand that a parking lot there was essential to the future success of the city and threw up bureaucratic roadblocks in the way of preservation efforts. City council finally prevailed, and the building was demolished in 1970. The site remains a parking lot thirty years later; only the stone retaining wall survives as a reminder that something more important once existed there. A new city office building eventually was erected behind the parking lot. As a token to the Conrad house, one of its finely carved Federal doorways was installed at the head of the office building's main stair. (Photograph: Virginia Department of Historic Resources)

MOLDAVIA (ALLAN HOUSE), in block bounded by Fifth, Main, Sixth, and Cary Streets, Richmond
Begun 1798 with later additions; demolished ca. 1890

The name Moldavia wittily unites the names of its first owners, Molly (Mary) and David Meade Randolph. By degrees the Randolphs acquired a full Richmond city block with magnificent views of the James River, and they began a brick house here in 1798. As their architect they picked the contractor George Winston, a major figure in the creation of Richmond who supplied bricks for the Virginia State Penitentiary (q.v.) and probably designed the final form of Clifton (q.v.).

The decline of the Randolphs' fortunes cost them Moldavia and propelled Mrs. Randolph into a career as a boardinghouse keeper and author of a celebrated cookbook. The rich miller Joseph Gallego and his wife bought Moldavia in 1804 and in 1805 hired James Oldham, one of Thomas Jefferson's workmen, to enlarge the building. Then-president Jefferson, after lending Oldham a copy of Palladio's book *I Quattro Libri (Four Books of Architecture)*, advised on the project himself. As of 1820, the date of the earliest known insurance policy on the property, the Main Street frontage was lined with outbuildings, from Oldham's icehouse at Fifth and Main to Winston's stable and carriage house at Sixth and Main. In 1825 the property passed to John and Frances Allan, whose foster son Edgar Allan Poe lived at Moldavia briefly in 1825 and 1826. After Allan's death in 1834 and by mid-1853, his second wife, Louisa, a prominent hostess, enlarged the dwelling. She had already subdivided the property to accommodate the Scott-Clarke house (1841) and the Barret house (1844), which still stand on vestiges of Moldavia's terraced, or falling, gardens. After an auction of furnishings in 1881, Moldavia was demolished around 1890. None of the estate buildings survives. Various museums have artifacts from the house, notably the Edgar Allan Poe and Valentine Museums in Richmond.

Moldavia represents the contest of alternatives in early-19th-century Richmond domestic architecture and the impact of the growing love of landscape on domestic design. Probably the original part of the house was the southerly block. This part, with its entry front facing Fifth Street on the northwest, had a two-tiered, temple-style piazza and a semioctagonal bow overlooking the river on the southwest. The bow was formed by an octagonal dining room on the first floor and an octagonal parlor on the second. The pattern of a bow projecting from the side of a block with a portico is Jeffersonian, and the combination of a two-tier portico with a polygonal bow at its side assuredly came from the first Monticello, which Jefferson had begun to transform into the second Monticello only in 1796. Jefferson, however, would have seen the fanciful Adamesque handling of the Tuscan and Doric orders on the Moldavia porch and the unclassical placement of pillars at the center of a portico as (in his language) "the barbarous & tawdry fancies of [an] individual workman."

As at Monticello, the Moldavia portico and bow were created for the enjoyment of splendid views. Indeed, making the most of James River scenery has been a major force in shaping the great houses of Richmond, and this was conspicuously so at the start of the 19th century. Col. Thomas H. Ellis, once a playmate of the young Poe's, recalled the portico as "the grand feature of the house; . . . as much used, in all favorable weather, for both family and company purposes, as any portion of the house" and easily reached from most of the principal rooms. In the bow, at the parlor level, the James River scenery had prompted the use of floor-length windows with iron balconies. The parlor had a number of false windows filled with mirrors, which may have been chosen to reflect the views through the real windows.

It appears that Gallego added the northerly wing of the house to hold his drawing room. In the contest of styles, this room presented an opportunity to Jefferson, who treated new buildings as chances to reform architecture by setting models, particularly models for the orders. Of the Corinthian order for the Moldavia drawing room, Jefferson wrote James Oldham in 1805 that "a single example of chaste architecture may guide the taste of the city." The president dictated the pattern of the rich frieze for this order and had the ornament cast in Washington, DC, in the molds made for the hall frieze at Monticello. The effect of Gallego's room on the "taste of the city" is not known. Almost certainly Louisa Allan transformed the wing into a larger block so that it would hold double parlors, with unknown consequences for the Corinthian detailing. (Photographs: Valentine Museum)
CEB, KLJ

BOYCE-MACFARLANE HOUSE, corner of Fifth and Leigh Streets, Richmond
Built by 1798; demolished 1903

This unusual house with three bowed wings has long been misidentified as a residence of William Wirt, the attorney general, attorney to Thomas Jefferson, and author of a popular biography of Patrick Henry. Possibly so small yet pretentious a building suggested to some observers that its cultivated owner possessed self-discipline, a quality that Wirt said guided the life of Henry and that he believed his own times required. Actually the house was built by Joseph Boyce no later than 1798, when it was first insured; by 1807 Boyce had added a second floor to the center section. The two flanking wings, as shown in this photograph, were semioctagonal. The rear wing was half-round, to judge from twelve of fourteen insurance policies issued for the building beginning in 1798. The house was lived in for much of the 19th century by William Macfarlane.

John P. Little, in his 1850 *History of Richmond*, commented about the "singular appearance" given to the city by "a large number" of residences that "seem to have been an imitation of the English bay window style"; that is, they had "part of the wall bulging out in the form of a half hexagon." Examples included not only the Boyce-Macfarlane house but also Moldavia and the Alexander McRae house (qq.v.). This architecture is linked at least tangentially to Thomas Jefferson, who had been the first in Virginia to work with polygonal shapes and who inspired a plantation tradition of tripartite domestic architecture. The Boyce-Macfarlane house predated both Moldavia and the McRae house; it may have influenced the latter, which was located just four blocks to the east and had the same basic plan of two side wings, with another to the rear. (Photograph: Valentine Museum)
KLJ

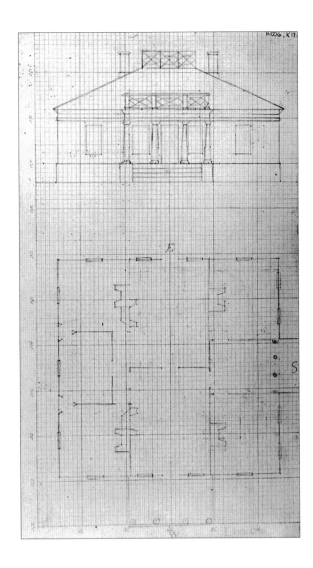

EDGEHILL, Shadwell vicinity, Albemarle County
Built 1798 and later; in serious disrepair by 1827, possibly standing as late as 1899

Thomas Jefferson first proposed this small, wooden, one-story Tuscan villa in 1790, the year that Thomas Mann Randolph, Jr., married his cousin and Thomas Jefferson's daughter Martha in a ceremony that took place at Monticello. The ties between the Randolph and Jefferson families had long been close. Thomas Jefferson's father, Peter, had acted as guardian for the senior Thomas Mann Randolph, and the two families had lived together for many years at Tuckahoe, the Randolph family seat. The Randolphs and the Jeffersons owned adjoining lands in Albemarle County. The eleven children of the younger Thomas Mann Randolph became greatly attached to their grandfather Thomas Jefferson; Randolph, however, became estranged from his father-in-law.

Begun in 1798, Edgehill was unfinished when the Randolphs first occupied it in 1800. The plan pictured here was drawn by Thomas Jefferson and was his preference for the house. Its awkward room arrangement, however, led Jefferson in the end to adopt instead for Edgehill the T-shaped plan he had developed at Monticello. Randolph, Jr., was frequently absent from Edgehill during his long career of public service. Among other positions, he was elected to the United States Congress twice and served as governor of Virginia on three occasions, during which time his family resided at Monticello.

Following the death of Thomas Mann Randolph, Jr., in 1828, his son Thomas Jefferson Randolph (the executor of Thomas Jefferson's estate) found Edgehill too small for his growing family. He replaced it in the same year with a larger, two-story brick house that still stands. The elevation of the second Edgehill was derived directly from that of the first. The second building was designed by Thomas R. Blackburn, one of Thomas Jefferson's highly skilled carpenters at the University of Virginia. By one account, the existing Edgehill was erected on the foundations of the original structure ("Colonel Thomas Jefferson Randolph, finding the old family dwelling at Edgehill too small, removed the old building for a short distance to the rear, and erected upon its site the front part of the present brick mansion"). While this cannot be verified, the similarity in dimensions between the footprints of the two buildings does not eliminate the possibility. What eventually happened to the original house is uncertain; it may have been standing as late as 1899. (Image: drawing by Thomas Jefferson, Massachusetts Historical Society)

ENNISCORTHY BARN,
Keene vicinity, Albemarle County
Built ca. 1800; demolished 1993

Built by Isaac Coles at his plantation Enniscorthy, this frame bank barn was one of the earliest and best-preserved historic barns in central Virginia. It featured a forebay and stone foundation, mortise-and-tenon hewn beams, wrought-iron strap hinges, beaded siding, and box cornices. The windows were fitted with diagonally set, horizontal wooden louvers. Germanic bank barns—so named because they were built against the bank or side of a hill—were used for grain storage and threshing on the upper level and the stabling of cattle below. They were popular because wheat had surpassed tobacco as the staple crop in Virginia at the turn into the

19th century. At Enniscorthy, the main level was used for milling wheat into flour, which fell through a wooden grating to the floor below. The grindstones were turned by a mule attached to a pole and walked in a circle. In 1993, the Enniscorthy barn and several outbuildings were thoughtlessly razed and the landscape changed by the construction of a new, paved road through the barn's site. (Photograph: Virginia Department of Historic Resources)
KEL

GARST LOG HOUSE, off Garst Cabin Road at intersection with Grandin Road Extension, Roanoke County
Built ca. 1800; demolished 1970s

Located on the top of a low hill, the so-called Garst log cabin (in reality a two-story log house from its inception) was built, according to oral tradition, by Benjamin Deyerle (1806–83), whose name is associated with many of the oldest houses in the area. He may have lived there. The original rough-hewn log house was rectangular with a chimney on the narrow end. Several years after construction, Deyerle, again according to local lore, built an addition and connected the two parts with an open passage, or dogtrot. George Washington Garst (1821–90), whose name was subsequently associated with the property, acquired the house about 1865. He was a prominent physician and miller who had a grist and saw mill on nearby Mudlick Creek. Garst is purported to have enclosed the open passage and built a rectangular addition in the rear, making the whole L-shaped. The house was never weatherboarded, and it was one of few double two-story log structures in the area. Despite efforts to preserve this landmark of Americana, it was demolished in the 1970s to make way for a housing development. The logs were preserved by the National Park Service for use in the restoration of old cabins on the Blue Ridge Parkway. (Photograph: Virginia Department of Historic Resources)
WLW

HOWERTON-WELLS HOUSE, Rocky Run vicinity, Dinwiddie County
Built ca. 1800; demolished ca. 1970

Few small, vernacular farm dwellings survive from the early Republican era in their original form. This example survived until recent years. With its steep, asymmetrical roof and differing wings, the Howerton-Wells house was an important architectural document. Its unusual plan included a large square room at the front with a narrow shed room across the rear. The chimney served the main room with a large cooking fireplace and extended back to provide a small fireplace in the shed room, at the end of the common wall. A diminutive, winding stair rose beside the chimney in the front corner, to the right of the door. The wing to the right was an early addition; the one to the left probably dated to the early 20th century. In the late 1960s about ninety pre-1840 dwellings remained in Dinwiddie County; at least a quarter of them no longer exist. The Howerton-Wells house was unlike any other. (Photograph: Virginia Department of Historic Resources)
JGZ, Jr.

MOUNT ATHOS, Kelly vicinity, Campbell County
Built ca. 1800, burned 1876

The enigmatic ruin atop a wooded ridge overlooking the James River has been the subject of speculation for many years. The house was built for William J. Lewis. Its elevated site, classical portico, one-story format, and demi-octagonal projections have led to the speculation that the design of Mount Athos was influenced by Thomas Jefferson, who used these features in his own works. Lewis family tradition holds that Jefferson and Lewis were friends and that Jefferson did indeed advise on the project. Mount Athos differed from Jefferson's works in the use of stone rather than brick construction. Only the simple drawing shown here records the exterior appearance before the house was

gutted by fire. Reporting the loss, the Lynchburg *Daily Virginian* stated, "It is sad to see an ancient abode of so much refinement, elegance, and hospitality swept away." It noted that the house held many valuable paintings and a fine library. (Image: Virginia Historical Society)

(SECOND) WHITE HOUSE,
on the Pamunkey River, New Kent County
Rebuilt early 19th century; burned 1862

The house pictured here was the second of at least three built on the same site prior to the 20th century. The one that preceded it, and which possibly dated to the 17th century, was the setting for the wedding of George Washington and Martha Dandridge Custis in 1759. The third White House, a Gothic Revival structure designed by Richmond architect Albert L. West, burned in 1880.

Col. John Lightfoot (d. 1709) is said to have built the first White House. Around 1735 the plantation was purchased by John Custis, the father of Daniel Parke Custis; the latter married Martha Dandridge in 1750. The couple lived at the White House until Daniel's untimely death in 1757. The house was probably the same size as the one shown here, as all three buildings report-

edly were constructed on the same foundation. The diminutive size of the first White House is significant because Martha's first husband was one of the wealthiest men in the colony, yet the couple did not live in a Georgian mansion. When Martha married George Washington, she moved to a residence that was at least as sizable as the first White House, and Mount Vernon was much more fashionably furnished. An inventory of the Custis holdings reveals that the family money had not been invested in architecture and decorative objects, but rather in land, slaves, and horses. Martha Custis would not have appeared to have suffered a loss in social status by marrying the young colonel Washington.

The first White House was rebuilt in the early 19th century by George Washington Parke Custis, Martha Washington's grandson, who inherited the plantation in 1798 and owned it until his death in 1857. The second building may have closely resembled the first, although there were changes, such as the treatment of the land-front porch and the addition of the bay window pictured here. Custis was himself resident at a much grander and more fashionable house, Arlington (now in Arlington National Cemetery), which he built, but he would not allow this historic landmark to deteriorate and disappear. He revered the setting of so famous a wedding, an episode that he later celebrated in his published recollections of the life of Washington.

The second White House holds interest for its Civil War history. At his death Custis willed the plantation to his grandsons and appointed his son-in-law Robert E. Lee as executor. George McClellan used the White House as a supply base, and it soon was burned by Federal troops. A note reportedly left on the door by Mrs. Mary Custis Lee is said to have read, to no avail, "Northern Soldiers who profess to revere Washington forbear to desecrate the home of his first married life." (Photographs: Benson J. Lossing, *A History of the Civil War*, 1912)

BATHURST, Essex County
Built early 19th century; demolished shortly after 1936

A classic example of Virginia's colonial architectural idiom, Bathurst was a one-and-a-half-story frame structure with brick foundation walls and end chimneys. The bond of the foundation walls was irregular, but the corbelled chimney, below the upper offset, was laid in Flemish bond with glazed headers. Above this point, the chimney was laid in an all-stretcher bond. Bathurst was covered with a clipped gable roof, giving it a picturesque outline; its walls were sheathed with beaded weatherboards. The front portion had a hall-passage-parlor plan.

At the time Bathurst was surveyed in 1936 by the Historic American Buildings Survey, it was in poor condition. Many sash and doors were missing, and all interior woodwork had been removed. However, only minor changes to the exterior had been made, such as the replacement of the original porch posts and floor. A meat house and a dairy photographed at the time of the survey are also now lost. (Photograph: Library of Congress)

MERCHENT HOUSE, Dumfries, Prince William County
Built ca. 1800; demolished 1940s

The Merchent house, named for Robert B. Merchent, who acquired it in the mid–19th century, rose one and a half stories from a stone foundation into a gable roof. Its prominent end chimney was laid up in four distinct bonds: Flemish, all-header, English, and common. The front of the house, articulated by two windows and a side-entry door, was faced with rusticated wood siding, perhaps inspired by Mount Vernon, one of the few Virginia houses to employ this architectural treatment. Here, however, the façade was probably painted a dull red. The side and rear walls may never have been painted. Until just before the house was photographed, a large frame barn, smokehouse, and corn house also stood on the site.

While oral histories recorded that the interior had been finely finished, most of the woodwork had been removed by the time the building was photographed. Measured drawings made in the 1930s note that the wood chair railing, door, cornice, and mantelpieces had been removed from the living room. On the second floor, the fireplace mantel, partition, and cuddy doors had also been taken out. The interior paint color closely approximated the red used on the exterior walls.

The storm of August 1933 that wrecked havoc on the historic structures of Dumfries may have inflicted damage on this house. The surveyor for the Historic American Buildings Survey concluded not long afterwards, "Unfortunately the remaining days of this building are numbered, for it is in a bad state of disrepair." (Photograph: Historic American Buildings Survey, Library of Congress)

GROVE HILL, Fincastle vicinity, Botetourt County
Built ca. 1800–1804; burned 1909

This large and elegant Federal-style mansion, which rivaled the best urban houses of the period, was built in a sparsely settled landscape. In 1800, Botetourt's courthouse was but a log structure, smaller than the thirty-six-by-twenty-foot stable at Grove Hill. The individual for whom this imposing structure was built was Gen. James Breckenridge, member of a family that gained prominence in both Virginia and Kentucky. By 1804, when Breckenridge first insured his plantation, the labor of the general's three hundred slaves had amassed a fortune for him. In 1825 his buildings and 3,385 acres of land were valued at the sizable sum of $46,063. Nothing in the county was comparable.

Grove Hill commanded a low hilltop above a rolling landscape. The house measured sixty by fifty feet. Its Federal-style doors, windows, and modillion cornice were handsomely crafted. Its unusual depth allowed five bays and an entry porch on both front and side, plus a distinctive interior. Large corner rooms were separated by a pair of halls set at cross angles. Those who knew the house before it burned remembered the unusual width of the halls and the elaborate woodwork of the mantels and staircases. Nearby was a remarkably large brick kitchen, two stories high, forty-seven by twenty-one feet, with an "open Piaser" (piazza) eight feet deep that ran the length of the building. Both structures were described in the insurance policy of 1804 as "elegantly finished." The Roanoke Valley lost its grandest early mansion when Grove Hill fell to flames in 1909. (Photograph: courtesy of Mr. Malcolm Bryan III)

MILES BOTT HOUSE, 216 Cowardin Avenue, Richmond
Built ca. 1802; demolished 1941

The Miles Bott house, located on a thirty-two-acre site in what is now south Richmond, was sheathed with beaded weatherboard. Huge chimneys framed a brick closet at each end of the building. In plan, the house was traditional; a central passage was flanked by pairs of rooms. The jewel it contained was its parlor, which was distinguished by an elaborate Adamesque mantel whose ornaments were probably derived from a plate in one of the popular pattern books of the period, such as those by William Pain or Asher Benjamin.

Miles Bott operated a grocery store on Main Street in Manchester (now Hull Street, Richmond) as early as 1801 and as late as 1829. Bott was also a part owner in the coal fields on Falling Creek in Powhatan County, known as the Creek Pits, and was in business with John Cunliffe in the firm Bott and Cunliffe, later known as Mills, Bott, and Cunliffe. He appears to have experienced financial reversals in 1815, when he sold his share in the firm to his partner Nicholas Mills. In 1819, he mortgaged his house, the coal mine, other business interests, farming equipment, and two slaves. He died in 1835. The house changed hands several times; the lot was subdivided and in 1867 purchased by Mrs. Elizabeth Baird. The house was occupied by Baird's granddaughter Miss Bessie Gill until her death in 1938, whereupon she left no will and many heirs at law. The city of Richmond prepared to purchase the house for use as a recreation center and branch public library for south Richmond. The City Council passed an ordinance to this effect, but Gill's heirs balked. The property was sold and the house demolished. Its loss was described by architectural historian Mary Wingfield Scott as "a calamity." (Photograph: Historic American Buildings Survey, Library of Congress)

ADAMS–VAN LEW HOUSE,
2311 East Grace Street, Richmond
Built 1802 and ca. 1836; demolished 1911

The stately Adams–Van Lew house, in Richmond's Church Hill neighborhood, had a series of storied occupants. Their biographies are entwined with the history of the city during two of its most critical and tumultuous periods, the explosion of growth that followed its designation as the capital of the commonwealth and, a half-century later, the Civil War.

The house was built in 1802 for Dr. John Adams, a Richmond physician educated at Edinburgh who also pursued politics, serving in the House of Delegates and as mayor of Richmond. In 1818, caught up in the financial downturn that consumed the real estate market in the capital, Adams was forced to mortgage both the Union Hotel (q.v.), which he controlled, and his house. The latter was purchased at auction by the United States Bank, which sold it to John Van Lew in 1836.

Wealthy from a hardware business, Van Lew was able to undertake extensive alterations that significantly improved the house and property. These are documented in a series of Mutual Assurance policies taken out before and after 1836. On the street façade he built a dwarf Doric portico that was elegant yet also substantial; it gave a strong classical presence to what had been a tame Federal design. On the garden façade he added a giant (two-story) Doric piazza, which had become a fashionable design element throughout the South following the dissemination of prints of George Washington's Mount Vernon and the use of the feature at many Virginia spas, as well as by Thomas Jefferson at the University of Virginia. He also developed an extensive garden, which cascaded down the steep slope at the rear of the house. The unobstructed view of the James River from the garden must have been spectacular.

Upon John Van Lew's death, in 1843, the house passed to his wife; at her death in 1876 it passed to their daughter Elizabeth Van Lew. Regarded as the most effective Union spy in Richmond during the Civil War, "Lizzie" made the house famous. Her messages to Washington, DC, were so accurate and timely that Gen. U. S. Grant sent troops to guard her dur-

ing the evacuation of Richmond. One of Van Lew's effective tactics was to wander the streets mumbling to herself, thus earning the widely circulated sobriquet Crazy Bet and undermining pervasive rumors about her spying. In reward for her service, President Grant appointed Van Lew postmistress of Richmond, the major political patronage position available at the time.

Lizzie Van Lew was generally despised in post–Civil War Richmond. Mary Wingfield Scott described her as "a legendary figure, a bogey" who would "frighten children." When she died in 1900, the house was purchased by the Virginia Club, which sold it to Dr. William H. Parker, who ran a sanatorium there for several years. In 1911 the property was condemned by the city to make way for the proposed Bellevue School. Whereas public opposition halted similar school proposals that would have demolished both the John Marshall house and the White House of the Confederacy, no one stepped forward to save a building with so unpopular a local history. (Photographs: Virginia Historical Society)

COLROSS, Oronoco Street, between Fayette and Henry Streets, Alexandria
Built ca. 1801; dismantled 1929 and reconstructed in Princeton, New Jersey

Colross belonged to a group of highly sophisticated Federal mansions in the Washington, DC, area that includes Tudor Place, Dumbarton House, Woodlawn, and Belmont, near Leesburg. The beautifully articulated composition was erected by local entrepreneur John Potts, Jr. Potts experienced financial difficulties immediately after completing the house and advertised it for sale, describing it in the *Alexandria Advertiser and Commercial Intelligencer* as a "large handsome brick house, fifty by forty feet with a Brick Stable, Smoke House, and Well of excellent water." The diplomat and Alexandria merchant Jonathan Swift purchased the property in 1803 and lived there until his death in 1824. It then was acquired by Alexandria attorney and judge Tomson F. Mason, grandson of George Mason. Union authorities seized Colross during the Civil War and reportedly executed several Union deserters there. Following tornado damage in 1927, the house was left in a state of neglect. John Munn soon purchased the structure and had it completely dismantled and shipped to Princeton, New Jersey, where it was rebuilt in 1929 as his residence. Following Munn's death in 1956, the house became the centerpiece of the Princeton Day School. (Photograph: Virginia Historical Society)

CLIFTON (BENJAMIN J. HARRIS HOUSE), Old Fourteenth Street
at the former Apricot Alley, Richmond
Built 1808–9; demolished 1905

Perhaps in 1807 or 1808, B. Henry Latrobe designed a grand villa for the Richmond tobacco and cotton manufacturer Benjamin J. Harris. Harris owned a site on what was then Council Chamber Hill with dramatic views of the city and the James River. Like many other Richmonders, Harris had business premises on the same lot as his house, and he meant Clifton to overlook his tobacco manufactory.

Latrobe's design for the house was in effect a critique of his design for the Harvie-Gamble house (q.v.). Once again he proposed a main block with a bowed garden front, hyphens leading to pavilions, and spaces distributed according to his passive solar principles of orientation, but the planning and the sure composition of the façades demonstrate how much Latrobe had matured since the late 1790s. In reentering the Richmond contest among bay window types, Latrobe again proposed a pair of polygonal bows, as he had at the Virginia State Penitentiary (q.v.), this time to overlook the James. In actuality, Latrobe did not originate this project for Harris; the proposal is a slightly revised version of a design that he had made in 1801 for Riversdale, the Stier-Calvert house in Riverdale, Maryland. Little or nothing of Latrobe survived in the execution of Riversdale (1801–ca. 1807), which is now open to the public.

Benjamin J. Harris, too, virtually rejected Latrobe's design. Harris likely had his house built by the prominent contractor George Winston, his brother-in-law, to whom much of the final design probably should be attributed. The mansion would have no recognizable connection to Latrobe but for a site plan that Latrobe drew for Harris's property. (Oddly, the voluminous documentation of Latrobe's life does not record the Harris project apart from this site drawing and a perspective of the proposed house.) In execution almost nothing survived from Latrobe's plan except the pair of garden bows. Insurance policies reveal that, by 1822 and perhaps from the first, these garden windows flanked a non-Latrobean feature, a loggia of at least one story that sheltered part of the south face of the house from the sun and formed an outdoor room commanding the outstanding view. This pattern of twin bows framing a porch is a major one in the story of neoclassical architecture in Virginia, the two most important examples being the Hancock-Wirt-Caskie house (1808–9, Richmond) and Point of Honor (ca. 1815, Lynchburg).

Clifton's departures from Latrobe had a twist. The deep exterior cornice and the blind arcade on the center pavilion probably did derive partly from Latrobe—from Latrobe's penitentiary and, in the case of the cornice, from the Harvie-Gamble house as well. These features, however, came by way of Richmond builders who reinterpreted these elements in the Adamesque vein that Latrobe disdained.

In 1814 Harris bought himself another mansion, Belvidere (q.v.), but kept Clifton until he lost his fortune by attempting to develop the area that is now

the Fan District. Clifton became a boardinghouse, a hotel, and a mission house—its main story stranded in the air by the lowering of the street—before it was leased to Sheltering Arms Hospital from 1889 to 1893 and demolished in 1905. Today, the site of the house, on Old Fourteenth Street, is a loading-dock yard overlooking Fourteenth Street. Commonwealth of Virginia employee parking descends through the site of Harris's garden and factory. Even so, one can still appreciate the sweep of the views that Clifton commanded. (Image: Library of Virginia)
CEB, KLJ

ALEXANDER McRAE HOUSE, 311 North Ninth Street, Richmond
Built 1804–9; demolished 1929

A Federal-period building, the Alexander McRae house was constructed in the form of three octagons, making its plan highly unusual if not odd. The evolution of the house was also unconventional. Alexander McRae, an eminent lawyer and later consul to Paris, purchased the property in 1802. By 1804 he had built a two-story octagonal office with front and rear two-tiered porticoes. An insurance declaration shows that McRae had moved his business to another building by 1808, when he converted the original single-octagonal office into a triple-octagonal dwelling with a rectangular central hall. Other insurance policies indicate that the new structure was largely in place by 1809, although it was not entirely finished until 1814.

Within the house, a staircase in the central hall ran parallel to the main façade, as at Point of Honor (ca. 1815) in Lynchburg, another double-bowed house. Damaged photographs of the first-floor octagonal wing rooms show ornate Federal mantels installed there. (In 1970 these and other trim were in the possession of noted antiquarian Joe Kindig, Jr.) The kitchen and dining room were located in the basement. In 1820, when the McRae house was advertised for sale, it was described as "convenient and roomy," while its desirable location (only a block from the Capitol) was ideal for any "genteel family." It would later house instead the offices of the Mutual Assurance Society of Virginia (1821–70) and the Catholic Male Orphan Asylum and School Association (1870–1929).

The McRae house was one of a group of Federal-era, bowed houses in Richmond. The type became popular in the city for reasons of both fashion and function; the bows allowed multiple windows and thus light and greater views of gardens, streets, and, in at least one instance, the James River. (Photograph: Valentine Museum; Image: Library of Virginia)
KLJ

DR. JOHN J. CABELL HOUSE, Main Street between Fifth and Sixth Streets, Lynchburg
Built ca. 1809; demolished after 1902

This handsome, Federal-style brick mansion stood on a hill overlooking the James River, adjacent to downtown Lynchburg and across Blackwater Creek from Point of Honor, home of Dr. Cabell's brother. As originally built, the house had only three bays and a side-hall plan; two additional bays were soon added, converting the plan to a center-hall type. Cabell, a physician and entrepreneur, was such an admirer of Andrew Jackson that in 1815, in anticipation of a visit, he papered his parlor with French scenic wallpaper. His descendants resided in the house until 1902, by which time it was surrounded by commercial establishments. Before selling it in 1902 to the Benevolent and Protective Order of Elks, who demolished it and erected a clubhouse on the site, the family had photographs taken of their ancestral home. In 1979, the clubhouse was demolished, the hill bulldozed, and the site utilized for the approach to the John Lynch Memorial Bridge. Only the album containing the photographs, of which this is one, remains. (Photograph: Jones Memorial Library, Lynchburg)
SAC, Jr.

ROANOKE, Randolph vicinity,
Charlotte County
Built ca. 1810; burned 1878

John Randolph of Roanoke so conspicuously defended the rights of his state as a congressman and senator that he was recognized internationally as a dynamic and eccentric spokesman for old Virginia ideals. He was self-identified by the name of the plantation that he loved. In 1775 Randolph inherited Roanoke, a remote property on and named for the Roanoke (Staunton) River, but he did not reside there until after 1810. He increased the tract considerably, to eight thousand acres, and invested just as liberally in the purchase of slaves (four hundred) and blooded horses. Randolph, however, was less interested in pretentious architecture, even though he championed the cause of the Virginia gentry ("I love liberty, I hate equality") and was himself an aristocrat, a descendant of William Randolph of Turkey Island through both his father and his mother (who were second cousins).

Eschewing the ideal of the Georgian mansion, Randolph lived in a complex of two small frame cottages surrounded by dependencies. In this way he reverted to a 17th-century Virginia tradition of domestic architecture. Randolph referred to these one-and-a-half-story structures as his winter and summer houses. In 1843 Henry Howe visited the site, describing it as "wild" and "primitive," more "the abode of a recluse, rather than that of a statesman." He prepared the sketch pictured here and explained that the building on the right, which was the one that was lost to fire, was much the larger and the summer dwelling. In it were two rooms; one was the library, which contained Randolph's sizable collection of books, and the other was a drawing room. A portrait of Randolph's ancestor Pocahontas hung in the latter. The cottage on the left, which still stands, was the winter residence, described as a "log structure, which is entered through a shed, paved with water-worn pebbles and supported by unhewn posts." Despite the "extreme simplicity" of the building, it was "furnished richly" with decorative objects and hung with portraits of Randolph (by Gilbert Stuart) and his servant Jupiter ("a fine drawing"). Outside the two cottages was a large, rough rock that Randolph reportedly used as a washstand and said should be placed over his grave. Like Patrick Henry, who lived nearby in Charlotte County in a similarly modest dwelling, Red Hill (q.v.), Randolph must have enjoyed the image of selflessness and integrity that these unassuming buildings projected. (Image: Robert A. Lancaster, *Virginia Homes and Churches*, 1915)

DUNLOP-BRYDON-TENNANT HOUSE, southeast corner of Adams and Washington Streets, Petersburg
Built ca. 1814, enlarged ca. 1829 and ca. 1875; demolished ca. 1947

This fine house was constructed in three phases spanning a sixty-year period, when architectural tastes shifted dramatically from classicism to eclecticism. The change in style was conspicuous in the finished building as pictured here. The main block was built by James Dunlop, Jr., a recent immigrant from Scotland, shortly after he purchased the property from Robert Bolling in 1814. Dunlop constructed a large, brick, two-story house set well back from both Adams Street, which it fronted, and Washington Street. Behind the house, on Washington Street, he built a one-story tobacco factory, one of the earliest in Petersburg. Following his death in 1827, the property was conveyed to Dunlop's nephews, David Dunlop and David Dunlop Brydon, and finally to Brydon alone. The two were apparently partners in the tobacco operation, but Brydon occupied the dwelling, to which, in 1829 or shortly before, a two-story brick wing was added on the north side (to the left in the photograph), apparently for use as an office. The wing soon became simply an integral part of the dwelling.

Following the death of David Dunlop Brydon in 1841, when ownership of the property passed to Brydon's widow, David Dunlop went into partnership with Brydon's nephew, David Brydon Tennant, to operate the factory. Tennant, who had been brought into the house by the Brydons, continued to live there with his aunt, and when she died he inherited the residence. It was Tennant who in the 1870s added the south wing (pictured here on the right). It was an elaborate addition, with brick paneling, bays with balustrades, intricate triple windows, and blind windows with iron window caps. These features suggest the hand of Harrison Waite, who designed William Mahone's house (q.v.) on Market Street in the same period. Tennant was the forebear of David Tennant Bryan of Richmond, publisher of Richmond Newspapers, Inc. The Dunlops, Brydons, Tennants, and their Scottish friends and business associates, such as Robert Leslie, were pioneers in the Petersburg tobacco-manufacturing industry, the mainstay of the city by the time of the Civil War. The house survived until 1947, when it was razed to make way for a Trailways bus station. (Photograph: Virginia Historical Society)
RDW, Jr.

BUENA VISTA
(NOZECTHOS), Henrico County
Built ca. 1815; demolished early 20th century

Buena Vista (later known as Nozecthos) was a Classical Revival farmhouse. It rose two stories from a slightly raised basement into a five-bay, Flemish bond brick structure with internal end chimneys covered by a shallow hipped roof. The house was distinguished by arcaded and rectangular recesses built into the brickwork to frame the window openings. The house was distinguished by shallow arcaded and rectangular recesses built into the brickwork to frame the window openings. The more powerful Greek Revival porch, with square Doric columns and a full entablature, probably was added later. Buena Vista was significant as an enthusiastic and unusual interpretation of Classical Revival influences. (Photograph: Valentine Museum)

MOUNT ERIN (FARM HILL, CAMERON CASTLE), east side of Adams Street between Apollo and Cupid Streets, Petersburg
Built ca. 1815, expanded 1862–66 and 1888; demolished 1943

Mount Erin began as a small, one-story brick house (twenty-four by eighteen feet), a *cottage orné*, standing on a sizable tract on the heights to the south of Petersburg. It was built, apparently, by the flour manufacturer Edward Stokes as his dwelling but expanded twice by the tobacco manufacturer William Cameron, first during the Civil War period and then again in 1888, when the value of the house nearly doubled.

In 1819, Edward Stokes sold his *cottage orné*, which he called Farm Hill, to the small-scale tobacco manufacturer John M. Ryan, who by that date already lived in the house. (Ryan had erected a small tobacco factory on the grounds.) After 1822, Farm Hill was conveyed to the merchant Joseph Caldwell. By the time Caldwell's widow, Eliza, insured the property in 1829, the brick walls of the house had been stuccoed and probably scored to resemble stone. She remarried (becoming Eliza Russell), bore more children, and called the property Mount Erin.

In 1854 William Cameron, a Scottish immigrant who had married one of the Russell girls and moved into Mount Erin, purchased an eighty percent interest in the property. Cameron's tobacco business burgeoned; in 1860, in partnership with Robert Crawford, he initiated construction of a factory building near Mount Erin. Then, in 1867, in partnership with his brother George, Cameron purchased the Riddle & McIlwaine Tobacco Factory, at the northwest corner of Perry and Brown Streets. Cameron's prosperity had enabled him to begin a sizable expansion of Mount Erin during the war, despite the turmoil, and the job was finished by the end of 1866. The result appears on the Beers map of 1877 as a cross-shaped dwelling much larger than the original house but not nearly the size of the final building.

The final expansion, in 1888, seems likely to have transformed the house entirely. It displays a sophisticated use of the Gothic Revival style, executed in stone and complete with an entrance tower, arcades, and turrets. In time the property became popularly known as Cameron Castle. Cameron's Scottish baronial fantasy was demolished in 1943 and became the site of Petersburg General Hospital, now Southside Regional Medical Center. (Photograph: Virginia Historical Society)
RDW, Jr.

CUNNINGHAM-ARCHER HOUSE, 101 North Sixth Street, Richmond
Built 1815–16; demolished 1927

Irish-born Edward Cunningham built what undoubtedly was one of 19th-century Richmond's most patrician and refined urban dwellings, a much-admired landmark on the corner of Sixth and Franklin Streets for over a century. Although its architect has not been documented, Robert Mills, America's first native-born professional architect, long has been thought responsible for the design. The house employs the restrained but inventive classicism that Mills so deftly incorporated into his compositions.

The stuccoed walls, paneled bays, and blind window arches seen here are characteristic features of Mills's work. The dwarf portico with its thin moldings is another Mills hallmark. Mills is also speculated to have designed the mansion at Howard's Neck, the Goochland County plantation home of Cunningham's son, Dr. John A. Cunningham, a work similar to the Cunninghams' Richmond residence.

Edward Cunningham sold the house to Dr. George Watson in 1825 and moved to Howard's Neck. Maj. Robert S. Archer, a member of a prominent Richmond family and Dr. Watson's son-in-law, purchased the Cunningham house from the Watson family in 1882. In 1920, Archer's widow, Ann Virginia Watson Archer, died in the Sixth Street residence after having lived there for ninety-three years.

Her heirs sold the property in 1927. The house and its famous garden were immediately destroyed to make way for a parking garage. Mary Wingfield Scott, in her acclaimed work *Houses of Old Richmond*, stated: "No house in Richmond was more full of atmosphere, both of the era when it was built and of the years following the Civil War. . . . The demolition of the Archer house was indeed the beginning of the end of that gracious life of old Richmond which centered on Franklin and Grace Streets from Monroe Park to the Capitol Square." (Photograph: Valentine Museum)

MARY GALT HOUSE, 1011 St. James Street, Richmond
Built 1815–16; demolished ca. 1970

The Mary Galt house stood in an area of Richmond known as Duval's Addition, an early suburb that housed free persons of color. It was constructed during the rush of development that followed the War of 1812 by John Leslie, apparently a real estate investor. Leslie may have intended to rent his property as a tenement for free blacks. However, the economic depression that began in 1819 apparently soured the investment. In 1821 John Galt purchased the property, along with two adjoining lots; he gave it to his former slave Mary Galt. Such a gift appears to have been unusual; most free African-Americans of the period purchased their own homes.

Though built by a white investor, the Galt house was representative of the type of architecture constructed and lived in by African-Americans during the antebellum period, a side-hall residence of modest scale. Features included a porch, symmetrically placed six-over-nine-pane windows, jack arches, and Flemish bond brickwork. Mary Wingfield Scott considered the large two-story outbuilding behind the house "probably the most picturesque one standing in

Richmond."

Mary Galt resided in the building until 1849, and a century later Scott found it still occupied by African-Americans. Scott prematurely congratulated the residents on its upkeep; by the time of the republication of her book in 1975 the building had vanished. The lot, in the neglected Gilpin Court neighborhood, remains vacant.

The fate of this structure was shared by nearly all of the homes of free blacks that are listed in the 1852 city directory. In the past fifty years, general neglect, the construction of the Richmond-Petersburg Turnpike, and land clearance for the ill-fated Jackson Place redevelopment have erased nearly all traces of these buildings. (Photograph: Valentine Museum)

TTP, Jr.

HAYES-McCANCE HOUSE, 801 East Leigh Street, Richmond
Built 1816, 1832–34; demolished 1893

As with the Adams–Van Lew and Hobson-Nolting mansions (qq.v.), as well as the surviving White House of the Confederacy, the distinctive feature of the Hayes-McCance house was its garden façade. Here, George Washington's design for the river front at Mount Vernon was carried to an urban site and into the era of the more archaeologically detailed Classical Revival style of architecture. The addition of a raised basement provided a new verticality to an old feature. With that adjustment, the colonial piazza was made to seem all the more imposing. The Doric entablature of the Hayes-McCance house, with its boldly detailed frieze of triglyphs and metopes, probably copied from a pattern book, served to rivet the eye to its lofty height.

The Hayes-McCance house does not carry the name of its most significant owner. The core structure was built in 1816 by Dr. John Hayes, who in 1832 sold the property to Thomas Green, a lawyer and speculator in land warrants. A decade later, Green sold it to Thomas McCance. According to insurance policies, it was Green who tripled the value of the house, from five to fifteen thousand dollars. He probably added both the piazza and a portico on Leigh Street to what was a handsome but simpler Federal house. Much of Green's expenditure was to improve the gardens, which extended to Clay Street and provided the type of expansive view that traditionally was enjoyed from a piazza. Robert Lancaster was able to describe the grounds two decades after the house was demolished: "Across the garden ran a deep ravine with a stream flowing through it. Mr. Green terraced the ravine and by checking the flow of the brook with a stone dam made a little lake, which was spanned by a rustic bridge. Upon the lake a small boat floated, and near the shore stood a tiny chalet-like cottage, covered with bark. In another part of the grounds was a bear-pit, containing several black bears, while here and there among the shrubbery and flowers gleamed pieces of white marble sculpture from Italy." (Photograph: Valentine Museum)

BARBOURSVILLE, Barboursville, Orange County
Built 1817–22; burned 1884

In 1817, James Barbour, a Piedmont planter who served as governor of Virginia, US senator, secretary of war, and ambassador to the Court of St. James in London, asked his friend and neighbor Thomas Jefferson to help him design a new house. Jefferson was "good enough" to draft a "plan" for him. In addition, the former president advised Barbour to send to him the workmen who would build this house so that they could "see [Monticello] and receive such verbal explanations as might facilitate their labours." Brickmason Edward Ancel and carpenter James Bradley made the trip to Albemarle County.

Barboursville resembled Monticello in many respects. It was a two-story structure designed to appear to be a single-story house. A turf ramp leading up to the portico concealed the raised basement, further strengthening the illusion. As at Monticello, a three-part bay projected under a garden-front portico. The center of the main floor was given to a two-story hexagonal reception area, behind which was a two-story octagonal drawing room. To either side of that central axis was a pair of square rooms separated by narrow hallways that contained small staircases. Barboursville was designed with a dome that was never built. All of these features were familiar elements of Jefferson's domestic designs.

Barboursville was the most highly valued estate in Orange County. For taxes it was appraised at twenty thousand dollars, twice the worth of its closest competitor in the county, James Madison's Montpelier. It was an extensive plantation. To the north of the mansion was an oval racetrack and stables for the horses that Barbour raised, a mill, many outbuildings, a cemetery, and a serpentine wall, another Jeffersonian feature, well known from those built at the University of Virginia.

Nearly a century after Barboursville burned, between 1977 and 1981, its ruins were stabilized through the efforts of Mario di Valmarana and the late Benjamin Howland, both of the University of Virginia's School of Architecture. Today the estate is well known for its vineyards. (Photograph: Virginia Historical Society; drawing by Thomas Jefferson, Massachusetts Historical Society)

MORRISON HOUSE, West Main and Liberty Streets, Harrisonburg
Completed by 1824; demolished 1982

The Morrison house, built for Joseph Thornton and later owned by the Morrison family, was a noteworthy example of the formality that could be instilled in the traditional vernacular architecture of Shenandoah Valley communities. One of Harrisonburg's few early houses to survive past World War II, the pleasingly proportioned dwelling stood in a state of near-perfect preservation, maintaining original window sash and simple but finely crafted interiors, including a handsome stair. The south wall was a rare use in the region of Flemish bond with a glazed-header pattern. Several years of effort aimed at preserving this local landmark came to naught when the Wetsel Seed Company leveled the registered historic landmark to clear space for half a dozen parking spaces. (Photograph: Richard Cheek for the Virginia Department of Historic Resources)

WITHROW HOUSE, Main Street, Waynesboro
Built ca. 1826; demolished ca. 1955

The Shenandoah Valley's early towns tended to develop in a linear fashion, following the precedent of communities in Pennsylvania whence many of the Valley's settlers emigrated. Houses and commercial buildings generally were situated on the front edges of their lots, giving the streets an urban character. This practice permitted deep yards beyond. A particularly dignified example of a large Federal town house so situated was Waynesboro's Withrow house, long a dominant feature of the downtown. The house seemed especially urban because it was attached to flanking buildings and included a shop in the northern end of the first floor. As was characteristic of Valley Federal buildings, the Withrow house was laid up in very even Flemish bond brickwork topped by a molded brick cornice. The latter device was used frequently on early Philadelphia buildings to make them less flammable. A wide center passage with wainscoting and a staircase dominated an interior filled with family possessions. The garden behind was noted for its shady, old-fashioned beauty. The stately, much-admired local landmark remained in the family until around 1955, when it was sold, demolished, and replaced by a J. J. Newberry store. The store, envisioned as an economic boon to the city, has since gone through several tenants and currently makes little contribution to an ailing downtown. Had it survived, the Withrow house today undoubtedly would be hailed as one of the community's leading cultural resources. (Photograph: Virginia Department of Historic Resources, gift of Mrs. Arthur Dugdale)

DUNLORA, Charlottesville vicinity, Albemarle County
Built 1828; burned 1916

Dunlora was the residence of Samuel Carr, the son of Dabney Carr, brother-in-law and close friend of Thomas Jefferson. It was designed by Thomas R. Blackburn, a craftsman and architect who began his career as a carpenter at the University of Virginia. It was built by Blackburn (as carpenter) and William B. Phillips (as bricklayer); Phillips was himself a former Jefferson workman and later a prolific builder. Dunlora was a significant example of Jeffersonian classicism as adapted to a smaller country house. Its design, like that of its near neighbor Bentivar (designed for Samuel Carr's brother John Carr and since demolished), ultimately was derived from Jefferson's design for Edgehill (q.v.). All of these houses were one story with an exposed cellar; they were double-pile in plan, with splayed fireplaces gathered into paired, internal chimneys. They were surmounted by a monitor and entered through a one-story Tuscan portico on the piano nobile that was reached by a prominent stair.

Dunlora passed in 1846 to William S. Dabney, a descendant who willed the western part of the property to his former slaves at the end of the Civil War; that tract became known as the Free State. In 1916, the house was burned by an arsonist. Following the fire, Dunlora was reconstructed in modified form by architect Eugene Bradbury, who, among other things, lowered the entrance to the ground floor. (Photograph: Manuscript Print Collection, Special Collections Department, University of Virginia Library)

WILLIAM H. BOWERS HOUSE, southwest corner of Sycamore and Bank Streets, Petersburg
Built 1828–29; demolished 1977

The urbanity and superb quality of Petersburg's Federal-era architecture was elegantly expressed in the town house erected for William H. Bowers in the heart of downtown. A merchant who had moved to Petersburg from New York in 1827, Bowers constructed a "large and elegant building," valued at twelve thousand dollars, that he may have used both as his home and as a store. His extravagant taste apparently was beyond his means, however, for he was forced to sell the structure to pay debts less than a year after its completion. He conveyed his fine new building, and others he had purchased, to Gardiner Green Howland and Samuel Shaw Howland of New York, who were among his creditors and who leased the property to dry goods merchants until 1841, when they sold it to George Ansley Davis, a member of a family of well-to-do Jewish merchants who had emigrated from London to Petersburg. In 1847, Davis conveyed the building to family member Goodman Davis, whose immediate family held it until 1881. At that point Davis's widow and sons, by then living in New York, sold the house to jeweler J. T. Young, whose shop had occupied the property for decades. It was apparently when the Youngs moved into the building, in 1859, taking over the stand of silversmiths/jewelers Lumsden & Shortt, that a marble and Gothic-style storefront was installed. For most of the 20th century, the building was home to a popular drugstore.

The Bowers house was said by Miss Mattie Spotswood to have been designed and constructed by James Noë and Theophilus Nash. Noë was Otis Manson's partner in the Bollingbrook Hotel project, and Nash executed what is now the Richmond Room in the American Wing of the Metropolitan Museum of Art and probably designed the wonderful A. L. Scott house on Market Street in Petersburg. Certainly the building was designed and constructed by highly skilled craftsmen; the elegance of its exterior seldom has been matched in commercial buildings in Virginia. The splendid dormers, the stepped and pierced gable, the ornamental panels between openings on every floor, the Palladian window on the attic level in the side elevation and the triple windows below it, enhanced with wrought-iron balconies, distinguished this remarkable structure. The interior must have been fine, but apparently neither photographs of it nor architectural elements from it survive. Both of the large wrought-iron balconies were saved, but they were badly damaged when the building was razed.

In 1977 the Historic Petersburg Foundation purchased the Bowers house, which was listed on the National Register of Historic Places, intending to restore it. Regrettably, when work began, a serious structural problem was aggravated, and the façade pulled away from the rest of the building. The local building inspector declared the Bowers house a safety hazard and ordered it demolished immediately. (Photograph: Historic American Buildings Survey, Library of Congress)
CCL and RDW, Jr.

DANIEL F. CARR HOUSE,
West Main Street, Charlottesville
Built ca. 1830; demolished 1975

Judging from its architectural character, this visually distinctive, *distyle-in-muris* brick house built for Daniel Carr undoubtedly was designed and constructed by one of Thomas Jefferson's master builders. Allegedly, it housed the town's first infirmary. The fabric incorporated mortise-and-tenon joinery, six-over-six sash, and four-panel doors. In 1975, the building was razed and sold for the price of its bricks. Demolition revealed that the columned façade was probably a midcentury addition, as with Christ Episcopal Church in Charlottesville. (Photograph: Prints Collection, Special Collections Department, University of Virginia Library)
KEL

ROSE HALL, 625 Ohio Street, Waynesboro
Built 1830; demolished 1963

Waynesboro's premier patrician mansion succumbed to the 1960s' notion of progress only three years before the passage of the National Historic Preservation Act of 1966. Had it survived that destructive decade, Rose Hall undoubtedly would be a registered landmark today and heralded as the foremost heritage site of this Shenandoah Valley city. A bland shopping center now occupies the place where this genteel homestead stood for more than a century.

Rose Hall was originally the home of Hugh L. Gallaher, Sr., a contractor who is said to have assisted with the construction of the railroad tunnel through Afton Mountain. Though built at a time when the Greek Revival style was the fashion, Rose Hall was architecturally conservative and in many ways resembled an 18th-century house more than a 19th-century one. Its tall, multipaned windows, modillion cornice, Flemish bond brickwork, and steep gable roof gave it the look of a Georgian plantation dwelling of the Tidewater. Inside were original mantels, chair rails, and a fine staircase with turned balusters and carved brackets. Several outbuildings and the remnants

of an old boxwood garden remained on the grounds. All survived to the end with little or no alteration.

It was in Rose Hall's parlor, on 12 January 1865, that Gallaher's daughter, Sally Bowen Gallaher, married Capt. Hugh Holmes McGuire, brother of the noted Confederate surgeon Dr. Hunter Holmes McGuire. Among the wedding guests were Gen. Thomas Rosser, Gen. Lunsford Lomax, and Maj. Fitzhugh Lee. Three months later, during the Battle of Waynesboro, on 1 and 2 March 1865, Gen. Jubal Early breakfasted at Rose Hall prior to the defeat of his troops by Gen. Philip Sheridan. Dr. McGuire was captured in the battle, but because he was a noncombatant he was permitted to go to Rose Hall. There he invited General Sheridan in for a hot meal. Out of gratitude Sheridan posted guards at the house to prevent its being looted and burned—an early instance of Federal preservation activity. (Photograph: Virginia Department of Historic Resources)

THE UNION, Palmyra vicinity, Fluvanna County
Built 1831; burned 1965

The Union, designed and built by former Thomas Jefferson workman Thomas R. Blackburn for John Timberlake at Union Mills, stood as part of an extensive mill complex. Thus the building was important both as an example of Jeffersonian classicism as spread by a carpenter who worked at the University of Virginia and as a reminder of Virginia's antebellum industrialization.

The Union was placed on a commanding site sixteen miles from Charlottesville that offered sweeping views of the Rivanna River and Mechunk Creek. The industrial complex surrounding it included a merchant mill, a sawmill, and a large brick cotton factory. This operation was begun by Timberlake in 1796 and grew as he enlarged the dam across the Rivanna River at Adams Falls. By 1835, the Virginia Union Factory, operated by Timberlake in partnership with John B. Magruder, was thriving. It ran fifteen hundred spindles and twelve power looms, which together produced several hundred yards of substantial cloth a day; the cloth was held in high repute throughout the state. More than one hundred operators were employed at the site and lived in a village around the mills that contained houses for eighteen or twenty families, a tanyard, a Methodist church, and "the elegant dwellings of the proprietors." This enterprise was what one would expect to see in the small mill villages of Connecticut or Rhode Island—not in Jefferson's shadow. As late as 1934, the factory and at least one other mill building remained; they were dismantled for their brick.

The Union was built in the style of Jeffersonian classicism, but the structure had been altered by the time it was photographed. A second-story porch and dormer window had been added and a Chinese lattice rail on the roof of the first-floor porch removed. The Jeffersonian triple-sash windows on the ground floor had been converted to standard double sash. On the interior the Union bore unmistakable connections to Jefferson's work. The dining room was given an elliptical arch (to frame a sideboard) derived directly from the dining room at Monticello, as well as a revolving serving closet door (called by Blackburn a "closet of convenience"). Interestingly, Blackburn's architectural drawings for the Union were mistaken for the work of Jefferson by Thomas Jefferson Randolph, Jefferson's grandson and executor, and became a part of the Coolidge Collection of Jefferson architectural drawings at the Massachusetts Historical Society.

The Union burned in February 1965. Only parts of the wall and portions of the front door survived. B. F. D. Runk, dean of the University of Virginia, purchased the ruins and commissioned Floyd E. Johnston to design for him on the site a Jeffersonian-style house, using materials from the Union where possible. (Photograph: Manuscript Print Collection, Special Collections Department, University of Virginia Library)

OVERSEER'S HOUSE, FOUR MILE TREE PLANTATION, Surry County
Built ca. 1838; burned 1980s

Four Mile Tree plantation became the property of Philip St. George Cocke in 1834, upon his marriage to Elizabeth Courtney Bowdoin. About four years later he erected on the property a romantic eclectic overseer's house, the L-shaped building that is pictured here. The precise location of the house is defined on an 1848 map of Four Mile Tree that survives in Cocke's letter book of 1809–61, preserved in the Cocke Family Papers at the University of Virginia. Also in the Cocke papers is a pencil drawing of the house dated 1838 and entitled "Elevation and Plan of Cottage for Overseer's House at 4 Mi Tree." (It is an amateurish drawing, not likely by the hand of Cocke, who was a West Point graduate and an unusually accomplished draftsman.) The drawing is an

adaptation of Plate XLII in *An Encyclopaedia of Cottage, Farm, and Villa Architecture* (London, 1833), pictured here, by British tastemaker John Claudius Loudon. As constructed, the overseer's house was a simplified version of Loudon's design. It burned in the 1980s; all that remains is a chimney.

Philip St. George Cocke was the son of John Hartwell Cocke, the builder of Bremo, Lower Bremo, and Bremo Recess in Fluvanna County. After his renovation and building projects at Four Mile Tree, the younger Cocke further advanced his father's architectural legacy with a more substantial undertaking. Philip St. George Cocke's letter book reveals that in 1838 he made an offer of thirty-five thousand dollars to William Old for "Belle Mead," an eighteen-hundred-acre plantation in Powhatan County. In 1845, Cocke wrote a letter to William Maxwell, his stepmother's brother, asking for help in securing an architect to design a mansion for "Belmead." The letter reaffirms Cocke's acquaintance with John Claudius Loudon; Cocke wrote, "The design given in Loudon's *Cyclopedia of Cottage, Farm, & Villa Architecture* [sic], page 920, as Trotman's *beau ideal* of a villa in this style comes nearer to my taste than any other design I ever saw—". In September 1845, a contract was drawn up between Cocke and prominent New York architect A. J. Davis for "building a dwelling house and kitchen offices at Belmead."

The small overseer's house at Four Mile Tree was the beginning of Philip St. George Cocke's interest in architecture. The Williamson House at Virginia Military Institute and the Lodge (qq.v.) were built as a result of Cocke's promotion of A. J. Davis among the Cocke family circle. (Photograph: Virginia Department of Historic Resources; Image: J. C. Loudon, *Encyclopaedia*, 1833)
MBR

SAMUEL FREEMAN HOUSE (DE SAUSSURE HOUSE), 316
East Main Street, Richmond
Built ca. 1839; demolished ca. 1940

Also known as the de Saussure house (for William D. de Saussure, a later owner), this Greek Revival residence was constructed in 1839 for Samuel Freeman. Rising two and a half stories above a raised basement, the building was impressive in scale. The brick walls were laid in Flemish bond with convex tooling. The windowsills, the panels over the first-floor windows, and the lintels all were of wood; the roof was slate. The entrance portico was tastefully designed with Ionic details. The interior woodwork was described as "of unusually delicate Greek character." A continuous stairway ran from basement to attic. At one time the building had a long iron balcony that hung from the raised first floor over the sidewalk. A series of rear extensions, servants' quarters, a kitchen, and a three-story rear porch all were lost by the time the building was photographed. (Photograph: Historic American Buildings Survey, Library of Congress)

VARNUM-MAHONE HOUSE,
42 South Market Street, Petersburg
Built 1839, enlarged and elaborated 1874; demolished 1954

In 1839 Jacob B. Varnum constructed a two-story, frame, side-passage house that was expanded in 1874 by Confederate general William Mahone into the building pictured here. In 1845 Varnum's trustees sold the house to Thomas White, whose family sold it in 1873 to Mahone, the hero of the Battle of the Crater, the builder of the Norfolk & Petersburg Railroad, and the consolidator of what became the Atlantic, Mississippi, & Ohio Railroad. Mahone's third and most important career, which he orchestrated largely from his basement office in this impressive house, was as the dominant political figure in Virginia for a long period in the 1870s and 1880s. Mahone became the leading proponent of readjusting the commonwealth's Civil War debt and allied himself with Republicans and African-Americans to accomplish that goal and other important social reforms. At the peak of his power, he controlled the General Assembly, the governor's mansion, and both senate seats. He helped to found two large institutions, Virginia State University (q.v.) and Central State Hospital of Petersburg. Both were designed by Maj. Harrison Waite, whom Mahone had employed to design his expanded house. Waite added wings to the south and rear of the Varnum house, changed the roof, and applied to the front of the building its square bay and porch.

In 1903 Mahone's widow, Otelia, received 430 veterans of Mahone's brigade on their way to reenact the Battle of the Crater; this reenactment is said to have inspired Douglas Southall Freeman to research and write *R. E. Lee: A Biography*. Mahone's family sold the house in 1943; it was demolished in 1954 and has been replaced by a discount bread store. (Photograph: A. M., *The City of Petersburg: The Book of Its Chamber of Commerce*, 1894) RDW, Jr.

CASERTA, Eastville vicinity, Northampton County
Built ca. 1836; burned 1975

Situated overlooking Mattawoman Creek, this Eastern Shore plantation dwelling had a curious side passage, the roof of which towered above the brick-ended main body of the house. The passage, both deep as well as tall, contained a dramatic open-well staircase that ascended to the attic. The high roof ridge provided headroom as the stair reached the top level. More typical of the region's traditional houses was the long service wing, which may have incorporated a small 18th-century dwelling. With this wing, Caserta thus had the "big house, colonnade, and kitchen" arrangement indigenous to the Eastern Shore.

The main part of the house was built circa 1836 for George P. Upshur, a US naval commander and brother of Judge Abel Parker Upshur of Vaucluse. He named the property after the Italian town near Naples that contains the famous royal palace and where he had spent many pleasant days. Following the deaths of his infant daughter and, in 1839, his wife and son, Upshur lost interest in the property; he sold it in 1847. He died in Spezia, Italy, in 1852 while in command of the USS *Levant*. His remains were returned to America, where they were buried in the Upshur family cemetery at Vaucluse.

Caserta had several owners following Upshur's tenure. Except for a later front porch, the house stood essentially unchanged until it was struck by lightning and burned to the ground in 1975, just five years after it had been listed on the Virginia Landmarks Register and the National Register of Historic Places. (Photograph: Historic American Buildings Survey, Library of Congress)

LEADBEATER HOUSE, 414 North Washington Street, Alexandria
Built 1840; demolished early 1960s

Named after its last owners, the Leadbeater house was a finely crafted and superb example of urban Greek Revival architecture. Rising two and a half stories over a slightly raised basement, this three-bay brick house was handsomely proportioned, partly due to the sizing and placement of window openings on three levels. The double front door was framed by sidelights and covered by an elegant Ionic portico with a full entablature. The façade was completed by a full-height Ionic cornice at the roofline. Actually, a full entablature was subtly suggested there. Below the cornice the brick was raised to outline both an architrave and a frieze punctuated by three grilled openings in the attic story. A delicate, finely wrought cast-iron fence enclosed the yard.

The Leadbeater house was described in 1959 by architectural historians from the Historic American Buildings Survey as "undoubtedly the best preserved example of the Greek Revival in town." The structure was demolished and replaced by a commercial office building. (Photograph: Historic American Buildings Survey, Library of Congress)

THE WESTMORELAND CLUB (GRAY-STANARD HOUSE), 601 East Grace Street, Richmond
Built 1840; demolished 1937

In 1835, James Gray purchased the southeast corner of Sixth and Grace Streets and set out to build an imposing mansion, one sure to draw attention to its owner. However, in the words of architectural historian Mary Wingfield Scott, "his affairs became involved," and in 1839 he sold the partly finished building, along with building material intended for the house, to Robert Stanard. Stanard completed the house the following year.

This dignified, Greek Revival, stucco-clad brick mansion rose two stories from a raised basement. Its three-bay façade, punctuated by three-part windows on both stories, was covered by a hipped roof pierced by two pairs of chimneys and topped by a baluster-wrapped monitor. The front door of the house was framed by a single-story Doric portico with full entablature and fluted Doric columns. The house bore a striking resemblance to the nearby Abram Warwick house at 503 East Grace Street (built 1834; demolished 1932), which may have served simultaneously as rival and model.

In 1879 the Gray-Stanard house was sold to the two-year-old Westmoreland Club, a prominent Richmond men's social club. In 1937, the storied Westmoreland Club ceased to exist; the house was sold and quickly demolished to make way for that greatest of civic ornaments—a parking lot. An undistinguished office block/parking deck now occupies the site, directly across Grace Street from the Carpenter Center for the Performing Arts, giving scant indication of what preceded it. (Photographs: Virginia Historical Society)

JAMES-DUNLOP HOUSE, Hinton (Friend) Street, in the block bounded by Hinton, Davis (Folly), Washington, and Market Streets, Petersburg
Built 1840, enlarged 1902; demolished 20th century

In 1840, the prosperous dry goods merchant Edwin James constructed an impressive two-story brick house, with a footprint of fifty-three by fifty-five feet and several large brick dependencies, on a large piece of land on the north side of Friend (now Hinton) Street long known as the Garden Lot. James spent twelve thousand dollars for the new house, a large sum for the time. In 1853 he sold the property to Judge Thomas S. Gholson, the first president of the Petersburg Library Association, who entertained former president John Tyler and Edward Everett in this house. The third owner, Robert A. Hamilton, saw his home serve in April 1865 as the headquarters for Union general Philip Sheridan. The house passed next to the Brown family and then in 1878 to tobacconist David Dunlop, whose father had amassed a substantial fortune in that business. Dunlop installed the handsome iron fence and brick walls that today are all that remain of the house above ground.

By the time he died in 1902, David Dunlop was the largest exporter of tobacco in the United States. Seven years earlier the newly widowed Dunlop had married Mary Corling Johnston, age twenty at the time of their wedding. Young "Molly" Dunlop brought great energy to the house, resulting in many changes, most dramatically a third-story ballroom addition completed in 1902 (and visible in this picture). In 1911 she married Archibald McCrea of Pittsburgh. The McCreas took up residence in the Friend Street house but also maintained residences at Brunswick Hall and in the Hotel Pierre in Manhattan. It was Molly McCrea who in 1928 purchased the colonial mansion Carter's Grove, which is now owned by the Colonial Williamsburg Foundation. (Photograph: courtesy of R. Dulaney Ward, Jr.)
RDW, Jr.

LUDLAM-ANDERSON HOUSE, 113 West Franklin Street, Richmond
Built 1844; demolished 1893

Located on the present site of the Jefferson Hotel in downtown Richmond, the Ludlam-Anderson house was built by Virginia architect F. C. Gravely for Henry Ludlam, a prominent Richmond merchant and banker. Initially, this austere yet refined Greek Revival building was simpler than what is pictured here; each of the wings was shallow and contained only a single room. The temple-shaped core was given a side hall that connected double parlors. Gravely probably took the design for the giant portico's four imposing and unusual columns from Asher Benjamin's *The Complete Builder's Guide* (1839); Benjamin's source was Stuart and Revett's publication of the ancient Greek order of the Tower of the Winds. Ludlam's house must have been the envy of the neighborhood, because only a year later its design, but in the Ionic order, was repeated across the street as the Taylor-Mayo house (now known as the Mayo Memorial Church House).

Ludlam occupied his house for but two years before he sold it to Joseph Reid Anderson, owner and president of Tredegar Iron Works. Anderson played a pivotal role in the history of Richmond and the Confederacy. Made a general by Robert E. Lee, he served until 1862, after which he directed Tredegar's manufacture of ammunition. Following the war he served in the Virginia House of Delegates.

Anderson altered Ludlum's house in two significant ways. In 1848 he removed the basement kitchen to a newly constructed outbuilding. In 1859 and 1860 he extended the wings to the depth of the center block, thereby providing more stately and practical living spaces. At Anderson's request F. C. Gravely left a detailed description and plan of the house that is a record of room use, dimensions, and even such details as the size of windowpanes and floorboards. The document describes a hot-air furnace and an elliptical, stained glass dome over the stair hall. When Anderson died, in 1892, his heirs sold the house to Maj. Lewis Ginter, who demolished it to make way for the Jefferson Hotel. Ironically, Anderson had been involved in the early planning of the hotel, never imagining that it would be built on the site of his own house. (Photograph: Valentine Museum)
KLJ

DOVER, Manakin-Sabot vicinity, Goochland County
Built 1845; burned 1933

In opulence, Dover stood apart from most of its neighbors. Its architect is not known. It was built for James Morson, a lawyer from Fredericksburg who was married to Ellen Bruce. Ellen Bruce's parents built the storied Greek Revival mansion Berry Hill in Halifax County; her father, James Coles Bruce, was one of the wealthiest men in the nation.

Dover's interior was a sumptuous display of classical detailing. The Corinthian order of the portico, using the Greek-style Corinthian of the Choragic Monument of Lysicrates, was repeated in the grand entrance hall and in remarkably ornate reception rooms. There the full entablature carried by the columns was so deep as to create an illusion of exceptional height and opulence. The ornamental ceiling medallions and imported marble mantels were akin to those at Berry Hill. The mantels were brought to Dover by the Morsons from the John Brockenbrough residence in Richmond, which they had purchased in 1844 and which later became the White House of the Confederacy.

Ellen Morson's sister Sallie Seddon lived nearby at Sabot Hill (q.v.). The sisters' retirement to Goochland was interrupted by the Civil War. In the course of serving the Confederacy, the Morsons relocated to Wilton, their sugar plantation in St. James's Parish, Louisiana, where Ellen died in 1862 and James died in 1868. Though Dover burned in 1933, nearby slave quarters survive. The ruins of the main house stood until the 1970s, when they were deemed a safety hazard and removed. (Photographs: Valentine Museum and Virginia Historical Society)

DREWRY'S MANSION, below Manchester, Richmond
Built ca. 1846–50; demolished 1964

Drewry's Mansion was a countryseat situated on a fifteen-hundred-acre tract in Chesterfield County and carved from a larger colonial estate called Falls Plantation. Today, the site lies within the boundaries of the city of Richmond. The builder was Maj. Henry T. Drewry, a veteran of the War of 1812. The house rivaled the best urban architecture. It was furnished with carved marble mantels, bronze chandeliers, and a giant, two-story piazza similar to those then fashionable in Richmond. Although in plan Drewry's Mansion followed the Classical Revival type, the house was detailed in a more avant-garde style, the Italianate. By tradition, construction began as early as 1846, only four years after Andrew Jackson Downing popularized Italianate designs in his *Cottage Residences* (1842).

Henry Drewry would enjoy tranquility in his new mansion for little more than a decade. In 1862 the Peninsula Campaign brought the Civil War perilously close to home when the battle of Drewry's Bluff halted a Union naval advance to Richmond via the James River. Drewry's Mansion had been a social center before the war; it regained that status later and in the 20th century. A newspaper account of 1900 stated, "Here gathered the fashionable of Richmond and Manchester." In 1964 the mansion was sold to the city and demolished to make room for a playground. (Photograph: Valentine Museum)

HOBSON-NOLTING HOUSE, 409 East Main Street, Richmond
Built ca. 1847; demolished 1950–51

The Hobson-Nolting house generally was considered to be Richmond's most impressive Greek Revival residence. A brick structure, it rose three stories at what was once one of the city's most architecturally distinguished locations, the intersection of Fifth and East Main Streets. Facing it were Moldavia (q.v.) and the Hancock-Wirt-Caskie house, which still stands. As with several other Richmond mansions, such as the Adams–Van Lew house (q.v.), the garden façade was given a giant, two-story piazza; its Doric columns were set on tall square pillars and topped by a full entablature. The interior was given lavish classical detailing employing the Greek Corinthian order of the Choragic Monument of Lysicrates.

John C. Hobson, builder of the house, was a tobacconist, owner of Howard's Neck plantation in Goochland County, and president of the Exchange Bank (q.v.). Upon his death in 1873 his mansion was sold to Emil Otto Nolting, also the owner of a tobacco company, as well as president of the Bank of the Commonwealth, the National Bank of Virginia, the Tobacco Exchange (q.v.), and the Chamber of Commerce (q.v.).

The builder of the Hobson-Nolting house was Robert McClellan, who later constructed the Exchange Hotel (q.v.). McClellan brought from Scotland several skilled craftsmen, one of whom was George Gibson, Sr., progenitor of a family of builders (John, George, William, and David). The senior Gibson would also build the Richmond Female Institute (q.v.). Richie V. Beazley and John D. Quarles were brickmasons for John Hobson's house.

The Hobson-Nolting house was little altered through the late 1940s, when it remained occupied by three of Nolting's children. It was then purchased by the Equitable Life Assurance Society of the United States, which in 1950 decided to raze the house, citing "the necessity for adequate parking facilities" for a new headquarters on the site. Gov. John S. Battle telegraphed the company in an effort to halt the demolition, to no avail. According to architectural historian Mary Wingfield Scott, at the time of its destruction the house needed only exterior paint. Many of the furnishings and some architectural details are preserved at the Valentine Museum. (Photographs: Valentine Museum and Historic American Buildings Survey, Library of Congress)

KINLOCH, Loretto vicinity, Essex County
Built 1847–48; burned 1948

The countryseat of planter-politician Richard Baylor, Kinloch was a Greek Revival structure of remarkable refinement for its setting in the fields of Tidewater Virginia. The design shows the hand of an experienced urban architect, Robert Cary Long, Jr., of Baltimore. A decade earlier, in 1839, Long had designed the Virginia School for the Deaf and the Blind in Staunton, one of the commonwealth's most imposing and harmonious Classical Revival buildings.

Kinloch's principal façade featured a one-story portico with paired Ionic columns topped by a superb iron rail and approached by semicircular stairs. The stairs were changed from Long's initial scheme; the effect was to soften the strong Greek character of this entrance. A one-story piazza stretched across the rear façade. In plan Kinloch was a square nearly sixty feet wide, with brick walls two and a half feet thick that rose four stories. Its observation deck, more than fifty feet in the air, offered a panorama of the Rappahannock River valley. Inside were twenty-one rooms, eighteen with fireplaces, plus long and large cross passages in the tradition of Virginia Georgian design of the colonial period. The mantels were marble, and the doors were finished with silver-plated hardware. Despite the size and elaborate appointments of the house, this structure seemed more elegant than massive. Its visual appeal derived from handsome proportioning and an understated use of Greek forms.

Construction of Kinloch began in July 1847, and by October the main roof timbers were in place. The house was completed in 1848. Robert Cary Long, Jr., brought from Baltimore virtually all of the workmen, as well as the building supplies. The craftsmen (bricklayer William Meakin, plasterer Samuel Bilson, carpenters Henry and Josiah Reynolds, stonemasons J. B. Sumwalt and Fred Green, stone carver Robert Hayes, tinner Henry Fouse, and smith Hugh Devlin) are all identified in the Baylor family papers at the Virginia Historical Society. So are the building supplies; these included granite sills, brick, window frames, lumber, cast-iron lintels, cast-iron handrails, marble mantels, and lime. Even the furnace and plants for the garden, which Long also had designed, came from Baltimore.

Today, only a depression in the ground marks the site of Kinloch; the ruins were raided for their brick. (Photograph: Virginia Historical Society)

CASTALIA, Cismont vicinity, Albemarle County
Built ca. 1850, enlarged late 1890s; demolished 1987

    This prodigious wooden mansion was one of the noted landmarks of the scenic Southwest Mountains region of Albemarle County. The property was included in the 1730 patent to Col. Nicholas Meriwether. In the 1830s it was acquired by Robert W. Lewis, who built the core of the mansion in 1850. Murray Boocock of New York City, a member of a prominent Brooklyn mercantile and banking family, purchased Castalia in 1894. Boocock hired architect Paul Pelz of Washington, DC, to draw up plans for improvements to the house. Pelz is perhaps best known as the original architect for the Library of Congress, though he also designed a number of notable buildings in the mid-Atlantic region, including the former Hotel Chamberlin at Old Point Comfort (q.v.). Pelz's remodeling included the taller, more picturesque roof with its large dormers, as well as a new front porch and rear porte-cochere with chamber above. These and other changes transformed a standard Greek Revival plantation house into a fashionable Colonial Revival mansion. The completed work was described by Edward C. Meade in 1898 thus: "Seated amid a dense grove of trees, its balustrades and lofty chimneys tower above the tree-tops . . . As we enter this handsome home of English type we are at once removed a century in time. . . ." Boocock later employed architects Henry J. Blauvelt of Philadelphia and Henry Wilkinson of Llewellyn Park, NJ, to design a north wing in 1911.

    Mr. and Mrs. R. Hitchcock purchased Castalia in the mid-1980s. Judging the house too costly to repair and modernize, too large to maintain or use, and architecturally unattractive, they demolished it and built a new house on the site. Some of the interior woodwork was salvaged and reused in the new residence. (Photograph: Virginia Department of Historic Resources)

ROCKLANDS, Gordonsville vicinity,
Orange County
Built 1850s (incorporating an older house); burned ca.
1905

Rocklands was built as a summer home for wealthy Richmond mill owner Richard Barton Haxall (see Haxall Mills, q.v.). The design of the house, which engulfed and enlarged a more modest earlier dwelling, was by Albert Lawrence West. Dr. George Bagby's essay "At Rocklands" describes the house and its inhabitants circa 1870, noting the house's setting in a lush landscape and its equally lush interior, which was richly decorated with oil paintings, marble statues, "plaques, majolica, fresh flowers, souvenirs of travel abroad and at home [and] everywhere . . . ample provision against the discomfort that so generally prevails in the country parts of Virginia." Bagby presciently observed that "With rare exceptions, the rule in the South hereafter will be what it has long been in the North and in Europe, that the handsomest country seats will belong to opulent men whose fortunes have been acquired at some pursuit other than farming." Rocklands burned circa 1905 and was replaced by the nucleus of the present Colonial Revival mansion there, built for the Atkinson family of Richmond and remodeled in the 1930s by William Lawrence Bottomley. (Photograph: Virginia Historical Society)
ALM

EASTWOOD, Manakin-Sabot vicinity, Goochland County
Built ca. 1850–60; burned 1941

Eastwood was an imaginative exercise in the application of largely Italianate detailing to the simple rectangular core of a traditional Classical Revival residence. Italianate brackets defined the cornice on all portions of the house, but it was the design of the porches, with their abundance of ornamentation, that distinguished Eastwood. Such a whimsical display was more frequently seen in the deep South during this period, on houses in the so-called Steamboat Gothic style, which mixed elements of almost any type. There, and at Eastwood, architecture served to convey prosperity, optimism, and exuberance. Virginia's economy enjoyed a revitalization during the 1850s, and Virginians experienced a renewed pride of place. A champion of the new commonwealth was the governor, Henry Wise, soon to become an ardent secessionist. Wise was the father-in-law of Plumer Hobson, for whom Eastwood was built.

Eastwood was totally destroyed by fire in 1941; a modern house was erected on the site in the 1960s. (Photograph: Virginia Historical Society)

SABOT HILL, Sabot vicinity, Goochland County
Built ca. 1851; burned early 1920s

The Sabot Hill estate was purchased by James and Ellen Morson when they built the Greek Revival mansion Dover (q.v.) nearby. They soon sold the property to Ellen's sister Sarah "Sallie" Bruce and her husband, James Alexander Seddon, who constructed the twenty-six-room mansion pictured here. Seddon served in the US House of Representatives from 1845 to 1861; he then became the fourth Confederate secretary of war, serving from 1862 to 1865.

Sabot Hill, along with Eastwood (q.v.) and Ben Dover, was one of three Italianate mansions erected in Goochland County at midcentury, following the popularization of the style by A. J. Downing in his *Architecture of Country Houses* (1850). Today the evidence is entirely gone; both Sabot Hill and Eastwood burned, while Ben Dover was remodeled in the Georgian style in 1921. Like Ben Dover, which had a tower and loggias, Sabot Hill was a true Italian villa; the house was picturesque in both its detailing and its asymmetrical floor plan. A two-story spiral stair was lit by a stained glass skylight. Even more unusual were the interior shutters, which were made of steel, apparently for security.

In 1864 Union troops burned the brick stable, barn, straw rack, and cattle sheds at Sabot Hill; slaves were able to extinguish other fires on the property. In 1937 the firm of Baskervill & Son designed for Mr. and Mrs. William T. Reed, Jr., the Georgian Revival house, also named Sabot Hill, that currently stands on the site of its Italianate predecessor. (Photograph: Valentine Museum)

THE LODGE (ELK HILL, RED LODGE), Genito Road and Route 609, Amelia County
Built 1851–52; burned by 1871; ruins demolished 20th century

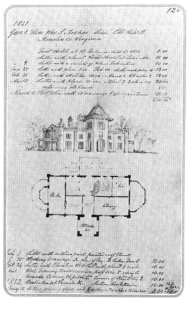

Sen. William Segar Archer of Amelia County served in the Virginia legislature and the US Congress for a quarter-century, but he is more interesting as a patron than as a politician. Archer commissioned a remarkable mansion on his plantation by one of the leading American Romantics, A. J. Davis of New York. For this important undertaking Davis even visited the site, but the house may not have been fully finished when Archer died in 1855, and it had burned by 1871.

The Lodge has left posterity with puzzles. The exact final form remains a question. The building seemingly followed the lines of Davis's perspective sketch, but the mansion is known almost solely from Davis's drawings, which show a series of alternatives. Another puzzle has been the style. Older historians often saw the conception as somehow Oriental—"a hybrid Italianate-Moorish-Hindu dwelling," in one writer's words. Instead, the house was an awkward but imaginative essay in reviving Tudor-Stuart architecture. The conception represents the union of an early form of Colonial Revivalism created in Virginia with the international, 19th-century search for nationalistic styles. This union occurred under the influence of Archer's relatives John Hartwell Cocke and Philip St. George Cocke, two of the great figures in Virginia's architectural history.

Working with the elder Cocke, John Neilson, one of Jefferson's favorite workmen, created a masterpiece of Jeffersonian Palladianism at Bremo (1816–20, Fluvanna County). Cocke learned to regret the expense and shallow roof of this house. He turned to reviving the Tudor-Stuart style of such buildings as Bacon's Castle (ca. 1665, Surry County), a Cocke family property, and he used this economical, practical manner for a series of structures. He also influenced his son, Philip St. George Cocke, to use this style at an overseer's house at Four Mile Tree (1838, q.v.). No doubt Cocke saw himself as reviving the first style to be used in both England and its North American domains, and presumably he wished to advertise his lineage, which stretched back to 17th-century Virginia.

Cocke's son Philip modified the elder man's approach, employing a professional architect, Davis, to design the Tudor Revival manor house Belmead (1845–48, Powhatan County). In the mid-19th century, a major mark of the search for national expression was the revival of Latrobe's decorative use of American plants at the US Capitol, and Davis included such Americanized detailing at Belmead. Cocke liberally promoted Davis's career in Virginia.

Responding to the younger Cocke, Archer had Davis devise an Elizabethan/Jacobean Revival manor house complete with curvilinear gables. Like the Cockes, Archer traced his lineage back to 17th-century Virginia, as the Lodge itself declared, and Davis gave the parlor porch a nationalistic character with a variation on Latrobe's corn order at the Capitol. The idea that Tudor-Stuart architecture belonged to American as well as British history would bear fruit at least into the 1920s. Thus, Alexander Wilbourne Weddell and Virginia Chase Weddell commissioned Virginia House (1925–28, Richmond) by Henry Grant Morse as their home, but ultimately they destined this tribute to the Anglo-American manorial past to house the Virginia Historical Society. (Photograph: Mary Armstrong Jefferson, *Old Homes and Buildings of Amelia County*, Volume 1, 1964; Manuscript: The Metropolitan Museum of Art) CEB

WILLIAMSON HOUSE, Virginia Military Institute, Lexington
Completed 1852; demolished ca. 1966

The Williamson house, on the grounds of the Virginia Military Institute, was a residence designed by A. J. Davis for Maj. Thomas H. Williamson, a professor at VMI. Davis, the architect of VMI, designed the Williamson house as the right-hand house of a pair, connected by an arcade, for Professors Williamson and Gilham.

Williamson was no stranger to architecture; he taught that subject and engineering to VMI cadets and published his own textbook, *An Elementary Course on Architecture and Civil Engineering* (Lexington, 1850). Davis first designed for him an asymmetrical Gothic structure with a wide, narrow floor plan, an octagonal two-story tower, and a taller, square tower. Both towers were to terminate in battlements similar to those that Davis had designed for the VMI Barracks. The plans for both the Gilham and Williamson houses were later altered by Davis, and in the end, the Gilham house was the only asymmetrical building he built at VMI. While the Gilham and Williamson houses were designed in the Gothic mode, they bear a striking resemblance to Hawkwood, the Italianate villa Davis was designing at the time for R. O. Morris in Louisa County. Using very nearly the same plan, proportions, and general layout, Davis simply transmuted the Gothic windows and turrets of the Williamson house into the round-headed windows and bracketed, hipped-roof tower of Hawkwood, offering striking testimony to the adaptability of mid-19th-century, picturesque styles.

The Williamson house, one of the few Davis buildings to survive the Civil War, stood on the VMI Parade Grounds until it was demolished to make way for the 1967 construction of Lejune Hall, a multipurpose cadet center. (Photographs: Virginia Military Institute and the Metropolitan Museum of Art, Harris Brisbane Dick Fund, 1924)

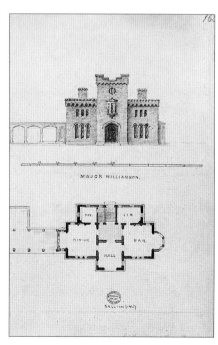

PRATT'S CASTLE, 324 South Fourth Street, Richmond
Built 1853; demolished 1956

For more than a century, from its construction in 1853 to its nationally protested demolition in 1956, few buildings caught the eye and captivated Richmonders more than did Pratt's Castle. This iron-plated, frame Gothic "fortress" was actually a modest-sized house. It was built at one of the most commanding points above the James River falls and the James River and Kanawha Canal on Gamble's Hill, a highly fashionable residential neighborhood in the 19th century. Pratt's Castle exemplified the picturesque aesthetic, universally popular at midcentury, and stood in stark contrast to the city's other, mostly stolid classical and vernacular structures. It was built by William A. Pratt, a talented entrepreneur who had moved to Richmond in 1845. His daguerreotype studio (q.v.) was located on East Main Street. As one of a number of his money-making schemes, he offered the house for sale in a lottery; but having few subscribers, he rescinded the offer.

Pratt's Castle had two floors set atop an English basement. Four crenelated towers of varying height added a particularly romantic flavor to the building's profile. In lieu of a moat, a high fence once surrounded the structure. Each of the house's rooms was irregularly shaped, and ceiling heights varied. The first-floor parlor and dining room contained a number of decorative features. The coffered living-room ceiling formed a chessboard pattern that included inset glass panels depicting chessmen. Elaborate stained glass windows admitted muted light into the spaces. A winding, cast-iron staircase led to three bedrooms on the second floor. On the lower level, a "dungeon" and tunnel fascinated visitors.

In 1858 Pratt moved to Charlottesville, where he was appointed superintendent of buildings and grounds at the University of Virginia. He sold Pratt's Castle in 1865, and it had a succession of owners until the mid-1950s, when it was purchased by Albemarle Paper Company. Despite strong protests, including appeals from the National Trust for Historic Preservation, the building was demolished in 1956 to make way for construction of Albemarle's corporate offices. (Photograph: Library of Virginia)
EJS, Jr.

JOHN WILLIAM MURRELL HOUSE, Second and Harrison Streets, Lynchburg
Built 1859–60; demolished 1940

Lynchburg's finest Italianate villa, this antebellum mansion boasted "twenty rooms, forty windows, five chimneys, and twelve marble mantels." It also contained its own water supply system and housed "a splendid ten pen [*sic*] alley" for bowling under the front porch. According to a son's manuscript, Murrell, a wealthy tobacco and sugar merchant, hired Thomas Eastlack, an architect from Philadelphia, to design the house. As work was nearing completion, Murrell went to New York to purchase furnishings. By the time they were ready, the Civil War had begun, and one of the two vessels carrying them sank while attempting to run the blockade. Pier glasses, paintings, and mahogany furniture intended for the library ended up instead in Davy Jones's locker.

During the war, the house served as one of Lynchburg's many emergency hospitals, and in 1868, Robert E. Lee stayed in it while attending an Episcopal convention. After an attempt to convert the house into a fine arts center failed during the 1930s, it was demolished. A greatly remodeled two-story servants' quarters, where family members lived while their house was under construction, remains. (Photograph: Jones Memorial Library, Lynchburg) SAC, Jr.

MOUNT SAN ANGELO, Route 29, Sweet Briar, Amherst County
Built 1870; burned 1979

Built for the W. Hamilton Mosby family, Mount San Angelo was a T-shaped Italianate villa with gable roofs and an impressive tower. The stuccoed façade was broken by single and paired arched windows set into arched, recessed panels. In 1901, when Sweet Briar College was founded, the house very nearly was purchased to serve as residence for the institution's first president; instead, seventy years would pass before the college acquired the property.

In 1909 Mount San Angelo was radically remodeled by new owners into a fashionable Georgian Revival mansion. The tower was removed, the walls were re-clad, the voids of the T-shaped floor plan were filled in to form a more symmetrical and rectangular mass, the fenestration was changed, and a balustrade was added, as were dormer windows and, most dramatically, a two-story Corinthian portico. Little evidence of the house's former appearance remained. The transformed residence was purchased by Sweet Briar College in 1972. While undergoing renovation for use as an arts space by the Virginia Center for the Creative Arts, Mount San Angelo was destroyed by fire. When a spokesman was asked about rumors that workmen had been burning old paint off the structure with blowtorches, thereby causing the fire, he retorted, "We had been scraping paint off with, not blowtorches, but propane." The building was a total loss. (Photograph: Virginia Department of Historic Resources)

MAPLEWOOD (VILLA NOUVA), Dolley Madison Boulevard near Capital Beltway interchange, Fairfax County
Built ca. 1873; demolished 1970

With its mansard roof, multiplicity of dormers, and central tower, Maplewood was a classic example of the American version of the Second Empire style, the neo–French Renaissance architectural mode fashionable during the reign of Napoleon III. Although the style was employed extensively in northern and midwestern states, few works of this type were erected in Virginia because of the disruption of the Civil War.

Originally called Villa Nouva, Maplewood was built for John L. Shipman, a prosperous contractor and dairy farmer. A house of such prominence and sophistication would likely have been designed by an architect, but the name of an architect has not surfaced. Shipman reportedly was the contractor for the 1872 British Embassy in Washington, DC; it has been speculated that he was inspired by that design. The embassy (razed in 1931) was designed by Washington, DC, architect John Fraser and had a general resemblance to Villa Nouva.

Shipman sold the property to Gen. William McKee Dunn in 1884 and moved to Washington, DC. Dunn, who renamed the place Maplewood, used it as a summer residence. Charles L. Brodt, owner of hotels in New York and Florida, purchased Maplewood from the Dunn estate in 1912. Brodt and his wife undertook an extensive remodeling of the interior in the Colonial Revival taste. In the late 1960s the western section of the property was lost to construction of the Capital Beltway and the cloverleaf serving Tyson's Corner. The Unfelder family, which owned Maplewood at the time, had the property rezoned and became instrumental in the development of the estate into an industrial park under the auspices of the Westgate Corporation. Fairfax County preservationists tried to convince Westgate to keep the house as a focal point of the development, but their concern was disregarded, and Maplewood was demolished in 1970. (Photograph: Historic American Buildings Survey, Library of Congress)

CAMERON LODGE, Gordonsville vicinity, Orange County
Built 1875–80; burned early 1920s

In the mid-1870s, Col. Alexander Cameron, son-in-law of Richmond mill owner Richard B. Haxall (see Haxall Mills, q.v.), who owned the adjoining Rocklands estate (q.v.), began to buy property on the top of the Southwest Mountains just north of Gordonsville. A native of Scotland and fiercely proud of his heritage, Colonel Cameron had first immigrated to Petersburg and then to Richmond. He married Mary Parke Haxall in 1868 and bought his first piece of Orange County land in 1875. Between then and his death in 1915, he accumulated 444 acres, spread over the crest of the Southwest Mountains above Gordonsville. Like his father-in-law and many other wealthy Victorians, Colonel Cameron maintained both an urban residence and a country estate. The centerpiece of his rural holdings was Cameron Lodge, a rambling, ornate country house with a multitude of porches, scrollwork brackets, a cupola, and a central, five-story tower, built by the colonel between 1875 and 1880. This was set in a model farm with pastoral landscaping, well-bred livestock, up-to-date agricultural buildings, and other support structures. (Regrettably, the designer of the house and other improvements is unknown.) Additional agricultural enterprises were carried out on a nearby secondary farm called simply Farm Number 2. Both Colonel Cameron and his wife died in 1915; their holdings were divided among their eight children. Eventually four of them built dwellings, all named after sites in Scotland, on or near the Cameron Lodge property. The original lodge burned in the early 1920s; however, several of its outbuildings and a gatehouse remain. (Photograph: Valentine Museum) ALM

HOUSE OFF GREEN SPRING (CENTERVILLE) ROAD, Toano vicinity, James City County
Built ca. 1880–90; lost ca. 1940

Harold Shurtleff established authoritatively in *The Log Cabin Myth* (1939) that the English settlers of eastern Virginia did not favor log buildings, which had virtually no known Albion origins. Property records show that in fact some log construction did take place in 17th-century Chesapeake, but archaeology has richly established that framed buildings with wooden supports dominated Virginia and Maryland farms into the 18th century. Many—probably most—of the houses had chimneys built of wood and clay, often at corners of the end walls.

By the early 19th century, modest houses across much of the South had a recognizable and common form: a single rectangular room served by

an exterior chimney centered on one end and opposing doors toward the far end of the long walls, balanced by one or two windows nearer the chimney. With varying degrees of quality, they housed many post-Revolutionary landowners as well as slaves. In the same era, even Tidewater Virginians increasingly used unhewn logs for the walls of relatively inexpensive structures, such as farm buildings and low-status houses. Building cost could also be saved by using wood and clay for chimneys instead of masonry.

As late as the 1930s, one or two such houses could still be found in most rural Virginia communities, with chimneys constructed of logs and/or posts and rails. They had already become common subjects for photographs and occasionally paintings that combined the popular taste for picturesque local color with romantic notions about blacks living in scenes thought still to resemble slavery. Boston designer Susan Higginson Nash took numerous photographs of this example near Toano between 1930 and 1934, while working on the Williamsburg restoration. The restoration's official photographer, Frank Nivison, was assigned to take large-format photos at the same time; one is reproduced here. Together, their images carefully detail the building's exterior, but neither photographer ventured into the then-occupied house.

It began, perhaps in the 1880s, as a rough but relatively sturdy house with a second room in the upper half-story (both sets of floor joists being visible between the logs). Its chimney, nearly twenty feet high, consisted of four hewn posts pierced by dowels giving support to the clay and straw walls. Such chimneys required annual maintenance as well as caution in use. While stories of push-away wooden chimneys are inflated, fire was a substantial danger, and the ladders on this house indicate conscious preparedness. An iron trammel set into the clay in the main room was used to suspend a pot for cooking, though it is possible that the detached smaller room served as a kitchen with a cookstove. (Photograph: Colonial Williamsburg Foundation)
EAC

HAWFIELD, Orange vicinity, Orange County
Built 1881 (incorporating an older house); burned 1937

Originally acquired by the Conway family in the 18th century, the Hawfield estate, then 770 acres, was purchased by Jonathan Graves in 1847 as a wedding present for his daughter and son-in-law, Fanny and William G. Crenshaw. Crenshaw, a partner in his family's Richmond-based milling and shipbuilding business, moved to New York and expanded his operations into fertilizer importation and manufacturing after the Civil War. He maintained Hawfield as a farming estate, buying additional acreage until his holdings exceeded three thousand acres, improving already fertile land through careful management and scientific farming methods, and acquiring purebred livestock. In the early 1880s, the Crenshaws returned to Orange County.

An earlier house on the property, built around 1790 by the Conway family, was enlarged in 1881 by an unknown designer into an expansive, fourteen-room frame structure, two stories high and with a four-story central tower. Front-gabled rooflines flanking the tower gave additional vertical emphasis to the principal façade, while the exterior as a whole was set off with a variety of drip moldings, cornices, brackets, and scrollwork. Large bay windows embellished the front and sides of the house. The interior, which boasted notably high ceilings even for its era, was fashionably furnished, with elaborate wallpapers and handsome mahogany furniture. On the first floor, a library and drawing room were placed on either side of a wide, parquet-floored center hallway; a focal point of the drawing room was its large, two-tiered, French blue porcelain chandelier, which once belonged to a nephew of Napoleon's. To the rear was a dining room with full-length windows looking out onto an enclosed garden. Eight bedchambers occupied the upper floor. Reportedly, minimal changes were made to the original portion of the house, which became a rear wing of the enlarged residence. Following the deaths of the senior Crenshaws in 1897, Hawfield was inherited by the three unmarried Crenshaw daughters, who continued to operate the farm according to the high standards set by their father. Still the home of the last Crenshaw daughter, the Hawfield residence burned in December 1937. Miss Fanny Crenshaw, a frail but determined woman of ninety, refused to leave Hawfield; she moved into a cabin on the property, where she lived out the remainder of her life. (Photograph: Valentine Museum)
ALM

WHITLOCK-GRAHAM HOUSE, 201

West Franklin Street, Richmond
Built 1883; demolished ca. 1970

The Whitlock-Graham house, built by Robert H. Whitlock, was one of dozens of grand, brick town houses erected along Richmond's fashionable West Franklin Street in the decades following the Civil War. The side-hall plan allowed a distinctive, pavilion-like bay to rise to a pediment that reflected French Renaissance influences. The cast-iron fence, which remains intact, exhibits the Eastlake influences popular in the late 19th century.

Although the Whitlock-Graham house was demolished, the remaining 19th-century houses in the 200 block of West Franklin were preserved through the efforts of the Historic Richmond Foundation. They remain an evocative architectural anchor amid the constantly changing face of downtown Richmond. Sadly, the former site of the Whitlock-Graham house remains an asphalt-paved parking lot, hardly appropriate between two Carrère and Hastings buildings, the Jefferson Hotel, and the Junior League Headquarters. The columned house next door had been demolished earlier. (Photograph: Valentine Museum)
EJS, Jr.

LABURNUM, Brook Road, Richmond

Built 1884–85; burned 1906

Polychromed in brick and stone, with mansard roofs, Stick Style dormers, ornamental ironwork, and an Italianate tower, Laburnum was a bold, elaborately detailed, and richly textured Victorian mansion. It was erected for Joseph Bryan, a Richmond attorney turned publisher and capitalist. The architect and builder was John Gibson. Gibson and three of his brothers, all from Scotland, were among the leading builders and contractors in 19th-century Richmond.

The New York design firm of D. S. Hess executed interiors for Laburnum that were as remarkable as its exterior. Hess provided designs for finishes, including woodwork, frescoes, inlaid flooring, stained glass, paint, and paper. The company also procured furniture, tapestries, and rugs. Several rooms were finished in ebony. Folding doors, with stained glass depicting a figure in 15th-century costume, separated the music room from the

dining room. Raised Japanese paper and a thistle-pattern fresco ceiling were used in the mahogany dining room. Correspondence between D. S. Hess and Joseph Bryan, detailing almost all aspects of construction and design, survive at the Virginia Historical Society.

Bryan replaced the house, which burned, with a huge Georgian Revival mansion that is now part of the Richmond Memorial Hospital complex. (Photograph: Valentine Museum)

SHELTON-BURTON HOUSE, 723
Main Street, Danville
Built 1884; demolished ca. 1961

In the early to mid-1880s, Danville's boom era produced at least half a dozen High Victorian Italianate mansions, each with polygonal bays; heavy, bracketed cornices; and cast-iron porches. These lavish brick dwellings, all attributed to the building skills of Thomas Benton Fitzgerald, were constructed for the contractor's business colleagues. Several, like himself, were pioneers in emerging local cotton mills, which soon added new wealth to pockets already overflowing with tobacco assets.

One such opulent dwelling was built for Mr. and Mrs. W. N. Shelton and their family. Just after the Civil War, Willoughby N. Shelton relocated from nearby Caswell County, North Carolina, to Danville, bringing with him knowledge of the lucrative tobacco trade. Like so many of their contemporaries, the Sheltons flourished in Danville. Retaining the Richmond architect Albert L. West, they removed an older dwelling in order to construct their mansion.

Completed in 1884 on one of the town's original, large antebellum-era lots, the new house stood in pleasing contrast to the crowded residential development on fifty-foot lots nearby. Residing with the Sheltons was their only daughter, Alice, and her husband, Mr. F. X. Burton, a leading tobacconist who also helped launch the city's textile fortunes, first in the Morotock Manufacturing Company and later as president of the Riverside Cotton Mills (q.v.). It was Mrs. Burton who over the decades gave this house its special presence, not only as a gracious hostess but also later as a philanthropist. After her death in 1929, Mrs. Burton's will established here a home for indigent ladies known as Sunnyside. Often called the Alice Burton Home, Sunnyside continued as a special project of Danville's First Presbyterian Church until 1955, when the Synod of Virginia relocated the institution to Massanetta Springs near Harrisonburg. The grand mansion stood vacant for several years thereafter, until it was sold to a local bank. Its site became the bank's parking lot in the early 1960s. (Photograph: *Art Work of Lynchburg and Danville, Virginia,* 1903)
GRG

ROSELAND MANOR,
Strawberry Banks, Hampton
Built 1886–87; burned 1985

Set amid landscaped grounds on the shore of Hampton Roads, Roseland Manor was a salient example of a Queen Anne mansion. The grandiose structure was built for Harrison Phoebus, owner of the Hygeia Hotel at nearby Old Point Comfort. Because of his many civic contributions, the adjacent community of Chesapeake City was renamed Phoebus in his honor. The mansion's architect was Arthur Crooks, a native of England who had worked as a draftsman for Richard Upjohn and established an independent practice in New York City by 1869, specializing in residential and ecclesiastical works. Taking advantage of its waterfront location and spectacular views of Hampton

Roads harbor, the house originally was outfitted with elaborate encircling verandas, all of which were later stripped off. Roseland Manor was an architectural rarity for Virginia; few houses of such scale and ostentation were built in the state in the aftermath of the Civil War. This vast edifice was long a landmark for thousands of motorists approaching the Hampton Roads tunnel. (Photograph: Virginia Department of Historic Resources)

MOUNT SHARON, Orange vicinity
Built 1888–90; demolished late 1930s

The land surrounding Mount Sharon traces back to patents granted to John and Francis Taliaferro in 1726 and 1727. It remained in the Taliaferro family for more than two centuries. In 1876, Charles Champe Taliaferro, then living in Georgia, inherited the property, which then comprised 711 acres; an earlier Mount Sharon residence, possibly of 18th-century vintage, had been destroyed a few years earlier. In the mid-1880s, C. C. Taliaferro returned to Virginia, and in 1888 he began to construct a new residence on the property. The result, completed in 1890, was the large and elaborate Second Empire–style country house pictured here. Standing three stories high over an English basement, this frame structure boasted elaborate decorative trim, including heavy cornices, and a slate roof. Although a designer has not been identified, the Baltimore firm of Frank D. Watkins & Co. has been documented as supplying the materials for the structure. The extensive grounds surrounding the house, framing views that extended to the Blue Ridge Mountains, were embellished with statuary.

Financial reversals and debts forced the sale of Mount Sharon in 1935. Unfashionable and deteriorating, C. C. Taliaferro's house there was demolished in the late 1930s to make way for the present residence, a finely proportioned Palladian Revival structure designed by New York architect Louis Bancel LaFarge. (Photograph: Valentine Museum)
ALM

NYDRIE, Keene vicinity, Albemarle County
Built 1889; demolished 1978

Grand Victorian mansions have proven to be among America's most vulnerable architectural types. Virginia's few examples of this domestic form have not been excepted. Among them was the fifty-room pile Nydrie on Green Mountain, perhaps the grandest Victorian house in Virginia's Piedmont. Begun in 1889, it was designed by architect D. Wiley Anderson for Harry Douglas Forsyth of New Orleans, who had made a fortune in sugar and banking. Inspired by Scottish baronial castles, the main dwelling was 68 by 175 feet, with brownstone trim and a slate roof. Its twenty-two-by-sixty-one-foot, two-story entrance hall served as a ballroom, above which was a musicians' gallery. Other features included a walnut library, drawing room, dining room, greenhouse with a swimming pool, quartered-oak staircase, and ash-paneled billiard room. Water tanks were enclosed in the castellated towers. In 1928 the house passed to the Van Clief family and was renovated by carpenter Ernest Hoover based on designs by Anderson, his father-in-law. Nydrie went unmaintained for many years and was finally razed in 1978. Its finely appointed stables were preserved and remain in regular use. (Photograph: Virginia Department of Historic Resources)
KEL

WESTBROOK, Westbrook Avenue, Richmond
Built 1888–92; demolished 1975

Westbrook was the country place of Lewis Ginter (1824–97), one of the great business leaders of post-Reconstruction Richmond. Ginter made his fortune in the tobacco industry and fostered several important ventures that contributed to the development of the city, including the Jefferson Hotel and Ginter Park, the city's first planned suburb. Around 1885, Ginter acquired Westbrook, a 125-acre farm in northern Henrico County, and transformed it into an impressive estate. His architect was Edgerton Rogers, son of sculptor Randolph Rogers, who opened a practice in Richmond in 1887 and also designed Maymont, the country house of James H. Dooley, and the Virginia Building for the World's Columbian Exposition, a model of Mount Vernon.

For Ginter, Rogers conceived a spacious Queen Anne dwelling of frame construction, which bore no resemblance to the simple farmhouse that had occupied the spot since 1815. Generous porches, the picturesque irregularities of dormers and balconies, a prominent tower, and the sweeping lines of the central gable together established an inviting, informal character befitting the typical American country house of the 1880s and early '90s. As recorded in photographs, newspaper articles, and documentation developed prior to its demolition, Westbrook's well-appointed, eclectic interiors combined Colonial Revival, Chateauesque, and Romanesque-style features carried out in overmantels and other detailing. Stained glass, fine woodwork, and parquet enriched the principal rooms. The elaborate complex of outbuildings included a carriage house, stable, conservatory, bowling alley, icehouse, and dairy. Neatly trimmed hedges, colorful bedding displays, and informal, naturalistically planted areas completed the landscape.

In 1911, Westbrook was converted for use as a psychiatric hospital. In 1975, following the sale of the original interior fittings and fixtures, the house was razed to make way for new hospital facilities. Thus Richmond lost one of its most exuberant expressions of Queen Anne style and an important example of the type of ornamental country place that flourished in the United States at the turn of the 20th century. (Photograph: Valentine Museum)
DCW

ROBERT WITHERS MASSIE
HOUSE, west corner of Federal and Tenth Streets, Lynchburg
Built 1899; demolished 1977

At the turn of the 20th century, Lynchburg's Massie Lumber Company was one of the largest operations of its kind in the Southeast. Robert Withers Massie, founder and president, showcased his product by erecting one of Virginia's largest frame houses. Its extensive façade incorporated weatherboards and shingles in a variety of patterns while elaborately turned posts supported the front porch and balcony. Judging from stylistic evidence, Massie likely employed Edward G. Frye as architect. The design encompassed all the requisite components of the Queen Anne style, but the abiding impression was one of magnitude, not finesse.

The well-established neighborhood where Massie built his house is characterized by antebellum brick dwellings. In 1977, the owner of one of the earlier houses, thinking the Victorian-era Massie house out of character and declaring it termite-ridden, acquired and demolished it. (Photograph: Jones Memorial Library, Lynchburg)
SAC, Jr.

MOUNT ATHOS, Somerset vicinity, Orange County
Built 1899–1900; burned 1903

Mount Athos, located near Somerset, was built as an elegantly appointed summer home for eccentric financier and bon vivant Walter George Newman. The house was a customization of a plan that appeared as Nos. 30 and 206 in various editions of George F. Barber's newly published *New Modern Dwellings* (after 1895). Mentioning the "slight changes" made to Newman's house from his stock plans, Barber noted that "the walls are of Tennessee brown stone, broken ashlar. The porch columns are of Tennessee marble, polished, with Ionic capitals carved from the same material. The roof is of red slate, and the finials on all towers are very elaborate, made of copper and gilded with pure gold leaf, and sparkle beautifully in the sunlight." The interior was decorated and furnished in florid Gilded Age taste, with expensive fixtures and furniture imported from New York. The first floor contained a reception area and large stair hall, parlor, library,

and dining room, with a kitchen and service areas to the rear. Four large chambers, two bathrooms, and servants' quarters were on the second floor. The attic held an additional chamber and servants' quarters, a children's playroom, and storage areas; the cellar contained a variety of service and storage rooms, a vault, and a wine cellar.

Landscape features included a lake, gazebos, a teahouse, extensive brick walkways and paving, and three thousand feet of decorative iron fence. There were several large and elaborate stone structures: a horse barn, observation tower (which also functioned as a water tower), gatehouse (pictured here), and icehouse. Additional structures included a boiler house, an overseer's house, a stock barn, and other agricultural buildings.

Mount Athos was the first house in Orange County equipped with electric power. Electric lights were installed in the residence, at the gazebos by the lake, along the driveway, and at the gatehouse; power was supplied by the estate's own electrical plant, which featured a fifty-horsepower generator. There was also a private telephone system; to be able to call his Wall Street contacts at will, Newman installed more than two miles' worth of telephone poles, extending from his house to the Somerset railroad station.

Harvey Abrames of Knoxville acted as general contractor for the project, and Woodruff Leeming of New York was employed as supervising architect for the construction of the house and outbuildings. Leeming apparently designed some of the outbuildings and some alterations to the house, and he may have been involved in the design of some of the landscape features as well. Prior to construction and at Newman's behest, an existing house on the property, a substantial structure built in 1893, was moved off the top of the hill and the hill raised five feet to make the building site the highest in the vicinity. Contemporary newspaper accounts claim that the house cost five hundred thousand dollars, although this appears to be a gross exaggeration; by George Barber's own statement the customized house cost forty thousand dollars (as opposed to ten to twelve thousand dollars for his stock design). However, the total cost of the land, site work, furnishings, support structures, and landscaping may have approached several hundred thousand dollars.

After the completion of the house, Newman and his wife divorced, and Leeming and Abrames, along with many other contractors and suppliers, went unpaid. In 1903, shortly after a court ordered that the property be sold and the proceeds divided between Newman and his former wife, and in the midst of lawsuits to recover the builders' fees, the Mount Athos residence mysteriously burned. Apparently Newman and Leeming had settled their differences by 1906, when Leeming designed a second Mount Athos dwelling, the construction cost of which was announced as several hundred thousand dollars. This structure, located near the site of the 1899 house, was later demolished; the present Mount Athos dwelling, built in the 1930s, is on the site of the 1899 structure. A few landscape features and stone gateposts remain from the 1899 construction. (Photographs: Orange County Historical Society)
ALM

LONGWOOD, East Main Street, Salem
Built 1904; burned 1968

Perched on a hill overlooking downtown Salem, Longwood was a grandiose Romanesque Revival country house built at a cost of one hundred thousand dollars for coal baron Thomas Henry Cooper. No architect has been linked to its design. The estate was typical of the period, boasting outbuildings and a landscaped park. Like many turn-of-the-century houses large and small, Longwood had irregular massing, a one-story wraparound porch, a porte-cochere, and a corner tower. The irregular roof was covered in orange Spanish tiles.

The city of Salem acquired the estate for $20,100 following Mrs. Cooper's death in 1942 and converted it into a municipal park. A fire of undetermined origin broke out in the residence's upper story on a snowy November afternoon in 1968. The wind was so strong that it prevented the streams of water from firemen's hoses from reaching the roof, and the house was gutted. Its walls were subsequently demolished. One of western Virginia's most ambitious Gilded Age monuments had been lost forever. (Photograph: Virginia Department of Historic Resources)

CEDAR HALL, Hampton
Built 1905–8; demolished 1976

Conspicuously sited on Hampton Creek, overlooking the venerable Hampton harbor, Cedar Hall was the architectural indulgence of "seafood king" Frank W. Darling. This opulent Colonial Revival house was constructed of Vermont granite and given handsome hand-carved interior trim. The large and complex structure took three years to build. Its exterior featured handsome and sophisticated stone cuttings, with quoins, jack arches, and a water table. Multiple porches were supported by columns with Scamozzi-style Ionic capitals. The interior was equally grand: a broad hall and impressive principal spaces on the first floor all featured a wealth of detailed carving, including pilasters, mantels, and built-in shelving.

Cedar Hall was eventually divided into apartments. Sentiment grew for its preservation, and some hope developed that the city of Hampton might acquire the landmark. Despite these efforts, however, the house was razed in 1976. (Photograph: Virginia Historical Society)
MRH

WHITMELL S. FORBES HOUSE, 3401 Monument Avenue (entire block), Richmond
Built 1914; demolished mid–20th century

The gigantic house built by Whitmell S. Forbes on Monument Avenue just west of Roseneath was one of Richmond's showpieces for several decades. Forbes was a prominent Richmond tycoon who owned a streetcar line, a wholesale grocery business, and interests in the Virginia Baking Company and the Richmond Guano Company. Ellen Glasgow, Richmond's great novelist of the early 20th century, caught some of the humor of Forbes's and other businessmen's conspicuous consumption in her 1916 novel *Life and Gabriella*. One of her characters exclaims, "'Look at that house now, that's one of the finest in the city. Rushington built it—he made his money in fertilizer, and the one next with the green tiles belongs to Hanly, the tobacco trust fellow you know, and this whopper on the next square is where Albertson lives. He made his pile out of railroad stocks . . .'"

Who designed the Forbes house remains unknown, but it probably was an out-of-town architecture firm that tried to capture the so-called Southern Colonial look, which featured conspicuous use of a giant portico. Constructed of yellow brick with large wings, a tile roof, outflung balustraded terraces, and elaborate details, the house's two-story, approximately forty-foot-tall entrance portico had four monumental Corinthian columns. Swags appeared in the entablature. The single-story porches on the side had row upon row of Ionic columns. This overdone quality set the teeth of many critics and architects grating. Joseph Everett Chandler, a proper Boston Colonial Revivalist, restorer, and scholar, pictured a house similar to the Forbes mansion in his book *The Colonial House* (1916), labeled it as "'Kickapoo' or 'Hoppigee'" or "'Virulent Colonial,'" and dismissed it as "an example of everything not to do." Forbes lost his money in the depression of the 1930s, and the house was demolished. A row of modest brick houses now occupies the site. (Photograph: Valentine Museum)
RGW

VIRGINIA STATE PENITENTIARY, Belvidere and Spring Streets, Richmond
Built 1797–1806, with later additions; last original portion demolished 1928, site cleared 1991–92

In 1796 Virginia revised its "sanguinary" penal code, restricting capital punishment to first-degree murder and providing for a place of humane confinement. In 1797 the commission for that place of confinement went to B. Henry Latrobe. He thereby received his first opportunity to build an American public building and the responsibility of working with one of the most important building types of the early modern period: a penitentiary.

In designing Virginia's penitentiary, Latrobe operated as a deliberate if inexperienced member of an international avant-garde, and his project must be assessed by international standards. He responded particularly to ideas from the British prison reformer John Howard and from Howard's orbit. Latrobe chose a semicircular, or peripheric, layout to permit surveillance of the main prison area. This kind of plan had been recently developed in Britain by William Blackburn, Howard's favorite architect, and Thomas Harrison. In accord with his own views on orientation, Latrobe made the main part of the prison face south, to take advantage of the sun's warmth in winter. Feeling confident of his measures for security, and perhaps responding to the ideas of Jeremy and Sir Samuel Bentham, he proposed remarkably low walls along the south edge of the penitentiary. He surely did so to promote the circulation of air as protection against typhus ("jail fever") and to admit the rays of the southern sun. Through his extensive use of vaulted masonry, Latrobe devised a landmark in American building technology. Erecting a novel kind of building, he wished to make the façade powerfully expressive, or "characteristic," of the nature of a penitentiary. Thus, in imitation of the threatening exterior of George Dance's Newgate Prison (1770–80 and later, London; since demolished), Latrobe's design for the lower story of the penitentiary featured rough stonework and garlands of chains.

Latrobe saw the commonwealth compromise his intentions repeatedly in 1797 and 1798, before he departed for the wider world of Philadelphia. Maj. John Clarke, a distinguished local architect, rethought the design extensively in finishing the building, and subsequently the original penitentiary became embedded in more and more additions. During the 19th century, such noteworthy Richmond architects as Albert L. West and Marion J. Dimmock contributed elements to the penitentiary complex.

Nationally and internationally, the future of penitentiary design lay not in Virginia but in New York and Pennsylvania. In Richmond, where the prison was the second grand public building (after the Capitol) to rise, the edifice wielded influence. The plan and detailing inspired Richmond's third monumental public building, the Virginia Manufactory of Arms (1798–1809; q.v.), by John Clarke. From the penitentiary and the manufactory came a repertory of motifs, including arcades, blind arches, and deep Tuscan cornices, that emanated from Latrobe but took on a highly Adamesque cast when they were applied to such buildings as Clifton (q.v.) and the Hancock-Wirt-Caskie house, both built in 1808 and 1809. Latrobe's double-bowed conception for the keeper's house may also have played a part in the contest of bow window types that took place in Richmond as the 19th century started. (Photograph: Valentine Museum)
CEB

CHAPTER II

Lost Civic Architecture

The lost civic buildings illustrated in the following pages served three primary functions. First, there were governmental structures that facilitated the administration of law and of general services and assured equitable commercial exchange. These municipal administrative buildings were of local, state, and federal origin; they include courthouses, post offices, customhouses, market houses, and armories. Second, there were civic buildings erected for social betterment and reform; these include prisons, hospitals, and homes for soldiers and orphans. Finally, there were civic buildings that served education, housing primary and secondary schools as well as colleges.

The most prominent of the lost administrative buildings were the county courthouses. The commonwealth produced an especially important collection of antebellum examples that stood as symbols of enlightened government and an ordered society. A significant number remain, but an ever-expanding need for additional court facilities has caused the loss of numerous structures that should not be forgotten. To cite an extreme statistic, five successive court structures had been built in Northampton County by 1795. The losses continued into the 20th century; three courthouses were built in Arlington County in the one hundred years between 1898 and 1997. Most of these losses inform about evolving needs in the commonwealth and about shifts in local status and self-perception. The history of courthouse demolition and reconstruction is often a record of local growth and prosperity that inspired change, as happened at Danville when its 1873 Renaissance Revival courthouse was built. Other lost courthouses suggest that architectural influences have been transmitted throughout the commonwealth with perhaps surprising frequency. To cite one example, the 1841 Roanoke County courthouse (demolished 1909) in Salem, which was a three-part structure with a porticoed center section and two-story wings, probably influenced the designs for the Botetourt (1848), Craig (1852), and Alleghany (1877) courthouses.

Federal civic buildings that are lost told different stories. The Alexandria Post Office and Customhouse (1856–58) was evidence of national progress at midcentury; the later post offices in Danville (1881–83) and Roanoke (1893) were products of Reconstruction. Market houses and armories, like Richmond's Seventeenth Street Market (1854) and Portsmouth's Romanesque Revival armory and market (1893), came to symbolize the shift from a rural to an urban landscape. The market house became the commercial, legal, and social center of the 19th-century Virginia town.

Lost civic buildings that served the social welfare of Virginians are remarkable for their ties to the peculiar social history of the region. For instance, B. Henry Latrobe's Virginia State Penitentiary (1797–1806) in Richmond was a monument to rationalized and humanitarian penology, yet Richmond's "Cage" (1814), a highly public lockup for the temporary restraint and shaming of miscreants, was not demolished until 1854. Libby Prison (ca. 1850), put into service in the same city during the Civil War, was a dirty and unhealthful environment. The Eastern Lunatic Asylum (1770 and later) in Williamsburg, the first public institution in America created solely for the care of the mentally ill, was a monument to the enlightened humanitarianism of Virginians who at the same time tolerated slavery.

Lost school buildings help to illustrate the progress of education in the commonwealth. The images and accounts gathered here resurrect histories of institutions that are now defunct, and they inform about the stylistic development of collegiate architecture in 19th-century Virginia, beginning with the Rotunda at the University of Virginia (1817 and later). By midcentury, when the picturesque was in vogue, a Gothic Revival Gatekeeper's Lodge (ca. 1856) had been added to that complex, despite the brilliance of Thomas Jefferson's Classical Revival buildings. The romantic styles of architecture found expression at a number of campuses. The Italianate came to be considered appropriate for institutions that housed women, as at the Richmond Female Institute (1853–54). Hayes Hall (1888) at Virginia College and Virginia Seminary in Lynchburg was Second Empire in style. The Gothic buildings at Virginia Military Institute influenced neighboring architecture, including the first Lynchburg College (1856–57) and Danville Military Institute (1890), a secondary school. The emergence and development of private secondary schools also can be traced in part through lost buildings. The progression begins with Liberty Hall (1793, Lexington). Margaret Academy (1806, Accomack County) took the form of a house. We find a noteworthy later example in Gordonsville Female Institute (1878, Orange County). In sharp contrast, as is evident from the example of the Fletcher School (late 19th century, Greene County), the architecture of rural, public secondary schools remained inadequate for many years. As the requirements for architectural facilities continue to increase, school buildings will always be prone to replacement. Fortunately, many historic schools are now acquiring new life through rehabilitation for alternative uses, but these represent only a fraction of those that have disappeared. Perhaps the greatest casualty of educational improvements are the one-room country schools, which, for better or worse, are practically extinct.

CHESTERFIELD COUNTY COURTHOUSE, Route 10, Chesterfield
Built 1749; demolished 1917

When John Booker was hired to build a courthouse, jail, and pillory for Chesterfield County in 1749, he was instructed that the courthouse was "to be the same dimensions and like materials as the present courthouse of Henrico County [at Varina] except the floors to be of plank." The building that he constructed had five bays and a hipped roof; as with other colonial courthouses, the brick was laid up in Flemish bond with glazed headers. Initially, it probably had no porch. The roof was altered after it burned during the Revolutionary War. In 1804 a wing was added to the back of the building, converting the courtroom to a T-shaped plan. Except for the period from 1871 to 1876, when Chesterfield County moved its seat to the town of Manchester, the colonial courthouse served the county until 1917, when it was demolished despite pleas that it be preserved. In 1976 and 1977, as a bicentennial project, a facsimile of the building was erected twenty yards north of the original site; it houses the Chesterfield County Historical Society. (Photograph: Virginia Historical Society)
JOP, MTP

ACCOMACK COUNTY COURTHOUSE, Accomac
Built 1758; demolished 1899

Completed in 1758, this courthouse replaced a two-story frame structure built circa 1710 in the Accomack County seat originally known as Matomkin. The community's name was changed to Drummondtown in 1786 and subsequently, in 1893, to Accomac. The builder of the courthouse was Severn Guthrey (possibly Guttridge). His use of Flemish bond brickwork with glazed headers, a prominent modillion cornice, and chimneys placed within the walls was typical of courthouse design throughout the colony. Exceptional features included the swallow-tailed roof and three dormers, which suggest that this building had a usable upper level, quite unlike most colonial courthouses. There appear to have been significant modifications to the brickwork over both the entrance and windows, which originally may have been arched openings. After long debate, the courthouse was altered in 1885, when its gable roof was converted to a mansard roof topped by a Victorian belfry. The structure was taken down when a new courthouse was built in 1899. (Photograph: Library of Virginia)
JOP, MTP

BEDFORD COUNTY COURTHOUSE, New London
Built 1766; demolished late 19th century

When this frame courthouse was constructed in 1766 at New London, then the seat of Bedford County, it replaced a crude structure of frame or logs known as a "rough house." New London, on the main road through the county (and no longer extant), was situated in what is now Campbell County. This courthouse sat on a brick foundation and measured twenty-four by thirty-six feet. It contained two jury rooms, each twelve feet square and with its own fireplace. The interior walls were "wainscoted four feet high and plastered above." The floor of the bench was elevated and "laid with plank," while the rest of the floor was "laid with brick or tile." It served as the county courthouse until 1782, when Bedford was divided to create Campbell County. (Image: Henry Howe, *Historical Collections of Virginia*, 1847)
JOP, MTP

EASTERN LUNATIC ASYLUM, bounded by Francis, Nassau, Henry, and Court Streets, Williamsburg
Built beginning 1770; burned 1876, 1885, 1902

With compassion sparked by the ideals of the Enlightenment, Lt. Gov. Francis Fauquier in 1766 alerted the burgesses to a "poor unhappy set of People who are deprived of their Senses and wander about the Country, terrifying the Rest of their Fellow Creatures." Pointing out that "every civilized Country has an Hospital for these People," Fauquier called for one in Virginia. It opened in 1773 as the first public institution in America created solely for care of the mentally ill. Robert Smith, an experienced Philadelphia master builder, was the architect. Thomas Jefferson judged this building (and the College of William and Mary) to be "rude, mis-shapen piles" that without their roofs would be mistaken for "brick-kilns," but most observers today would disagree. In 1985 the building was reconstructed by the Colonial Williamsburg Foundation.

In the middle decades of the 19th century several buildings were appended to Smith's Georgian hospital, forming a sizable forecourt on the principal façade (facing Francis Street to the north); two medieval structures were placed to the rear. According to Joseph Martin's *Gazetteer* of 1835, an increase in patient population during that decade brought about the first "addition . . . to enlarge the building"; by circa 1840 Smith's two-story hospital had risen to three stories, with a cupola and Greek Revival portico, and was flanked by and connected to two structures of virtually the same classical design. From 1841 to 1862, during the tenure of John Minson Galt as superintendent, Eastern Lunatic Asylum grew to the nine-building hospital pictured here. In 1859 alone, the patient population more than doubled, from 125 to 299.

Galt was an advocate of "moral management," a philosophy newly initiated in England whereby mental patients were not subjected to "confinement and restraint" but instead were shown "kindness" and reintroduced to the lifestyle of the sane. In his 1857 report to the legislature, Galt endorsed British "objections to the erection of isolated, single, symmetrical masses of buildings studded over the grounds"; preferable were "detached buildings . . . of the character of cottages." This would account for his pride in the asylum's midcentury medieval buildings, a Jacobean hall that more resembled a house and a Gothic Revival building that housed African-American patients; Galt chose to illustrate these as the frontispiece to his 1857 report in lieu of a view of the symmetrical and massive north courtyard. The architects of these additions to the asylum are not known; the work may have been done by builders who simply took cues from Smith's design and from nearby structures, like the Jacobean Custis house in Williamsburg and the Gothic Revival Cabin Point Episcopal Church in Surry County (both now lost). Albert L. West of Richmond was architect of a later addition to the asylum; that building has yet to be identified.

By 1857 gas lighting was in place; it may or may not have caused the fires that a few decades later destroyed most of the complex. The Gothic Revival building burned in 1902. (Images: unidentified lithograph of north courtyard, Lyon G. Tyler, *Williamsburg: The Old Colonial Capital*, 1907; *Report of the Eastern Lunatic Asylum*, 1857)

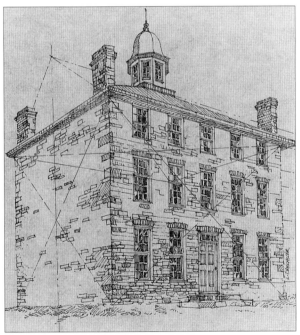

LIBERTY HALL, WASHINGTON AND LEE UNIVERSITY,
Lexington
Built 1793; burned 1803

Liberty Hall was the first substantial structure of the fledgling classical academy that eventually became Washington and Lee University. Although the university traces its origins to 1749, it was housed in various wood and log buildings in several locations before it settled on a 120-acre site just west of Lexington in 1782. In 1793, the board of trustees contracted with William Cravens, a stonemason from Rockingham County, to build a main building and a steward's house. The detailed specifications that survive describe a building thirty by thirty-eight feet and three stories high, with a square roof, belfry, and corner chimneys.

The four corner chimneys were an unusual feature. Several other buildings in the Lexington area had a similar arrangement, most notably the Alexander-Withrow house (1786); it may have been a regional variation. An 1890 Michael Miley photograph shows not only the chimneys but also the remains of plaster and chair rails. The stone building served as both classroom and dormitory, housing some forty to fifty students in the upper two floors and classes, scientific apparatus, and the library on the first floor.

Extensive archaeological work in the mid-1970s unearthed evidence of a sophisticated lifestyle for the school's occupants. Rather than the rifles and wild game that might have been expected on the 18th-century frontier, researchers found instead Chinese and English export porcelain, bones from domesticated animals, and many clay pipes, as well as slate boards and marbles.

In November 1802, the trustees insured the building for $3,333.34. It was a timely move, for in January 1803, the roof caught fire. As the *Richmond Recorder* of 18 January 1803 reported, "the flames had got to such an extent that all exertions to extinguish them proved fruitless. The library and college apparatus and students' property were generally saved. It is believed the building . . . was injured." In fact, the building was gutted, and workmen reported that the walls could not "be repaired without more expense than profit."

In the aftermath of the fire, the trustees decided to move the school closer to town, but the substantial stone walls of William Cravens's building survived as a picturesque ruin. In the 1940s the university reinforced them with concrete abutments and iron crossties to ensure their preservation. Today the ruins are a registered historic landmark and much prized as the last physical remnant of the 18th-century origins of Washington and Lee University. (Photograph: Virginia Historical Society; Image: drawing by Larry Dreschler in *The Architecture of Historic Lexington*, by Royster Lyle, Jr., and Pamela Hemenway Simpson, 1977, courtesy of Historic Lexington Foundation)
PHS

NORTHAMPTON COUNTY COURTHOUSE, Eastville
Built 1795; demolished 1899

One of the oldest counties in Virginia, Northampton had four courthouses before this brick building was erected in 1795 at a cost of four hundred pounds. It was a traditional five-bay, one-story brick structure, laid up in Flemish bond, with a simple gable roof and a water table with English bond below. It is speculated that the hexagonal belfry, a feature found on many Virginia court buildings, was added at a later date; its placement at the far right-hand roof ridge, rather than centered over the entryway, was unusual. The window shutters served the practical purpose: keeping the courthouse cooler in the summer and helping retain the limited heat produced by a single fireplace or stove in the cooler months. The prosaic building served the Eastern Shore county until 1899, when it was replaced by a larger brick structure. (Photograph: Virginia Historical Society)
JOP, MTP

VIRGINIA MANUFACTORY OF ARMS/RICHMOND ARMORY, southern terminus of Seventh Street at the James River, Richmond
Built 1798–1809; burned 1865, demolished ca. 1900

The Virginia Manufactory of Arms was established to produce armaments for the Virginia militia and to function as a depository for them. Maj. John Clarke served as the first superintendent of the manufactory and oversaw its construction.

Integral to the siting and design of the manufactory was its position on the James River and Kanawha Canal, the swift water of which was harnessed to power the machinery used for production. The complex faced north and extended 310 feet along the canal. A large arched tower marked the center of the stucco-clad brick buildings and provided entrance. Above it was perched one of the earliest large domes built in Virginia (twelve feet tall and sixty-one feet in circumference). Atop the dome stood a small cupola with a bell. The long wings that provided space for offices, storage, and a kitchen were handsomely articulated by the pattern of their windows, which were set in arched recesses and flanked by pilasters. Rear wings housed the shops of the manufactory and extended around a parade area. Nearby were a foundry and a boring mill.

In 1822 the manufactory ceased production and functioned simply as a warehouse for the storage of arms. In 1861, however, the Confederate government reactivated the facility by installing equipment salvaged from the United States Armory at Harpers Ferry. Renamed the Richmond Armory, the building produced munitions until 3 April 1865, when it was largely destroyed by the Richmond evacuation fire. A portion of the refurbished ruins served briefly as a militia barracks after the war. The site served as a local tourist attraction until the ruins were leveled around 1900.

The building's elongated form inspired the design of the east building of the Ethyl Company's headquarters, which now sits on the hill above the site. (Photograph: Valentine Museum)
TTP, Jr.

MARGARET ACADEMY, Cheriton vicinity, Accomack County
Built 1806; destroyed late 19th century

Prior to Thomas Jefferson's development of the University of Virginia in the early 1800s, and despite the presence throughout the 18th century of the Wren building at the College of William and Mary, few Americans sought to conceive a distinct genre of academic architecture; educational buildings simply resembled domestic ones, the type universally known then to owners and craftsmen. Margaret Academy, at least on the exterior, was a Georgian mansion; it was a symmetrical brick building with features familiar to the type, including a hipped roof and windows graduated in height and capped by flat stone arches with keystones. A side door visible in the photograph is little reason to believe that the floor plan differed significantly from the usual domestic type of center passage and four corner rooms; nothing is known about the building itself beyond this image.

Margaret Academy was one of the earlier schools established in the commonwealth. In 1786 the Virginia General Assembly granted a charter to seven trustees, residents of the Eastern Shore, for "establishing a School of learning either in the county of Accomack or North Hampton" to be known as Margaret Academy. The name reportedly honored Margaret Pettit, a resident of the Eastern Shore. She apparently was not a benefactress; a lack of money delayed construction for two decades, and the academy did not open until 1807. Among the graduates were many of the 19th-century civic leaders of the Eastern Shore, including Henry Wise, the Virginia governor and Confederate general. In 1893 the academy trustees, after struggling with finances and enrollment in the aftermath of the Civil War, voted to move the institution to a more central location, Onancock, much farther north. The circumstances surrounding the disappearance of the original school building are unknown. (Photograph: Robert Lancaster, *Virginia Homes and Churches*, 1915)

CULPEPER COUNTY COURTHOUSE, Davis Street, Culpeper
Built 1809; demolished 1870

The seat of Culpeper County was originally, if confusingly, named Fairfax. It was there in 1809 that the building shown here was erected to replace a frame colonial courthouse. The new building was two stories and rectangular, with a gable front, modillion cornice, and four interior chimneys. Not long thereafter, a somewhat peculiar structure was added to the front. Although the addition incorporated the traditional courthouse motif of a brick arcade, it also included an elaborate, two-tiered belfry and a balcony, which was rare, if not unique, among Virginia courthouses at the time. In the photograph, Confederate prisoners can been seen hanging their laundry on the balcony's railing. In 1870 county supervisors decided to build a new courthouse on a different site; materials from the 1809 building were sold. The local paper lamented that the "spot which has resounded with the eloquence of a Wirt, a Barbour, a Pendleton, a Scott . . . is now desecrated by the daily sale of wet groceries and tobacco." (Photograph: Library of Congress)
JOP, MTP

THE WASHINGTON LANCASTERIAN (FREE) SCHOOL, Washington Street, Alexandria
Built ca. 1812; demolished before 1903

Ever conscious that his own schooling had been defective, George Washington developed a passion for education. He gave serious thought to the subject during the Revolutionary War, when his troops continually impressed upon him their ignorance and provincialism. Before the war was over, and then throughout his later years, Washington took an enlightened stance that linked the education of America's citizens to the fulfillment of the nation's destiny.

Immediately after the Revolution, Washington began to look for ways to better the new nation's educational opportunities. Because the general knew what it meant to be fatherless and had seen the abject poverty of many of his soldiers, he took a particular interest in schools for children whose parents were deceased or indigent. In 1785 he made a donation, which was amplified in his will by a bequest of four thousand dollars, to the nearby Alexandria Academy "for the purpose of educating such Orphan children, or the children of such other poor and indigent persons." The funds were used to establish the Free School, which was originally housed on the third floor of the Alexandria Academy, visible in the left background of this photograph (and still standing). In the foreground is the Washington Lancasterian School, given an elegant accent by its lunette of intersecting tracery. Apparently, the Free School moved into this building, entered through a pair of doors (one for boys, the other for girls), at a later date.

Washington's commitment to education is best known through his gift to the fledgling Liberty Hall Academy in Rockbridge County (q.v.), a gift that enabled the academy to become Washington College (now Washington and Lee University). This building is evidence of his even earlier commitment to the cause of education in Virginia. (Photograph: Virginia Historical Society)

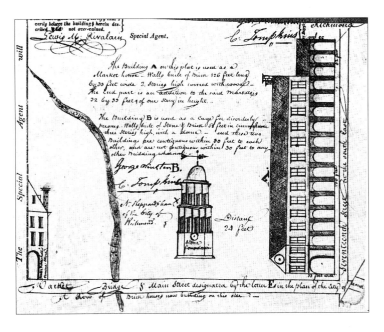

THE CAGE, Seventeenth Street Market, Seventeenth and Main Streets, Richmond
Built by 1814; demolished 1854

Among the diverse civic and commercial activities undertaken at Virginia's market houses was the punishment of criminals. Punishment was generally meted out swiftly and always in public. The idea that people should be incarcerated and thus do penance for their crimes (e.g., be placed in a penitentiary) was still an emerging notion in this period (see the Virginia State Penitentiary, q.v.). Those guilty of capital crimes were hanged by the neck. Noncapital criminals frequently were whipped or locked into stocks or cages. Market houses frequently had what was called a lockup, or cage, a public cell for the temporary restraint of miscreants. Whipping posts and stocks commonly surrounded the lockup.

A traveler in 1814 defined one Virginia cage as "a small room on the ground floor of jails for the confinement of unruly persons. It is generally in a public part of town, and the gate being formed of iron bars, the culprit is of course exposed to the view of the passengers [passersby]." Much more elaborate than most was the lockup constructed by 1814 at the Seventeenth Street Market in Richmond, a three-story, circular building fifty-eight feet in circumference and surmounted by a dome. In his memoirs, a Richmond resident recalled that "This cage, of octagonal form, had open iron gratings on three sides, about ten feet above the street, and the floor of this prison was arranged ampitheatrically [sic] so that each occupant could see, and what was worse, be seen from the street."

These two passages make clear the essential fact that the punishment meted out for violation of corporation law was a public act; both accounts emphasize that the offenders could be seen in the cage and that this public shaming was an essential part of the punishment. It is also important that this punishment took place in what was the busiest public place in town: the market. (Photograph: Mutual Assurance Society policy, Library of Virginia)

LYNCHBURG MARKET, Ninth Street, between Church and Main Streets, Lynchburg
Built 1814; demolished after 1873

In Virginia the market house precinct consisted of two basic components: the market house itself and the yard or enclosure surrounding it. The market house generally was given an open, arcaded lower story for the display and sale of foodstuffs and sometimes an enclosed upper story or stories, used as meeting rooms for such civic organizations as the town council or the corporation (city) court. The scale of market buildings varied greatly with the wealth and needs of the local government, ranging from the Seventeenth Street Market in Richmond (q.v.) to this single-story example at Lynchburg.

In 1814, Lynchburg replaced its 1805 market house with a newer though still modest structure. A committee assembled by the town council to finish the market specified "that the space between each Pillar be enclosed with Locust posts, Rails and Substantial Bench, that a Suitable Gate be put at each end of the House, that eight Stalls be erected, that the floor be paved with Brick, and that the Roof and Cornice be painted, the probable expense of which will be about $200." The market house was soon completed and quickly became a bustling place. However, with only twenty-two feet on either side of Ninth Street left to accommodate the ever-increasing traffic at Lynchburg's busiest intersection, the market house was doomed to demolition.

Toward the end of its life, the Lynchburg Market became the object of considerable local attention. While Edward King thought the "open air market [as] picturesque as any in Italy or Spain" and illustrated it in his book *The Great South* (1875) and Flavius Fisher, one of Lynchburg's foremost 19th-century artists, painted it, others were not so generously inclined. George W. Bagby, in his article "An Intoxicated View of Lynchburg," wrote, "I observed in my rambles . . . some admirable diluvian remains, the principle of which is a market house, found [sic] here by the first settlers a few centuries ago, the timbers in this edifice, its elevation above tidewater, and the incrustations on the butchers' blocks, attest its hoary antiquity. The best students are agreed that it is a distinct and lineal relic of Noah's Ark." The market house was sold at auction in 1873 for $112. It was subsequently demolished. (Photograph: Virginia Historical Society)

(FIRST) VIRGINIA MUSEUM, Twelfth Street between Bank and
G (now Grace) Streets, Richmond
Built ca. 1816; demolished after 1836

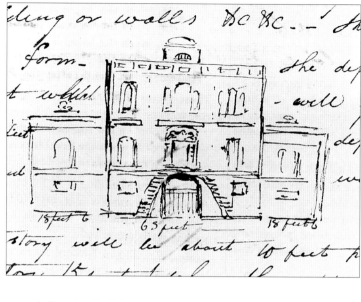

Many today know the Virginia Museum of Fine Arts (founded in 1936),
but few have heard of the first Virginia Museum, which opened in 1817; it ex-
hibited rare and unique objects and offered special events to the public.
Founded by James Warrell, an English painter, with the help of such prominent
Richmonders as Thomas Ritchie (editor of the Richmond Enquirer), Chief Justice John Marshall, and Governor Wilson Cary Nicholas, the museum was
granted by the General Assembly a small parcel of land on Capitol Square;
the plot was described at the time as "an unsightly ravine." The building was
to be constructed using private funds. Initial community support was so great
that forty out of fifty available shares sold almost at once.

The only known image of the museum is the sketch pictured here, which
appeared in a letter written by Warrell to the artist Charles Bird King in July
1816. It shows a neoclassical building with an English basement and a two-
story central block with wings on either side. The center section was to have
had a cupola to light a Hall of Paintings below. Warrell mentioned plans to "have an arch through the building. To pass into the Capitol Square" and gas-
lights for illumination. Warrell's goals were ambitious, however; it is likely that they were scaled down. According to one account, the façade was "entirely
devoid of ornament." A Mutual Assurance Society policy of 1818 describes a brick building with a stucco finish, two stories high, ninety-one by fifty feet.

Although the Virginia Museum was an initial success, it had begun to fail by the mid-1820s. Warrell departed Richmond to travel and paint, leaving the
museum in the hands of managers. By 1836 visitation and revenue were virtually nonexistent. The building and grounds reverted to the state, and the collection was dispersed. (Image: Virginia Historical Society)
LC

RICHMOND CITY HALL,
facing Broad, Capitol, and Eleventh Streets,
Richmond
Built 1816–18; demolished 1874

"The City Hall is at last ordered to execution. The testimony is all against it, and
is damning. No man . . . dares to say a word
in its defense, and down the old building
must come." In 1874, these words in the *Richmond Dispatch* signaled the demise of one
of two major Robert Mills commissions in
Richmond that were within sight of each
other: the surviving 1814 Monumental
Church and the first city hall.

Situated between Richmond's grand
boulevard, Broad Street, to the north and
Thomas Jefferson's Capitol to the south,
City Hall had a stately presence at the center of the city. Its north and south façades
were identical and imposing, with monumental porticoes in the Doric order. A third
entrance, to the east on Eleventh Street, provided access to a pair of curving stairs that
served the second floor. The principal feature of the interior was a large circular
courtroom with a low dais for city officials and judges. Offices for the mayor, jury rooms for trials, and rooms for other city functions were grouped
around its perimeter, except at the east entrance hall, where openings in the drum of the central rotunda were paired with exterior windows to brighten the
interior. The principal light source for the rotunda was a lantern in its dome.

In 1865, City Hall was the site of the formal surrender of Richmond at the end of the Civil War. It continued to serve as the center of municipal affairs
until the 1870s. Modifications in 1850 to the drum of the rotunda had structurally weakened the building, impairing its use. This, combined with mounting
hysteria about the condition of Richmond's public buildings that had been generated by the catastrophic collapse of a courtroom in the Capitol in 1870,
caused the outcry in 1874 for the demolition of City Hall. The site remained vacant until 1887, when work was begun on the Victorian Gothic city hall that
replaced its predecessor. (Photograph: Library of Virginia)
SR

THE LEXINGTON ARSENAL, Valley Road, Lexington (now Virginia Military Institute campus)
Built 1816; demolition begun 1851

In 1816, the Virginia legislature established three arsenals, including this one in Lexington. For this arsenal, a four-and-a-half-acre tract on a high bluff above the North River, located between Woods Creek and Valley Road (later US Highway 11), was selected; soon an adjacent three acres were added to the site. Maj. John Staples, superintendent of the Virginia Manufactory of Arms in Richmond (q.v.), developed plans for the new arsenal. The brickwork was executed by Lexington brick mason John Jordan, who later erected the principal buildings of Washington and Lee University.

During the mid-1830s, the idea was conceived to allow the young men who were guarding the arsenal to continue their training in a strict military setting while pursuing a course of scientific studies at nearby Washington College. From this idea, and in the Lexington Arsenal building, grew the Virginia Military Institute, which would first be housed in the Lexington Arsenal some twenty-three years later.

While the exact steps that led to the establishment of VMI are unclear, it is generally accepted that Col. John T. L. Preston, a Lexington lawyer and graduate of Washington College, originated and formulated the concept, actively promoting the idea in the mid-1830s. The educational program for VMI was modeled on that of the United States Military Academy and L'Ecole Polytechnique in Paris. In 1839, Francis H. Smith, a young West Point graduate then teaching mathematics at Hampden-Sydney College, was selected as VMI's first superintendent. Col. Claudius Crozet, a graduate of L'Ecole Polytechnique, was named the first president of the board of visitors, the school's governing body. Smith described the arsenal on his arrival in Lexington in 1839 as "a large and substantial brick building, in the center of a small courtyard. In front were the soldiers' barracks, embracing a small two-story brick building in the center, with five rooms; and two wings of one story each having two rooms. The sally-port was closed by a large iron-bound gate, and the court was enclosed by a brick wall fourteen feet high. The windows of the first story of the barracks were guarded by substantial iron bars; the whole establishment presenting the appearance of a prison, and such it was to the old soldiers."

The Lexington Arsenal, a building with "the appearance of a prison," housed VMI's first matriculating class in 1840. Under Smith's guidance, VMI quickly expanded and soon "exceeded the accommodations of the old Arsenal buildings." Through the influence of Philip St. George Cocke, A. J. Davis, perhaps the most prominent American architect of the day, was hired in 1848 to design an expanded VMI. To make room for Davis's new buildings (including the Williamson House, q.v.), the Lexington Arsenal was demolished over the course of a few years beginning in 1851, while Davis's Barracks was under construction. (Image: Virginia Military Institute)

THE ALAMO, HAMPDEN-SYDNEY COLLEGE, Prince Edward County
Built 1817 and 1822; burned and demolished 1994

Until it was finally lost in 1994, the Alamo was the oldest building on Hampden-Sydney's venerable campus. The earliest portion of the structure, the rear wing, was erected in 1817 to serve as the residence of the college's vice president. However, the intended resident died before its completion, and the house thus became the home of the professor of chemistry. This straightforward, Federal-style country dwelling had only two principal rooms: a parlor/dining room on the first floor and a bedroom above. It was in this section that President Woodrow Wilson's parents lived when the senior Wilson was a professor at the college. The larger and more formal front section was added, at an oblique angle, in 1822. The building acquired its distinctive name following a remodeling in the 1870s, because it was thought that the changed façade resembled the building famous in Texas history.

The Alamo served the college until 1990, when the administration determined that it was in deteriorated condition and would be too costly to repair. Its demolition was thus decreed and formally approved by the board of trustees. This decision attracted preservation sentiment not only among the college community and alumni but also among the preservation community statewide. In addition to being the college's most senior building, the Alamo had been designated a contributing historic resource when Hampden-Sydney was listed on the Virginia Landmarks Register in 1969 and, in 1970, the National Register of Historic Places. Various architectural experts from the Virginia Department of Historic Resources and the Colonial Williamsburg Foundation eventually prevailed upon the college to stabilize the building rather than demolish it. This holding action removed the building from harm's way until it mysteriously caught fire in 1994. Though not destroyed, the Alamo was badly damaged, and it was formally condemned as too unsafe to repair and was subsequently demolished. A new college housing complex occupies its site. (Photograph: Virginia Department of Historic Resources)

ROTUNDA, UNIVERSITY OF VIRGINIA, Charlottesville
Built 1817–26; burned 1895

Today, the Rotunda at the University of Virginia is routinely described as having been designed by Thomas Jefferson. Then it is added, yes, Stanford White, the famous New York architect, rebuilt it after the great fire of 1895, but it has been restored to Jefferson's original conception. This is only partially true, for while the interior approximates Jefferson's original, the dome room of which is shown here, the exterior retains many elements of Stanford White's design.

Jefferson's Rotunda and Robert Mills's Annex to it (q.v.) were gutted by fire on 27 October 1895. Constructed of brick, some stone, and wood—especially the interior floors and roofs, including the dome—the entire core of the building and much of its contents went up in flames; all that remained were brick walls. After some initial floundering with another architectural firm, the university's board of visitors hired McKim, Mead & White of New York, quite easily the leading and most prestigious architects in the country, to rebuild the Rotunda and add to the grounds Cabell, Cocke, and Rouse Halls. Stanford White took charge of the project. White claimed that his design of the Rotunda's interior was what "Jefferson himself would have adopted had the Rotunda been intended solely for use as a Library." Instead of Jefferson's three levels, with the library only on the third floor under the dome, White created a tall, soaring space with a

circle of Corinthian columns carrying the book stacks. On the exterior, White maintained Jefferson's elevation on the Lawn side but added terraces or esplanades to the north elevation matching those on the south and connected to them by colonnades. In the most dramatic change, White added a new north portico and steps that paid homage to Jefferson's south portico, though it is not as deep. White claimed that this was "evidently Jefferson's intention." Finally, to make it fireproof, Guastavino tile vaulting was used for the dome and interior floors. The result was a different building: one entered up the north flight of steps into the great Pantheon-like space and then exited on the south side, with the magnificent vista of the Lawn stretching away (though terminated by White's new Cabell Hall in the distance).

A monumental conception, White's library proved to be no more efficient than Jefferson's; how could it be expanded? By the 1930s the Rotunda had become outmoded, and the new—and rectangular—Alderman Library was built. The Rotunda fell into disuse except for official functions. Between 1973 and 1976 White's interior was removed and an approximation of Jefferson's interior inserted by Ballou and Justice, Richmond architects, with Frederick Doveton Nichols, professor of architectural history at the university, as adviser. The exterior, however, retains White's terraces, north portico, and steps. As such, the Rotunda is unique not simply for the conjunction of two great architects in a single work, but because a genuine original space (White's) was removed for an approximation of another space (the lost Jefferson interior). (Photograph: Valentine Museum)

RGW

LOUISA COUNTY COURTHOUSE,
Louisa
Built 1818; demolished 1905

Louisa County's third courthouse, completed in 1818, was built by Samuel Ragland during a transition period in Virginia court-house design, when Georgian, Federal, and Classical Revival ideas and motifs all found expression. While many designers abandoned the small, one-story colonial type for buildings with giant porticoes, Ragland adhered more to the former. In his design, one-story wings for offices and jury rooms flanked a taller central block measuring forty by twenty-five feet. The building was essentially Georgian not only

in its proportioning but also in the detail of its window lintels, which held keystones. The semicircular fanlight over the doorway, however, was a Federal motif. This courthouse was replaced on the same site in 1905 by the county's fourth courthouse, a monumental domed and porticoed work, which is still in use. (Photograph: Louisa County Historical Society)
JOP, MTP

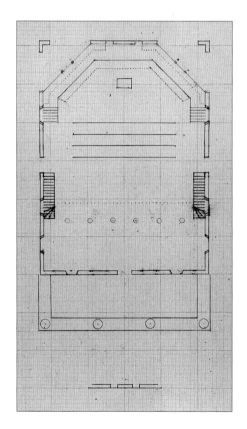

BUCKINGHAM COUNTY COURTHOUSE, Buckingham Court House
Built 1822; burned 1869

On 12 July 1821, on behalf of the Buckingham County commissioners, Charles Yancey wrote to Thomas Jefferson, "I have taken liberty to trespass upon your time and talents (a common stock) which we all have the right to draw upon . . . to draft for us a plan of our Court house." Jefferson responded two weeks later with a plan, specifications, and a letter of explanation: "Everything proposed in them is in the plainest style, and will be cheap, altho' requiring skill in the workmanship . . . I cannot but therefore recommend to you to get the work undertaken by some of the workmen of our University." Buckingham courthouse was built the next year by former University of Virginia workman and Staunton brickmason Dabney Cosby.

Yancey asked Jefferson for a brick building "48 to 52 feet square," fronted by a two-story portico that would extend the plan an additional "10 or 12 feet." There were to be three jury rooms on a partial second floor, with galleries extending along the side walls. The galleries would have to be moved to the center to make room for stairs, but otherwise Yancey's detailed request was answered. What Jefferson added were aesthetic and practical elements that turned the specifications of the commissioners into architecture. He carefully defined the dimensions of "the Order Tuscan," providing diameters and heights of columns and entablatures both on the exterior and within. He was particularly careful "to give light and air" to the interior. Deviating from ancient examples, Jefferson opened each back corner of the building with a pair of arches. In this way he maintained the integrity of the temple form while allowing light to reach the diagonally set justices' benches.

Buckingham is one of two courthouses designed by Jefferson for which documentary evidence survives. The other is the Botetourt County courthouse (1818), also destroyed by fire, in 1847. No doubt the Charlotte County courthouse, 1823, is by his hand also, because it was described in 1835 as "built on a plan furnished by Mr. Jefferson." These three buildings, which adapted the Classical Revival style of Jefferson's Richmond Capitol to a different civic role, were enormously important because of their influence on the rural landscape of central Virginia. Some fifteen other county courthouses repeat the type. A number of those buildings are by workmen formerly in Jefferson's employ. For instance, Dabney Cosby also built the courthouses in Goochland and Sussex Counties, simply by reapplying what he had learned at Buckingham. The present Buckingham County courthouse, erected in 1873, was designed to resemble Jefferson's building. (Image: drawing by Thomas Jefferson, Massachusetts Historical Society)

HENRICO COUNTY COURTHOUSE,
Twenty-second and Main Streets, Richmond
Built 1825; demolished 1896

In 1752 the county seat of Henrico was moved from Varina to the new town of Richmond, where a courthouse was built on land donated by the Cocke family. The second courthouse to stand on that site was the building pictured here, erected in 1825 by Samuel Sublett. It was described in a contemporary insurance policy as having "walls of brick" and a roof "covered in slate"; it was sketched in elevation to show its Doric portico. This courthouse was large by early-19th-century courthouse standards and featured a clerk's office attached to the rear. All of the deeds and wills of the city of Richmond were housed in this structure until the Civil War. Sometime in the late 1830s or early '40s, the building was moved from its original site in the middle of Twenty-second Street to the southwest corner of Twenty-second and Main Streets. Damages incurred during the evacuation fire of 1865 were repaired, and it was not until 1896 that the courthouse was demolished to make way for an imposing Victorian structure. (Image: Virginia Historical Society)
JOP, MTP

ANATOMICAL THEATRE, UNIVERSITY OF VIRGINIA,
McCormick Road opposite Hotel A, Charlottesville
Built 1826–27; demolished 1939

The Anatomical Theatre was the only building at the University of Virginia designed by Thomas Jefferson but not constructed during his lifetime. Nor was it an integral part of his grand rectangular plan, being positioned in solitude opposite Hotel A, at the edge of a hilltop site. This plain brick architectural afterthought shared little of the grace or the classical formality of its neighboring buildings. Instead, it was a more modern, more utilitarian structure.

Jefferson's idea for a dissection laboratory was seemingly straightforward and simplistic on paper. The original sketches suggest a building of two principal stories with a gruesome charnel space beneath. Windows were shown in simple linear arrangements on two floors, as semicircles arrayed across front and rear façades. The second-story interior was to receive an octagonal arrangement of tiers—a theater in the round—to accommodate viewers as dissections took place at the center. The center appears to have had a stair from below, suggesting a Lazarus-like entry for both professor and corpse. The purpose of the lower floor, aside from entry, was unclear, and corner stairs connecting the two floors make little sense as drawn.

As built, the structure departed in many respects from Jefferson's sketch. Its siting allowed a two-story front elevation in reasonable harmony with Hotel A and similar in overall proportions to the drawing. But side and rear walls extended almost two stories downward as the building perched at the edge of the roadway now known as McCormick Road. Photographs prove that window placement and shape varied from the plan and suggest difficulty on the interior in making the tiers fit within a second floor that was insufficiently tall. How the several stairs worked and how the first floor was arranged are not known. Over the years a linear skylight was replaced by a large boxlike cupola, and the first-floor interior was divided into small rooms. By 1939 the building had been replaced by a more functional operating amphitheater at the University's medical school. No longer needed, not particularly appealing, and seemingly unnecessary on a campus filled with other Jefferson buildings, the Anatomical Theatre, unique though it was, was demolished to make room for Alderman Library. (Photograph: Manuscript Print Collection, Special Collections Department, University of Virginia Library)
JMH

FRANKLIN COUNTY COURTHOUSE, Rocky Mount
Built 1831; demolished 1909–10

Two courthouses preceded the building pictured here. The first Franklin County court met in 1785 "at the house of James Callaway, at his iron works." By 1786, a permanent log courthouse had been constructed on the site of the present one.

The Franklin County courthouse of 1831 closely resembled those of the counties of Patrick (1822) and Bedford (1833, q.v.). In all three, the Jeffersonian influence was evident in the tripartite format and Tuscan portico, although the Patrick and Bedford courthouses were erected on high basements. Franklin's portico, unlike the others, was graced by a lunette with intersecting tracery identical to that of Pavilion IV at the University of Virginia. The building was the work of local artisans Silas Heston, contractor, and Abram Paul, brickmason, overseen by commissioners appointed by the county court. No direct connection has been established between the builders and Jefferson, although the father of one of the commissioners had been a friend of his and had resided near Jefferson's Bedford County estate, Poplar Forest.

The arrangement of the interior is not known; presumably the court met in the central section while the wings held a jury room and a chamber for the justices. This handsome expression of Jeffersonian ideals was demolished to make way for the current courthouse. (Photograph: Virginia Department of Historic Resources)
JS

PRINCE EDWARD COUNTY COURTHOUSE, Worsham
Built 1832; demolished early 20th century

The 1776 Prince Edward County courthouse was replaced by the structure shown here, completed in 1832. The county justices adopted a plan submitted by William A. Howard, who had undertaken the 1822 courthouse at nearby Cumberland. Like many courthouses, including that at Cumberland, the primary entrance probably was on the long side of the building. During the final days of the Civil War, a detachment of Federal cavalry visited the Prince Edward County seat but inflicted no damage. This building was abandoned as a courthouse with the removal of the county seat to Farmville in 1871. It subsequently served as a private school for boys, beginning in 1874. Known as Hampden Institute and later Prince Edward Academy, the school's primary purpose was to prepare students for nearby Hampden-Sydney College. The building was abandoned in the early 20th century and subsequently torn down. Its bricks were used to build a residence in Farmville. (Image: Library of Virginia)
JOP, MTP

SMYTH COUNTY COURTHOUSE,
Marion
Built 1832–34; demolished 1905

In 1832, when the court of Smyth County appointed commissioners to see to the building of a new courthouse at Marion, officials specified that they wanted a structure like the one in Scott County. The Scott County courthouse (1829) had been designed by James Toncray of Wythe County, the most prolific courthouse architect and builder in southwest Virginia prior to 1850. The Smyth County commissioners accepted plans submitted by Toncray that were similar to those for his Scott County courthouse but awarded the construction contract to John Dameron and Thomas W. Mercer. Noteworthy in addition to Toncray's signature two-story wings are the high hipped roof on the central block and the octagonal, domed cupola. The building, completed in 1834, was practically identical to Toncray's Montgomery County courthouse (1836, q.v.) and the courthouse that Mercer built for Giles County in 1836, which still stands at Pearisburg. (Photograph: Smyth County Historical Society)
JOP, MTP

BEDFORD COUNTY COURTHOUSE, Main Street, Bedford
Built 1833; demolished ca. 1930

This Roman Revival courthouse in the Doric order was built at Liberty, now Bedford, in 1833. Thomas Jefferson's Poplar Forest was located in the county, and the Jeffersonian influence on the region's builders was significant. With its three-part configuration, high basement, tetrastyle portico, and tall steps, the building appears to have been influenced as well by the 1822 Roman Revival courthouse in Patrick County. It was not unusual for a jurisdiction to adopt the design of the courthouse in an adjacent county. In 1849, neighboring Campbell and Pittsylvania Counties also built Classical Revival courthouses in this same configuration. The Bedford courthouse remained in use until about 1930, when it was replaced by an imposing new building on the same site. (Image: Library of Virginia)
JOP, MTP

ROCKINGHAM COUNTY COURTHOUSE,

Harrisonburg

Third courthouse: built 1834; demolished 1873 (shown left)
Fourth courthouse: built 1874; demolished 1896 (shown above)

Rockingham, one of the Shenandoah Valley's most prosperous counties, has had four courthouses prior to the present one. The first, a thirty-by-twenty-foot, two-story log structure, was built in 1780. The second was built in 1792 by Brewer Reeves, a local tavern keeper; it was a simple, two-story, Federal-style brick building with a bull's-eye window in the front gable and what were presumably stone lintels over the windows. That building was replaced in 1834 by a far larger two-story brick structure with a hipped roof and a handsome hexagonal cupola; the cost was approximately five thousand dollars. The builder was Isaac S. Pennybaker. Improvements to the building took place in 1859, and it was this building that saw soldiers in both blue and gray marching by during the Civil War. The fourth courthouse to serve the county was completed in 1874 by the Holmes and Rust construction firm of Charles Town, West Virginia. It was a large building with a stone foundation, a two-story portico, and a square-domed cupola with a clock. Fewer than thirty years later, the 1874 building was demolished to make way for the present stone courthouse, which still serves the county today. (Photographs: Library of Virginia)
JOP, MTP

AUGUSTA COUNTY COURTHOUSE, northeast corner of South Augusta and East Johnson Streets, Staunton
Built 1835–36; demolished 1900

This incarnation of the Augusta County courthouse—the fourth of five built on the same site—was designed and built by former Jefferson workman Thomas R. Blackburn and completed in 1836. Its immediate predecessor, a two-story, square stone building constructed in 1789, was in use until its removal in 1835, at which point all buildings on the site were cleared. The courthouse designed by Blackburn was at the center a high, two-story building fronted by giant Doric columns, surmounted by a prominent two-stage cupola, and flanked by a pair of lower two-story wings housing the clerk's offices.

The design of this courthouse closely follows Thomas Jefferson's bold use of classical elements; in fact, of all the courthouses built by former Jefferson workmen, this was perhaps the purest example of Jeffersonian classicism. Its architectural merit did not escape notice in the press of the day. In a footnote added just before publication to his 1836 *Gazetteer*, Joseph Martin noted, "Since this was written, the court has contracted for the erection of a new C.H. [court house] which will be unquestionably the finest building of the kind in any county in the state." As to Blackburn, in addition to several houses in Staunton and Augusta County, Blackburn's designs for public buildings in Staunton included the United States District Courthouse, a Masonic hall, and a variety of projects for the Virginia School for the Deaf and the Blind. Blackburn had become superintendent of buildings at Western Lunatic Asylum as early as 1838 and remained in that position until the end of his career, around 1858, completing numerous additions and new structures there.

The 1835 courthouse was razed in 1900 to make room for the present courthouse, completed in 1901 on the same site and designed by T. J. Collins, a prolific Staunton architect. (Photograph: *Art Work of Scenes in the Valley of Virginia*, 1897)

MONTGOMERY COUNTY COURTHOUSE, Christiansburg
Built 1836, remodeled 1909; demolished 1978

This structure was built by James Toncray on the site of an 1815 courthouse for the sizable sum of four thousand dollars. Modeled on Toncray's Smyth County courthouse (1832–34, q.v.), it incorporated a tall central block, high hipped roof, octagonal cupola, and two-story wings. By 1908, the county needed a larger courthouse. Instead of building a new one, the supervisors chose to renovate the 1836 building and commissioned Harry Hartwell Huggins of Huggins and Bates in nearby Roanoke to draw the plans. At the time Huggins was designing a new courthouse for Roanoke County, as well as one for Franklin County, both similar in type and completed in 1910. The renovations at Montgomery were so extensive that the building took on an entirely different appearance; Beaux Arts elements were added to the simpler structure of the earlier courthouse. The renovated building, which was rededicated in 1909, had a portico that was removed in 1925. It served the county until 1978, when it was demolished after a new courthouse with little architectural distinction had been completed. Only the imposing metal eagle that topped the dome survives, perched on a pedestal in front of the 1978 courthouse. (Image: drawing by Lewis Miller, Virginia Historical Society)
JOP, MTP

ALEXANDRIA COURTHOUSE,
Columbus between Queen and Princess Streets,
Alexandria
Built 1838; demolished ca. 1905

This Greek Revival courthouse for the city of Alexandria was designed by Robert Mills when he was resident in Washington and prominent there as architect of the Treasury Building (1836–42) and Patent Office (1836–40 and later), both of which are among the nation's grandest Greek Revival monuments. It was Mills who had introduced the Greek orders into use in Virginia, through the still-extant Monumental Church in Richmond (1812–17).

For the Alexandria commission, Mills fused Virginia traditions with ideas for courthouses that he had developed in South Carolina during the 1820s and with ideas borrowed from B. Henry Latrobe's US Capitol. Virginia tradition called for raised, apsidal seating for the magistrates, a lawyer's bar across the center of the courtroom, and two jury rooms positioned opposite the bench. In his South Carolina courthouses Mills had replaced the traditional wooden, one-story type with what he would repeat for Alexandria; the court spaces were raised on the second level, above a ground-floor, vaulted "basement" given to offices and fireproof record-storage. Mills had learned how to build vaulting from Latrobe. It was also Latrobe whose semicircular Hall of Representatives in the US Capitol influenced Mills to borrow that shape for the Alexandria courtroom, except that Mills placed the bench on the curved wall, not at the center of the diameter as Latrobe had done. In that way Mills updated the traditional Virginia apsidal-ended room, changing a rectangle with a curved end into a semicircle.

The raised courtroom at Alexandria gave the building a monumental scale, almost creating the illusion that this temple to justice was elevated on a hill. The severity of the design was softened by graceful, curving stairs leading up to the portico. Mills covered the courtroom with a wooden half-dome, probably built on the Delorme method of laminated-plank construction that Thomas Jefferson had championed and that Mills had employed at Monumental Church. In 1851 part of the dome caved in and was replaced by the cupola pictured in this photograph. (Photograph: Virginia Historical Society)

ROANOKE COUNTY COURTHOUSE, Main Street,
Salem
Built 1841; demolished 1909

Shortly after Roanoke County was created in 1838, the county court appointed a committee to bring in "models" for a new courthouse. For inspiration the committee might have looked to the tripartite courthouses with two-story central blocks and two-story wings that James Toncray had designed for Scott County (1829), Smyth County (1832–34, q.v.), Montgomery County (1836, q.v.), and Grayson County at the Old Town location (1834). Those buildings, however, showed restraint in the use of classical forms. In contrast, the central block of the Roanoke County courthouse that builder William C. Williams completed in 1841 at Salem was

fronted by a giant portico. The building incorporated two-story wings used for office space, as was common on many courthouses in southwest Virginia at the time. In 1865, several local lawyers were given permission to build single-story additions at both ends of the courthouse in which to house their offices. This important building, which introduced the Classical Revival portico to courthouse architecture of the Southwest, probably influenced the designs for the Botetourt (1847), Craig (1852), and Alleghany (1877, q.v.) County courthouses. It was razed in 1909 to make way for a new courthouse. (Photograph: William McCauley, ed., *History of Roanoke County, Salem, Roanoke City, Virginia and Representative Citizens*, 1902)
JOP, MTP

APPOMATTOX COUNTY COURTHOUSE, Appomattox National Battlefield Park
Built 1846; burned 1892

Appomattox County was established in 1845; one year later it erected this courthouse, a vernacular building that made spare use of Greek ornamentation. The courthouse was closed on Palm Sunday 1865, when Lee surrendered to Grant in Wilmer McLean's farmhouse across the road, thereby ending the Civil War. The 1846 courthouse was a two-story, hipped-roof building with running bond brickwork and tall flights of steps leading upward on two elevations to centered entry porches on the principal level. A fire in 1892 either destroyed or inflicted substantial damage on the building. The citizens then voted to move the county seat to Appomattox Depot, which is now known simply as Appomattox. The 1846 courthouse was reconstructed in 1963 and 1964 by the National Park Service to serve as the visitor center at Appomattox National Battlefield Park. (Photograph: Library of Virginia)
JOP, MTP

AMELIA COUNTY COURTHOUSE, Amelia
Built 1850; demolished 1924

The Amelia County courthouse of 1850 was built on a two-acre tract donated by Lewis E. Harvie when the route of the new Richmond and Danville Railroad was projected through the center of the 1792 courthouse. The 1850 structure was described as "a plain substantial building of Doric architecture, roomy and well ventilated." Its pedimented portico was supported by square piers rather than traditional columns; these appear to have been covered in stucco. The courthouse and the surrounding village stood in a strategic position in the closing days of the Civil War, as Confederate forces gathered before the surrender at Appomattox, but the building and its records suffered little damage then. It was removed in 1924 for construction of a new, more commodious courthouse that repeated its general configuration. (Photograph: Valentine Museum)
JOP, MTP

ANNEX (NEW HALL), UNIVERSITY OF VIRGINIA, Charlottesville
Built 1850–53; burned 1895

Despite the great symbolic power and beauty of Thomas Jefferson's design for the University of Virginia, its inadequacies had become only too evident by the late 1840s. The library in the Rotunda, which initially served also as a public hall, became too crowded with books to serve either purpose. In addition, new spaces were needed for classes in the different disciplines, which, with the exception of natural history and chemistry, were forced to share classrooms. The board of visitors contracted with Robert Mills to design an annex, or New Hall, to be attached to the north or back side of Jefferson's Rotunda. The Annex would be Mills's last major commission. The structure was physically attached to the Rotunda at the basement level by a triple-arched arcade that provided access to the new building and separated on the upper two floors by a thirty-foot colonnade. Mills also placed a duplicate of the Rotunda's south portico on the far north end. The roofs of the two buildings were united, and the entablature of the Rotunda was continued around the Annex. Mills's New Hall attempted to maintain Jefferson's architectural vocabulary of red brick and white trim, but Mills's Corinthian columns were built with cast-iron capitals. On the interior, new classrooms were provided on the ground and third levels, and a large public hall capable of seating twelve hundred occupied the second floor. In this space a copy of Raphael's *School of Athens* was hung.

Robert Mills had studied briefly with Jefferson between about 1800 and 1803. That study had been followed by an apprenticeship with B. Henry Latrobe, after which Mills had designed many notable buildings in Virginia, South Carolina, Washington, DC, and elsewhere. In a sense the "court architect" of the Jackson administration, Mills provided initial designs for the Washington Monument, the United States Treasury Building, and the old Patent Office in Washington, as well as many customhouses around the country. Hence the board of visitors's choice of Mills as the architect appears entirely logical.

Sentiments on the Annex have varied, and while it received some praise for its "commodious hall," the outer form proved less than popular. Prints published at the time make it appear as a long tail overwhelming its host. The fire that consumed the Rotunda in October 1895 began in the Annex, and apparently neither the board of visitors, the faculty, nor the various architects consulted ever suggested rebuilding it. If its loss was little mourned, the Annex did serve to make visible a problem that has continued to bedevil architects: how to make additions to Mr. Jefferson's design? (Photograph: Manuscript Print Collection, Special Collections Department, University of Virginia Library)
RGW

LIBBY PRISON, 2001 East Cary Street, Richmond
Built ca. 1850, moved to Chicago 1888; demolished 1900

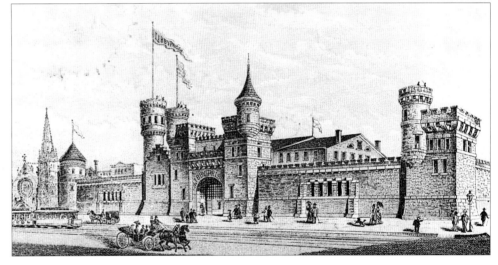

In 1816, the construction of what is now known as the Richmond Ship Canal prompted the building of warehouses and factories along its length. At midcentury John Enders, a local industrialist who was involved in constructing the Richmond dock, undertook one of the most ambitious developments along the waterfront: a row of fourteen warehouses located between Eighteenth and Twenty-first Streets that were built to store goods shipped by the vessels moored nearby. The warehouses would be uniform, each one hundred by forty feet and either three stories (on Cary Street) or four stories tall (on Dock Street, due to the slope of the site).

The project brought disastrous consequences to many associated with it. During construction Enders fell through flooring and was killed. In the 1850s several of the warehouses burned, allegedly from fires set by Enders's slaves, who were disgruntled at not having been freed upon his death. Additional buildings were destroyed in a fire of 1864 that began in the Confederate coffee factory at Eighteenth and Cary Streets. Luther Libby, a ship chandler, leased the warehouse at the southeast corner of Twentieth and Cary, a building that the Civil War would give the worst notoriety.

Following Libby's death, the Confederate government in 1861 seized from his estate the warehouse on the wall of which his business sign was still prominent. That building and the two adjoining it were converted into a prison that was dark, dirty, unheated, poorly ventilated, and unsanitary. Libby Prison became infamous because in the thirty-two thousand square feet of its eight rooms that were used to hold prisoners, as many as twelve hundred Union officers were confined at a time. Some thirty thousand Union prisoners were housed there during the course of the war.

From 1865 to 1868 the Libby buildings were used to imprison former Confederates; afterward, for twenty years, they served as a fertilizer factory. In 1888, businessmen in Chicago purchased Libby Prison and moved it there to be viewed as a relic of the late war. Philadelphia architect Louis Hall supervised the relocation, which involved dismantling, numbering, and loading the prison's materials onto thirty-two boxcars. On its new site the reconstructed building was surrounded by a massive turreted and castellated stone wall and filled with various war artifacts and artwork. The Libby Prison War Museum opened in 1889 to disappointingly small crowds, although it did become an attraction during the Chicago World's Columbian Exposition of 1893. In 1900 the building was demolished, and the Chicago Coliseum rose in its place. (Images: Virginia Historical Society)
TTP, Jr.

RICHMOND FEMALE INSTITUTE, Tenth Street between Marshall and Clay Streets, Richmond
Built 1853–54; demolished 1924

The Richmond Female Institute operated independently for half a century until 1914, when it merged with the University of Richmond. The founders of this Baptist-sponsored institution sought to create a women's seminary comparable to the University of Virginia. The architect selected by the founders was Thomas Tefft of Rhode Island, a former schoolteacher and protégé of educational reformer Henry Barnard's. Tefft had established a reputation in school design, and he was well placed in Baptist circles.

For the Richmond commission, Tefft conceived an Italianate design; that style, perhaps for its association with Osborne, the Italian villa–style retreat of Queen Victoria on the Isle of Wight, had become popular in 19th-century America for institutions that housed women (see the Lynchburg Female Orphan Asylum of 1872 and Tefft's Richmond College building of 1855, qq.v.). The most prominent feature of this building was its central section with two towers, one of which held a bell and the other "an observatory, commanding an extensive view of a most beautiful landscape, . . . suited also for astronomical observations." Tefft's drawings for the institute show end pavilions, never built, that would have extended its length.

The Richmond Female Institute was one of only a few monumental civic commissions that Tefft executed before his premature death at age thirty-three in 1859. It led to a significant sequel, the design for Vassar College (1856), but that project had to be transferred to James Renwick, best known for his design of the original Smithsonian Institution. The Richmond Female Institute would influence Virginia architecture; it was imitated in the rebuilt Wren building at the College of William and Mary by Henry Exall and Eben Faxon, completed in 1859 and burned in 1862. (Photograph: Valentine Museum)

CHESAPEAKE FEMALE COLLEGE (later, SOLDIERS' HOME), Hampton
Built ca. 1854; demolished 1913

Built at midcentury, this handsome and imposing building overlooking Hampton Roads initially housed the Chesapeake Female College, an institution of higher education for women. The college rose five stories, the upper four of which were each given a full-façade veranda; above was a huge dome set on an octagonal drum. Financial problems and the advent of the Civil War contributed to the school's closure in 1861. Confederate forces reportedly occupied the vacant structure and used its dome to spy on the Union army at nearby Fort Monroe until Northern forces seized the building after the Battle of Big Bethel and converted it into the Chesapeake Military Hospital. With the construction of the Hampton Military Hospital for enlisted men, the Chesapeake Military Hospital became an officers' facility. Union general Benjamin Franklin Butler acquired the property and then sold it to the United States government to house the recently established Southern Branch of the National Home for Disabled Volunteer Soldiers. (General Hospital #43 [q.v.] was added to this complex in 1885.) The former college was converted into a dormitory for soldiers and was known as the Main Building until its demolition in 1913. (Photograph: Virginia Historical Society)
MRH

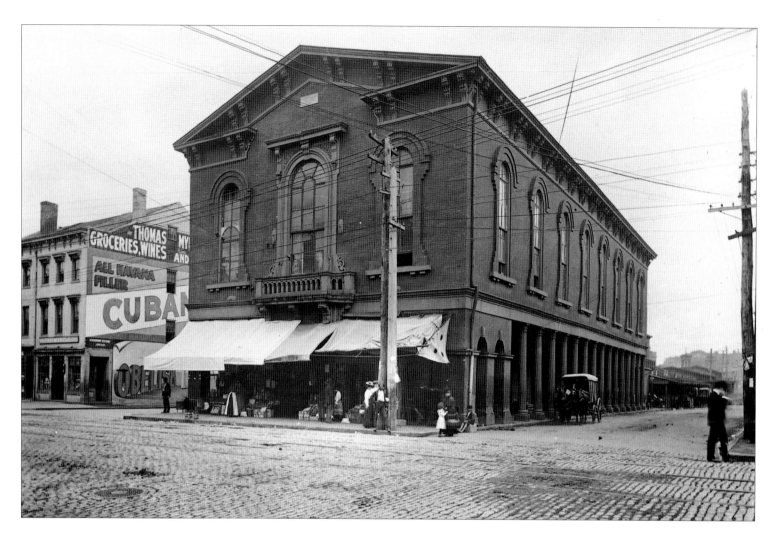

SEVENTEENTH STREET MARKET (NEW MARKET),
Seventeenth and Main Streets, Richmond
Built 1854, second story added probably by 1868; demolished 1913

At the center of Virginia's 19th-century incorporated towns stood market houses, the most important civic structures in those early municipalities. Politically, the market house (through the courts and council chambers sometimes housed within) symbolized the emerging importance of towns as the landscape of Virginia became more densely populated and as cities (especially Richmond and Alexandria) began to challenge the economic, political, and social hegemony of the agrarian countryside. On another level, market houses were the commercial, legal, and social centers of towns. They were places where merchants, beggars, and farmers selling their produce all vied for attention; where carts displaying vegetables rested against lockups and whipping posts; and where, in the evening, the market yard might be swept and the upper rooms transformed into the setting of an elite assembly or ball open only to the most wealthy.

This incarnation of the Seventeenth Street Market replaced an earlier version built circa 1794 and demolished in 1854. It was first a single-story market (shown at left), with sides screened by a rank of cast-iron columns with Tower of the Winds capitals and terminated by brick arcades; above was a two-stage cupola with a square base, hexagonal drum, and a dome. The building was covered with a gable roof, which may have sheltered a second-floor loft. At some point the building was altered by the addition of a full second story, as shown in the second photograph above. The change was made at least by 1868 (when the enlarged market appeared in an engraving of the market yard published in *Frank Leslie's Illustrated Newspaper*). The Italianate detailing so prominent on the second level dramatically altered the appearance of the market. With so long a colonnade, the building formerly projected a strong sense of civic might; the Victorianized market evoked new associations of refinement and enlightenment.

As an integral component of the day-to-day life of Virginia's towns and cities, the market house was a place of social stratification, where the levels of Virginia society were literally visible. In the market yard were common merchants and farmers displaying their products, while inside the market house was the clerk—the common council's agent—ensuring the fairness of the ensuing transactions. Also "below" were the lockups, stocks, and whipping posts used in the enforcement of corporation law; these were not used primarily for the punishment of transgressors among the gentry, whose punishments were financial, not physical. Also, literally above the market floor were the council chambers, in which the town leaders—invariably members of the local gentry or well-heeled local merchants—controlled the city's finances and made its laws. Also above the market floor were the corporation (city) courts, in which the laws made by the councilmen were applied to the people "below." On this level were found the various high social functions located in the building, such as assemblies, balls, church services, and the like, generally reserved for the upper social classes. Finally, "above" this were found the town clock, bells, and cupola, which (both visually and aurally) represented the town and its corporate authority over all of its citizens below. People from all levels of society experienced the market house, and, while for each of them it may have held a different meaning, it was nonetheless one of the focal points of the Virginia urban experience. (Photographs: Library of Congress and Valentine Museum)

RICHMOND COLLEGE, MAIN BUILDING, in the former block bounded by Ryland, Franklin, Lombardy, and Broad Streets, Richmond
Built 1855, 1873, and 1876; demolished ca. 1920

The University of Richmond, now located in Richmond's far west end, traces its history to 1830, when a Baptist seminary was opened in Powhatan County. Two years later the school moved to Spring Farm in Henrico County, near today's Bryan Park. In 1834 the school relocated to a former residence, "Columbia," a building still standing at the northeast corner of Lombardy and Grace Streets. In 1840, when Richmond College was chartered to replace the seminary, it continued to occupy Columbia and other buildings nearby. What would become the college's landmark edifice, the Main Building, was built in at least three phases beginning in 1855. The first building was designed by Thomas Alexander Tefft, a Rhode Island architect who in 1853 had designed another prominent commission for local Baptists, the Richmond Female Institute (q.v.) on Tenth Street between Marshall and Clay. The Main Building was built in 1855 near the western city limits. Like the Richmond Female Institute, this structure also resembled an Italianate villa, with three floors set atop an English basement. Its one-story entrance portico faced Broad Street.

Following the Civil War, a movement was begun to update and expand the college's facilities. In 1873, a tower and central section were added. These were designed by Alexander Y. Lee, an architect who worked in Richmond from 1869 to 1874. Finally, in 1876, the southernmost wing (probably also designed by Lee) completed the ensemble. The five-part structure, now fronting Ryland and on an axis with Grace, was successfully unified by a mansard roof. The central tower, however, was crowned by a two-story, top-heavy confection in the French Second Empire style. When the building was partially destroyed by a fire in 1910, plans were already under way for a new campus on two hundred acres in Richmond's suburban Westhampton area. In a sentimental gesture the granite steps to the portico that once faced Broad Street were reinstalled at the new campus (just south of Jepson Hall).

The Main Building again saw academic service during World War I when, for financial reasons, the university leased its new campus to the US government for use as a hospital and moved back temporarily to the old campus. In the early 1920s, the university sold its old campus; Grace Street was extended westward, and apartment houses were built along it. Today, the former campus is marked by imposing granite classical piers that flank the Lombardy and Ryland Street boundaries of the 1100 block of West Grace. (Photograph: Virginia Historical Society)
EJS, Jr.

TEMPERANCE HALL, UNIVERSITY OF VIRGINIA, Main Street, Charlottesville
Built 1855; demolished ca. 1914

The flat arches, pilasters, and whimsical frieze of this classical structure repeated motifs that had been given resonance a short distance away in Thomas Jefferson's academical village. Temperance Hall was erected to serve as a refuge where students at the University of Virginia could engage in wholesome activities away from the vice of alcohol. Total abstinence was the goal of the Sons of Temperance (later the Friends of Temperance), a group that met in the hall's second-floor assembly room.

Temperance Hall was built by George Wilson Spooner, Jr., who two years earlier had supervised the construction of Robert Mills's Rotunda Annex (q.v.) at the university. Spooner's association with the institution was long-lived. Born in Fredericksburg in 1798, he first worked under one of Thomas Jefferson's principal builders, John Neilson, at Upper Bremo, the home of John Hartwell Cocke. Cocke, a president of the National Temperance Union, helped fund Temperance Hall. By 1819 Spooner was employed at the university. In that year he wrote to the proctor that he was boarding with another Jefferson builder, John M. Perry, because it was more convenient to his university work. Within two years he married Perry's eldest daughter. Spooner was the principal carpenter for Hotels C and E and for several student rooms at the university. He also worked for James Dinsmore on the Rotunda and for Neilson on Pavilion IX. During the 1845–46 academic year, he became acting proctor of the university.

The temperance movement at the University of Virginia had been initiated about 1842 by librarian William Wertenbaker; it was interrupted by the Civil War and waned afterward, when Temperance Hall reverted to the university. The building was in use as a bookstore when it was photographed circa 1913. (Photograph: Manuscript Print Collection, Special Collections Department, University of Virginia Library)
KEL

118

(FIRST) LYNCHBURG

COLLEGE, in block bounded by Wise, Tenth, Floyd, and Eleventh Streets, Lynchburg
Built 1856–57; demolished ca. 1870 and 1960s

Not to be confused with the present institution that carries the name, the antebellum Lynchburg College was housed in this phenomenal picturesque Gothic structure, two portions of which survived for more than a century. In plan the complex formed an L. It was designed by James T. Murfee, a faculty member who had graduated first in his class at Virginia Military Institute in 1853. A. J. Davis, America's master of the Gothic Revival who had designed the VMI campus (Williamson house, q.v.), voiced the hope that "cadets returning to their homes should be enabled to serve on building committees and have a competent knowledge of Castellated, Collegiate, Memorial, and Domestic Gothic." Murfee made his mentor proud. Lynchburg College was as relentlessly Gothic as could be wished.

The institution, a casualty of the Civil War, began its last session in February 1861. During the ensuing conflict, the college served as the city's General Military Hospital, and after Lee's surrender, it became barracks for Federal troops stationed in the city. Vagrants who followed vandalized it so completely that portions had to be demolished. Later, two of the city's leading families purchased the two remaining sections and converted them into houses. Both were demolished in the early 1960s by the neighboring Westminster Presbyterian Church. (Photograph: Jones Memorial Library, Lynchburg)
SAC, Jr.

GATEKEEPER'S LODGE, UNIVERSITY OF VIRGINIA, Charlottesville
Built ca. 1856; demolished 1937

The Gatekeeper's Lodge, also known as the Château or the Château Front and Back, stood near the present day intersection of Ivy Road (a continuation of University Avenue and US 250 Business) and McCormick Road. It was demolished to make way for the construction of Alderman Library. Designed as one of the entrances to the University of Virginia's grounds, the lodge was occupied by faculty for many years. Entrances on two sides led to the popular nickname Front and Back. The term Château refers rather inaccurately to its style and gives a clue to the architectural illiteracy of Virginians with regard to the Romantic revivals.

Designed in the Gothic Revival cottage mode popularized by A. J. Davis and Andrew Jackson Downing in the 1840s, the Gatekeeper's Lodge, with its steeply pitched roofs, elaborate bargeboards (or vergeboards), pointed windows, and finials, exemplified this style. It was constructed of random fieldstone reputedly taken from a demolished observatory designed by Thomas Jefferson that had stood on Observatory Hill.

The architect of the Gatekeeper's Lodge was William A. Pratt, who would serve as superintendent of buildings and grounds at the university from 1858 to 1865. He designed the lodge before he took on the larger task of the university. Born in England, Pratt came to the United States in 1832 and lived first in Washington, DC, and Alexandria before moving to Richmond, where he designed several residences, including his well-known Pratt's Castle (q.v.). Devoted to the Romantic, or Picturesque, mode of composition, Pratt even proposed a Gothic Revival chapel for the university in 1859 that would have stood in the middle of the Lawn, facing Jefferson's Rotunda. The Civil War interrupted fund-raising for the structure, and it was never built. The present chapel at the university dates to the years 1884–90 and was designed by Charles E. Cassell. Pratt's full career has never been treated; he submitted designs for the University of the South in Sewanee, Tennessee, and after leaving the University of Virginia in 1865 practiced in Staunton, Virginia. (Photograph: Manuscript Print Collection, Special Collections Department, University of Virginia Library)
RGW

ALEXANDRIA POST OFFICE AND CUSTOMHOUSE, southwest corner of Prince and South St. Asaph Streets, Alexandria
Built 1856–58; demolished 1930

Designed by noted Federal architect Ammi Burnham Young, this imposing Italianate edifice was Alexandria's first purpose-built post office and customhouse. Previously, the federal government had conducted its custom duties in Alexandria from a former bank building. The Alexandria Customhouse was one of several dozen federal buildings designed by Young, the first supervising architect for the Department of the Treasury's Office of Construction, established in 1852, which oversaw the design and construction of government structures throughout the nation. These included customhouses, hospitals, post offices, and courthouses, for which Young developed a set of economical and standardized designs in response to increased national demand. Young drew from his early experience in New England designing public buildings, as well as from the contemporary English architect Sir Charles Barry's Italian palazzo–inspired clubhouse designs.

If restrained in ornament, Young's Alexandria Customhouse evoked the grandeur of the Italian Renaissance palazzo while retaining elements of the popular Greek Revival style. Its heavy, articulated granite base was surmounted by a two-story-high brick "colonnade" defined by pilasters and topped by a full classical entablature. Originally designed with a three-bay façade facing South St. Asaph Street, the building was expanded to five bays in width in 1904. The Alexandria Customhouse was not only stately but also incorporated state-of-the-art, fireproof construction methods in its structure. Young used wrought-iron beams set on cast-iron columns, solid brick walls, and iron windowsills, shutters, and door frames to render his building sturdy and impervious to conflagration. Despite its durable construction, however, after seventy-two years of service the building was demolished to make room for a larger federal building that was designed to house the US district court and a federal post office. Completed in 1931, the current courthouse faces South Washington Street. The site of the former customhouse now serves as a parking lot at the rear. (Photograph: Virginia Historical Society)
KGS

PAVILION FOR HENRY CLAY STATUE,
Capitol Square, Richmond
Built 1860; demolished 1932

The movement to erect a monument to Henry Clay in Richmond's Capitol Square was initiated in 1844 by the "Whig Ladies of Richmond," who by this effort came to be known also as the "Ladies Clay Association." This group engaged the Kentucky-born sculptor Joel T. Hart, who in 1846 sketched his state's favorite son at Clay's Kentucky home, Ashland. Hart's full-length image of the Great Pacifier was sculpted in Florence and unveiled in Richmond in 1860. It was positioned in Capitol Square almost in the shadow of Thomas Crawford's monumental equestrian figure of George Washington, which had been commissioned in 1850 and received in 1857. Thus, the dedicatory address for the Clay sculpture, given by B. Johnson Barbour, saluted both the Kentuckian, whom he described as "next to Washington, the foremost man of all our country," and the "Southern matrons and Southern maidens [who had recently] rescued Mount Vernon from dilapidation and decay and made it the trysting spot of the nation."

The cast-iron pavilion that shielded the marble sculpture from the elements was designed by Richmonder Henry Exall and executed at the local foundry of Andrew J. Bowers. Its eight Corinthian columns were connected by a Greek-inspired iron rail, and above were anthemia, but the roof was given an exotic ogee profile.

The Clay statue has led a peripatetic life. It was removed to the Capitol rotunda before 1885 "because of repeated mutilations by bad boys"; the sculpture was "artistically restored" during the administration of Governor Fitzhugh Lee and returned to its pavilion, only to be removed a final time in 1930 to the Old Hall of the House of Delegates in the Capitol. The little-remembered pavilion is one of three lost buildings in Capitol Square, the other two being the first Virginia Museum (q.v.), demolished after 1836, and the General Court Building, erected on the site of the Virginia Museum and burned in the evacuation fire of 3 April 1865. (Photograph: Virginia Historical Society)

PRINCE EDWARD COUNTY COURTHOUSE, Farmville
Built 1872; demolished 1939

Following the close of the Civil War, sentiment grew for the removal of the Prince Edward County seat from Worsham to the thriving community of Farmville, which was well situated on the canal-navigable Appomattox River and had rail lines linking it directly to Richmond. The General Assembly authorized a referendum with the understanding that the town would pay for both the special election and the construction of new court buildings should the move be approved by the voters, which it was. The cornerstone of a new courthouse was laid in 1871, and court sessions were held there in the spring of 1872. The new building was a tall brick structure, later painted white, with an impressive belfry tower and a main entrance on the second floor. In addition to the standard courtroom and jury rooms, the courthouse contained a large hall suitable for the meetings of the Farmville town council. The building served the county until 1939, when it was replaced by a new courthouse. (Image: Library of Virginia)
JOP, MTP

LYNCHBURG FEMALE ORPHAN ASYLUM, Memorial Avenue, Lynchburg
Built 1872; demolished 1959

Samuel Miller, a wealthy 19th-century tobacconist, left a portion of his estate to build this orphanage, directing that it be "han-some [*sic*] . . . and constructed of good and durable materials." The trustees abandoned plans that A. J. Davis had prepared and instead selected a little-known architect, Gen. John Ellicott of Baltimore, to carry out the donor's wishes. Ellicott used good and durable brick, but it is doubtful if anyone ever considered his building handsome. The uncompromising Italianate structure contained the entire institution, including two parlors, offices, dormitories, a chapel, a dining room, and classrooms. Matrons had their own quarters in the two upper floors of the towers that flanked the main entrance. Miller Home, as it became known, was demolished in 1959, and a shopping center now occupies its site. The institution continues, now happily housed in a far less daunting building. (Photograph: Jones Memorial Library, Lynchburg)
SAC, Jr.

THE FLETCHER SCHOOL, rural Greene County
Built late 19th century; abandoned early 20th century

Even well into the 20th century, public secondary schools in rural Virginia could be the simplest and crudest of buildings, akin to the residences that housed many of the pupils. The Fletcher School in Greene County was little more than a shack constructed on a drystone foundation. Such a structure was not out of the ordinary, to judge from one writer's description at the turn of the century of a typical schoolhouse as "more unsightly often than the corn houses or the tobacco barns" and "frequently situated in some out-of-the-way place, where somebody gave a half-acre of land to have the school near him." These were impermanent buildings that existed only as long as the noncompulsory schools attracted their student populations. (Photograph: Library of Virginia)

EQUESTRIAN FOUNTAIN, intersection of Hull Street and Cowardin Avenue, Richmond
Built late 19th century; demolished early 20th century

This finely crafted cast-iron fountain, a monument to horses, once dominated the intersection of Hull Street and Cowardin Avenue in south Richmond. It was surmounted by the classical figure of Hebe, the Greek goddess of youth, bearing a jar in her right hand and holding forth a bowl in her left. The figure is derived from the Danish neoclassical sculptor Bertel Thorvaldsen's second sculpture of Hebe, the more discreet (and more clothed) of his two versions. The monument featured a hierarchy of fountains for the refreshment of animals and passersby. The large troughs, fed by streams of water emitting from large horse heads, were intended, if one couldn't guess, to water horses. On a smaller scale and on opposite sides of the monument were what appear to have been the heads of ponies, loosening streams of water into smaller troughs that were fitted with dippers and intended for the refreshment of passing men and women. At the very bottom of the monument and at all four corners were small dogs' heads, which passed water into four small receptacles for the watering of dogs.

When horses were rendered obsolete by the efficiency of automobiles, this dignified and functional piece of civic art was deemed an impediment to modern traffic and removed from the intersection. A special urban spot was thus converted into an ordinary one. (Photograph: Virginia Historical Society)

DANVILLE COURTHOUSE, 505 Patton Street, Danville
Built ca. 1873; demolished 1926

Danville's first important public place following Reconstruction took shape in the early 1870s on Patton Street, diagonally across from Neal's Warehouse, where the "Danville system" of auctioning tobacco in piles of loose leaves was born in 1858. This permanent courthouse, which the tobacco boomtown had lacked since a hustings court had been established about 1841, may have derived from hand-me-down plans. As part of his research on some of the commonwealth's Jefferson-designed courthouses, Washington and Lee University historian Delos Hughes has determined that in the wake of the fire that destroyed Buckingham County's Jefferson-designed courthouse in 1869, the county "secured plans from Albert Lybrock for a new one. After the failure of a bond referendum, they abandoned Lybrock's plans. Very quickly afterwards, Danville built their new courthouse." It appears possible, then, that Lybrock's proposal for the Buckingham County courthouse may in fact have been the one picked up by Danville. Recycled or not, these plans produced for Danville a remarkably handsome building from one of Richmond's premier practitioners of Italianate design. Even so, Albert Lybrock, who studied architecture at the Polytechnic School of Karlsruhe in his native Germany, is remembered chiefly for a Gothic-inspired tour de force—James Monroe's cast-iron tomb, which graces Richmond's Hollywood Cemetery.

The cornerstone of Lybrock's Danville courthouse, which also housed the town's municipal offices, was laid on 21 August 1873. Its symmetrical Renaissance Revival façade of two stories was distinguished by arched windows between dignified pilasters on the main level. Its brick construction was stuccoed and scored in an ashlar pattern, rusticated on the first level. A commanding octagonal clock tower assured the structure's place in the public eye. The courthouse served the community until the mid-1920s, when, despite the completion in 1890 of a separate, new municipal building on Main Street, the need for judicial and municipal services continued to mushroom with the city's population. Danville elected to consolidate the courts and city services on Patton Street, sacrificing the 1873 courthouse and an adjacent fire station. They were replaced by a massive three-story structure of limestone and brick designed by Heard and Chesterman. Occupied in 1927, the opulent building continues as the seat of city government and courts to this day. In 1999, an adjacent annex expanded court facilities further within a design that recalls, at least in classically inspired form, its long-destroyed 1873 predecessor. (Photograph: *Art Work of Lynchburg and Danville, Virginia*, 1903)
GRG

TOBACCO EXCHANGE, Shockoe Slip at Thirteenth Street, Richmond
Built 1876–77; demolished 1955

In early-19th-century Richmond, tobacco was marketed primarily by auction at various tobacco warehouses. After 1858, when the Richmond Tobacco Exchange organized, a building was erected, only to burn during the Richmond evacuation fire of 1865. It was rebuilt as the structure pictured here, square in plan, with each side about ninety feet in length. In conjunction, the cavernous Shockoe Tobacco Warehouse was put up nearby to house the crops that would pass through the exchange.

The Tobacco Exchange was designed by J. Crawford Neilson of Baltimore; Marion J. Dimmock, a Richmond architect, supervised construction. With brick arches, piers, corbels, and recesses, the two-story building was one of the most modern in reconstructed Richmond. At the same time, however, the exchange was an eclectic Victorian structure; its prominent, round-arched windows evoked association with Italianate and even Romanesque design. The center bay contained a wagon entrance to allow passage of crops in and out; the flanking bays contained offices. The second floor was given to a large trading floor. The tall windows and hipped clerestory roof provided light essential for inspecting tobacco and ventilated the space. An elaborately carved auctioneer's pulpit was a focal point of the large room.

The Tobacco Exchange stood initially as a symbol of the recovery of Richmond following the Civil War, and for almost a century it gave evidence of the importance in Virginia of the tobacco industry. It was demolished to make way for a parking lot in 1955, thus disfiguring one of Richmond's most picturesque urban quarters. A thoughtfully designed structure was erected on its site in the mid-1990s. Much of the neighborhood, part of the Shockoe Slip Historic District, has been rehabilitated since the 1970s. (Photograph: Valentine Museum)
TTP, Jr., and THR

ALLEGHANY COUNTY COURTHOUSE, Covington
Built 1877; demolished 1911

Shortly after the 1870 arrival in Covington of the Chesapeake and Ohio Railroad and the prosperity that accompanied it, Alleghany County replaced its first courthouse (ca. 1824) with this Classical Revival building, a very late expression of the style. It had a tall, two-story, temple-form central block flanked by two-story wings with low hipped roofs. The tetrastyle portico had unfluted columns with a plain entablature and pediment. This courthouse was similar to the ones in neighboring Botetourt (1848) and Craig (1852) Counties, which influenced its design. It was built by H. J. Shomo and John H. Plunkett for seventy-two hundred dollars, with seven hundred dollars deducted for materials salvaged from the earlier courthouse. A large hall on the second floor was used by the town council of Covington. The entire courthouse square was enclosed by an iron fence similar to ones that survive at the Botetourt and Craig County courthouses. This building served until 1911, when it was replaced by the current courthouse. (Photograph: Alleghany Historical Society)
JOP, MTP

GORDONSVILLE FEMALE INSTITUTE, Baker Street, Gordonsville, Orange County
Built 1878, extensively altered early 20th century; demolished mid-1960s

Gordonsville Female Institute was built in 1878 as a private school for young ladies. During the next twenty years, the complex continued to serve as a private girls' school under a number of names: Gordonsville Female College, Central Female Institute, a second Gordonsville Female College, and, beginning in 1902 and continuing for a number of years, Woodlawn Seminary and Musical Institute. The main building, designed in the Second Empire style, was a large frame structure three stories high and capped by slate roofs with elaborate iron crestings. Several surviving brochures describe the interior. The eight first-floor rooms included a chamber, a music room, and a dining room forty feet long. The second-floor rooms included a chamber, a parlor, and a substantial schoolroom forty by twenty-seven feet; the movable partitions of the adjoining recitation rooms could be opened to form a concert hall forty-one by forty feet. The third floor was occupied by a dormitory that could accommodate forty girls.

The brochures also describe the curriculum. In the 1880s, two areas of concentration were offered: literary and ornamental. The former offered courses in English, Latin, French, German, mathematics (including trigonometry and bookkeeping), logic, natural sciences (including geology, chemistry, and astronomy), and music. The ornamental curriculum offered drawing, painting, embroidery, waxwork, and lace making, along with calisthenics.

This building was later acquired by the Orange County public school system and, after remodeling and additions, became a public school that was demolished in the mid-1960s. (Photograph: Orange County Historical Society)
ALM

BIGGERS SCHOOL, Fifth and Clay Streets, Lynchburg
Built 1881; demolished after 1966

Named for Lynchburg's first superintendent of schools, Abram F. Biggers, this public elementary school was so big that it was generally referred to as Biggers University. When it was completed, the local press described the school as "plain but well proportioned" and pointed out its iron cresting and finials. Those elements, along with the triangular vents in the expansive roof of the main block and the flanking mansard towers, were found in many buildings designed by August Forsberg, who served as the first city engineer. Biggers, which can be regarded as something of a precursor of Lynchburg's 1890s boom, served its purpose until 1966, when it was closed. When the property was later proposed as the site for a public library, the then-vacant school was demolished. The library was never built, and a public playground now occupies the site. Only the stone wall facing Fifth Street and the stone steps trod by generations of students on their way to and from classes remain. (Photograph: Jones Memorial Library, Lynchburg)
SAC, Jr.

US POST OFFICE AND FEDERAL BUILDING, 530 Main Street, Danville
Built 1881–83; demolished 1937

Bristling with gables and chimney stacks and terminating in a lofty octagonal clock tower, Danville's Post Office and Courthouse did not just enliven the downtown skyline; this eclectic pile of red brick, with brownstone and granite trim, all produced or quarried in Virginia, also signaled Danville's arrival as a city of the New South, one that was rich from tobacco and textiles. This was the fourth, and by far the most opulent, post office since Danville's late antebellum days, when the first facility dedicated specifically for that purpose was erected. Before that time, Danville's postal service, established in 1800, was a storefront operation only. Maj. James G. Hill, supervising architect for the United States Treasury Department from 1876 through 1883, is said to have followed in this Danville commission the same exuberant style visible in his Bureau of Engraving and Printing (1878–80), built in Washington, DC. Its compact form was highly embellished, characterized in *The Making of Virginia Architecture* as "a wild concoction of Romanesque, Flemish, English and American Colonial details." Breaking ranks with the dense alignment of its commercial neighbors, this important civic monument stood prominently within a wide half-acre lot in the middle of the 500 block of Main Street. After fifty years of service, the post office lost its place as "the heart of the town" to a Depression-era facility of stripped classicism, built in 1932 and 1933 just two blocks up Main Street. Prior to its destruction in 1937, the old building was proposed as a site for an expanded Danville Public Library, then housed in the historic Sutherlin mansion, a former residence. That and other suggestions failed, and the structure was pulled down for salvage, a portion of its site occupied for some time thereafter by a parking lot. Until recent years the headless remnant of its terra-cotta Federal eagle, once mounted just above the front door, languished in a private campground near Danville. (Photograph: *Art Work of Lynchburg and Danville, Virginia*, 1903)
GRG

SPRINGWOOD TRUSS BRIDGE, Springwood, Botetourt County
Built 1884; demolished 1985

Until it was dismantled following damage from the 1985 floods, this graceful, three-span structure was the state's last major wooden bridge across the James River. It was built by the Richmond and Allegheny Railroad Company and acquired by the Virginia Department of Highways when it took over the county roads in 1932. Supported by tapering stone piers, the superstructure was composed entirely of timbers, except for some wrought-iron reinforcing members. Its overall length was 240 feet. The bridge had been closed to vehicular traffic for several years prior to its destruction. A visually uninteresting concrete bridge now spans the river just upstream. (Photograph: Virginia Department of Historic Resources)

Covered bridges are an American icon. As many as ten thousand of these structures were erected between 1800 and 1920, adorning rural byways across the nation. Virginia once had an impressive collection of its own. Fifty of them were in use as late as 1936. Today only about a half-dozen remain in the whole state, four in public ownership and two or so on private property. Only one, Meems Bottom Covered Bridge in Shenandoah County, still carries automobile traffic. Few other structures excite such intense sentiment as covered bridges, and few traveling experiences offer such fun as driving across a covered bridge. These wooden structures were roofed and sided not to provide sheltered crossings but to prolong the strength of their timbers. The picturesque result has provided a nostalgic image that has inspired poets, painters, and photographers ever since.

Included here is a small sampling of the commonwealth's many covered bridges now preserved only as photographs or memories. The Maury River Covered Bridge in Lexington was among the best known. It was erected in 1870 and gone by the 1950s. The Rock Castle Creek Covered Bridge in Patrick County was probably erected in the early part of the 20th century and disappeared in the 1950s. Patrick County, however, preserves two covered bridges: the Jack's Creek Covered Bridge and the Bob White Covered Bridge. The Mill Creek Covered Bridge in Shenandoah County was a casualty of the 1940s. Otter Creek's vine-covered span in Campbell County also disappeared in the 1940s. Rockbridge County's 1878 covered bridge across Buffalo Creek was replaced by a modern structure in 1940 and razed five years later. Carroll County's covered bridge across Little Reed Island Creek also stood beside its concrete replacement for five years but was swept away in a 1940s flood. Floods have been particularly hard on covered bridges; the lightweight, flat-sided structures can barely withstand raging waters. A covered bridge in Campbell County was lost to flooding as late as the 1990s.

MAURY RIVER COVERED BRIDGE,
Lexington
Built 1870; replaced 1935, demolished 1944
(Photograph: Library of Virginia)

ROCK CASTLE CREEK COVERED BRIDGE,
Patrick County
Built early 20th century; demolished 1950s
(Photograph: Library of Virginia)

MILL CREEK COVERED BRIDGE, Shenandoah County
Built late 19th century; demolished 1940s
(Photograph: Library of Virginia)

OTTER CREEK COVERED BRIDGE, Campbell County
Built late 19th century; demolished 1940s
(Photograph: Library of Virginia)

BUFFALO CREEK COVERED BRIDGE, Buffalo Forge, Rockbridge County
Built 1878; replaced 1940, demolished 1945
(Photograph: Library of Virginia)

LITTLE REED ISLAND COVERED BRIDGE, Carroll County
Built late 19th century; destroyed by flood 1940s
(Photograph: Library of Virginia)

VIRGINIA HALL, VIRGINIA STATE UNIVERSITY, Ettrick, Chesterfield County
Built 1883–88; demolished 1937

Founded in 1882, Virginia State University is the nation's oldest state-supported land grant college for African-Americans. Originally called the Virginia Normal and Collegiate Institute, the school was a creation of the Readjuster Party, led by William Mahone, which pledged to have the commonwealth establish an institution of higher learning for former slaves and their descendants. Virginia Hall, its first building, was a testament to the seriousness of the state's commitment to the program.

Designed by Harrison Waite, a native of western Virginia, this four-and-a-half-story, multisectional behemoth was Virginia's largest collegiate building and housed the entire school—dormitories, classrooms, offices, and laboratories. It was decked out in the then-fashionable Second Empire style, with mansard roofs and a central, towering, pyramidal cupola. It was outfitted in the most modern manner, with fireproof stairways, elevators, lavatories, baths, water closets, steam radiation heat, and the "Edison incandescent electric light system." Crowning a bluff above the Appomattox River, Virginia Hall was a landmark conspicuous from downtown Petersburg. Its general form and character were consistent with the structures being built for the many newly established land grant colleges around the country.

One can scarcely believe that such an enormous and solid facility could be vulnerable to replacement, but in 1937 an engineering report found that it had been constructed on inadequate footings and required either prohibitively expensive stabilization or demolition. The latter path was chosen, making way for the Charles M. Robinson–designed campus that we see today. (Photograph: Virginia Historical Society)
CCL and RDW, Jr.

HAYES HALL, VIRGINIA COLLEGE AND VIRGINIA SEMINARY, DeWitt Street, Lynchburg
Built 1888; demolished 1988

The institution now known as Virginia College and Virginia Seminary was authorized in 1886 at the nineteenth session of the Virginia Baptist State Convention, held in Lynchburg's First Baptist Church. First known as the Lynchburg Baptist Seminary, it was one of several Virginia schools of higher education founded in the late 19th century to bring the state's African-Americans into the mainstream of society. Despite several name changes, it remains the oldest institution of higher learning in the Lynchburg area. The school originally espoused the self-help educational principles advocated for African-Americans by Booker T. Washington. Virginia College and Virginia Seminary was a pioneer in the field of African-American education, placing emphasis on the training of teachers and ministers for work within the African-American community. Shown here is its first brick building, begun in 1888, a large and imposing structure in the Second Empire style containing classrooms, a recitation hall, and dormitories. The building was later named Hayes Hall in honor of Gregory Willis Hayes, the institution's second president.

Though it was the college's architectural centerpiece, Hayes Hall fell into disrepair in the mid-1970s and was later abandoned. Efforts to raise money for its restoration were unsuccessful, and the deteriorated building was demolished in 1988. (Photograph: Virginia Department of Historic Resources)

GENERAL HOSPITAL #43, Hampton
Built 1885; demolished 1961

This hospital was constructed as part of the Southern Branch of the National Home for Disabled Volunteer Soldiers; the complex was established on the grounds of the former Chesapeake Female College (q.v.) in Hampton. The building was oriented to enjoy a view of Hampton Roads and sited within an attractively landscaped complex. At the core of the hospital was a three-story, hipped-roof building. Long, galleried barracks wings, connected to the core section by breezeways, extended east and west and terminated in small towers. The innumerable porches enabled patients to enjoy fresh air and sunshine, which were thought to be beneficial to recovery. The complex was eventually absorbed into the Veterans Administration. From 1938 until its demolition in 1961, the hospital served as an administration building. (Photograph: Virginia Historical Society)
MRH

ARMORY, CITY OFFICE, AND MARKET BUILDING,
City Hall Avenue between Brewer and Monticello Streets, Norfolk
Built 1890; market sheds demolished 1923, armory building demolished 1955

This handsome Romanesque edifice was erected in 1890; two long projecting sheds were added to the north end of the building sometime after 1900. The armory was a multipurpose facility, housing not only offices for various governmental and social service organizations but also a large civic auditorium that was a venue for banquets, concerts, and military tattoos. The sheds accommodated Norfolk's market, which had outgrown its previous address nearer the water. In 1923, the market sheds were demolished and a "state-of-the-art" stone Art Deco market building constructed north of the armory. The building suffered partial demolition when ornamental features that were deemed unsound were removed; total demolition of both the armory and the 1923 market occurred in 1955. A public referendum had been launched in an unsuccessful effort to save the complex. It was replaced by speculative office buildings, which have since been demolished to make way for the MacArthur Center Shopping Mall. (Photograph: William Stewart, *History of Norfolk County Virginia and its Representative Citizens*, 1902)
MRH

DANVILLE MILITARY INSTITUTE, southwest corner of Kemper Road at South Main Street, Danville
Built 1890; demolished 1974

Danville Military Institute (DMI) was modeled after Virginia Military Institute, both architecturally and programmatically. As at VMI, the Gothic Revival style was appropriately and effectively used at Danville to simulate a medieval castle where young warriors were housed. This preparatory school, however, never enjoyed the financial stability of the state-supported college. The school traced its origins to the Civil War, when Danville Male Academy, under the direction of a VMI graduate, became the Danville Military Institute. It was soon defunct, but in 1890 a second Male Academy in Danville was transformed into a military school, and the name Danville Military Institute was revived, again by a VMI graduate. Inspired, it is said, by VMI's Jackson Hall, DMI was roughly I-shaped; it was designed by the Norfolk-based architect George C. Moser. Among the early instructors at the new DMI was George C. Marshall. Financial problems closed the school in 1906 and 1918. In 1933 the Presbyterian Church assumed control of DMI and discontinued the military tradition there. The school was closed and vacant during World War II, when its buildings housed German prisoners of war. After the war, the campus was adapted and expanded to house the Danville Technical Institute as well as a Danville satellite of Virginia Polytechnic Institute. By 1968, both schools had been absorbed into the commonwealth's community college system as Danville Community College (DCC). In 1974, DCC demolished this building and an accessory structure, the DMI superintendent's quarters and dining room, designed by Danville architect E. R. James and built in 1922. (Photograph: *Art Work of Lynchburg and Danville, Virginia*, 1903)
GRG, WMSR

RANDOLPH-MACON ACADEMY, Front Royal
Built 1892; burned 1927

Founded in 1892, Randolph-Macon Academy began as a preparatory school in the former Randolph-Macon system of colleges and academies. The system was established by the Methodist Church in 1890 and at one time embraced three preparatory schools and two colleges. The Front Royal school initially offered military training for males. The main academy building, completed in 1892, was a remarkably romantic, castle-like structure in the then-fashionable Romanesque Revival style. It was dramatically sited on a hill overlooking Front Royal, the same hill on which Stonewall Jackson had positioned his cannons during the

Civil War battle of Front Royal. The building's architect likely was William M. Poindexter of Washington, DC, who also designed the 1889 Randolph-Macon Academy building in Bedford County and the grand, Queen Anne–style main building of Lynchburg's Randolph-Macon Woman's College, begun in 1891. The Front Royal structure was outfitted with finely appointed dormitories, classrooms, study halls, a social hall, and other school facilities. The huge building, appearing so solid and enduring, proved to be far from permanent when it was completely destroyed by fire on 10 January 1927, only thirty-five years after completion. Following the fire, students were housed in local homes; classes were conducted in a Methodist church until a new fireproof building was completed on the site. Sonner-Payne Hall, the Georgian-style replacement structure, continues to serve as Randolph-Macon's main building. (Photograph: Virginia Historical Society)

CLIFTON FORGE YMCA, Ridgeway Street, Clifton Forge, Alleghany County
Built 1893; demolished early 20th century

This fashionable, Queen Anne–style structure, with a picturesque profile and shingled surfaces, was erected to accommodate the increased traffic to Clifton Forge that followed its virtual creation by the Chesapeake and Ohio Railway Company in 1882. The building stood as a symbol of the progressiveness and promise of the new railway center. The C&O had made the town a division point on the line, constructing track yards and shops there. Before that date, Clifton Forge had been the village of Williamson, named after the family that owned much of its land. Like many places in the Valley and farther west, in 1890 and 1891 the town enjoyed a boom, enhanced by both the railroad activity and the revival of the local iron industry that had given Clifton Forge its name. With the Panic of 1893, however, the bottom fell out of the local land market. Clifton Forge would continue to grow, but at a far slower pace than anticipated; its first YMCA was doomed to a short life. (Photograph: Alleghany Historical Society)

SEABOARD MARKET AND ARMORY, corner of County and South Streets, Portsmouth
Built 1893; demolished 1945

In the late 19th century, Portsmouth's market ran down the center of Crawford Street for an entire block. The Seaboard Railroad, in exchange for a right-of-way in the center of Crawford Street, built this imposing Romanesque Revival building for the city of Portsmouth in 1893. Designed by the Norfolk firm of Carpenter and Peebles, the armory and market stood like a fortress at the corner of South and County Streets until 1945. The principal elevations were given large arched openings at the street level, with diminished, arched fenestration above. Corner towers with slit windows and a heavy use of crenelation, combined with the sheer mass and bulk of the building, reinforced its role as an armory that housed the Grimes Battery. The Seaboard Market and Armory served almost as a symbol of its era, a time when many Virginia cities built an imposing armory as part of the downtown fabric. (Photograph: William Stewart, *History of Norfolk County Virginia and its Representative Citizens*, 1902)
MRH

UNITED STATES POST OFFICE, Church Avenue at First Street, Roanoke
Begun 1893; demolished ca. 1933

In the aftermath of the Civil War, Virginia was awarded a series of federal post offices and courthouses designed in Washington, DC, by the supervising architect of the treasury and built by his office. From 1876 through 1883 the position was held by James G. Hill, who designed the US Post Office and Federal Building in Danville in 1881 (q.v.). From 1893 to early 1895 Jeremiah O'Rourke held the title; he designed the building pictured here. O'Rourke's signed drawings for the Roanoke post office, like Hill's for Danville, are preserved in the National Archives. .

In his private practice O'Rourke, an Irish architect who immigrated to Newark, NJ, in 1856, produced a number of Roman Catholic church designs, often working as a creative medievalist. Toward the end of the 19th century he found inspiration in the Romanesque designs of Henry Hobson Richardson. For the Roanoke post office, O'Rourke conceived a building that as drawn seems Richardsonian; it lies close to the ground, anchored by broad arches and the weight of massive stonework; a vertical lift is provided by its tall tower. As constructed, however, with a proliferation of light stone trim, this polychrome building seemed more Victorian Gothic than medieval. Even the "Romanesque" arches, slightly pointed at the apex, appeared to soar.

On its completion, this turreted and gargoyled structure may have seemed as enduring as a medieval castle or cathedral. Tastes would soon change, however. O'Rourke signed his drawings for Roanoke on 8 July 1893; that summer, in Chicago, the World's Columbian Exposition initiated a revival of Renaissance-style architecture that would make medievalist design seem passé rather than enduring and would doom the Roanoke post office to a short existence of only four decades. (Photograph: William McCauley, *History of Roanoke County, Salem, Roanoke City, Virginia*, 1902)

ARLINGTON COUNTY COURTHOUSE, Arlington
Built 1898, 1960, enlarged 1929, 1950; demolished 1959, 1997

In 1896, the voters of Alexandria County (renamed Arlington County in 1920) decided to move their courthouse from the city of Alexandria to Fort Myer Heights. Architect A. Groenner designed a symmetrical, three-story Romanesque structure with a central tower that was typical of many public buildings erected during the Victorian period. The building, dedicated in 1898, was expanded by the addition of a south wing (1929) and a north wing (1950) to meet the needs of a burgeoning population.

In 1959, the 1898 structure (but not the wings) was demolished to make room for a new central block. This second courthouse was designed by John M. Walton and Associates with Albert D. Lueders. It combined vestiges of the Moderne, Art Deco, and International styles; decorative elements were concentrated around the massive entrance. This building, dated not only by its style but also by its usefulness, was demolished in 1997 after only thirty-seven years. The older wings were leveled as well. The short history of the 1960 building illustrates the rapidity with which court buildings can become outmoded and be replaced to serve the needs of justice in a society that is growing and changing at an ever-increasing pace. (Photographs: Arlington County Historical Society)
JOP, MTP

SURRY COUNTY COURTHOUSE, Route 10, Surry
Built 1907; burned 1922

After its 1895 Victorian courthouse was destroyed by fire in 1906, Surry County erected this two-story brick building, with a six-column Ionic portico with full entablature, a shallow parapet, a cupola, and round-arched windows on the second story. So bold a use of classical forms was typical of public architecture in the Beaux Arts tradition. The courthouse bore a close resemblance to the United States Post Office and Courthouse being built in Charlottesville at precisely the same time. The structure stood for only fifteen years, after which it too went up in flames, bringing to four the number of Surry courthouses lost to fire. The county decided to model its new courthouse (completed in 1923) on the newly lost building, utilizing the same footprint and even some of the salvaged brick. The cupola was eliminated to cut costs. (Photograph: Valentine Museum)
JOP, MTP

WILLIAMSBURG–JAMES CITY, COURTHOUSE, Francis Street at South England Street, Williamsburg
Built 1932; demolished ca. 1984

The creation of Colonial Williamsburg at the core of an existing 20th-century town required complex negotiations, as well as property purchases on a remarkable scale. In 1930, the city and James City County still used the 1770 courthouse, which the community had restored after a fire in 1911.

The John D. Rockefeller, Jr.–backed museum acquired the old

courthouse in exchange for building a more capacious one south of Market Square in 1932. Perry, Shaw, and Hepburn designed the new courthouse as a five-part ensemble with a Georgian, houselike central block. Placing the main courtroom in a high second story created a distinctive piano nobile elevation slightly reminiscent of Stratford Hall. The designers emphasized the secondary quality of the lower story by borrowing the design of a gauged-brick door surround from the 1748 Secretary's Office and the 1751 Carter's Grove, pushing its pediment up through the belt course.

An essential design objective was to provide space for municipal offices as well as courtrooms while minimizing the building's presence when viewed from Market Square. The architects handled this by treating the north end as a small, loggia-fronted colonial courthouse of the King William and Hanover County variety. (They rendered this and other elements in a pre-Revolutionary idiom, unlike Merchants Square, which generally draws for inspiration on later buildings.)

The north building was also designed to protect archaeological remains of the Francis Street house occupied by Robert Carter Nicholas and, later, by President John Tyler. The sizable office and laundry that flanked the Nicholas-Tyler house were reconstructed as part of the 1932 civic complex. In one of the more esoteric chapters of Williamsburg's building history, the outbuildings were reconstructed in brick to satisfy city requirements and subsequently cased with wood. These outbuildings remain, but the courthouse was demolished after its functions moved to a new building in 1969. Following the long tradition of scavenging architectural elements, residents reused the dormers and interior woodwork in several Williamsburg and Charles City houses. The reconstruction of the Nicholas-Tyler house has yet to take place. (Photograph: Colonial Williamsburg Foundation)
EAC

EASTERN SHORE CHAPEL, London Bridge vicinity, Virginia Beach
Built 1755; dismantled 1952

The Anglican Church was the government-established religion in colonial Virginia. Thus, compared to other colonies, Virginia had an unusually large number of houses of worship serving this denomination. As many as three hundred Anglican churches may have been erected in Virginia during colonial times. Of that number some fifty remain, more than in any other state. Though the majority of the commonwealth's vanished colonial churches disappeared in the years following the 1784 act disestablishing the Anglican Church, Eastern Shore Chapel was lost through unusual circumstances in 1952.

Taking its name from its location near the Atlantic coastline, or eastern shore (not the Eastern Shore peninsula), this diminutive house of worship, only twenty-five by thirty-five feet, was commissioned by the vestry of Lynnhaven Parish in 1754 as a successor to two earlier parish churches. Typical of Virginia's simpler colonial churches, Eastern Shore Chapel had a gable roof skirted by modillion cornices. The side walls featured round-top windows with gauged-brick arches, which served to distinguish small churches from domestic architecture. In the late 19th century the original crown glass windows were replaced with stained glass, and the modillion cornices were replaced with Italianate bracketed cornices. A small belfry was added over the front gable.

The construction of the Oceana Naval Air Station in the decade after World War II required the confiscation of the Eastern Shore Chapel tract. Recognizing the historic importance of the venerable building, the congregation proposed dismantling its brick walls and rebuilding them a short distance from the original location. The church was taken down in 1952, but the bricks were found to be unusable; the replacement church, completed in 1954 on Eastern Shore Chapel Road, is an entirely new building. Only selected remnants of interior fabric, including the gallery steps, the gallery pew, and the stained glass window above the entrance, were reused in the new building. Some of the old bricks were put down to make a walkway. (Photograph: Virginia Historical Society)

CHAPTER III

Lost Religious Architecture

A history of religious architecture in the commonwealth would be difficult to compile without reference to the lost buildings because so many Virginia churches and synagogues have been destroyed during the past four centuries. The losses began early, in the colonial period. Because the Anglican faith was government supported, as many as three hundred Anglican churches may have been erected in colonial Virginia. Today, however, only about fifty remain. Buildings were abandoned when populations shifted and parish lines were redrawn, as well as in the aftermath of a 1784 act disestablishing the Anglican Church. Few survived as long as did the Eastern Shore Chapel (Virginia Beach, 1755), which was lost in 1952. The destruction of church buildings continued through the 19th century. Gone today are soaring urban Gothic churches that date to that period, such as Richmond's Pace Memorial Methodist Church (1886) and Grace Street Presbyterian Church (1872), the spire of which rose 210 feet.

The religious landscape of Virginia has been in constant flux. Old buildings have been destroyed because congregations have disassembled, built new structures on the same site, or relocated entirely. New buildings have appeared not only with the rebuildings and relocations, but also when entirely new congregations have formed. One example of a building that fell victim to the dwindling size of its congregation is Aetz Chayim Synagogue (Danville, 1912). This was the center of the city's Orthodox Jewish community until the early 1980s, when the remaining members chose to desanctify their house of worship; it was pulled down in 1986. An example of a congregation that rebuilt because the existing structure no longer seemed large enough is the First African Baptist Church of Richmond (ca. 1780); in 1874 the national press reported that its members were "preparing to demolish and rebuild their ancient house of worship." An example of a building lost because it was abandoned by its congregation is Christ Episcopal Church in Norfolk (1828). In 1910 its members joined with those of St. Luke's Church to build a stately new structure in a more fashionable neighborhood. A half-century later, the old church was demolished by the Norfolk Redevelopment and Housing Authority despite the building's inclusion on the Virginia Landmarks Register and the National Register of Historic Places.

The congregation of Norfolk's Christ Church is but one of many in Virginia that have relocated, causing the loss of one building and the creation of another. Such shifts generally occurred in urban areas, where congregations moved from one neighborhood to another. Second Baptist Church of Richmond moved in 1841 to a new location at Main and Sixth Streets that was "free from the many disadvantages" of the previous site. In the process its members built a structure that the leadership considered not only "capacious, but indeed an ornament to the city." The new church was itself demolished in 1906, when the congregation built a newer church. The congregation of Richmond's First Presbyterian Church, organized in 1812, has met in five buildings as it repeatedly changed locations. As with other congregations in Richmond, the path of the First Presbyterian buildings followed the westward growth of the city.

New congregations have formed almost routinely in Virginia, in the process changing the religious landscape. In the colonial era the westward settlement of the region brought new parishes, new congregations, and new church buildings. Once the commonwealth was settled, new congregations emerged primarily in the cities. For example, the congregation of All Saints Episcopal Church in Richmond grew out of that of Monumental Church in 1883. (The first two buildings erected for the new All Saints congregation no longer survive.) Such moves have not always been amicable. Second Baptist Church in Richmond formed in 1820 from Richmond Baptist Church (later renamed First Baptist Church); a dispute over the propriety of conducting a school for children in the church gallery prompted creation of the new church by the school's promoters. (Neither the Richmond Baptist Church building nor the new structure erected for Second Baptist survives.) The 1850 minutes of Lynchburg's Third Street Methodist Church state that "Fifty-six members have withdrawn from this church to build one up on the hill to serve the devil in." Those members formed the Court Street Methodist Church. (Neither the Court Street Methodist Church nor the Third Street Methodist

Church's newer building, which was erected ten years later, survives.)

As to the style of church architecture in Virginia, tastes changed in the different time periods, as happened with probably all building types. Minutes recorded in 1852 by the congregation of Richmond's First Presbyterian Church (1852–53) called for "an edifice corresponding in Architectural taste and beauty with others in the City, and in which the worship of God could be celebrated by his people with more comfort and convenience." In the colonial period, prevailing taste called for simple Georgian classicism. Following the turn of the century, a more archaeologically accurate variation of classical architecture was favored. Some Baptist congregations in antebellum Richmond were even influenced stylistically by one another; they built fairly similar Classical Revival structures in order to "correspond . . . with others in the city." But the 19th century saw

multiple styles that evoked a variety of historic images. To cite two unusual examples, Lexington's Baptist Church (1879) was an eclectic combination of English Tudor and Queen Anne details. Zion Baptist Church in Albemarle County (1871) was an octagon; the shape of this simple country building recalled the earlier and more sophisticated Monumental Church in Richmond.

Like public buildings, churches are constantly pressed by changing needs, changing tastes, and changing demographics. Today, as earlier, congregations continue to outgrow their buildings or diminish in number and require more modest quarters. Congregations continue to relocate and require new buildings in new locations, leaving the future of their former houses of worship to fate. Their loss has been a particularly poignant erosion of Virginia's architectural legacy.

PAYNE'S CHURCH,
Ox Road, Fairfax County
Built 1766–68; demolished by
Union soldiers 1862

Payne's Church, the appearance of which is known only through this dim photograph, was one of only two buildings whose designs can be solidly attributed to John Ariss, a mysterious figure who is today known because Thomas Tileston Waterman, in his 1945 book *The Mansions of Virginia*, attributed to him many of the great houses built in Virginia between 1750 and 1770.

Ariss, born in Westmoreland County, Virginia, around 1725, was educated both in the colonies and in England; in 1751 he advertised in the *Maryland Gazette* as having arrived "Lately from Great Britain" and being familiar with English architectural pattern books. His first known commission of signifi-

cance was awarded in 1752 for Trinity Church in Charles County, Maryland; the brick building was to be 55 feet long by 30 feet wide, with a 22½-by-30-foot wing on the north. Trinity Church was torn down in 1786 by the parish and rebuilt in a different manner on the same foundations. Only part of the interior woodwork of Ariss's 1752 church survives today.

Between 1749 and 1759 John Ariss trained nine apprentices. In 1762 he was in Richmond County; in 1764 he moved to Fauquier County. In 1766 he submitted a plan and estimate for Payne's Church in Fairfax County. Payne's Church was similar in size to Trinity Church: 53½ feet long by 30 feet wide. It was built by Truro Parish churchwarden Edward Payne, who was paid 579 pounds of Virginia currency for superintending the building of a church that over time took his name.

John Ariss died in 1799 in what is today Jefferson County, West Virginia. He left his entire estate to his wife, Elizabeth; at her death there were three sales, beginning in 1808. Inventoried at that time were carpenter's tools and drawing instruments. (Photograph: Fairfax County Public Library)
SATJ

FIRST AFRICAN BAPTIST CHURCH,
corner of College and Broad Streets, Richmond
Built ca. 1780, with additions in 1803 and 1827; demolished
1876

In 1874, a writer for *Harper's Weekly* lamented: "Another relic from the olden time is about to disappear from the face of the earth. The members of the First African Baptist Church, Richmond, Virginia, with true American lack of veneration for old things and old buildings, are preparing to demolish and re-build their ancient house of worship, the oldest colored church in America, if not the world."

First African Baptist was certainly the oldest African-American congregation in Richmond, but the architectural "relic" that housed the congregation and dated to the Revolutionary War era initially belonged to a predominantly white congregation, First Baptist (originally called Richmond Baptist). From an early date First Baptist had welcomed African-Americans, though it relegated them to the galleries during services. By 1841 the African-American congregants (1,700) so outnumbered the white members (387) that the latter voted to leave the extant structure and build a new one at the corner of Broad and Twelfth Streets. (That new building, by Thomas U. Walter, still stands.) The older structure was then sold to the African-American members of the congregation for the sizable sum of sixty-five hundred dollars.

The "relic from the olden time" had a storied history. During the 1811 theater fire (a half-block away), it was used to shelter the dead and dying. As the largest gathering space in Richmond outside of the Capitol, it was the site of political gatherings, including debates surrounding the 1829 Virginia Constitutional Convention, Jefferson Davis's last speech as president of the Confederate States of America, and the first Republican convention in Virginia, which convened in 1865.

As was typical of most early-19th-century Protestant churches, the building began life as an auditorium-style preaching barn, thirty-eight by sixty feet. Then wings were added to it, much in the same manner that nearby St. John's Church, the site of Patrick Henry's famous "liberty or death" speech, was dramatically altered. The congregation of the First African Baptist Church more than doubled its size in the three decades following the church's inception. In the 1870s, under the direction of Rev. James Holmes and with nearly four thousand communicants, it was one of the largest congregations in the South. The old building, despite its additions, no longer seemed adequate. "The plans for the new building which is to rise on its site [were] already in the hands of the builder" in 1876; it was completed the next year. The replacement structure is today owned by the Medical College of Virginia (part of Virginia Commonwealth University), which purchased it in 1955. In that year the First African Baptist congregation moved to 2700 Hanes Avenue. (Photograph: Valentine Museum; Image: Virginia Historical Society)

NORFOLK PRESBYTERIAN CHURCH, Catherine (now Bank) and Charlotte Streets, Norfolk
Built 1802; demolished ca. 1900?

This early building housed the congregation of what was the Norfolk area's mother church of Presbyterianism. Previously, local Presbyterians had met in private homes. In 1800 they launched a subscription drive for the construction of a church building; eighty-seven residents contributed. Completed two years later, the brick, gable-fronted structure was particularly notable for its bell tower, which was the first of its kind on a Norfolk church. The building was often referred to as the Bell Church. In the 1830s the congregation divided, and a large contingent built Second Presbyterian Church on Church Street. In 1837, the congregations reunited to form First Presbyterian Church at the new location; the Bell Church was closed. The congregation later moved to a location in the fashionable Ghent neighborhood, into a building designed by Ferguson, Calrow, and Taylor. The Bell Church was used by other congregations until it was demolished. (Photograph: Virginia Historical Society)
MRH

BETH SHALOME SYNAGOGUE, Mayo Street
(east side) north of Franklin Street, Richmond
Built 1822; demolished 1934

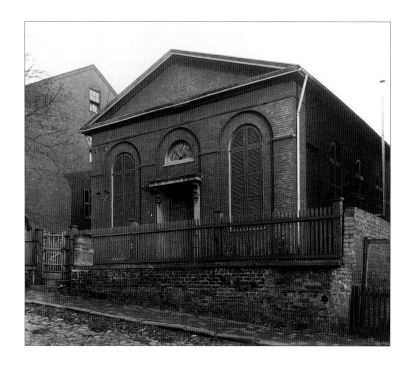

Beth Shalome, the sixth-oldest Jewish congregation in the United States, was founded in 1789. It worshipped initially in a private home on Nineteenth Street before moving its services in 1811 to a small brick structure on the northwest corner of Nineteenth and Cary Streets. That building was undermined by excavations for the neighboring Union Hotel (q.v.) and abandoned in 1817. A lot on Mayo Street was purchased in 1818, and the congregation consecrated a new building there in 1822. The Mayo Street Synagogue (Beth Shalome) was the first structure consecrated as a synagogue in Virginia.

No genre of synagogue architecture was established in early America; most Jewish houses of worship looked much like any Christian church. The Mayo Street building was a modest one-story brick structure with tall, arched windows and an unadorned pediment on its façade. The interior, decorated in white and gold, was orthodox in orientation. The pews ran lengthwise, and a reading platform was at the center of the room. The ark and pulpit were placed at one end of the sanctuary. A gallery was provided for the female members of the congregation.

Congregation Beth Shalome sold the building to the Sir Moses Montefiore congregation in 1891 and worshipped in rented quarters until 1898, when Beth Shalome merged with Beth Ahabah and used the latter's facility (q.v.). (Photograph: Valentine Museum)
SSB

TABB STREET PRESBYTERIAN CHURCH,
Tabb Street, Petersburg
Built 1823; burned 1841

Although there had been Scots Presbyterians in Petersburg since the town was laid out, and despite attempts to organize a church since the Rev. Samuel Davies's visits between 1746 and 1750, it was not until 1813 that the Rev. Benjamin Holt Rice was able to establish a congregation in Petersburg. This church was completed on Tabb Street in 1815. It was an unadorned, two-story brick building, gable-fronted, with an elliptical fanlight above a broad front door. After an extremely successful revival in 1822, a cornerstone was laid for a new church (illustrated here) on the south side of Tabb Street to serve the rapidly growing congregation.

The new church was completed in 1823 and described in a local newspaper as the most beautiful in town. The building was sixty-four feet wide, seventy-eight feet deep, and thirty feet high at the eaves. Judging from the first Mutual Assurance Society of Virginia insurance policy, the façade was articulated, and a seventeen-foot-wide, three-story steeple projected forward about three feet. The church entrances flanked the tower. As the churchgoer entered the sanctuary, however, he or she was facing the congregation; the pulpit was placed in the center, against the steeple tower, and reached by steps on either side. A pyramidal chandelier with crystal pendants hung from the ceiling.

The drawing by William S. Simpson shown here is thought to be the only known image of the second Tabb Street Presbyterian Church. Instead of an accurate representation of the building, however, this drawing appears to be an 1827 proposal for improvements that would have included a portico with Corinthian columns and a much taller, octagonal steeple. Simpson seems to have been suggesting closing the flanking doors, providing a much wider central doorway, making the lower two sections of the tower octagonal, and surmounting those sections with massive scrolls, an octagon, a dome, another octagon, and a steeple, in that order. Simpson's proposals, however, were never put into effect.

On the morning of 7 November 1841, fire broke out in the stables of Dr. Walter F. Jones, who lived immediately to the west of the church. The blaze spread eventually to the church, burning it to the ground. The steeple was described as looking "like a solid coal of fire before it tottered and fell to the ground." The following day, a subscription was begun for a replacement, resulting in the present church designed by Thomas U. Walter. (Image: Virginia Historical Society)
RDW, Jr.

CHRIST EPISCOPAL CHURCH, block bounded by East Jefferson,
Water Street, Second Street, NW, and First Street, Charlottesville
Built 1824–26; demolished 1895

Christ Episcopal was the first church in Charlottesville. As early as 1857 Bishop William Meade attributed its design to Thomas Jefferson; more likely, it was built over time by several Jefferson builders. A letter written by the rector of Fredericksville Parish in 1824 suggests that John M. Perry was the builder. In 1838 William B. Phillips enclosed the churchyard with a brick wall costing five hundred dollars. In 1853, George Wilson Spooner, Jr., attached a *distyle-in-muris* façade to the building similar to the one added that same year to the 1834 St. Thomas's Church in Orange. Originally, the front of the church simply had two doors in a plain brick façade, similar to Phillips's Christ Church in Glendower (which still stands in southern Albemarle County). Five years later a chancel with cruciform wings was added, and William A. Pratt submitted to the vestry his drawings for a new steeple; it was built but collapsed in a windstorm eleven years later. In 1873 a belfry was added to the roof and a new bell installed. The building was razed by Spooner's son to make way for the present stone church, but the original, thirty-five-foot-wide stone foundation still exists within the cellar. (Photograph: Manuscript Print Collection, Special Collections Department, University of Virginia Library)
KEL

CHRIST EPISCOPAL CHURCH, East Freemason Street at Cumberland Street, Norfolk
Built 1828; demolished 1973

A remnant of antebellum Norfolk, Christ Church replaced an earlier church on the same site that was destroyed by fire. With its temple form and Tuscan portico *in muris*, the building had a strong but coincidental resemblance to Christ Church in Charlottesville (q.v.). Levi Swain, who also designed the Capitol Square Bell Tower in Richmond, was the church's architect. Thomas Williamson, a parishioner and amateur designer, assisted him.

The parish traced its origins to Elizabeth River Parish, which constructed its first church circa 1637. The building pictured here served the Episcopalians until 1910, when the parish moved to a new location and eventually combined with St. Luke's Church in the stately Gothic Revival edifice on Olney Road. A Greek Orthodox congregation then worshipped in Swain's building for a number of years. Between 1955 and 1960 it served as one of the numerous "heavens" of the flamboyant African-American religious leader Sweet Daddy Grace. It was during this time that the exterior columns were patriotically painted red, white, and blue. The Norfolk Redevelopment and Housing Authority purchased the church in 1960 as part of the city's massive urban renewal program. Despite its being listed on both the Virginia Landmarks Register and the National Register of Historic Places, the authority turned a deaf ear to preservation interests and demolished the building in 1973. Although the church had been declared structurally unsound, the nave's floor did not give when a bulldozer drove across it. (Photograph: William Edmund Barrett for Virginia Department of Historic Resources)

ST. JAMES'S EPISCOPAL CHURCH, Fifth and Marshall Streets, Richmond
Built 1837–40, 1878; demolished 1912

The first St. James's Church in Richmond was designed largely by its vestry, which in 1837 agreed upon a floor plan. Inspiration was taken from a nearby landmark, Robert Mills's Monumental Church. The floor plan was not the long and narrow basilica type more routinely chosen but rather was almost square, akin to the wide plan of the Mills building. St. James's was the first Episcopal house of worship erected on Shockoe Hill in the quarter-century that had passed since Monumental Church was built. Construction was begun in 1838 by a little-known figure, Joseph Boyd, who apparently served as contractor; the estimate submitted by Otis Manson, the experienced architect who designed the elegant Union Hotel (q.v.), was rejected, probably on the basis of cost. In these years the congregation's efforts at fund-raising were faltering. In 1840 the vestry corresponded with a leading national architect, William Strickland of Philadelphia; perhaps even then it was apparent to many that the exterior of the church would need embellishment. In 1878 the rear wall was removed to expand the chancel, the side windows were enlarged, and the temple portico pictured here was added to the Fifth Street façade by Richmond architect Marion J. Dimmock. These changes transformed what had been a simplistic exterior into a more overtly Classical Revival one akin to those of the several Greek and Roman Revival churches that had been erected in the city at midcentury, mostly by Baptist congregations. The Doric columns of the portico each rested on a separate, raised pedestal; the building stood too low to the ground to allow a more traditional treatment.

Under its articles of incorporation, St. James's Church was to be demolished should the congregation move; thus a place of worship would not be desecrated by commercial use. The building was duly demolished in 1912, when the congregation moved to a new church on West Franklin Street, an imposing Georgian Revival edifice designed by Noland & Baskervill. (Photograph: Virginia Historical Society)
WMSR, DRT

HIGH STREET PRESBYTERIAN CHURCH, south side of High Street between Market and Davis Streets, Petersburg
Built 1839; demolished 1869

In 1837, the former minister of Tabb Street Presbyterian Church, Dr. William Swan Plumer, was instrumental in separating the Presbyterian Church in the US into two assemblies, the Old School and the New School Assemblies, in order to resolve problems caused by the 1801 Union Plan of cooperation between the Congregational and Presbyterian Churches. A minority at Tabb Street Presbyterian Church decided to align themselves with the New School Assembly, withdrew, and organized the High Street Presbyterian Church. In 1839, they recruited as their pastor a Congregationalist minister from New England, the Rev. Abner J. Leavenworth, who was then conducting a school in Warrenton. Under his energetic leadership, the congregation quickly completed its new church. Following the Civil War, Leavenworth was a primary participant in the establishment of both the Petersburg and the statewide public school systems.

High Street Presbyterian Church was a jewel, judging from the 1842 drawings of William S. Simpson, one of which is pictured here. Constructed on the former site of the dwellings and shops of the carriage-builder Christopher F. Jones, on the south side of High Street, the front of the brick church was articulated as a classical temple front, with a pediment over a full entablature supported by four brick pilasters. Each end bay contained a large blank window capped by a stone lintel and filled with unplastered brick. The center bay, reached by stone steps, was pulled back beneath the entablature to protect a large and handsome doorway in the Greek Revival manner. The pediment also was faced with unplastered brickwork. The three-part tower above the central bay was the crowning glory of the church. Its upper entablature was surmounted by scrollwork in the Greek Revival manner.

Given the timing of the construction of this church and its considerable similarity to Calvin Pollard's St. Paul's Church on Sycamore Street, one has to suspect here the hand of Pollard and/or James Berrian, who were concurrently working on the courthouse, St. Paul's Church, and the Exchange Building, all in Petersburg.

Soon after the departure of Reverend Leavenworth, the New School congregation was reabsorbed into Tabb Street, but in 1851 a decision was made to create a new congregation, Second Presbyterian, which occupied the old High Street structure. On the eve of the Civil War, however, the new congregation undertook the construction of a new church, in the Gothic style, on Washington Street. The High Street edifice was used during the war as a shot tower and was replaced in 1869 by a row of three-story brick dwellings known as Baltimore Row. (Image: Virginia Historical Society)
RDW, Jr.

SECOND BAPTIST CHURCH,
Main and Sixth Streets, Richmond
Built 1840–42; demolished 1906

A dispute over the propriety of conducting a school for children in the gallery of the Richmond Baptist Church led the school's promoters to form the Second Baptist Church in 1820. Growth of both the parent (renamed First) and the daughter churches led to the simultaneous construction of new buildings designed by the accomplished Philadelphia architect Thomas U. Walter. First Baptist Church relocated to H (Broad) and Twelfth Streets; Second Baptist to Main and Sixth. First Baptist Church spent $40,222 on its building project; Second Baptist, $40,186. First Baptist Church occupied its new facilities on 17 October 1841; Second Baptist, on 6 January 1842. Second Baptist Church had reported to the Dover Baptist Association the preceding September, "The church early last spring vacated the M. H. [Meeting House] which we have occupied for so many years, and removed to the basement of the new house, which we have at great cost & personal sacrifice now nearly completed—in this change we have secured a location free from the many disadvantages of our present location & a house which is not [only] capacious, but indeed an ornament to the city."

The Second Baptist Church was fronted by six huge Doric columns that screened three large entry doors; above was a tall steeple that became a landmark of the city skyline. The entry door opened to a wide center aisle and smaller side aisles that gave access to 114 pews. There were seven pews on either side of the pulpit, six open seats at the front, and galleries on three sides of the room. The church seated twice as many as the congregation's previous building.

On 29 September 1896, a severe windstorm sent the steeple of Walter's church plummeting onto Main Street, ripping off a fifteen-foot section of the roof and damaging the YMCA building across Main Street. While the roof was repaired, the steeple was not replaced, because the congregation anticipated a move farther west, which would occur a decade later. The last services were held in the building on 15 October 1905; it was demolished to make way for commercial development soon thereafter. (Photograph: Valentine Museum)
DRT

COURT STREET METHODIST CHURCH, Court and Seventh Streets, Lynchburg
Built 1850–51; demolished 1901

In 1850, a scribe recorded this terse passage in the minutes of Lynchburg's Third Street Methodist Church: "Fifty-six members have withdrawn from this church to build one up on the hill to serve the devil in." At its first meeting, the board of trustees made plans for the new church. An ambitious Greek Revival building, it was built by George C. Curle "after the same order and model of the Charles Street Church in Baltimore, except the portico, which is dispensed with." Double stairs in the vestibule led to a spacious second-floor sanctuary with a balcony on three sides and a large Ionic reredos serving as a backdrop for the pulpit. The interior was originally equipped with cuspidors, proof positive of the popularity of tobacco in antebellum Lynchburg. In 1901, the congregation erected a new, larger sanctuary on the site. Although the exterior of the 1901 church is emphatically Romanesque Revival in style, the interior has a number of classical features, perhaps subtle reminders of the now vanished 1850 structure. (Photograph: Jones Memorial Library, Lynchburg)
SAC, Jr.

ST. PAUL'S EPISCOPAL CHURCH,
Seventh and Church Streets, Lynchburg
Built 1850–51; reconstructed for secular use
early 20th century

The second church built by Lynchburg's oldest Episcopal parish, St. Paul's, was an architectural descendant of the 15th-century King's College Chapel in Cambridge, one of the masterpieces of Perpendicular Gothic architecture. Its architect, William S. Ellison, arrived in Lynchburg in 1849 as a division engineer with the Virginia and Tennessee Railroad. Although built of brick, the church was stuccoed and colored to imitate brownstone both inside and out. While its revivalist architecture looked backward, its equipment was quite up to date. When the church was consecrated in November 1851, the newspaper reported that "the whole building [was] warmed by one of Chilson's Ventilating Furnaces." After serving for almost half a century, the church was replaced by a larger building several blocks away. The vestry kept the 1850s building for a while to use as a chapel and lecture room but eventually sold it. Now completely remodeled and bearing no resemblance to its original appearance, the former church serves as a ladies' fashion salon. Inside, portions of the original timber roof framing remain, and—if one looks hard enough on the exterior—a ghostly outline of one of the Gothic arched windows can be seen on a side wall. (Photograph: Jones Memorial Library, Lynchburg)
SAC, Jr.

MAPSICO EPISCOPAL CHURCH, Charles City vicinity, Charles City County
Built 1856; collapsed 1950s

This board-and-batten Gothic Revival gem is all but forgotten—a church that lost membership adequate to support it and thus fell victim to changing demographics. The church took its name from nearby Mapsico Creek, itself an Indian name, on Weyanoke Peninsula. It was built in 1856 to replace an 1834 frame church, St. Thomas's, which had been destroyed by fire on Christmas day in 1854. The new structure, consecrated as Mapsico Church by Bishop Johns, was a classic example of the many antebellum wooden country churches cast in a medieval mode. Such churches were expressions of the Romantic Revivalism that swept the nation in the first half of the 19th century and were frequently referred to as Carpenter's Gothic. With its large window of intersecting tracery and flanking, crenelated towers, Mapsico was more sophisticated than most, the work of an informed builder or possibly even an architect. Its general form referenced that of English collegiate chapels. The design itself was probably adapted from one published in the many architectural pattern books being produced in that period.

Mapsico's most distinguished parishioner was President John Tyler, who lived nearby at Sherwood Forest. Unlike many rural Virginia Episcopal churches in areas of military action, Mapsico remained in service during the Civil War. Regular services were held until 1920, when Mapsico's remaining members joined Westover Parish Church. The building was left untended and finally sold in 1946 to a private individual for $127.50 with the provision that it be removed and the site cleaned by July 1948. A small graveyard and a marker commemorating the church remain at the site. (Photograph: Virginia Historical Society)

FIRST PRESBYTERIAN CHURCH, Tenth and Capitol Streets (dismantled and reconstructed 1884–85 at Grace and Madison Streets), Richmond
Built 1852–53; demolished 1955

Organized in 1812, the congregation of Richmond's First Presbyterian Church has met in five buildings at six different locations. As with other congregations in Richmond, the path of church structures has followed the westward growth of the city. The congregation's fourth building, pictured here, may have been the most architecturally significant. Constructed in the years 1852–53, it originally stood at the northwest corner of Tenth and Capitol Streets, overlooking the Washington Monument in Capitol Square. The talented John McArthur, Jr., later the architect of Philadelphia City Hall (begun 1872) and a resident of that city, designed the building, his only known Virginia commission.

Church minutes of 1852 called for "an edifice corresponding in Architectural taste and beauty with others in the City, and in which the worship of God could be celebrated by his people with more comfort and convenience." The contractors, John and George Gibson, housebuilders and carpenters active in Richmond from 1845 through the end of the 19th century, were given seventeen months to build the church. Thirty years later John Gibson would remove and reconstruct this building on its second site.

In the 1853 *Presbyterian Magazine* the new structure was described as "in the Byzantine style." The base of the tower formed "a vestibule, or porch, to the principal entrance." Inside, galleries were carried by "octagonal iron shafts . . . surmounted with rich Byzantine capitals, from which [sprang] cusped spandrels or archivolts, giving the whole ceiling a vaulted appearance." According to Richmond's *Daily Dispatch*, the wood trim inside and out was painted to imitate oak. The walls imitated ashlar, the ceiling was panel work, and the columns, capitals, and corbels imitated bronze. The exterior was covered with stucco in imitation of stone. The height of the spire was 160 feet.

In 1882, when Richmond looked to build its Victorian city hall on the block next to the church, leaders of the congregation decided to dismantle their building and reconstruct it at the northwest corner of Grace and Madison Streets. They were aided by the Richmond engineer's office, headed by Wilfred Emory Cutshaw; the church reopened for services in 1885. By coincidence, the new site was across the street from another building that had been moved from the Capitol Square area, the Daniel Call house, which had been built in the 1790s at Ninth and Broad Streets. In 1911, when a number of Richmond church steeples were judged unsafe by city engineers, the First Presbyterian steeple was removed. In 1943 the congregation moved to its sixth location, farther west, in the 4600 block of West Cary Street. The building at Grace and Madison was sold to the Acca Temple. In 1955 it was razed to make way for a parking lot. (Photograph: Virginia Historical Society)
RB

BROAD STREET METHODIST CHURCH,
1000 East Broad Street, Richmond
Built 1859; demolished 1968

One of the first designs by Richmond architect Albert L. West and considered his greatest, Broad Street Methodist Church was Italianate in style and imposing in scale: thirty-eight feet wide and seventy-one feet long. The most unusual feature of the building was its polygonal portico and steeple base. A probable source for so unusual a base is Samuel Sloan's *City and Suburban Architecture*, published in 1859. Sloan's tower was slightly smaller than what was built in Richmond, and his building was much larger overall, sixty-two by eighty-four feet. Sloan described the design as a spire superimposed on an otherwise secular building. To his thinking, if a Protestant church is a preaching box focused on the pulpit, then he would promote as appropriate for Protestants the Italianate style, not the Gothic that was associated with the medieval Roman Catholic cathedral.

In 1876 the steeple of Broad Street Methodist was heightened by twenty feet; this remarkable landmark of the Richmond skyline was taken down around 1900, however, when a hurricane scare caused the city to order the removal of steeples. In December 1961, the congregation began holding services in a new church west of the city. By 1962, the Broad Street building was vacant. Demolition of the old building was threatened for nearly ten years before it was finally torn down in 1968 to make way for a parking lot. (Photographs: Valentine Museum and courtesy Stephanie Jacobe)
SATJ

POPLAR GROVE CHURCH, Poplar Grove National Cemetery, off Vaughan Road south of Flank Road, Dinwiddie County
Built 1865; demolished 1868

The 50th New York Engineers, attached to the 6th Corps, was engaged in the Battle of Peebles Farm from 19 September through 1 October 1864, after which the unit set up winter camp in the vicinity on the farm of Thomas Flowers. There the soldiers remained until the spring of 1865, when they broke camp in preparation for the final assault on Petersburg. During the winter months, they engaged themselves in working on the siege fortifications, as well as making improvements to their own camp, which they transformed into a small, semipermanent settlement. In February 1865, they turned to building a church for themselves.

Poplar Grove Church was designed by Capt. Michael H. McGrath, commander of Company F, in part to replace the Poplar Springs Church that had been destroyed during the Battle of Peebles Farm. The new building, which seated about 225, was built entirely of materials gathered from the woods, including stripped logs, saplings, and bark. Soldiers brought their own three-legged stools into the church with them. Intended as an auditorium for profane as well as sacred uses, it was first utilized, for a strolling minstrel show, on 4 March. The following day it was dedicated in a church service led by the Reverend Duryea. Religious services were held in it on Sundays and some weekdays until the 50th Engineers pulled out later in the spring. Many tourists were brought to visit the church during March, including Mrs. U. S. Grant.

In 1866, Lt. Col. James M. Moore, who had developed military cemeteries at Andersonville and in the vicinity of Washington, DC, chose the tract around Poplar Grove Church for a national cemetery, in part because of its centrality but largely because of the presence of the church. More than six thousand Union soldiers who had been killed in the Petersburg and Appomattox campaigns were buried there, some brought from as far away as Lynchburg. In late April or early March 1868, the church was demolished because funding had not provided for its upkeep. (Photograph: Virginia Historical Society)
RDW, Jr.

ZION BAPTIST CHURCH, Crossroads, Albemarle County
Built 1871; demolished 1975

Orson Squire Fowler, in his book *A Home for All, Or, The Gravel Wall and Octagonal Mode of Building*, first published in 1848, suggested that people's lives would be much enhanced if they lived, worked, and worshipped in multisided buildings. His recommendations increased the popularity of octagonal and other nonorthogonal structures. As late as 1871 Zion Baptist Church, an African-American congregation, built this frame decahedron church. The building was donated by Andrew Hart of Sunny Bank. Legend had it that its base was from a carousel left by a traveling carnival that had come through the county, but demolition revealed no support for the story. This unique building was razed in 1975 and replaced by a characterless concrete-block edifice. (Photograph: Manuscript Print Collection, Special Collections Department, University of Virginia Library)
KEL

GRACE STREET PRESBYTERIAN CHURCH, northwest corner of Grace and Fourth Streets, Richmond
Built 1872; dismantled 1920

The great fire that consumed much of central Richmond during the evacuation at the close of the Civil War had but one religious casualty, the United Presbyterian Church at the corner of Franklin and Eighth Streets. The Rev. Dr. Charles Read, minister since 1849 of what had suddenly become an impoverished congregation, traveled to New Orleans, through Texas, and to California seeking donations to rebuild the church. These travels, plus gifts from friends in the North, netted twenty-five thousand dollars, which funded construction in 1868 of the basement lecture room of a new structure, pictured here. The bulk of the church was completed in 1872, just in time for a meeting of the General Assembly of the Southern Presbyterian Church.

The body of Grace Street Church was the work of Richmond architect Maj. Charles H. Dimmock. The tower and steeple, which soared to 210 feet, were the work of Dimmock's brother, Capt. Marion J. Dimmock; these were not completed until 1881. When the steeple and scaffolding ignited from firepots left behind by tinners, there must have been a sense of déjà vu; however, no serious damage resulted. A three-thousand-pound bell in the tower, a gift to the congregation from a friend in Cincinnati, was claimed to be the heaviest in Richmond. In 1906 Tiffany Studios of New York redecorated many components of the church's interior, including the walls, gallery, choir loft, stained glass, and electric light fixtures. In 1915 Grace Street Church merged with the Church of the Covenant at another location. The Grace Street building was dismantled in 1920 and taken to the city's north side, where it was rebuilt, somewhat reconfigured, as Ginter Park Baptist Church. (Photograph: Valentine Museum)
DRT

ST. ANDREW'S EPISCOPAL CHURCH,
corner of Laurel and Beverley Streets, Oregon Hill, Richmond
Built 1875; demolished 1950

This board-and-batten structure was a charming and simplified interpretation of the style called Carpenter's Gothic. It is the earliest documented church designed in Richmond by architect Marion J. Dimmock. Dimmock built at least three other similar Episcopal churches, all of which survive: St. Mary's on River Road, Goochland County; St. Luke's in Clover, Halifax County; and the Confederate Memorial Chapel in Richmond.

The St. Andrew's congregation had outgrown this small structure by 1901. The building was sold and moved to 2000 Grove Avenue, where it was reconstructed as the first Church of the Holy Comforter. The board-and-batten siding was replaced by horizontal weatherboarding, and a wing was added. The building was sold again in 1949, when its second congregation outgrew the space and moved to the west end. It was demolished a year later and apartments built on the site. Locally, the church was important as the birthplace of two still vital congregations, St. Andrew's and Holy Comforter. (Photograph: William N. Glenn, *St. Andrew's Episcopal Church and Its Environs*, 1978)
THR

BAPTIST CHURCH, East Nelson Street, Lexington
Built 1879; demolished 1919

Lexington's Baptist Church was a late-19th-century eclectic combination of English Tudor and Queen Anne details. Its half-timbered gables and upper tower contrasted with brick corbelling and stone coursing for a distinctive polychromy. J. Appleton Wilson of Baltimore, son of a Baptist minister, designed Baptist churches in Berryville, Leesburg, and Winchester, as well as nearly a dozen in Baltimore. Appleton's drawings for an 1884 addition to Lexington's Baptist Church survive, and although the attribution is conjectural and based on similarity of style, it seems likely that he was the original architect as well.

The church had a distinctive weathervane with a corkscrew finial. Lexington's Presbyterian Church, designed in 1845 by Thomas U. Walter, was right next door; its spire had a copper ball on it that was rumored to have been recycled from a local still. That led to a local joke about the Baptists having the corkscrew to open the Presbyterians' store of liquor. The Baptist church was torn down in 1919, when the congregation built a new, larger classical structure. (Photograph: Historic Lexington Foundation, courtesy Washington and Lee University)
PHS

BETH AHABAH SYNAGOGUE, Eleventh Street between Marshall and Clay Streets, Richmond
Built 1880; demolished 1957

Beth Ahabah was founded in 1841, but for the first seven years of its existence the congregation worshipped in rented quarters. The Eleventh Street site was purchased in 1847 for nineteen hundred dollars, and a synagogue was constructed there the following year. The builders were John D. Quarles, Richie V. Beazley, and Otis Manson. That building was demolished and replaced in 1880 by another synagogue, the one pictured here, on the same site. Its architect was Albert Lybrock, a German native who had moved to Richmond from New York in 1853; the general contractors were Jarvis and Glinn. This impressive structure was evidence of the growing affluence of Jewish congregations in America and their desire to imitate their Christian neighbors. With its round arches and minaret-like towers, the Lybrock building was a combination of Romanesque and Middle Eastern elements. The façade was given elaborate terra-cotta tile work by the Perth Amboy Company of New York and was described in one news account as unique in Richmond.

The Eleventh Street synagogue could seat 500 worshippers on the main floor and 250 more in the galleries. Its red and blue interior was described as "oriental" in a local news account. The ark, reading desk, and pulpit were placed together at the front of the sanctuary, as was common in Reform synagogues. William Nickle carved the ornate white and gold ark. A Hook and Hastings organ was installed in the balcony.

Congregation Beth Ahabah worshipped in this building until 1904, when the Franklin Street Synagogue, designed by Noland & Baskervill, replaced it. The Eleventh Street building was then sold to the Sir Moses Montefiore congregation; it was demolished in 1957 by a later owner, the Medical College of Virginia. (Photograph: Beth Ahabah Archives)
SSB

PACE MEMORIAL METHODIST CHURCH, 700 West Franklin Street, Richmond
Built 1886; burned 1966

In the intricate design and bold scale of its towers, the abundance of two-dimensional patterning, and the varied colors of its fabric, this Victorian Gothic structure seemed to soar with energy. The steeples of Pace Memorial Methodist Church, which rose to heights of 110 and 168 feet, were sculpted forms; even a four-faced clock, more often found in secular architecture, was added to the spire of the taller steeple to extend upward the theme of Victorian embellishment. Every break in the façade and every structural line afforded the architect an excuse to add patterns of detailing, what Victorians considered both "unnecessary" and the key to good architecture. The building was polychromatic, with blue granite set off against dark red brick. The plan was for a building measuring ninety-six by sixty-six feet.

Park Place Methodist Episcopal Church South shortened its name in 1921, following the death of benefactor James B. Pace. In 1875 he had donated the lot opposite Monroe Park on which the church illustrated here was built. The massive memorial window over its front entrance, twenty-five by twelve feet, was dedicated to members of the Pace family. This church was a landmark in the city of Richmond before it was destroyed by arson in 1966. The congregation built a new church on the site, hardly more than a tiny chapel, where it remained until it disbanded in 2000. (Photograph: Valentine Museum)
SATJ

(FIRST) ALL SAINTS EPISCOPAL CHURCH, Madison Street between Franklin and Grace Streets, Richmond
Built 1887–88; demolished 1935

Richmond architect Marion J. Dimmock, a lifetime member of the congregation, designed the first All Saints Episcopal Church, the building pictured here. This structure served the church, however, for little more than a decade, after which a larger building was needed and built on adjoining property. The new building bore a distinct resemblance to the one it replaced, but it was larger and more ornate.

All Saints, built in the Romanesque style that had been made popular in post–Civil War America by the designs of Henry Hobson Richardson, was the first large, auditorium-style church designed by Dimmock. It would serve as the prototype for other churches he designed, such as the first Grove Avenue Baptist Church, which now serves as the performing arts center for Virginia Commonwealth University.

The original All Saints building was demolished in 1935 after it was deemed unsafe. (Photograph: *All Saints Church . . . from Christmas 1888 to 1903*, 1904)
THR

(SECOND) ALL SAINTS EPISCOPAL CHURCH, 300 West Franklin Street, Richmond
Built 1898–1900; demolished 1961

The second All Saints Episcopal Church was one of Richmond's most successful examples of Romanesque Revival architecture. Its congregation grew out of a Sunday school and evening services program established in 1883 at Monumental Church. The members first met in the nearby Daniel Call house. In the years 1887–88 they commissioned from Marion J. Dimmock a restrained Romanesque brick church building (q.v.) that was constructed on Madison Street. Church minutes record that in 1897 a new structure was proposed to accommodate the growing congregation. Built on adjoining property, it was similar to the first building but more ornate. By 1898 six different architectural firms, including Dimmock's and New York's Carrère and Hastings, had submitted plans. The commission was awarded to the New York firm of Barney and Chapman, which designed the building illustrated here. John Stewart Barney served as consulting architect.

The design of All Saints was related, in style if not in size and scope, to Barney and Chapman's Grace Church Mission Chapel and Dispensary (1894) and Holy Trinity Church (1897), both in New York City. Those buildings show the influence of the Romanesque Revival work of Henry Hobson Richardson. Barney's All Saints also resembled his first Richmond commission, the 1894 Church of the Holy Trinity. Although All Saints was slightly larger and more elaborate, both buildings had a rough granite façade, round arched entrances, and a polygonal corner tower. At All Saints, however, the tower was more ornate, with pairs of gargoyles at each corner. A rose window filled its front gable. Several memorial stained glass windows were designed by Tiffany Glass and Decorating Company.

Services were first held in All Saints in January 1901. When the congregation moved in 1958 to its third and present location at 8787 River Road, most of the memorial windows were incorporated into the new building. The old structure on West Franklin Street was demolished in 1961 to make way for the Berkshire (1963), a high-rise apartment building. (Photographs: Virginia Historical Society and *Richmond Times-Dispatch*)
RB

FIRST BAPTIST CHURCH, 407 North Jefferson Street, NW, Roanoke
Built 1900; burned 1995

When completed, Roanoke's First Baptist Church housed what was at the time western Virginia's largest and most prominent African-American congregation. Designed by the ambitious local architect H. H. Huggins, the church, standing just two blocks north of the famed Hotel Roanoke, was declared by the *Roanoke Times* to be "the handsomest colored church in the city."

The origins of First Baptist's congregation date to 1855, when Dr. Charles L. Cocke, founder of what is now Hollins College, established a Bible class for slaves in Big Lick (now Roanoke). The class evolved into a full congregation, and by 1876 it was able to purchase a former Episcopal church. The congregation was greatly expanded by an influx of workers following the arrival of the Norfolk and Western Railroad in the area in 1882. Church membership peaked in the 1930s at more than two thousand. The congregation left the building in 1982, when it constructed a new church a block away. Plans were in the works to convert the landmark building into a performing arts center when it was gutted by fire in 1995. Attempts to preserve the roofless walls and tower proved futile, and the site was cleared. (Photograph: Virginia Department of Historic Resources)

FIRST CHRISTIAN CHURCH, Main and Fifth Streets, Lynchburg
Built 1903, 1911; damaged by fire and demolished after 1959

Architects Edward G. Frye and Aubrey Chesterman designed the first portion, the Sunday school, of this Romanesque Revival church, and the firm of McLaughlin, Pettit, and Johnson followed their design leads in conceiving the sanctuary a decade later. Perhaps more strange than beautiful, the church was strategically located at the northwestern edge of downtown Lynchburg, where its twin towers served as familiar landmarks. The building was smaller than it appeared; the sanctuary, with curved pews arranged on a sloping floor, seated only four hundred. As the local newspaper announced when it was completed, however, "when the Sunday School lecture room is thrown open there will be seating for nearly 700." The congregation abandoned the crowded site for greener pastures in Rivermont in 1959, taking only the communion table and a portion of one of the stained glass windows as mementos. Rearrangement of streets and changes in topography have obliterated all evidence of the site's original condition. (Photograph: Jones Memorial Library, Lynchburg)
SAC, Jr.

FIRST BAPTIST CHURCH, northeast corner of East Jefferson and Second Streets, Charlottesville
Built 1904; burned 1977

The Baptists were the third denomination to appear in Charlottesville. In 1833 they erected their first church, on a site two blocks from the building pictured here. In 1852 they moved to a larger structure, a classical, pilastered brick building that had been constructed by George Wilson Spooner, Jr.; it was razed in 1904 to clear the site for the (third) First Baptist Church. The third church, illustrated here, was a unique structure, built of brick in the Romanesque Revival style and positioned diagonally on the corner to respond to what became Lee Park. It was given wide bands of windows so that its expansive, vaulted interior was dramatically lit. The congregation had already begun work on its new church on Park Street when fire destroyed the Romanesque building in 1977. About a decade later the Queen Charlotte Square Apartments were built on the site.

Charlotte "Lottie" Digges Moon became associated with this Charlottesville church. She was born at nearby Viewmont (q.v.) and graduated with a degree in French from what is now Hollins College. In 1858 she was converted at a revival in the second building. She became famous as a Baptist missionary to China from 1873 until her death in 1912. (Photographs: Holsinger Studio Collection, Special Collections Department, Manuscripts Division, University of Virginia Library)
KEL

AETZ CHAYIM SYNAGOGUE, 728 Wilson Street, Danville
Built 1912; demolished 1986

"Under its vaulted roof," wrote a descendant of one of its founders, "a small but tenacious Orthodox congregation took hold of its tradition and drew strength, joy, and inspiration from it." Dedicated in 1910, this tall, confident building was the center of Danville's Orthodox Jewish community, mostly Eastern European immigrants then living in the shadow of its twin ogee-curved domes. As the only Orthodox synagogue in the region, Aetz Chayim, or Tree of Life, was used for seventy-five years as a house of study and prayer for area residents, professionals, and college students in south-central Virginia and neighboring North Carolina. The interior, reminiscent of Touro Synagogue in Newport, Rhode Island, was arranged so that the rabbi occupied the center of the sanctuary, nearly surrounded by the congregation—men downstairs and women in the gallery. Exotic "onion domes" gave its otherwise straightforward, Romanesque Revival exterior of red brick a dramatic silhouette visible from many parts of town. The building was designed by local draftsman and architect Joseph H. Parker. By the 1970s and early 1980s the remaining members, who then were meeting primarily at their rabbi's home, decided to desanctify their house of worship. They removed ritual items, sent the sacred ark to Israel, and sold the building to a local construction company, which demolished it and sold the vacant lot to a local restaurant for parking. The removal of this massive landmark from the top of Wilson Street in 1986 completed the commercialization of what had been Danville's principal residential antebellum thoroughfare. (Photograph: city of Danville, Virginia)
GRG

EXCHANGE BANK, 1104 East Main Street, Richmond
Built 1841; burned 1865. Rebuilt 1865 and 1910; demolished 1935

In 1840, while working on Richmond's Exchange Hotel (q.v.), noted Boston architect Isaiah Rogers received the commission for this building, shown here following the evacuation fire of April 1865. In ruins—even more so than when standing—the Exchange Bank resembled a building from antiquity. The *distyle-in-muris* portico that served as the entire front of the bank was distinctive; its elegant columns were derived from the Tower of the Winds as published by Stuart and Revett. Each was carved from a single block of Quincy, Massachusetts, granite, so that the façade was one of the more expensive built in antebellum Richmond. The interior housed offices and a large domed hall lit by a stained glass skylight. Marble mantels and a cast-iron vault were shipped by Rogers from Boston.

When Richmond's burnt district was rebuilt, the bank's façade was incorporated into a replacement building. But that structure was itself destroyed in 1910, when construction on the adjoining lot undermined its foundations. "With a crash that could be heard for two blocks," the rear of the building collapsed into an excavation pit; only the heroics of workmen kept the portico in place. Construction of a third building behind the Rogers façade preserved it as a landmark in Richmond's financial district until 1935, when the Parcel Post building was built on the site. Because they had survived the evacuation fire and had come to symbolize it, the magnificent columns of the Exchange Bank were at that time salvaged and brought to rest at the Robert E. Lee Camp for Confederate Veterans on Richmond's Boulevard. Alexander Weddell, president of the Virginia Historical Society, reportedly wanted to re-erect the columns as a folly on the grounds of the Society. In 1959, the Commonwealth of Virginia sold the columns as scrap. They were reduced to granite chips. (Photograph: Valentine Museum)
TTP, Jr.

CHAPTER IV

Lost Commercial Architecture

The commercial landscape of 19th-century Virginia was marked by the prominence of several building types that answered contemporary needs but now are mostly gone. There were places of lodging that were unique for their time and place—taverns, the first urban hotels, hotels at the mineral and thermal springs, and Victorian resort hotels. There were sizable mills in both Richmond and the countryside. There were picturesque railroad stations, bank buildings that were architecturally significant, and business shops that could serve only the pace of a simpler time. They all disappeared when they could no longer fulfill their primary function, making money.

Taverns first served the lodging needs of travelers. One of many lost examples is Gordon's tavern (1790s, Gordonsville, Orange County), a well-known stopping place that Thomas Jefferson described as a "good house." Some of these buildings, like Warren tavern (1804, Albemarle County), were actually houses adapted to serve a new function. Superior accommodations were offered to the traveler in early urban hotels, which were considered such an advance that the absence of one in early 19th-century Richmond was labeled a "mortification" by a contemporary newspaper. The Union Hotel (1817), which introduced high-style neoclassical architecture to the city, was said to provide legislators and visitors with "genteel accommodations." The Jefferson Hotel (1827) in Charlottesville had "every necessary out convenience"; these were a kitchen, smokehouse, icehouse, well, stable, carriage house, post office, and shops. The Crawford House (1835) in Portsmouth, another prototype hotel, was also unlike the more homespun inns and taverns; it had public rooms above its first-floor shops and three upper floors of well-appointed guest rooms. The Crawford House boasted such visitors as US presidents Martin Van Buren, John Tyler, James K. Polk, and Millard Fillmore. The Exchange Hotel (1840–41) in Richmond was immediately celebrated as one of the great buildings in the nation. Calling it "the Lion of the day" at its opening, the *Richmond Whig* reported that this mammoth and multipurpose structure housed a "Hotel, Post Office, Reading Room, Baths, Stores, &c." All of these early hotels

were lost when dramatic improvements in plumbing, heating, and lighting made them obsolete.

Also highly visible in the commercial landscape of 19th-century Virginia were the hotels of its many mineral springs, the majority of which have long been closed and forgotten. Western Virginia (including several counties that in 1863 became part of West Virginia) was dotted with these spas, which by the middle decades of the 1800s were fairly accessible by roads; visitors came from across the state and from northern cities. They went for sightseeing, social interaction, and to be cured of ailments. The mythology of the Old South is even partly rooted in this setting. Some spas are completely gone; Montgomery White Sulphur Springs (1855, Montgomery County), for example, is entirely farmland now. Little remains at the site of Fauquier White Sulphur Springs (1834–35, Fauquier County) to remind that the hotel there attracted such distinguished visitors as John Marshall, James Madison, James Monroe, Martin Van Buren, and Henry Clay. At Rockbridge Alum Springs (ca. 1852, Rockbridge County) the hotel and most of the other three dozen buildings once there are lost. At Yellow Sulphur Springs (late 1880s, Montgomery County), the Victorian hotel is gone. Other springs, such as the Homestead (ca. 1848 and later, Bath County), saw dramatic growth in the form of enlargements and rebuildings, so that the original architecture there is lost.

Numerous Victorian resort hotels were built in the commonwealth in the late 19th century, particularly in the Shenandoah Valley. Impetus came from the popularity of the antebellum springs and from a real estate boom around 1890. Speculators accumulated huge tracts of land that they platted into whole new towns, offering lots for sale. A large hotel generally was built to entice investors and customers; these buildings tended to be towered and turreted structures that were visually arresting and evoked European grandeur. The Alleghany Hotel (1890–91) in Goshen was to have "no superior in the United States." The deHart Hotel (1891) would make Lexington "the most beautiful and profitable city in the South to live in." Resort hotels were built in other parts of the commonwealth following the Panic of 1893, in the east (Hotel Chamberlin, 1890–96, Hampton) and Southside (Mecklenburg Hotel and Sanitorium, 1903).

Virginia's early commercial landscape also was one of mills. Countless wooden gristmills operated in the countryside; the smaller windmills were picturesque, as were the larger, water-driven wood structures, like Byrd Mill (1740) in Louisa County. Richmond became a city of gigantic flour mills. The Haxall (begun 1790), Gallego (1835 and later), and Dunlop mills (1852) surpassed their national competitors in the annual volume of flour produced and transformed the landscape of the Richmond waterfront. These massive "houses" of industry carried the traditional house form to an unprecedented scale, a height of eight to twelve stories. They signaled progress, as did Riverside Cotton Mills in Danville later in the century. With the addition of Mill #6 in 1894 and 1895, the Riverside complex became the South's largest in terms of the number of spindles in operation.

Railroad stations are gone from the Virginia commercial landscape because of the decline of rail traffic in the mid-20th century. Fewer than twenty railroad stations in Virginia still serve their original function. Small, picturesque depots, like the ones in Leesburg (1887) and Woodstock (1889), are lost. Lynchburg's Union Station (1890), though hemmed in by tracks on both sides, was an expansive structure that gave visitors a grand first impression of the city. Virginia had few truly monumental rail terminals, but one of those, Norfolk's Terminal Station (1912), is lost. Designed by Reed and Stem of New York City, the Norfolk station offered an elegant waiting room; above was a nine-story office tower.

Any 19th-century architect commissioned to design a bank was confronted with the question of what form to give it. Banks were new then in North America; bank architecture had no set patterns, and architects could only experiment. Frederick Graff was one of the first to try in Virginia, at the United States Branch Bank (ca. 1800) in Norfolk. Isaiah Rogers's Exchange Bank (1841) in Richmond resembled a building from antiquity; the columns of its distinctive portico were derived from the ancient Tower of the Winds in Greece. Later, when the American Savings Bank (1905) in Roanoke was built, classical architecture was revived in a new way. The bold Beaux Arts appearance of that small bank was common to the American Renaissance movement that motivated city fathers and civic leaders to revive and beautify cities. These banks were intended to convey a sense of solidity, security, and permanence.

Early shops, several of which are pictured in this section, were given windows in front, which served to showcase goods, and long interior walls on which to display them. In many instances these photographs of lost stores are the only record of their nature. The type had become probably the most common nondomestic building in the Virginia landscape by the end of the 18th century; stores were found in towns, at crossroads, and even on plantations. Also lost from the Virginia commercial landscape are urban business buildings of the 19th century, such as the one that housed the journal *The Southern Literary Messenger* (1813, Richmond) and Pratt's Virginia Sky-Light Daguerrean Gallery (1846) in the same city.

Lost commercial buildings tied to the African-American experience in Virginia carry histories of tragedy and progress. The Alexandria Slave Pens (ca. 1828) were evidence of the misery suffered by thousands of slaves who passed through that place. Conversely, St. Luke Penny Savings Bank (1909, Richmond), a Renaissance Revival structure, stood as a notable symbol of African-American progress because it was financed, designed, built, and occupied by African-Americans.

PROVIDENCE FORGE MILL, Providence Forge, New Kent County
Built beginning ca. 1725–49; demolished after 1933

Gristmills were equipped with machinery for grinding grain, typically wheat into flour and corn into meal. Gristmills contained millstones, gears, and other machinery connected to a source of power, in this case water channeled from a millpond through an undershot waterwheel—that is, a wheel turned by water flowing beneath it. Field survey notes made circa 1933 record the condition of the Providence Forge mill as "poor, to be destroyed." It was one of scores of such traditional industrial structures lost in this period, being supplanted by more modern facilities. (Photograph: Historic American Buildings Survey, Library of Congress)

BYRD MILL, Louisa vicinity, Louisa County
Built 1740; burned 1968

When it was consumed by fire in December 1968, Byrd mill had been in continuous operation since 1740; its full complement of millrace, millstones, and water turbine (with wooden bearings) was still functioning. Built for miller John Garth by a contractor known only by the surname Byrd, it was one of very few pre-Revolutionary commercial buildings in Virginia that in the 20th century were still used for their original purposes. In 1967, the mill was processing more than 750,000 pounds of grain a year, milled primarily into cornmeal but also into flour and an assortment of convenience mixes. (Photographs: Ron Jennings)

GOLDEN BALL TAVERN (RICHARD HANSON HOUSE), southeast corner of Old and Market Streets, Petersburg
Built ca. 1764, enlarged ca. 1820; demolished 1944

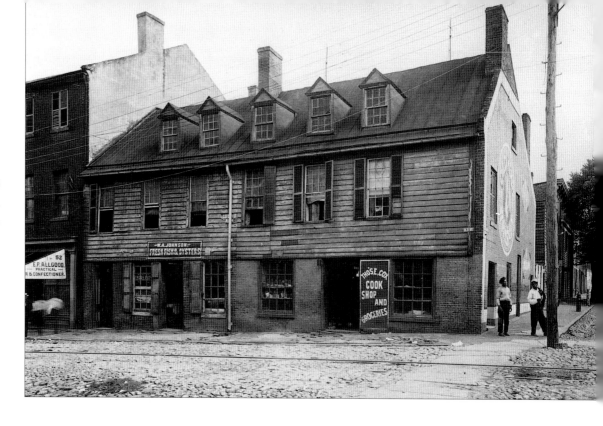

In the early 1760s, when this property was sold by Peter Jones of Folly Castle to the tobacconist Richard Hanson, of the large London firm Lionel Lyde, there seem already to have been structures on the site. However, when Hanson offered the property for sale on 6 November 1766, he spoke of the "houses" on the property as "lately built, and well finished, and will want no repairs for many years."

It is unclear whether Hanson ever used the new "houses" or leased them as an inn, but it is clear that John King, to whom he seems to have sold the property, probably in 1776, did run it as the Golden Ball Tavern. The Petersburg Jockey Club met there, British officers were quartered there in 1781, and the tavern was established in 1784 by act of the General Assembly as the first meeting place of the courts and the common council of Petersburg. By that date, the property consisted of two major buildings: a large brick structure at Old and St. Paul's Lane, and a brick-and-frame structure at Old and Market Streets, the latter traditionally known as the Golden Ball Tavern.

The property continued in use under a succession of tavern owners who leased it from John King's estate until the loyalist Richard Hanson recovered it circa 1790 and sold it to the Glasgow tobacconist David Buchanan. Buchanan and his partner, Robert Pollok, lived and conducted their business there. However, the common council and courts of the town moved to Armistead's tavern on Sycamore Street. After the deaths of Pollok and his brother Allen, the property was sold in 1815 to the merchant Pleasant Akin, who held it until his death in 1847. He seems to have lived in the brick house and leased the other building as a tavern. By 1820 he had somewhat enlarged the tavern building, linking it with the brick building and expanding it to the rear, probably rebuilding the wall at the western end and very likely altering the upper story and roof configurations, which may have begun as a "Dutch roof" as described in the 1766 advertisement. Insurance policies show a kitchen and other facilities to the rear of the brick house, as well as structures along Market Street that were leased to doctors and barbers.

The main buildings continued to be used as hotel facilities until shortly after the Civil War, and for a series of other retail uses until 1944, when the tavern building was torn down to make way for a parking lot by a feed-and-grain operation located diagonally across the street. Demolition of the brick house had preceded the tavern by perhaps a decade. The property has been a parking lot ever since. (Photograph: Petersburg Department of Planning) RDW, Jr.

ROGERS SHOP, Covington
Built ca. 1770; demolished 1924

In 1822, Alleghany County was established in response to demands from residents of the Jackson River area who had great difficulty reaching the existing courthouses across mountainous terrain and often impassable roads. The first county court met in Covington at this log structure, which had been erected a half-century earlier and was known as Rogers Shop. The building was also being used as a Methodist meeting house at the time. It was customary for courts to meet temporarily in meeting houses, residences, or even taverns before permanent court buildings could be completed. This log building housed court business for only two years; a two-story brick courthouse opened in Covington in 1824. (Photograph: Alleghany Historical Society) JOP, MTP

MARSHALL HOUSE HOTEL, King and Pitt Streets, Alexandria
Built ca. 1785; burned 1873

Alexandria became a prosperous port following the American Revolution and produced some notably urbane architecture. Located at a busy intersection on the city's principal street, the three-and-a-half-story Marshall House hotel, with its pediment articulated by modillion cornices, could easily have stood in downtown Philadelphia or Boston. Though it was significant as an accomplished example of Federal-style design, the Marshall House is best remembered for an incident occurring in the first days of the Civil War. On 17 April 1861, James W. Jackson, an ardent secessionist who acquired the hotel in January 1861, raised a Confederate flag over the establishment. On 24 May, Union colonel Elmer Ellsworth and his troops entered the city to secure it for the North. The banner was noted on their march up King Street, and Ellsworth entered the hotel and hauled it down. Incensed by this action, Jackson shot Ellsworth as he carried the flag. The deceased thus earned the dubious distinction of being the first Union officer mortally wounded in the Civil War. Jackson was bayoneted on the spot by a Union corporal and in turn became the first Southerner killed in action. (Photograph: Virginia Historical Society)

GORDON INN (GORDON'S TAVERN), at the intersection of Routes 15, 33, and 231, Gordonsville, Orange County
Built 1790s, 1802; demolished 1947

In 1787, twenty-four-year-old Nathaniel Gordon, son of Col. James Gordon of Lancaster County, purchased 1,350 acres near the Southwest Mountains in southern Orange County adjoining the plantation of his brother-in-law, Presbyterian "Blind Preacher" James Waddell. Gordon's land contained the crossroads of the Richmond Road and the Fredericksburg Road, major routes connecting Richmond, the Valley of Virginia, Fredericksburg, northern Virginia, and Charlottesville and points southward. Gordon built a house at the crossroads and, quick to sense an opportunity, had opened a tavern there by 1794. His plantation/tavern complex, originally called Newville, soon became a stage stop as well, and Gordon's business and his fortunes expanded. By the early 1800s, Gordon's tavern was a well-known stopping place; it was described as a "good house" by Thomas Jefferson in 1802. By the 1810s, the popular name of Gordonsville had supplanted the earlier Newville; a Gordonsville post office was established there in 1813, and the town of Gordonsville subsequently grew up around the tavern complex.

The tavern originally took the form of a story-and-a-half frame structure measuring thirty-six by eighteen feet. It had been enlarged to forty-two feet in length by 1802, when Gordon added a thirty-eight-by-twenty-six-foot, two-story frame wing as a residence for his family. The roof of the original structure was subsequently raised to two stories. The interiors of both wings were embellished with wainscoting and well-executed Federal-style mantels, and at least one room had a carved cornice. The building continued in use as a tavern until circa 1830, after which it was a private school and a residence. It was demolished to provide space for a parking lot in 1947. (Photograph: Library of Virginia)
ALM

HAXALL MILLS, southern terminus of Twelfth and Thirteenth Streets and part of what is now Browns Island, Richmond
Begun 1790, rebuilt or expanded 1830, 1853, 1865, 1874; demolished after 1891

As early as the 1780s, wheat production in Virginia had surged, prompting the pioneering in the Shenandoah Valley of machinery for harvesting the crop, as well as the building of new mills throughout the commonwealth. Richmond soon became the center of a new and prospering flour industry; it was situated where mills could harness the hydraulic force of the falls of the James, below which the river was navigable to ocean vessels.

Mills were constructed on both sides of the falls in the 18th century. The first mill built by Scotsman David Ross was perched on rocks in the James River and swept away by flooding in 1784. Around 1790 he set up a mill nearby that was better protected, on the millrace that still bears his name and that of his successors on the site, the Ross-Haxall millrace. He called his business the Columbia Mills, a name that was at times reintroduced after the Haxall family had purchased the site from his creditor, in 1809. During the Civil War era the operation was known as the Haxall-Crenshaw Company.

Through the early decades of the 19th century, the Haxall operation maintained a pattern of prosperity and growth comparable to that of its local competitor, Gallego Mills (q.v.). The business survived the depression of the early 1820s and conflagrations in 1830 and 1853; fires were all too frequent at flour mills because of the volatility of grain dust. Tax records show a steady increase in the value of the Haxall property as four-story and two-story brick buildings went up in 1834 and 1842. In the 1850s the Haxall mills nearly matched the output at Gallego, as both companies marketed successfully to South America, especially Rio de Janeiro, and to California. In 1853, when fire damage prompted additional construction at Haxall, three hundred thousand barrels of Richmond flour arrived in San Francisco; most of it had been ground at the two mills.

The Haxall complex was situated below the Gallego property and set apart by a stretch of canal built along the Ross-Haxall millrace. Following the evacuation fire of 3 April 1865 that ended the Civil War in Richmond and gutted the Gallego buildings, the Haxall mills were still standing. Alexander Gardner, who photographed the burned city, explained that they "escaped the torch . . . owing to a favorable wind." Damages reportedly were incurred during the evacuation, but the mills were quickly restored to operation. Nonetheless, the company did not fare well in the post-war market. At least part of the complex burned in a major fire in 1874. The mills closed in 1894, following the financial panic of 1893, and within two decades a hydroelectric plant had been built on the site. (Photograph: Valentine Museum)
TTP, Jr., and WMSR

BRANCH BANK OF THE UNITED STATES,
Granby Street at College Place, Norfolk
Built ca. 1800; demolished ca. 1910

The first Bank of the United States, the government fiscal agency conceived by Alexander Hamilton, had branches in eight American cities. The bank established its Norfolk branch in 1799, and the commission to design the building went to a Philadelphian, Frederick Graff, the first major pupil of B. Henry Latrobe. (In 1804 Latrobe himself wrote a laudatory account of how the younger man had handled the commission.) Graff, who would prove to be a minor architect but a great engineer, later won a distinguished place in American history by supplanting Latrobe's problem-ridden Philadelphia Waterworks (1799–1801 and later) with the brilliantly successful Schuylkill Waterworks (1812–15, 1819–22, and later), for which Graff also created one of the most memorable neoclassical architectural compositions in America.

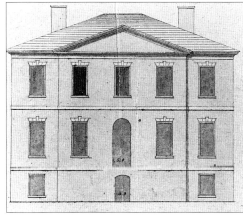

Around 1800, the young Graff was still feeling his way architecturally. Banking was a new institution in North America, and bank architecture did not have set patterns. From prehistory onward, one of the most important models for new kinds of buildings has been the house, and nowhere is this truer than during the multiplication of building types internationally in the decades between the 1760s and the 1860s. It is thus not surprising that Graff designed his Norfolk bank in the form of a dwelling. (In fact, the building incorporated the residence of the chief officer of the branch on the upper story.) Graff, who during the 1790s had schooled himself in Adamesque neoclassicism, decorated the exterior of the bank building in this style, which had already fallen out of fashion in England. The only external traces of Latrobe's cosmopolitan and up-to-date version of neoclassicism were the twin guard boxes, which echoed the pair that Latrobe had just built in front of a marvel of the period, the Bank of Pennsylvania (1799–1801, Philadelphia), the construction of which Graff had superintended.

Graff's building did not fulfill its function for long, because in 1811 Congress rejected the petition of the Bank of the United States for a renewal of its charter. The bank's Norfolk building subsequently took on a variety of functions, including serving as a private dwelling and later as an early home for the Norfolk Public Library. It was demolished to make way for a commercial block around 1910, but it is survived by a set of nine of Graff's revealing working drawings, one of which is pictured here, now in the Winterthur Library. (Photograph: Andrew Morrison, ed., *Pictures in Maritime Dixie . . .*, 1893; Image: Winterthur Library, Joseph Downs Collection of Manuscripts and Printed Ephemera, No. 76x138.2a)
CEB

OLD STONE WINDMILL, Winter Harbor,
Mathews County
Built ca. 1800; destroyed early 20th century

Windmills once dotted the exposed shorelines of colonial Virginia, adding a picturesque, Old World quality to the landscape. Intricately balanced and durable structures that had been developed in medieval Europe, windmills functioned well in Tidewater Virginia and along the Eastern Shore when positioned on wind-swept promontories, such as those that shelter inlets. Useful to sailors as landmarks, they were sometimes recorded on late-colonial maps. Some were built of stone; some of wood. The first was in operation in 1621, set up by Lt. Gov. George Yeardley on his plantation near the falls of the James River. In 1649 four of nine mills in the colony were driven by wind. Most were built later, however, after the turn into the 19th century, when wheat replaced tobacco as the principal crop of the region and additional mills of all types were needed.

Mathews County was at one time supplied with flour from ten wind and two tide mills; only one water-powered gristmill was in operation there because of the unbroken flatness of the land. Accordingly, mill operation in Mathews was unaffected by drought, which could cripple other regions. The early windmills, however, were highly vulnerable to the New World's sudden, violent storms and tidal surges and long ago were so destroyed. (Photograph: Robert Lancaster, *Virginia Homes and Churches*, 1915)

Taverns of all sizes and degrees of architectural sophistication were once a common roadside fixture in Virginia. They served as havens that provided much-needed rest and sustenance for travelers venturing out on Virginia's taxing roads as well as places of entertainment and gathering. The prices they charged for lodging, food, drink, and stableage were strictly regulated by the local courts. The tavern became the venue for such public and private diversions as assemblies, balls, concerts, business meetings, dinners, cockfights, and horse races. Accordingly, by the middle of the 18th century, many taverns had specialized rooms and fixtures, such as well-appointed assembly and long rooms, dining rooms, and bars.

The group of taverns illustrated here suggests the variations that were built in early Virginia. Some were rural and some urban. Some were modest and convenient; others were more ambitious. The South Hill example, about which little is known, is representative of the smaller taverns that once dotted the Virginia landscape. Alexandria's Catt's tavern, though located in what became a more populous area, was comparable. Catt's tavern was known as a drover's tavern, since it was where cattle sales took place. Warren tavern in Albemarle County, a plain gable roof structure with a towering chimney, probably was built by the future governor, Wilson Cary Nicholas of Mount Warren (q.v.), whose wheat-shipping business was the impetus for the growth of Warren and the consequent need for a tavern there. Goddin's tavern was a more substantial building that accommodated farmers traveling to Richmond to sell their products at the market there (see the 17th Street Market, q.v.). The Effingham tavern, with its front galleries characteristic of rural county-seat taverns, was a more impressive landmark that provided accommodations for those traveling to Cumberland Court House when the court was in session.

TAVERN, South Hill, Mecklenburg County
Built early 19th century (?); demolished after ca. 1940
(Photograph: Historic American Buildings Survey, Library of Congress)

CATT'S TAVERN, intersection of Duke and Diagonal Streets, Alexandria
Built 1815; burned 1896
(Photograph: Virginia Historical Society)

WARREN TAVERN, Warren, Albemarle County
Built 1804; demolished ca. 1970
(Photograph: Special Collections Department, University Archives,
University of Virginia Library)

GODDIN'S TAVERN, 821 Brook Avenue, Richmond
Built 19th century; demolished 1912
(Photograph: Valentine Museum)

EFFINGHAM TAVERN, Cumberland Court House, Cumberland County
Built late 18th or early 19th century; demolished before 1950
(Photograph: Valentine Museum)

THE COLONNADE BUILDING AND WARM SPRINGS HOTEL, Warm Springs, Bath County
Begun ca. 1810–12; demolished 1925

Early travelers to Warm Springs noted the appealing landscape there of two parallel ridges of mountains. They were drawn to the spot, however, by the ninety-eight-degree temperature of the waters. In 1785 Thomas Jefferson reported that these "sulphureous" waters would "relieve rheumatisms." By then, an octagonal men's bathhouse had been constructed. In 1836 a slightly larger women's bathhouse was built. Unlike the other buildings at Warm Springs, both are still in use; the former is one of the oldest spa structures in the nation.

Warm Springs enjoyed its greatest popularity prior to the Civil War, when in season its hotels and cottages housed more than three hundred guests. The first of the hotels there, called the Colonnade Building, is the structure illustrated here carrying a giant piazza across its front; the design was unabashedly derived from Mount Vernon. The much larger building to its left, called the Warm Springs Hotel, was constructed not long afterward. In the 19th century, as pictured in both Sir William Fox's 1853 watercolor view (National Library of New Zealand) and Edward Beyer's 1857 lithograph of the complex, the motif of the two-story piazza was repeated at the hotel; the dates of its removal and of this photograph are unknown. The piazza, which did much to give the building the aura of both Southern and resort architecture, ran the long expanse between two wings that housed a ballroom and a dining room. Across from the hotels were rows of brick and log cottages.

Throughout the 19th century Warm Springs was more famous than the Homestead (q.v.) in nearby Hot Springs, five miles to the south. But in 1890, at the peak of the economic boom that fueled a craze for resort hotels, the Southern Improvement Company purchased both properties and devoted its resources not to Warm Springs but to developing the Homestead into one of the nation's great hotels. The principal buildings at Warm Springs, which were suspected to be structurally unsound, were doomed to abandonment and destruction. (Photograph: Bath County Historical Society)
TTP, Jr., and WMSR

SOUTHERN LITERARY MESSENGER BUILDING, 1501 East Main Street, Richmond
Built 1813; demolished 1916

On its two upper floors, this commercial structure once housed the *Southern Literary Messenger*, the influential literary journal that published the first short stories of Edgar Allan Poe and that was edited by him for two years, beginning in 1835. Here Poe established his career and national reputation. (The first floor of the building was given to Archer's Shoe Store.) The structure to the right in this photograph, also lost, was the commission house of Ellis and Allan; one of its principals, John Allan, was Poe's foster father. The *Messenger* building stood for a century before it was demolished in 1916.

After 1916 portions of the *Southern Literary Messenger* building enjoyed a second life, just down the street at Richmond's so-called Old Stone House, long believed to be the oldest house in Richmond (though not of 17th-century origin). In this coda, in 1921 Mr. and Mrs. Archer Jones conceived the idea of transforming the house, which actually had no associations with Edgar Allan Poe, into a shrine to him. In the following year, the Old Stone House was refurbished as a museum, and a garden was created behind it. At the north end of the garden a summerhouse was constructed out of bricks salvaged from the *Southern Literary Messenger* building; salvaged woodwork was installed inside the stone house. That structure is today owned by the Association for the Preservation of Virginia Antiquities and operated by the Poe Foundation as a museum honoring the author's ties to Richmond. (Photograph: Virginia Historical Society)
TTP, Jr,. and BCG

UNION HOTEL, Main and Nineteenth Streets, Richmond
Built 1817; demolished 1911

The Union Hotel introduced to Richmond high-style neoclassical architecture of the type that Charles Bulfinch had developed in private and public buildings in Boston. It stood in the Shockoe district, below and east of Thomas Jefferson's Capitol, where it provided legislators and visitors with "genteel accommodations," the absence of which had been a source of "mortification," according to a contemporary newspaper account. The architect was Otis Manson, a carpenter-builder from Framingham, Massachusetts, who worked in Richmond for some forty years, beginning about 1810. Manson also designed Richmond's Linden Row, which survives as evidence of his sound grasp of classical detailing and proportioning. The hotel reportedly could house one hundred guests. The main public spaces, including a ballroom in which Lafayette was entertained in 1825, were situated on the second floor.

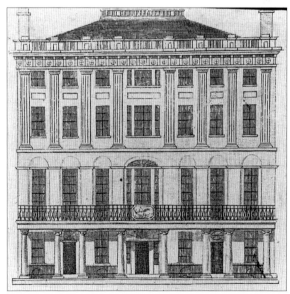

Though highly fashionable in 1817, the Union seemed antiquated by the 1830s, when a new hotel type was introduced in the North by Isaiah Rogers, soon to be the architect of Richmond's Exchange Hotel (q.v.). Rogers offered the traveler larger and more opulent public spaces, as well as central heating, running water, and toilets. The Union served its original function for only two decades. By 1838 it had been leased to Hampden-Sydney Medical School; it later served as a hotel again, a hospital (during the Civil War), and finally a school. The Union was demolished well after newer warehouses and factories had changed the nature of Shockoe from a neighborhood of houses and shops to a thoroughly commercial district. (Images: Virginia Historical Society)

BOLLINGBROOK STREET THEATRE ([THIRD] PETERSBURG THEATRE), northeast corner of Bollingbrook and Phoenix Streets, Petersburg
Built 1818, burned 1850, rebuilt 1854, burned again 1866; demolished 1867

This well-appointed theater opened on 12 October 1818 under the leadership of James H. Caldwell, the English light comedian and manager who was one of the most important figures in the westward expansion of the American theater. The Petersburg Theatre Company, apparently under the leadership of Thomas Jones, had engaged the English architect Charles A. Busby to design the building. Interested in modern technology, Busby had been experimenting in England with iron structures, but the failure of one of them sent him scurrying to America, where he remained about two years. His later career included a long series of commissions at Brighton and Hove. His Petersburg theater, designed in 1817, was to be his only American work. He took advantage of the natural slope of the land to create a large auditorium circled by three tiers of balconies supported by iron columns. The elegant façade (which predated the photograph shown here) was marked by three central entries beneath a semicircular Ionic portico.

Times were booming, and in the first four months after it opened, the Bollingbrook Street Theatre cleared half of its construction costs of twenty thousand dollars. On 29 October 1824, Bollingbrook was the scene of a gala held for the nation's guest, the Marquis de Lafayette. Following a revival in the 1830s, the theater seems to have encountered increasingly difficult times. On 11 February 1850, the building was consumed by fire. In September 1854, a new owner, Francis Pace, opened a new theater named Phoenix Hall, illustrated here, using what remained of the Busby structure. It was a much-diminished building, but Edwin Booth played on its stage, Edward Everett lectured there, John Letcher was nominated as candidate for Virginia governor by a Democratic state convention held there, and Roger A. Pryor delivered his rousing secession speech there. Damaged during the siege of Petersburg (1864–65), Phoenix Hall burned on 18 November 1866; what remained was pulled down on 9 May 1867 to protect pedestrians from the teetering walls. (Photograph: Frederick Bell Collection)
RDW, Jr.

JEFFERSON HOTEL, Court Square, Charlottesville
Built 1827; demolished 1926

In 1813 John Manoah Carr sold John Winn a property on Court Square just to the east of the Eagle Tavern in Charlottesville. Winn served as town postmaster for many years and built the three-story brick Jefferson Hotel there within a year of Thomas Jefferson's death in 1826. Proprietor George Garrett advertised that the apartments were commodious and "from many a delightful prospect of landscape scenery [offers a] view of the mountain of Monticello." The next year Winn proclaimed that "this house, 95 by 40 feet . . . [included] every necessary out convenience—a brick kitchen, . . . brick smoke house; a good icehouse; a well of most excellent water . . . and a brick stable 103 by 30 feet containing 44 stalls. . . . A carriage house large enough to contain 8 or 10 carriages will be put up as soon as it may be wanted." The first floor of the hotel housed a post office and shops. About a century later, in 1926, the nine-story brick Monticello Hotel designed by Lynchburg architect Stanhope S. Johnson replaced the earlier buildings. The Eagle Tavern, shown at the left, still stands. (Photograph: Albemarle County Historical Society)
KEL

ALEXANDRIA SLAVE PENS (FRANKLIN AND ARMFIELD OFFICE), 1300 block of Duke Street, Alexandria
Built ca. 1828; demolished 1870

In 1828 Isaac Franklin, a New Orleans slave dealer, and John Armfield, a North Carolina stagecoach driver, formed a partnership for the buying and selling of human beings and established their headquarters on Duke Street in Alexandria. The location was chosen because the area had a surplus of slaves available at low prices. Franklin set up sales offices in New Orleans, Louisiana, and Natchez, Mississippi, where slaves brought the highest prices, while Armfield remained in Alexandria. Typical of the firm's advertisements is one stating: "We will give Cash for one hundred likely YOUNG NEGROES of both sexes between the ages of 8 and 25 years. Persons who wish to sell, would do well to give us a call, as the negroes are wanted immediately. We will give more than any other purchasers that are in the market or may hereafter come into the market." The newly purchased slaves were held at Duke Street—which also served as Armfield's residence—until they could be transported south. During the day, the slaves were kept in a series of partially roofed courts or pens behind the high brick wall attached to the three-story house. At night they slept in a two-story rear wing whose doors and windows were grated like those of jails. Franklin and Armfield's dubious enterprise grew into the largest slave-trading operation in the antebellum South.

The business passed to different owners in 1846, 1858, and 1861 but was shut down in 1861, when Alexandria came under Union occupation. Ironically, during the Civil War, Union forces used the complex to imprison captured Confederate soldiers. The circa 1865 photograph of the interior (to the left) shows a Union guard at the cell-block door. The cells, slave pens, and perimeter wall were removed in 1870, when the property was purchased by Thomas Swann, a railroad builder. Swann added a mansard roof to the house and erected a row of town houses on the former site of the slave pens. The Armfield-Swann house still stands, in remodeled form, and is used for offices. Because of the historic significance of the site, it was designated a National Historic Landmark in 1978. Little tangible evidence remains of the misery suffered by the thousands of African-American slaves who passed through this place. (Photographs: Library of Congress)

BOLLINGBROOK HOTEL (IMPERIAL HOTEL, STRATFORD HOTEL), northeast corner of Bollingbrook and Second
Streets, Petersburg
Built 1828, extensively remodeled and enlarged 1857, remodeled 1906; demolished 1933

When Niblo's tavern, where Lafayette had been entertained in 1824, burned in 1827, John Niblo put together a group of investors to found a new and grander hotel, to be located on a vacant lot a half-block to the east. Among the investors were Otis Manson, who had designed the Union Hotel (1817, q.v.) in Richmond, and James Noë, who with his partner Theophilus Nash was concurrently engaged, in the years 1827–28, in the design and construction of the Bowers house (q.v.). It appears Noë and Nash were in partnership in the design and construction of the Bollingbrook as well. By December 1828, the hotel had been completed and leased back to Niblo. At a cost of twenty-two thousand dollars, and with more than twenty thousand square feet, it was Petersburg's finest and largest hostelry for decades. It was a three-story building with a 100-foot principal front and 106½ feet on Second. Both of these elevations were "plaistered or rough cast" and scored to resemble ashlar masonry. The Bollingbrook Street façade had a slightly projecting center section, five bays wide and pedimented above the cornice, with a portico at ground level. The travel diarist Anne Royall called the hotel "one of the best taverns in the Atlantic country."

In 1857, in response to calls for a new first-class hotel, a fourth story was added and the façade restyled in the Italianate manner, featuring a bracketed cornice, cast-iron segmental window caps, and a cast-iron balcony across the center section that replaced the portico. Confederate officers were quartered there during the siege of Petersburg. By 1870 the hotel was closed and the subject of many civic lamentations until it was reopened with renovations in 1875. About 1906, when it was called the Imperial, the hotel was modernized by Harrison Waite and experienced a new era of popularity under a third name, the Stratford. In 1915, however, its owners constructed the new Petersburg Hotel, with 118 rooms and an elegant dining hall, thereby dooming the Bollingbrook, which was razed in 1932 to make way for construction of a filling station. (Photograph: Virginia Historical Society)
RDW, Jr.

FAUQUIER WHITE SULPHUR SPRINGS HOTEL, on the Rappahannock River, Warrenton and Opal vicinity, Fauquier County
Built 1834–35; destroyed by shelling 1862

With a giant piazza extending the length of the building and rising with impressive verticality, the Fauquier White Sulphur Springs Hotel (also known as the Warrenton Springs Hotel) resembled Greek Revival urban mansions like the Hayes-McCance, Adams–Van Lew, and Hobson-Nolting houses (q.v.) in Richmond, all of which owed a debt to Mount Vernon and George Washington's conception of what Virginia architecture of distinction should be. Since this resort was but fifty miles southwest of the seat of that most respected of Virginians, some of its guests must have been reminded of Mount Vernon by the similar use of classical forms to match the self-image and climate of the South. Proximity to the nation's capital brought Fauquier such distinguished visitors as John Marshall, James Madison, James Monroe, Martin Van Buren, and Henry Clay. In 1849 the Virginia legislature took refuge there from a cholera outbreak in Richmond.

Beginning in 1828 the resort was developed by Hancock Lee IV and Thomas Green. A simple lodge had been built there in 1792 by Hancock Lee III. In 1835 the younger Hancock Lee boasted that the new accommodations were "probably unsurpassed." The four-story brick hotel measured 188 by 44 feet. The Doric columns of the porch rose about forty feet. A similar piazza was planned for the eastern façade, along which the public road ran, but the prepared timbers were destroyed by fire prior to construction. The ground floor was given to a large dining room (144 by 30 feet), with a kitchen and servants' hall; the second floor held a ballroom (100 by 40 feet) and two sitting rooms. These public rooms were "supplied with water, by pipes." The third and fourth floors contained some seventy private rooms. Additional lodging, pushing the total number of rooms to 230, was available in small cabins and two- and three-story buildings that reached westward like dependencies on a plantation. An octagonal Greek temple, nearly forty feet in diameter and with Doric columns, marked the sulphur spring; Lee called it "costly and handsome." In the notes to Edward Beyer's *Album of Virginia* (1857), the source of the image shown here, the "well shaded ground" was said to be "beautifully laid out, and ornamented by walks, flowers and shrubbery," including "a pretty fountain." The notes point out as well the deer park, where a herd of sixty or seventy fallow deer afforded the pleasure of the hunt over a one-mile track. On nearby flatland mock medieval tournaments were staged.

The Civil War hastened the decline of Fauquier White Sulphur Springs Hotel. In 1862 Union troops firing on Confederates encamped there reduced the resort to ruins. It was rebuilt in 1879 on a more modest scale. The property became a military academy in 1895 but went out of business when the main building burned in 1901. The property became the home of the Fauquier Springs County Club in 1953. (Photograph: Virginia Historical Society)

CRAWFORD HOUSE HOTEL, 450 Crawford Street, Portsmouth
Built 1835; demolished 1970

Until the Portsmouth Redevelopment and Housing Authority demolished it, the Crawford House was perhaps the oldest and least altered urban hotel in the commonwealth, even preserving its original stone storefronts. This dignified brick structure, the city's first hotel and for a time its tallest building, was erected for J. W. Collins and named for William Crawford, founder of Portsmouth. In its heyday the Crawford House boasted such guests as US presidents Martin Van Buren, John Tyler, James K. Polk, and Millard Fillmore. Unlike the more homespun inns and taverns, this prototype hotel had public rooms above its first-floor shops and three upper floors of guest rooms. Although it had passed out of service by the 1960s, the building was in excellent condition when it fell victim to the mindless Federal urban renewal program of that period. The Redevelopment and Housing Authority made no attempt to find an alternative use for this landmark. An unmemorable structure currently occupies the site. (Photograph: Virginia Department of Historic Resources)

GALLEGO MILLS, Twelfth Street between Cary and Canal Streets (at the former James River and Kanawha Canal Turning Basin), Richmond
Built 1835, rebuilt or expanded 1848, 1860, 1865, 1904; demolished after 1930

On the eve of the Civil War, Richmond's massive Gallego and Haxall mills surpassed their national competitors in annual volume of flour produced. The Gallego mills of 1860, the complex pictured here in ruins following the evacuation fire of 1865, topped the list, achieving an output rated at 190,000 barrels. The production of Haxall Mills (q.v.) was put at 160,000 barrels. The architecture of these mills transformed the Richmond waterfront at the falls of the James River into an industrial center made up of some of the largest structures then standing in America.

The first Gallego mill was established at the falls as early as 1796 by Joseph Gallego, a Spaniard whose name became the most famous in Richmond's flour-milling history. He was associated in business with a Frenchman, Jean Auguste Marie Chevallié; the two were married to sisters. Their buildings burned repeatedly, and the site was vulnerable to flooding; after the turn of the century they moved most of their operations farther west along the James River and Kanawha Canal, which had been built to circumvent the falls and which matched the river as a source of industrial waterpower. The new site was near what would become the western boundary of Hollywood Cemetery. The progress of these "upper mills" can be traced in the tax records of Henrico County.

Although there was inactivity during the depression years 1819–23, the operation was enlarged in 1832 and 1833.

Following a catastrophic fire at the upper mills in 1834, the Gallego operation relocated close to where it had started, although farther back from the river, at the eastern end of the canal turning basin. Two new mills, three and four stories tall, were built there. Following another fire, in 1848, an even taller, five-story masonry mill was erected on the site (by new owners Warwick and Barksdale) and described as the largest on the eastern seaboard, 164 by 94 feet and 127 feet high. The line of buildings was extended farther toward the river in 1860, when the tallest of all the mills was built. Samuel Mordecai reported that year with awe that this structure was to be "of great dimensions, twelve stories high." It would house thirty-one pairs of millstones propelled by six waterwheels, which would use "the same water-power repeated." As the largest building in Richmond, this became perhaps the most prominent ruin of the burned district at the close of the Civil War. In a series of somber photographs of the ravaged city, the stark shells of the Gallego buildings loom before the tranquil basin or reach upward with fragile pinnacles of brick; these images capture the magnitude of the loss.

Although at least one of the major Gallego buildings was rebuilt to a height of seven stories, as pictured here, the post-war operation was unable to compete effectively with competition that emerged in the Midwest. The business finally shut down in 1930, after the mill's waterpower rights were lost to the Chesapeake and Ohio Railway Company. The Gallego complex was slowly dismantled during the next forty years. (Photographs: Valentine Museum) TTP, Jr., and WMSR

EXCHANGE HOTEL, southeast corner of Franklin and Fourteenth Streets, Richmond
Built 1840–41; demolished 1900–1901

In 1839, as Richmond recovered from two decades of economic stagnation, city business leaders established a stock company to fund a palatial hotel that would stimulate urban growth. The commission was awarded to the nation's premier architect in this genre, New Englander Isaiah Rogers, who had achieved prominence following his work in Boston, New York, New Orleans, Cincinnati, Louisville, and Nashville. Rogers would also design the nearby Exchange Bank (q.v.) and a number of houses in Richmond, only one of which, built for Horace Kent, survives, in altered form as the Kent-Valentine House.

Richmond's Exchange Hotel soon became celebrated as one of the great buildings in the nation. Calling it "the Lion of the day" at its opening in 1841, the *Richmond Whig* reported that this mammoth and multipurpose structure housed a "Hotel, Post Office, Reading Room, Baths, Stores, &c." and that its location was ideal. The hotel was close to "the Railroad and Steamboat communications, . . . Banks, Custom House and Tobacco Brakes," and scenery "of the most picturesque beauty, with extensive landscape" of the James River basin, could be viewed from the hotel's "Observatory, Portico, &c."

Rogers gave the Greek Revival Exchange Hotel a handsome and distinctive exterior. The 130-foot façade on Franklin Street, which rose three stories above a rusticated granite basement, featured giant engaged Ionic columns, derived from those at the Temple on the Illisus, flanked by elliptical bays that were set off by three-story pilasters. Serving as a roof "observatory" and focal point was a variation of the Choragic Monument of Lysicrates, another survival of Greek antiquity that became renowned in the 19th century.

The interior spaces and appointments were as impressive as the façades. The traveler entered a "vestibule, with arched ceiling, supported by pillars of variegated marble of every hue. Between each [were] statues, emblematic of the seasons." Next the traveler came to "the great hall, with pillars from floor to roof, well proportioned. The view [there seemed] palace-like." To the left was "the Ladies' Drawing Room, the interior of which [was] in the best taste of Louis XIV." Adjoining were the ladies' dining room and "Bathing Rooms," where a woman could "live as private as a hermit in London, or as public as [she] please[d]." Opposite were the "Gentlemen's Drawing Rooms." To the rear were the "Ball Room," "Reading Rooms," and "Gentlemen's Ordinary," where "upwards of 300 persons" could dine. Above were "the greatest of all accommodations, parlors for private families, with rooms privately connected to them, in which a man [might] think himself in his own house." The guest rooms totaled 160. Charles Dickens, who visited the Exchange the year of its opening, judged it "very large and elegant" and reported that he was "well entertained" there. Several years later Edgar Allan Poe gave a public reading at the hotel of his poem "The Raven."

In 1851 the hotel was acquired and refurbished by John Ballard, whose Ballard House Hotel fronted it across Franklin Street. Ballard linked the Greek Revival structure to his newer Italianate one with a Gothic Revival cast-iron bridge. In 1867 the Gothic walkway was replaced by the nondescript pedestrian bridge illustrated in this photograph. The Exchange Hotel prospered until competition in 1895 from the new Jefferson Hotel forced its closing the following year. The vacant building was demolished at the turn of the century, and a warehouse was built on the site. (Photograph: Virginia Historical Society) TTP, Jr., and WMSR

FORD'S HOTEL (THE POWHATAN HOUSE), 1101 East Broad Street, Richmond
Built ca. 1840; demolished 1911

Although situated in a mostly residential neighborhood, Ford's Hotel (named for its owner, A. J. Ford) sat strategically at the epicenter of the social, political, and business worlds of mid-to-late-19th-century Richmond. The Capitol and City Hall (q.v.), as well as the First Presbyterian (q.v.), Broad Street Methodist (q.v.), First Baptist, and Monumental churches, were located just one block away. The hotel, which originally was called the Powhatan House, occupied the entire western half of the block defined by Broad, Eleventh, Capitol, and Twelfth Streets. This sprawling brick structure had a restrained Italianate façade on its Broad, Eleventh, and Capitol Streets sides. A prominent and unifying bracketed entablature crowned the building. A one-story colonnade of paired, slender columns was set into the Broad Street front; it wrapped the corner and continued for four bays along Eleventh Street. From this corner, horse-drawn omnibuses made continuous rounds to the city's several railroad stations. The hotel lobby, paved in marble, had entrances from both Broad and Eleventh Streets. The dining room, located on the building's south side, afforded patrons excellent views of Capitol Square. As with other Richmond hotels of the period, a barroom and barbershop were in the basement.

Significant events took place at Ford's Hotel. In 1842, the remains of Mrs. John Tyler (the first wife of a US president to die in the White House) were brought to the hotel for viewing prior to her burial. In 1848, Virginians just back from the Mexican War were feted here by the General Assembly. In 1851, President Millard Fillmore was entertained here prior to giving a speech at the Capitol. Edwin Booth, the famous actor, was among the notable figures who stayed here. In 1911 the city of Richmond purchased the site for a municipal courthouse, and the cleared lot was used as an aviation recruiting station during World War I. In 1938, however, the Virginia State Library and Supreme Court Building was constructed on the site. (Photograph: Valentine Museum)
EJS, Jr.

SPENCER'S HOTEL (later THE COLONIAL INN),
Duke of Gloucester and Queen Streets, Williamsburg
Built ca. 1840, expanded 1890–1900; demolished ca. 1938

Prominently sited at the core of colonial Williamsburg (on the site where Chowning's Tavern was later reconstructed), Spencer's Hotel once served as a conspicuous reminder of Williamsburg's commercial 19th-century past. Named for a former owner and operator, Col. Jack Spencer, the hotel was constructed in three phases. The earliest unit was the central structure, which on two sides (and possibly four originally) was faced with a broad, two-story piazza; these porches and an octagonal cupola gave the building considerable visual appeal.

After a half-century of use, Spencer's Hotel was expanded along Duke of Gloucester Street and to the rear and renamed the Colonial Inn. The smaller wing to the east continued the picturesque theme of the original structure; at one time this unit contained two shops downstairs and hotel rooms above. The sizable addition to the rear provided individual chambers, as well as a large sitting room and a dining room that also served as a ballroom. The expanded building accommodated tourists who were increasingly visiting the colonial town at the turn of the century. Among the patrons in the 1890s was novelist Ellen Glasgow. The new traffic to the town would eventually lead to the hotel's removal; ironically, the Colonial Inn was demolished in the process of restoring colonial Williamsburg. (Photograph: Historic American Buildings Survey, Library of Congress)

PRATT'S VIRGINIA SKY-LIGHT DAGUERREAN GALLERY, 145 East Main Street,
Richmond
Built 1846; demolished ca. 1900

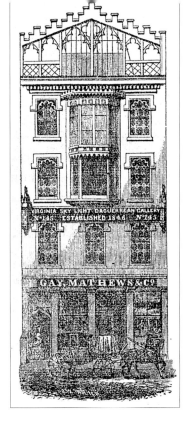

The multitalented William A. Pratt was his own architect for the remodeling of "Pratt's Virginia Sky-Light Daguerrean Gallery," where he made and sold daguerreotypes. The gallery took up the second, third, and fourth floors of a brick building that was part of a row on Main Street known as Eagle Square. The Gothic window in the topmost floor was both an eye-catching folly and a means of screening a large skylight that provided the brilliant illumination crucial to the making of daguerreotypes. The Gothic was almost Pratt's signature in architecturally conservative Richmond; he not only advertised his studio as "At the Gothic Window, 145 Main Street," but he lived in Richmond's premier Gothic-style mansion, Pratt's Castle (q.v.), another of his designs. (Among Pratt's other known works are the Gatekeeper's Lodge [q.v.] at the University of Virginia.)

Pratt advertised that visitors to his studio would be ushered into a semicircular reception room decorated with statuettes, divans, draperies, carpets, mirrors, and stained glass, all designed, "with their subdued tones and admirable contrast, to produce a harmonious whole, well adapted to show the daguerrean pictures which grace the walls, to the best advantage." At the rear of the floor was a "Ladies retiring room, which has been fitted up and furnished with taste." Above were the "operating rooms." There Pratt could "obtain an unobstructed light from a Northern point of the horizon, by means of sky-lights thirty feet in height by twelve feet in width." He believed that "this sky-light, in combination with the gothic window, constitute[d] the distinguishing feature of [the] Gallery, and enable[d] him . . . to surpass all other operators in his art, in this meridian, at least." (Image: Virginia Historical Society)

(FIRST) HOMESTEAD, Hot Springs, Bath County
Built ca. 1848 and 1890s; burned 1901

In 1750 Dr. Thomas Walker remarked about the waters of Hot Springs, "Very clear and warmer than new milk. It will be famous." There were nine separate baths of varied temperatures. In the notes to Edward Beyer's *Album of Virginia*, published a century later, these waters were said to be "excelled by nothing ever known to the human race. Their alternative and curative powers are unsurpassed by those of any mineral water on the face of the Globe." Nonetheless, it was not until the 20th century that Hot Springs eclipsed neighboring resorts. The 19th-century traveler was more frequently drawn to nearby Warm Springs, five miles to the north.

By 1848 there were enough visitors to Hot Springs that the owner there, a physician and entrepreneur named Thomas Goode, was compelled to build a large hotel that he named the Homestead. Beyer depicted it in his *Album*; the notes accompanying the lithograph recorded that the accommodations for 250 guests were "first class." This large wooden structure appears to have been modeled, at least in part, on Warm Springs Hotel (q.v.), and in turn on Mount Vernon; a giant, two-story piazza stretched across the center section of its north (main) façade.

In 1890 the Homestead was purchased by the Southern Improvement Company, which set out to develop it into a world-class resort. The grounds were expanded more than fourfold, and a massive construction project was initiated. In 1892 Philadelphia architects Yarnell and Goforth built a classical bathhouse. A Queen Anne–style hotel, named the Virginia, was erected at the terminus of a new line of railroad tracks. By the next year another building in the same style, the Casino, had been completed; the bathhouse, Virginia hotel, and Casino all survive. Also by 1893, the main wooden hotel had been greatly enlarged, as shown here. The Elzner and Anderson firm of Cincinnati had transformed the 1848 building into a quadrangular structure and extended it with a long, four-and-a-half-story northwest wing that reached toward the bathhouse. The Mount Vernon motif was replaced by one borrowed from another white house, the one built in Washington, DC, to house the president; this was a double-story, rounded Ionic portico. In 1901 a fire that had originated in the hotel's bakeshop leveled the building, including the large new wing. The hotel was rebuilt in brick the next year and survives today as the core of the present Homestead. (Photograph: Virginia Department of Historic Resources)

MOSS TOBACCO FACTORY,
Clarksville, Mecklenburg County
Built 1850s; demolished 1980

Built in two stages in the 1850s, the three-and-a-half-story, brick Moss Tobacco Factory housed a complete tobacco manufacturing operation until 1862. By 1872, however, Clarksville had ceded its primacy in tobacco manufacturing to Richmond and Petersburg, and the building was converted from manufacturing to use as a warehouse for the sale and exchange of tobacco. In time, the Southside tobacco market became concentrated in Danville, and this structure ceased to have any connection to the tobacco industry. It survived, however, as a rare example of an antebellum industrial building, until it was demolished in 1980. (Photograph: Virginia Department of Historic Resources)

DUNLOP MILLS, Manchester district, Richmond
Built 1852; burned 1949

Like the large steamboats that carried cotton to New Orleans at midcentury, the giant flour mills of Richmond were highly visible evidence of the industrialization of the 1850s, which radically changed the traditional perception that the Old South was a rural plantation society frozen in time. These massive "houses" of industry carried the traditional house form to an unprecedented scale, a height of eight to twelve stories. Each contained multiple pairs of millstones (even dozens) that were propelled by multiple wheels. Wheat was carried in volume to these complexes by the extended James River and Kanawha Canal and by newly constructed railroads that reached even beyond the boundaries of Virginia. Production peaked in the 1850s, when Richmond flour was shipped to California to meet a new demand brought about by the gold rush of 1849. The Richmond mills signaled progress and measured the extent to which the city's flour industry had grown.

Dunlop, Moncure, and Company erected buildings at midcentury on the site of a mill established in the 1700s by William Byrd II and later enlarged by the Mayo family; the business would operate for nearly a century. Situated on the south bank of the James River, these mills reportedly suffered damage during the fall of Richmond in 1865, but they were not burned like the Gallego mills; photographs taken after the evacuation of the city show the complex still standing. It was large, then; two four-and-a-half-story structures that once flanked the principal buildings were gone by 1936, the date of the image shown here. During the decades immediately following the war Thomas W. McCance, part owner of the Dunlop firm, proved to be a particularly able businessman when he doubled the mill's productivity. Earlier, he had transformed his residence, the Hayes-McCance house (q.v.), into a showplace.

Richmond's mills produced flours that resisted spoilage in tropical climates. Haxall Mills (q.v.) shipped almost entirely to South American markets, primarily Brazil (which shipped coffee in return to Richmond). Gallego Mills (q.v.) developed markets there as well as in Great Britain. With the collapse of those markets as the century neared its close, the Haxall company failed, and the Gallego company faltered. The Dunlop business served a domestic market, in the south and southwest, which kept it operating at a greater capacity until 1932. Its mills continued to produce flour for yet another decade as the Dixie Portland Flour Co. (Photograph: Historic American Buildings Survey, Library of Congress)

MONTGOMERY WHITE
SULPHUR SPRINGS, Blacksburg
vicinity, Montgomery County
Built 1855; destroyed by flooding, fire, 1903

In the notes written in 1857 to accompany Edward Beyer's series of lithographs entitled *Album of Virginia*, mention was made of "the rapidity with which [Montgomery White Sulphur Springs had] come into notoriety." After only two years of existence, this spa "promise[d] to be the most agreeable place in the Mountains." One reason was its ease of accessibility; the Montgomery was located only one and a half miles from the Virginia-Tennessee Railroad line. A newspaper writer in 1855 applauded the development of the new spring,

stating that the neighboring ones, while numerous, were already too crowded.

The architect for Montgomery Springs was Richmonder Henry Exall (who would soon design the pavilion for the Henry Clay statue on the grounds of the Capitol [q.v.]). The plan he devised for Montgomery was described thusly in the 1855 newspaper account: "On each side of the beautiful valley is a row of cottages corresponding with each other and, in the center, not far from the spring, is the house where the guests are received and registered." The complex was depicted by Beyer (shown here). Beyer illustrated twenty-two cottages that flank a lawn of several acres laid out with shade trees, walkways and carriageways, and even a riding track. The spring was located near the juncture of the rows of cottages. The "house where the guests are received," the hotel, was the large structure to the left in Beyer's lithograph; it measured 110 by 60 feet according to a promotional brochure written after the Civil War. The lower level was given to a huge dining room; three parlors and a hall were on the second floor, and sixteen bedrooms on the third. Part of the appeal of the other buildings was their varied size; there were sixteen-room cottages, as well as twelve-, eight-, six-, and two-room buildings. In all, there were 223 guest rooms. Reportedly, a thousand guests could be accommodated.

During the Civil War years, Montgomery White Sulphur Springs was commandeered as a military hospital where victims of smallpox, which then had no known cure, were isolated, and many died. The resort was revived in the 1880s; among the new visitors were Confederate veterans, who reveled in the recent history of the spring. Today nothing remains on the site, which is entirely farmland. (Image: Virginia Historical Society; Photograph: General Photograph Collection, Special Collections Department, University Libraries, Virginia Tech, Blacksburg, Virginia)

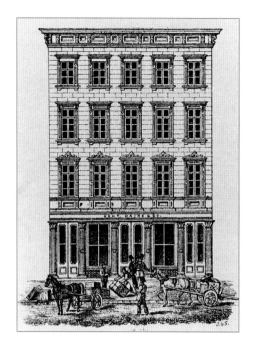

KENT, PAINE AND COMPANY HEADQUARTERS, Main Street between Eleventh and Twelfth Streets, Richmond
Built ca. 1858; burned 1865

Horace Leavitt Kent came to Richmond from Suffield, Connecticut, in 1821. He established a dry goods business that was highly successful and enabled him to acquire several significant properties. In 1845 he built an Italianate residence with Gothic Revival interiors at 12 East Franklin Street, designed by the Boston architect Isaiah Rogers and now the headquarters of the Garden Club of Virginia. In 1863 he purchased Melrose Castle, a Gothic Revival villa in Fauquier County. By that time he also owned one of the more impressive business buildings in Richmond.

By 1858 Kent's business was known as Kent, Paine and Company, and it had settled on Main Street. The property was insured for the large sum of fifty thousand dollars, an indication of the high value of both the building and its inventory. The storefront, as pictured on Kent's business letterhead of circa 1858, was Italianate; it rose five stories and was built of cut stone. Samuel Mordecai, the Richmond chronicler, linked Kent, Paine and Company to the merchant princes of New York, calling "the splendid store of Kent, Paine and Co., the first specimen in Richmond of the Broadway style of dry goods palaces." The building's architect is not known. This building was lost during the Civil War, in the evacuation fire of 1865. (Image: Virginia Historical Society)
LC

ATLANTIC HOTEL, Main, Granby, and Randolph Streets, Norfolk
Built 1858; demolished 1976

This massive Second Empire structure, with its fashionable mansard roof, opened on Norfolk's waterfront on the eve of the Civil War. The continuous colonnade and three-part façades of the Atlantic Hotel gave both visual appeal and scale to a building so large that it could accommodate "1000 guests." In a later broadside the hotel was touted as "new" because it offered the most modern appointments; in the premodern hotel business these routinely lured the traveler. The Atlantic provided "five stairways, three iron fire escapes, . . . electric lights throughout the hotel, electric bells, elevators, [and] hot and cold baths." "Tourists and invalids" were invited to enjoy "the fine climate of Norfolk." The Atlantic burned twice, in 1867 and 1902; it was demolished as part of the urban renewal of 1976. (Photograph: Valentine Museum)

PETERSBURG LIBRARY HALL,
Sycamore and Bollingbrook Streets, Petersburg
Built 1859; burned 1878, demolished 1932

The Petersburg Library Association was founded in 1853. Petersburg printer Thomas S. Pleasants was named librarian, and a new, handsome Italianate building was soon erected. It housed several rental retail spaces on the ground floor; above were an assembly hall and a library containing several thousand volumes. The first occupant of the principal retail spaces was the large firm of E. P. Nash & Co., booksellers, stationers, and piano dealers. The assembly hall saw an ambitious program of lectures, as well as balls, social events, and Masonic meetings. During the siege of Petersburg (1864–65), hosts of Confederate soldiers found relaxation in the library. In 1878 Library Hall burned but was not destroyed and was soon rebuilt, probably with few alterations. However, the building was used primarily for its ground-floor stores and no longer as a library. It never recovered its original tax value, which suggests that the upper floors were never fully restored.

In 1910, Virginia Railway & Power purchased the building to serve as its local headquarters and as the Petersburg terminus of its interurban line to Richmond. When the company built a new building in 1925, Library Hall fell on troubled days and was demolished in 1932. (Photograph: collection of Russell Wayne Davis)
RDW, Jr.

IRON FRONT BUILDING, west
side of Sycamore Street just south of Tabb Street, Petersburg
Built 1861–63; burned 1889

The Iron Front Building was one of the most ambitious architectural projects ever carried forward in Petersburg. The site was storied—Washington had been entertained there, at Armistead's Tavern in 1791, and two successive buildings housing Powell's Hotel had occupied the address until the end of 1858. On 16 September 1859, the *Daily Express* announced a "Heavy Transaction in Real Estate"—the sale of the "fine Sycamore street property known as Powell's Hotel, . . . there is none more desirable in Petersburg," to three local merchants, James Weddell, Samuel Drummond, and Augustus P. Spencer, for $35,750. Their intention was to demolish the hotel and erect "five first class storehouses, four stories high, with ornamental fronts, and all the latest improvements." By 10 February 1860, the three advertised for carpenters, bricklayers, and stonemasons to submit proposals. The process of construction seems to have been slow—one of the five buildings was brought to completion in 1861, two more in 1862, and the final two in 1863. It is impressive that one of the buildings actually was built four stories high, with a façade entirely of iron, particularly since the project was jeopardized by the war. Weddell, a Scottish immigrant to Petersburg in 1827 and grandfather of Alexander Wilborne Weddell (benefactor of the Virginia Historical Society), seems to have been the force behind the project.

The Iron Front Building was enormous, with about eighty thousand square feet and extremely high ceilings throughout, towering above its neighbors. The elaborate iron façade consisted of three tiers of arcades, ornamented identically but of descending height, and an enormous, bracketed, Italianate cornice, all carried at ground level by a slender Corinthian colonnade. The proportion of glass to structural elements was probably far beyond anything Petersburg had seen before. Each arch contained a pair of round-headed, double-sash windows, with a glass transom above. But it was on the ground floor that glass truly predominated: everything between the storefront cornice and the bulkhead was filled with huge sheets of glass. Moreover, the upper floors were painted white; the ground floor, black. As seen from an angle, as the building usually was, the row of piers and columns on the ground floor appeared fully capable of carrying the weight above. As one approached, however, the weight of the ground floor dissolved. While Weddell and his partners constructed the building cooperatively, each of the five stores was separately sold. Eventually, Anthony Rosenstock owned and occupied number one; he was the only owner to rebuild a store of equal size after a fire destroyed the building in 1889. (Photograph: collection of Howard D. Brown)
RDW, Jr.

PETERSBURG ACADEMY OF MUSIC,
northeast corner of West Bank Street and St. Paul's Alley, Petersburg
Built 1871, extensively remodeled 1888; demolished 1930

This theater, known as the Academy of Music, was the principal venue of an ambitious music community in post–Civil War Petersburg. Those supporters were led by tobacco manufacturers like C. W. Spicer, who in 1868 purchased the old Petersburg banking house of the Bank of Virginia and demolished it to make way for the academy. In 1870, Albert Lybrock of Richmond presented the academy with plans for a structure similar to Niblo's Garden and Theater (1827) in New York City. B. J. Black was awarded the contract for the carpentry and brickwork. The building was dedicated in October 1871.

The Academy of Music quickly encountered financial problems and failed. Its trustees then sold the building to the firm of Williams, Black & Co., which continued to operate the theater under its old name. In the 1880s, a new Petersburg Musical Association began holding large annual music festivals in the academy. In 1886, tobacconists John Q. Jackson and Heinrich Noltenius, principals in the new association, purchased the academy building and turned it over to their group, which immediately invested in a major overhaul of the structure under the direction of "Oscar Cobb, Architect." The new theater, illustrated here, could seat between fourteen hundred and fifteen hundred for music festivals, and the stage could accommodate four hundred performers at once. A great deal of attention was given to comfort and safety. The new façade, called Romanesque at the time, was a strange and vigorous composition, a far cry from the chaste

1871 elevation. Rental spaces flanked the cast-iron and slate marquee that spanned the sidewalk. The marquee, the semicircular arch on the second floor, the circular openings interrupted at their base on the third floor, and the scrolled central gable gave the façade considerable liveliness. The new theater opened with the Fifth Annual Petersburg Music Festival in 1888, but after 1891 the association's drive petered out, the festivals ceased, and the theater was sold in 1896 to David Dunlop. The academy continued to be operated as a theater, however, serving vaudeville troops, among other acts, at least until 1918 and perhaps until its demolition in 1930. (Image: Virginia Historical Society)
RDW, Jr.

GRAND PAVILION, YORKTOWN CENTENNIAL EXHIBITION, Yorktown
Built 1881; demolished 1881

The Yorktown Centennial Exhibition was the last great exposition that celebrated the American Revolution. It lasted but three days, and none of the buildings were permanent. Nonetheless, more public figures were present at Yorktown than at any other exposition of the period, including the great centennial event in Philadelphia in 1876.

The Yorktown celebration began to take form in 1879, when the governors of the original thirteen states met at Independence Hall in Philadelphia at the invitation of the governors of Virginia and Pennsylvania. Through their efforts Congress appropriated twenty thousand dollars for the exhibition and one hundred thousand dollars for a monument to commemorate the surrender of Cornwallis and his forces. Such a monument had been approved by Congress in 1781, but funding had never been appropriated. The Victory Monument, designed by architects Richard Morris Hunt and Henry van Brunt with sculptor John Quincy Adams Ward, was not completed until 1884, but the laying of its cornerstone was a showpiece of the 1881 celebration. Twenty-five thousand visitors converged on Yorktown; twelve hundred army hospital tents were put up as temporary housing.

The Grand Pavilion, shown in the left of the image, was one of the exhibition's few wooden buildings. The imposing structure was designed by Richmond architect Albert L. West. The exhibition was illustrated in both *Harper's Weekly*, the source of the image illustrated here, and *Frank Leslie's Illustrated Weekly*. (Image: Library of Virginia)
SATJ

FOREST LODGE, Mountain Road at the Richmond, Fredericksburg & Potomac track crossing, Glen Allen, Henrico County
Built ca. 1882; demolished 1992

Capt. John Cussons, an English-born Confederate veteran, settled in Glen Allen following his marriage to Susan Sheppard Allen shortly after the Civil War. Allen was a widow whose family included prominent landowners in the farming community just north of Richmond. Cussons established a successful printing company near Mountain Road at the Glen Allen railroad crossing and built a fortune printing druggist labels and calendars. In the early 1880s he used his wealth to finance his dream project, the construction of Forest Lodge, a pleasure resort serving wealthy northerners.

The six-story, Italianate frame hotel had 135 rooms and three-story verandas on two sides. The public rooms were lavishly decorated with hand-painted murals. Peacocks roamed the grounds, and the lodge offered a hunting preserve, four stocked fishing lakes, and a golf course. Cussons worked for twelve years to enhance Forest Lodge according to his own designs. The resort, however, never turned a profit, perhaps because of Cusson's overbearing personality. After his death in 1912 the hotel was converted into apartments but continued to decline. It was demolished in 1992. (Photograph: Library of Virginia)
EJS, Jr.

THE MOZART ACADEMY OF MUSIC, North Eighth Street between Franklin and Grace Streets, Richmond
Built 1886; burned 1927

The Mozart Association was established in 1876 to advance musical activity in Richmond. The group first met on the second floor of a building at Fourth and Broad Streets and sponsored a series of musicales each season. But in 1886 the association built the Mozart Academy of Music on Eighth Street, on the site of an existing assembly hall.

The academy was designed by Albert Lybrock, a German-born architect who had arrived in Richmond in 1852. Lybrock had been supervising architect for the Richmond Customs House (now the Lewis F. Powell Federal Courthouse), and he designed the cast-iron tomb of President James Monroe in Hollywood Cemetery. He gave the academy a three-part classical façade with a slightly recessed central bay that formed the entrance. Three grand arched windows marked the second floor. The elaborate entablature featured prominent brackets and garlands.

In addition to musical programs, the academy building was also used for political and theatrical performances. Congregational preacher Henry Ward Beecher lectured there, and actresses Sarah Bernhardt, Maude Adams (who in 1905 originated the stage role of Peter Pan), and Ethel Barrymore all performed there. This celebrated institution came to an abrupt end in 1927, when a fire destroyed the building. (Photograph: Valentine Museum)
EJS, Jr.

IRON GATE HOTEL, Iron Gate, Alleghany County
Built late 1880s; demolished 1945

Iron Gate, two miles south of Clifton Forge, is the site of Rainbow Arch, a remarkable rock formation described by its name and well known to travelers since the beginning of the 19th century. An early iron furnace at the site, however, gave the town its name. Following the arrival of the Chesapeake and Ohio Railroad at Clifton Forge in 1882, iron mines in Alleghany County were opened, and the Alleghany Iron and Ore Company built blast furnaces in Iron Gate; these operated until 1919, when forced out of business by competition from Minnesota. Iron Gate was a boomtown of the 1880s; its resort-style hotel with long verandas provided fifty-two rooms for guests and served as a social center for the community. In the next decade, however, land prices dropped to one-fiftieth of their former value. Nonetheless, the Iron Gate Hotel survived for half a century. The hotel was demolished when it interfered with the path of an expanded Route 220. (Photograph: Alleghany Historical Society)

RICHMOND & DANVILLE RAILROAD (LATER SOUTHERN RAILWAY) DEPOT,
Leesburg
Built 1887; burned 1969

In 1881 the Richmond & Danville Railroad Company hired architect J. F. Z. Caracristi to design a depot that would be reproduced at multiple locations along its line. It would need to be capable of modification to suit local needs: at some sites the depot would serve passengers only, with a separate freight building; at others it would house passengers and freight. The Richmond newspaper *The State* described the style of architecture as "Modern Swiss" and suggested that this "tasteful design" would "add much to the picturesqueness of the scenery" wherever it was placed. Those locations were the Virginia towns of Clifton, Clarion, Remington, Gainesville, Rapidan, and Franklin Junction (now Gretna) on the railway's main line and East Falls Church and Leesburg on its Bluemont branch. The Leesburg depot served passengers only. Rapidan depot is the only survivor of the group. (Photograph: W & O D Railroad Regional Park)
DRT

BALTIMORE & OHIO RAILROAD/SOUTHERN RAILWAY DEPOT, Woodstock
Built 1889; demolished 1954

The rail line up the Shenandoah Valley was operated jointly by the Baltimore & Ohio Railroad and the Southern Railway. It is likely that the Woodstock depot was constructed by the B&O, although it was later owned by the Southern. This was a relatively grand and costly little station; three explanations have been offered as to why it was awarded to so small a stop. The first, more engaging than probable, is that through a mistake in the bill of lading, stone destined for Woodstock, Maryland, arrived in the like-named Virginia town, and citizens lobbied to keep it. Another, told by the son of the former station agent, is that following the death of area residents in a train wreck, a new, modern station was erected to generate goodwill. According to this story, a Mr. Billinglea, an architect, arrived from Baltimore with instructions to build the stone depot. The third explanation, more plausible, is that the new station answered complaints about B&O accommodations that periodically were made in the local newspaper by a US senator who owned the paper and lived in Woodstock. After a half-century of use, the building was sold for twenty dollars and dismantled for its materials. (Photograph: Southern Railway, Donald R. Traser collection)
DRT

THE ROCKBRIDGE HOTEL, Glasgow, Rockbridge County
Built 1889–92; demolished mid–20th century

In the years that preceded the national Panic of 1893, Rockbridge County was gripped by a land speculation boom. In 1889 in Buena Vista and Glasgow, and in the following two years in Goshen and Lexington, land development companies were established to transform farmland into urban property. Financing was provided in part by northern capitalists attracted to the Valley's natural resources and new railroads. Common to the four Rockbridge schemes, and the first structure to be built at each site, was a hotel to house investors and events. Each hotel was a large and rambling structure, an imaginative exercise in creative eclectic design. The architects, all of them Pennsylvanians, manipulated picturesque skylines and varied textures and colors to devise an imaginative environment. The *Baltimore Sun* reported that "every town in this section of Virginia just now seems to have a separate and distinct boom [hotel] of its own, each like Barnum's Circus." The first hotel to be built, and one of two to survive, was at Buena Vista; the Buena Vista Hotel now serves as the main building of Southern Virginia College.

Three land companies attempted to develop the village of Glasgow. According to a local newspaper account of the time, this "city" was not to have a grid of streets but to follow instead a "modern plan with crescents and circles." A picturesque hill above the James River valley was set aside for the centerpiece of the plan: the Rockbridge Hotel. It was designed by Edgerton S. Rogers and Walter R. Hignam of Philadelphia. The *Rockbridge County News* described it as "the queen of Virginia's hotels," with "tall towers and wide bays, sweeping piazzas and impressive stone-cut fronts and pillars." Its two hundred rooms and suites were all "finished in meticulous and expensive detail." There was even a roof garden.

The gala opening of the Rockbridge Hotel in September 1892 was spoiled when creditors arrived on the same evening. Investors and guests panicked as stock and land values plunged. The hotel, which cost $135,000 to build, was sold for $10,500. In the ensuing years the building served only as a storage barn where neighboring farmers might store their hay. It was eventually demolished. (Photograph: Rockbridge Historical Society, courtesy Washington and Lee University)

PRINCESS ANNE HOTEL, Twenty-fourth Street and Oceanfront, Virginia Beach
Built ca. 1890, 1922; demolished 1963

This was the second Virginia Beach hotel to be given the name Princess Anne. The core of the structure was a private Queen Anne–style residence built for the Groves family that was remarkable for its prodigious use of stone, which was an uncommon and expensive building material to use at this time and place. Porches on the east and south elevations pivoted from a striking three-story tower at the house's southeast corner. In 1922 Garrett Smith purchased the house and built the hotel addition to the west and north. The three-story hotel was given a mansard roof with dormer windows and verandas. It was representative of a generation of Virginia Beach and Princess Anne County hotels that were appealing because of their proximity to the oceanfront and almost domestic scale and feeling. (Photograph: Edgar Cayce Foundation Archives)
MRH

UNION STATION, Jefferson Street between Eighth and Ninth Streets, Lynchburg
Built 1890; demolished 1966

Union Station opened in the spring of 1890, in time to participate fully in Lynchburg's extraordinary, if short-lived, 1890s boom. The expansive structure, hemmed in by tracks on both sides, served several railroad lines that converged near the banks of the James River, three blocks from Main Street. Union Station gave newcomers and potential investors a grand first impression of the city. Covered platforms sheltered passengers in inclement weather, while louvered ventilators topped by baroque cupolas helped air circulation within. The building was similar to contemporary depots erected in other cities, notably in Bedford and Bluefield, West Virginia. The distinctive mansard roof was removed in the mid–20th century, when the station was remodeled. Eventually, with the decline in passenger traffic, the building was demolished. (Photograph: Jones Memorial Library, Lynchburg)
SAC, Jr.

THE ALLEGHANY HOTEL, Goshen, Rockbridge County
Built 1890–91; burned 1920s

In the late 19th century the village of Goshen was not unknown. It served as a watering spot that was situated close to popular Rockbridge Alum Springs and Cold Sulphur Springs. Its "Victoria" iron furnace was once the largest in the state. The main line of the Chesapeake and Ohio Railroad made the region accessible.

As part of the Shenandoah Valley land speculation boom around 1890, the Goshen Land and Development Company set out to build a hotel there that would have "no superior in the United States." Architects Yarnall and Goforth of Philadelphia, whose design for the Hotel Altemonte in nearby Staunton would never progress beyond the drawing board, devised a fantastic towered and turreted structure of considerable size and seeming European origin. Remarkably, it was actually built. Set in the rugged landscape beside the Maury River, the Alleghany Hotel nearly resembled a medieval town, one tied together by modern verandas. The *Goshen Blade* reported that this "magnificent building" offered 160 rooms, tennis courts, and swimming pools; it was to be "lighted with electricity and have all the modern conveniences." The building cost $150,000.

The Alleghany Hotel survived until the 1920s, when it was purchased by doctors who planned to convert it into a hospital. The building burned before they could do so, thereby depriving the region of what was probably its most fantastic architectural creation. (Photograph: Rockbridge Historical Society, courtesy Washington and Lee University)

HOTEL CHAMBERLIN, Old Point Comfort, Hampton
Built 1890–96; burned 1920

The Chamberlin was one of a series of hotels to grace Old Point Comfort, on the peninsula containing Fort Monroe and marking the entrance to Hampton Roads harbor. As early as 1820, entrepreneurs planned, built, and operated hotels in the immediate vicinity. One was the Greek Revival Hygeia Hotel, which was razed only six years after the opening of the more modern Chamberlin.

The first Hotel Chamberlin, illustrated here, was the brainchild of restaurateur and gaming magnate John Chamberlin, who had owned and operated entertainment venues in New York State and Washington, DC, before selecting Tidewater Virginia as the site to which he would relocate his family. He chose Smithmeyer and Pelz, architects of the Library of Congress, to design the hotel. This massive Queen Anne establishment was to feature the latest in amenities, including an on-site ice plant, laundry, billiard rooms, a bowling alley, and an electrical plant, as well as shops and railroad and telegraph offices. The public spaces were impressive. The dining room was given a large gallery to house the dinner orchestra and large windows affording a view of Hampton Roads. The ballroom was one thousand square feet and equipped with a spring floor. An enclosed Palm Garden, popular for afternoon tea, stretched along the hotel's south side. An adjoining pier carried an iron and glass pavilion for outdoor dancing. An enclosed saltwater pool was lit by a skylight.

Easily accessible by steamship and rail, the Hotel Chamberlin quickly became a popular stop for travelers en route to and from resorts in Florida, especially for honeymooners and retired military officers, some of whom took up permanent residence there. The Chamberlin's proximity to Fort Monroe ensured that young female guests would find officers with whom they might dance at the numerous soirees and balls. The Chamberlin burned in 1920, and a new, Georgian-style Hotel Chamberlin was built on its site in 1928. The adjoining wharf was demolished in 1960. (Photograph: Virginia Historical Society) MRH

TRUE REFORMERS HALL, 604 North Second Street,
Richmond
Built 1891–95; demolished ca. 1955

William Washington Browne (1850–1897), one of America's most important yet least remembered African-American leaders, conceived the Richmond True Reformers Hall and led the project to completion. Browne headed what W. E. B. DuBois called "probably the most remarkable Negro Society in the Country": the Grand Fountain, United Order of True Reformers. Browne, a proponent of African-American self-reliance, attempted to make the hall both a product of and monument to self-reliance. To this end, the African-American membership of the Grand Fountain financed the hall, and one of Richmond's leading African-American builders, George Boyd, constructed it. Because there were no African-Americans practicing architecture in Virginia at the time, Bernard Black, a white man, was hired to design the building.

Completed at a cost of twenty-four thousand dollars, the hall was Romanesque in style. The first floor contained the lobby of the True Reformers Bank, the Grand Fountain offices, and other commercial tenants. The stair tower provided access to meeting rooms on the second floor and a galleried concert hall on the third and fourth floors. The True Reformers proclaimed their building "one of the finest public halls ever erected by the Negroes of this country." It was one of the first of its kind in the nation. Successors, such as St. Luke Building in Richmond and the True Reformers Hall in Washington, DC (both 1903), as well as countless other halls around the nation, owed a debt to Browne's architectural experiment. A nondescript hotel ultimately replaced Richmond's True Reformers Hall; that building is now vacant and condemned. (Photographs: D. W. Davis, *Life of William Washington Browne*, 1910, and W. P. Burrell and D. E. Johnson, Sr., *Twenty-Five Years History of the Grand Fountain of the United Order of True Reformers, 1881–1905*, 1909)
TTP, Jr.

HALL, for the GRAND FOUNTAIN, UNITED ORDER OF TRUE REFORMERS, Fulton
neighborhood, Richmond
Built between 1887 and 1895; demolished early 1970s?

This two-story, frame, bracketed storefront building served as a neighborhood meeting hall for the True Reformers in Fulton, a once-thriving African-American neighborhood in Richmond. Citing repeated damage caused by the flooding of the James River, municipal authorities demolished the town center of Fulton in the early 1970s. No trace of this building, or the other commercial structures that once lined the streets of Fulton, remains.

The hall was built by Daniel J. Farrar, Sr., an African-American born in 1862 in Richmond and educated in public schools there. At age eighteen, he learned carpentry from his father, Joseph E. Farrar, a prominent Richmond contractor and builder.

In 1887, Joseph E. Farrar retired from his contracting and building business and was succeeded by his son, along with Henry J. Moore (b. 1856 and probably the brother-in-law of Daniel Farrar, Sr.) and a brother, John E. C. Farrar. In October of the same year, John withdrew from the new firm, which was then called Farrar & Moore and operated from the corner of Third and Duval Streets. The Richmond *Daily Planet* wrote of the partners in 1895: "Some of the handsomest dwellings in the city have been built by them." Farrar & Moore dissolved between 1897 and 1900, at which point both Daniel J. Farrar, Sr., and Henry J. Moore independently advertised as contractors. Farrar continued to advertise his services as a builder and contractor until 1923, the year of his death at age sixty-one. His son Daniel, Jr., followed the example of his father and grandfather, becoming at least the third generation of Farrars to become a carpenter and contractor. (Photograph: G. P. Burrell and D. E. Johnson, Sr., *Twenty-Five Years History of the Grand Fountain of the United Order of True Reformers, 1881–1905*, 1909)

LAW BUILDING, 807 Main Street, Lynchburg
Built 1891; demolished 1948

This massive, six-story, Romanesque Revival building brooded over Lynchburg's Main Street for half a century. When it opened, it was the city's tallest commercial structure, housing shops and a café on the ground floor and offices above. The Law Building was well named; the 1897 city directory listed twenty-seven law firms among its tenants. The façade, utilizing brownstone and brick, was embellished with carved lions' heads in the keystones of the prominent second-story arches, while menacing gargoyles glowered from the cornice high above. In all probability, the architect was William Poindexter of Washington, DC. When the building was demolished, some of the more notable ornamental features were saved. (Photograph: Jones Memorial Library, Lynchburg)
SAC, Jr.

WESTOVER HOTEL (later WESTOVER HALL, LYNCHBURG COLLEGE), West Lynchburg
Built 1891; demolished 1970

As one astute Lynchburg resident observed in 1890, "Old Virginia is 'on the boom' these days." Throughout the state, speculators accumulated huge tracts of land, usually near established communities, platted them into lots, and offered them for sale. More often than not, these "boomers" envisioned a large hotel on a prime parcel as part of the package to entice investors and customers. The West Lynchburg Land Company planned the Westover Hotel as the centerpiece of a one-thousand-acre tract and hired a New York architect, Charles Frederick Rose of Rose and Stone, to design it. By the time the Chateauesque frame building opened on 4 July 1891, the parent company had been reorganized because of financial difficulties. After several summers of fitful operation, the hotel was bought by a group of citizens to serve as the first building of Virginia Christian College, now Lynchburg College. It served its new purpose for well over half a century but eventually came to be regarded, with some justification, as an obsolete firetrap. It was demolished in 1970. A memorial plaque on the campus now marks the location of a notable building in Virginia's economic and educational history. (Photograph: Virginia Historical Society)
SAC, Jr.

THE DEHART HOTEL,
Lexington
Built 1891; burned 1922

In October 1890 the *Rockbridge County News* announced "Lexington's great awakening": "The old town has aroused from her lethargy, she has caught the spirit of the times," it reported. With six passenger trains arriving daily, Lexington seemed destined to become a railroad center of the South. Local citizens and outside investors alike envisioned a modern-day migration of settlers to the expanded city. The Union Steel Company of Louisville prepared to relocate there. The Lexington Development Company sold "$100,000 Of Stock . . . in Two Hours," according to a headline in the *Lexington Gazette*. With the proceeds, the company purchased 1,275 acres west of the city, where it planned to lay out streets and lots, provide a water supply, and erect two grand hotels. It would make Lexington "the most beautiful and profitable city in the South to live in."

One hotel was built, the deHart. The architect was S. W. Foulks of New Castle, Pennsylvania, who a year earlier had designed the nearby Buena Vista Hotel (which still stands and is today Southern Virginia College). Working in the creative eclectic style of the day, Foulks used medieval forms to signal modernity. The picturesque profile, sweeping verandas, and prominent tower and dome of the hotel made it a building that could not go unnoticed in the Lexington landscape. Promoters pointed to its elevator and "several bathrooms on each of the upper floors."

The deHart Hotel remained unopened when the *Rockbridge County News* announced the Panic of 1893: "It's a bust! The boom's busted." The Lexington Development Company folded. Today foundations for the Union Steel Company's projected plant lie buried beneath tennis courts at Washington and Lee University. The deHart Hotel was boarded up for nearly two decades. Around 1908, and until the early 1920s, the building was used as a student dormitory by the university and as a summer hotel. Plans to convert it into a preparatory school were abandoned when it burned. (Photograph: Rockbridge Historical Society, courtesy Washington and Lee University)

INTERMONT HOTEL, area of Fudge, Prospect, Highland, and Monroe Streets, Covington, Alleghany County
Built 1891; demolished 1913

In the 1890s the Intermont was described by its promoters as the finest hotel between Washington, DC, and Cincinnati. Nestled in the heart of the Allegheny Mountains, within walking distance of two springs and but a twenty-mile ride from others, including Hot, Warm, White Sulphur, Old Sweet, and Sweet Chalybeate Springs, and eight miles from the famous Falling Spring, the Intermont was a resort destination. At the same time, the hotel overlooked the main line of the Chesapeake and Ohio Railroad, which underlay its creation and would bring industry to Covington. Like other boomtown hotels of the period, this one was the creation of a local Improvement Society. What was different at Covington was that the group there actually achieved its goal of urban growth. During the following years, when the nearby Homestead and Greenbrier resorts expanded, Covington became increasingly industrial. As a result, the Intermont folded.

A promotional brochure from the 1890s boasted that this hotel was equal to any in the entire South. It offered the traveler dancing, walking, riding, touring, rowing, tennis, golf, hunting, and fishing. There were one hundred rooms, luxurious because they were reached by elevator and equipped with the latest amenities, including steam heat, gaslight, and hot and cold water baths. The dining room seated two hundred guests. Despite this grandeur, the hotel was short-lived; it was pulled down only twenty-two years after it opened. (Photograph: Alleghany Historical Society)

THE GABLES HOTEL (formerly THE ELKTON), Elkton, Rockingham County
Built 1891; demolished 1957

The Gables was yet another of the numerous Victorian resort hotels built in the Shenandoah Valley during the real estate boom of 1890. Like most of these Queen Anne creations, it was a visually arresting assemblage of towers, gables, porches, and shingles. As with several other hotels, its design was popularly attributed to the famed architect Stanford White. This was wishful thinking, however, for the *Manufacturer's Record* of 19 July 1890 lists Marion J. Dimmock of Richmond as the architect.

Completed in 1891, the 120-room hotel attracted guests from Washington, DC, and eastern Virginia seeking fresh air and cool summer nights. Unlike many of the other Valley resorts, the Gables survived the Great Depression and continued to offer accommodations well after World War II. Declining fortune forced Stewart Houston, the last owner, to close it in 1956 and offer it for sale. However, he soon took it off the market and donated it to the Methodist Church, which had indicated an interest in using the building as a conference center. The Methodists quickly changed their minds and had the building razed in 1957. (Photograph: Virginia Historical Society)

CHAMBER OF COMMERCE BUILDING, Ninth and Main Streets, Richmond
Built 1892–93; demolished ca. 1913

A competition for the Richmond Chamber of Commerce building was staged in 1891 and won by local architect Marion J. Dimmock. His design, which shows the influence of the new high-rise buildings being pioneered nationally by Henry Hobson Richardson, Louis Sullivan, and McKim, Mead, and White, was published in *American Architect and Building News* (27 July 1891). As constructed, however, the building was given a more chaste façade than in the drawing, and absent was an ornamental corner tower that the architect had proposed. However, it boasted six floors of offices, a courtyard covered by a skylight, an auditorium, a restaurant, and a vault. The latest technology was used, including iron girders and fireproofing. The façade was faced with Petersburg granite on the ground level and brick above.

Dimmock's Chamber of Commerce was one of the first "modern" office buildings in Richmond, a symbol of the end of the Victorian era and the beginning of a new century. It was short-lived, however. In 1911 the property was sold to First National Bank, which constructed a new bank building on the site. Some of the ground-floor stonework was reused in a building on Governor Street. (Photograph: Virginia Historical Society)
THR

For three centuries, a broad cross section of Virginians—rich and poor, male and female, black and white—has experienced the world of business behind the walls of retail stores. With the rising scholarly interest in commerce and culture, these buildings are gaining fresh interest as some of the most important institutions and places of everyday life.

Colonial stores were usually built to exchange crops (often tobacco) for goods (often imported). Such specially built structures remained uncommon, however, until the second quarter of the 18th century, when the increase and spread of population and an exploding desire for consumer goods led to strong competition. By the end of the 18th century, retail stores were perhaps the most common nondomestic buildings on the Virginia landscape—in towns, at crossroads, and on plantations.

It is easy to recognize early purpose-built stores. In Richmond, the clothing store on Gay Street, recorded in a photograph around the time of the Civil War, shows one of the two most common forms. The most obvious distinguishing feature is the fenestration, the placement of windows and doors. The entrance is on the gable end, and a customer could step directly into the storeroom, where goods were stored and displayed. Without windows or doors, the long wall perpendicular to the street shows the need for long, uninterrupted shelving in the interior, a zone of display probably fronted with some kind of counter space. The chimney was placed at the rear to heat the office, which was a separate space where the merchant could court patrons and keep accounts. A similar version was found in the Petersburg store at 412 Hurt Street, built circa 1835 in a workers' housing area known as Pig Alley.

While the basic unit of store and counting room or office was most common, the placement of the rooms on the lot, alignment to the street, addition of other rooms, and location of doors and windows differed. An alternate version of the plan put the office and storeroom side by side, as shown in the photograph of the White Marsh store. The number of dormers suggests upstairs sleeping space for a merchant or more likely an assistant. This was a common feature to provide inexpensive housing and additional security for valuable goods. Finally, the merchant's increasing need to entice passersby from the street is shown by the large windows in Benjamin Barton's urban row store in Alexandria.

The evolution of store architecture in Virginia is one important index of economic and social change. Slowly changing agricultural practices in broad swathes of Virginia predicted that a customer—black or white—would continue to buy goods on credit and pay with staple crops in similar rural stores. Gill's store in Charles City County, for one, was an enlarged version of the colonial store type that continued to serve as a local gathering place. As shopping became a more important form of entertainment, women and girls became more common visitors. In all, as consumers became more particular about the kinds of things they wanted to buy, merchants had to compete by providing better shopping experiences. As the technology of making glass windows improved, more and more light was provided for customers to scrutinize goods and for displays to entice passersby, as seen at a grocery in Norfolk at the turn of the century. By that time, the retail store was the cornerstone of downtown development. In larger towns, the department store was the appropriate environment for the powerful desires of consumer demand to unfold. After World War II, the suburban challenge to downtown began, and those cores of commerce spread in new patterns and in new architectural forms. All of these architectural spaces tell us something about business—and us—and are being lost at a rapid pace.

ASM

GAY STREET CLOTHING STORE, Gay Street, Richmond
(Photograph: Cook Collection, current location unknown)

STORE, Pig Alley, Petersburg
(Photograph: Historic American Buildings Survey, Library of Congress)

WHITE MARSH STORE
(Photograph: Historic American Buildings Survey, Library of Congress)

BENJAMIN BARTON'S STORE,
Alexandria
(Photograph: Virginia Historical Society)

GILL'S STORE, Charles City County
(Photograph: Cook Collection, current location unknown)

TAGLIAVERA GROCERY STORE, 908 1/2 East Main Street, Norfolk
(Photograph: Norfolk Public Library, print in collection of Virginia Historical Society)

MILL #6, RIVERSIDE COTTON MILLS, in the block between the Main and Worsham Street bridges, along US Route 58 and the Dan River, Danville
Built 1894–95 (with later additions); demolished 1995

With the addition of Mill #6 in 1895, Riverside Cotton Mills became the South's largest in terms of the number of spindles in operation; twenty thousand were in Mill #6 alone. Looming five stories above the Dan River, Mill #6 was a powerful visual symbol of the "cotton factory fever" that gripped the city beginning in the 1880s and 1890s. Its construction marked the crest of Riverside Cotton Mills's initial wave of rapid expansion under the direction of T. B. Fitzgerald, the company's first president and, until the end of the 19th century, the "supervising architect" of the firm's first seven mills, all water powered. Capitalizing on the wealth generated by Danville's post-Reconstruction tobacco and textile boom, Fitzgerald also made a name for himself either as the designer or building supervisor of a number of the city's most lavish Victorian-era dwellings and churches. In contrast, his designs for tobacco factories and textile mills were fairly plain. Mill #6 was typical of these handsome, if austere, brick structures. All were vernacular versions of the popular "slow burning construction," which avoided enclosed attics and covered joists within a standard factory of thick brick walls, heavy timber framing, and plank floors. Mill #6 featured Fitzgerald's ubiquitous decked gables, with the walls enhanced subtly by recessed brick panels. Upon completion of the last of a series of accessory structures in 1923, the Mill #6 complex filled the entire block between the Main and Worsham Street bridges. As Dan River, Inc., the owner of Mill #6, continued to consolidate operations elsewhere in Danville, the facility ceased production in the mid-1980s, and the block was demolished in 1995. (Photograph: Virginia State Chamber of Commerce)
GRG

MONTICELLO HOTEL,
Granby Street and City Hall Avenue,
Norfolk
Built 1896–98; demolished 1976

The Monticello is remembered as the grandest of the early hotels of Norfolk. Its walls of arched and heavy masonry introduced to the region the creative eclectic style of the Romanesque as it had been popularized by Henry Hobson Richardson and Louis Sullivan; the architects were Carpenter & Peebles of Norfolk and Scott, Edelsvard & Fortin of New York. Following a fire in 1918, the Monticello was restored on the interior with the most modern amenities, including telephones in each room and lighting powered by the building's own electric plant. It was here that important visitors to the Jamestown Exposition of 1907 were housed and Woodrow Wilson announced his candidacy for the presidency.

The Monticello was refurbished in 1956, but its neighborhood remained in decline. In Norfolk's decades-long attempt to remake its image by demolishing its inner city, the Monticello was pulled down only twenty years after its refurbishment; a federal office building now occupies the site. (Photograph: Virginia Historical Society)

CASINO, Rivermont Park, Lynchburg
Built ca. 1901; demolished 1920s

At the turn of the 20th century, the Lynchburg Traction and Light Company, hoping to boost ridership, erected this elegant casino in Rivermont Park, a short streetcar ride from downtown. Its asymmetrical towers were Queen Anne in spirit, but its plethora of classical details heralded the coming Colonial Revival. The casino, actually a theater, served as a summer venue for performances of all sorts. One entertainer, Prince Giovanni, who was advertised as a "grotesque eccentric comedian," so offended a 1903 audience that the local papers printed a public apology. No apology was printed when the casino was taken down in the 1920s. Today the site of the park, on Rivermont Avenue between Belvedere Street and Langhorne Road, is occupied largely by apartment houses. (Photograph: Jones Memorial Library, Lynchburg)
SAC, Jr.

ROMAN EAGLE MASONIC LODGE,
southeast corner of Main Street at South Union, Danville
Built 1901–2; burned 1920

Established in 1820, Danville's Roman Eagle Lodge No. 122 has built and maintained three temples on the corner of Main Street at South Union since 1851. John W. Cosby, the son and associate of Dabney Cosby and one of North Carolina's foremost antebellum builders, designed the first, a three-story, cubic brick structure topped with a cupola. The competition for the second and larger structure pictured here was won, apparently, by the prolific southern architect Frank P. Milburn; at the time he was also the designer of the city's new Southern Passenger Depot (1899). Begun in 1901, the temple was an urbane, four-story brick edifice, its top floor sheltered by a Chateauesque mansard roofline with peaks and dormers worthy of Cornelius Vanderbilt II's Fifth Avenue mansion. It was typical of Milburn's eclectic designs, which were alternately praised and derided by critics. Of the successive Masonic temples on this site since the mid–19th century, the 1901 edition had by far the shortest useful life, fewer than twenty years. On 3 January 1920, a disastrous fire that began in a store nearby consumed nearly the entire block, including this structure. Recalling the sad scene, a lodge member lamented, "Sunday morning found the smoldering ruins of the Temple and adjoining buildings covered with a mantle of snow which had fallen during the night."

The Masons insisted on fireproof construction for its successor, the present temple, a "modern gothic" building clad in white terra-cotta. The first of Danville's two skyscrapers, this ten-story office building designed by Fred F. Farris of Wheeling, West Virginia, continues to house professional offices and the lodges. (Photograph: *Art Work of Lynchburg and Danville, Virginia*, 1903)
GRG

MECKLENBURG HOTEL AND SANITORIUM, Chase City, Mecklenburg County
Built 1903; burned 1909

Chase City was incorporated in 1873; two mineral springs there provided opportunity for the economic development of the town. Mecklenburg Mineral Water soon was marketed nationally; it won gold medals for quality at the world expositions of 1893 and 1904 in Chicago and St. Louis. A tourist trade developed around the springs, if slowly, via the railroad.

By the turn into the 20th century a luxury resort hotel seemed feasible at the Mecklenburg County springs. The developers no doubt were outsiders, probably northern investors; they commissioned a Boston architectural firm, Kendall, Taylor, & Stevens. The resulting 150-room structure was imposing because of its size and classical design, yet at the same time it was appealing as leisure architecture, because it was wrapped in porches. Brochures that publicized the hotel mention a ballroom, lecture hall, gymnasium, sunrooms, and chambers for billiards, reading, cards, and smoking. The sick, who were lured by the presumed medicinal properties of the spring waters, could engage in the various healthful activities of a sanatorium; not only was bathing offered, but also available were hot air cabinets, electric treatment, and vibration and massage therapy. On the extensive grounds of the complex, guests could golf, bowl, shoot, play tennis, ride horseback, hunt, or simply walk.

The Mecklenburg Hotel and Sanitorium was so popular an attraction that special excursion trains were sent there on occasion from Richmond and Durham, North Carolina. Among the famous visitors were composer John Philip Sousa and novelist Ellen Glasgow. The resort operated for only six years, however, before the principal building, like so many of its ilk, was destroyed by fire. Today only concrete foundations mark the site. (Photographs: Prestwould Foundation Collection)

AMERICAN SAVINGS BANK, 116 Campbell Avenue West, Roanoke
Built 1905; demolished early 20th century

    The bold Beaux Arts appearance of this small bank was common to the American Renaissance movement, which during the first three decades of the 20th century motivated city fathers and civic leaders to revive and beautify cities with classical architecture. In this way the American urban landscape would replicate Old World settings that appealed for their charm and heritage. The American Savings Bank was an early expression in Virginia of the new style; the architect of the building is not known, but he was influenced by national figures like McKim, Mead, and White. They typically drew inspiration from architecture of the Italian Renaissance and ancient Rome. Here, the prototype was a Roman triumphal arch, a form that seemed appropriate for a modern bank because of its associations with achievement, bounty, and permanence. The American Savings Bank, however, proved to be short-lived; it was defunct by 1910, when the tenant pictured here, Colonial Bank and Trust Company, opened its doors. (Photograph: George S. Jack and E. B. Jacobs, *History of Roanoke County*, 1912)

NEGRO BUILDING, JAMESTOWN TERCENTENNIAL EXPOSITION, Norfolk
Built 1906–7; demolished 1907

    The Negro Building was designed for the Jamestown Tercentennial Exposition by William Sidney Pittman, an African-American architect practicing in Washington, DC, who had trained at Tuskegee Institute in Alabama and Drexel Institute in Philadelphia. Pittman's brick building rose two stories into a high hipped roof. Giant, freestanding Ionic columns supported the projecting pediment of the entrance façade. This commanding Beaux Arts structure, 213 by 129 feet, was apparently the first major exhibition building designed by and the first government commission awarded to an African-American architect; all contractors and workmen associated with its construction also were African-Americans.

    The exhibitions in the Negro Building, some 9,114 in number, celebrated the achievements of African-Americans. At the cornerstone laying on 14 February 1907, Giles B. Jackson, director general of the Negro Development and Exposition Company, proclaimed, "The showing we will make in this building will startle the world, it will astonish those that are unfamiliar with the true condition of the Negro and it will be stimulating to our race." A temporary structure, the Negro Building was designed only to last the life of the exposition and was demolished the year that it opened. (Photograph: *The Official Blue Book of the Jamestown Ter-Centennial Exposition*, 1907)

PEACOCK BALLROOM, SEASIDE PARK, Thirtieth to Thirty-third Streets, Virginia Beach
Built 1906; burned 1955

Seaside Park, which stretched along the oceanfront just outside the town limits of Virginia Beach, was developed by the Norfolk Southern Railroad in 1906. Special trains aptly titled the One-Step Special and Two-Step Special brought scores of revelers to the complex. This speculative entertainment venture provided the railroad with revenues from both concessions and transportation. The complex included restaurant and amusement buildings that were set back from and parallel to the beach. Large end pavilions extended east; the south pavilion housed the famed Peacock Ballroom, and the north pavilion housed the bathhouse.

The Peacock Ballroom was enclosed by a massive gable broken by long shed dormers of clerestory windows. At the east, huge glass panels provided magnificent ocean views that gave the interior a sense of openness and light that was amplified by the minimal nature of the interior architecture. Except for piers supporting the roof structure at the dormer level, the whole interior was an undifferentiated and unpartitioned space beneath a series of enormous scissor trusses. The ballroom hosted the top entertainers of its era, including Fats Waller, Duke Ellington, Cab Calloway, and Tommy Dorsey. The park burned in 1955, and although some elements were rebuilt, it never achieved its pre-incendiary prominence. Ultimately the entire site was razed for redevelopment. (Photograph: James Jordan, *Virginia Beach: A Pictorial History*, 1974)
MRH

LARKIN COMPANY PAVILION, JAMESTOWN TERCENTENNIAL EXPOSITION, Norfolk
Built 1906–7; demolished 1907

The Larkin Company Pavilion, designed by Frank Lloyd Wright for the Jamestown Tercentennial of 1907, is the earliest example of what could be called Modern architecture in Virginia. The pavilion must have stood in dramatic contrast to its neighbors in what was called a "Colonial city"; most buildings constructed for the exposition were red brick with white trim, or imitation marble ("staff," a mixture of plaster of paris and horsehair), and they followed the symmetrical, columned, and pedimented language of classicism. Wright's pavilion was instead horizontal and asymmetrical; its design was driven by abstract geometry instead of historical allusion.

Stylistically, the Larkin Pavilion emerged from Wright's Prairie-style domestic architecture, which he had developed in the Midwest beginning in the late 1890s. The architect described that work as a response to the midwestern landscape. For the Buffalo-based Larkin Company, which manufactured soap, Wright had earlier designed a headquarters (since demolished) and a series of Prairie-style houses for its executives. Although the Larkin Pavilion was a radical design for its time and place, it was awarded one of the few gold medals for architecture bestowed at the exposition. It was demolished when the fair closed. (Photograph: *The Official Blue Book of the Jamestown Ter-Centennial Exposition*, 1907)

FIRST NATIONAL BANK, 503–7 King Street, Alexandria
Built 1908–9; demolished 1968

Until it was demolished by the Alexandria Redevelopment Housing Authority in one of the typically misguided urban renewal projects of the 1960s, this austere Neoclassical Revival bank was a prominent component of the streetscape of urban Alexandria. The First National Bank was designed in 1908 by the Washington, DC, architects Vogt and Morrill and was built by the Washington construction firm Charles J. Cassidy Co.

An imposing one-story structure measuring fifty by seventy-five feet in plan, First National Bank was constructed of brick and concrete, with the King Street front sheathed in marble. This handsome façade was remarkably bold and simple in design; a broken Doric pediment with full architrave, frieze, and cornice framed a massive recessed arch and window, penetrated by the entrance to the bank. Inside was an equally impressive space, a large, forty-by-seventy-foot banking room, finished with white brick and covered by a vaulted ceiling punctuated by skylights. The arched window of the façade was repeated at the rear of the building above the bank vault. When built, First National Bank was described by the *Alexandria Gazette* as "an ornament to the city." (Photograph: Historic American Buildings Survey, Library of Congress)

ST. LUKE PENNY SAVINGS BANK, southeast corner of Marshall and First Streets, Richmond
Built 1909; demolished ca. 1970

In 1909, Maggie Lena Walker, president of the St. Luke Penny Savings Bank, set out to replace the outgrown quarters of her institution in Jackson Ward, Richmond's African-American business district or "Black Wall Street." To design a new building she commissioned Charles T. Russell, a Richmond native who had studied at Hampton Institute and taught carpentry and mechanical drawing at Tuskegee Institute. This was Russell's first commission; it enabled him to start what was probably the first architectural practice in Virginia by an African-American . A local African-American contractor executed Russell's design.

The completed St. Luke Penny Savings Bank had prominent street-front elevations in the Renaissance Revival style, each with distinctive cast-stone signage. The corner of the building was given to an ornate, fireproofed banking lobby with a mezzanine. The upper floors accommodated twelve apartments. The building stood for nearly sixty years as a notable example of African-American progress; it was financed, designed, built, and occupied by African-Americans. Around 1970, Consolidated Bank and Trust Company, the successor to the St. Luke Bank, demolished this local landmark when it constructed a bland new facility across First Street. The site of the bank is today a parking lot. (Photograph: Valentine Museum)
TTP, Jr.

TERMINAL STATION, Main Street, Norfolk
Built 1912; demolished 1963

Virginia had few monumental rail terminals, excepting the extant Broad Street and Main Street stations in Richmond. Norfolk's Terminal Station, however, was a close contender. It was designed by Reed and Stem of New York, one of two firms responsible for that city's famed Grand Central Terminal. The Norfolk depot served trains of the Norfolk Southern, Norfolk & Western, and Virginian railways. More tracks than were actually needed were provided in hopes that the other rail lines serving the city would route their trains into the station; this never happened. An elegant waiting room featured extensive marble decoration and a coffered ceiling; above was a nine-story tower that housed offices of the three rail companies. As highways and airlines eroded the railway's passenger base, Norfolk Southern and Virginian discontinued their passenger trains, leaving Norfolk & Western the sole occupant of Terminal Station in 1956. Norfolk & Western moved its business to a smaller facility and closed the terminal on 26 December 1962. Prohibitive costs prevented a number of interested parties from converting Terminal Station for other uses, and it was demolished in the spring of 1963. (Photograph: Donald Traser collection)

DRT

CENTURY THEATRE, southeast corner of Sycamore and East Bank Streets, Petersburg
Built 1918; demolished 1972

Several generations of Petersburgers remember the Century with great fondness, as the principal first-run movie theater in the area, but it began life as a vaudeville theatre in 1918. J. F. Sachs of Roanoke (and later Baltimore) and Walter Sachs of Petersburg bought the property at the southeast corner of Sycamore and East Bank Streets in 1916 and immediately began construction of the theater. The building cost fifty thousand dollars, far more than any previous Petersburg theater. Its straightforward modern design was a clear reaction to the elaborate façade of the Academy of Music (q.v.), a block to the west, and a gesture to the new century. It was equipped with more than 850 seats, an upstairs lobby with Victorian furniture, stage rigging and machinery, and, perhaps from the beginning, motion picture equipment. In 1923, trustees sold the theater to Robert L. Thomas of Charlottesville, beginning a decade and a half of frequent ownership changes. This ended in 1937, when Petersburg Theatres, Inc., purchased the building; until the late 1960s it served as the flagship of movie houses in the Petersburg area. In 1970 the building was sold to an automobile dealer who demolished it to make way for a used-car lot in 1972. (Photograph: collection of Howard D. Brown)

RDW, Jr.

CONOCO SERVICE STATION, Richmond Road at Scotland Street, Williamsburg
Built 1939; demolished ca. 1974

Petroleum companies sought to assuage public distaste for gasoline stations in residential neighborhoods by casting them in traditional styles as early as the 1920s. The colonial idiom was, of course, favored in Virginia, where motorists often stopped for fuel en route to the state's historic sites.

Continental Oil Company took this approach to an extreme when it demolished an old house on the main road into Williamsburg to build a station in 1939. Conoco consulted with the Colonial Williamsburg Foundation and Singleton P. Moorehead, the museum's most skilled long-term architect. Moorehead provided details from existing buildings and, after much discussion, ultimately designed the elevations.

The plan was conventional service station fare, with a large front window lighting the office, beside wide front and rear doorways to a washing and greasing bay. A men's restroom opened into the office, while a door to the women's room was discretely located at the rear.

Moorehead cast all this as a prim edifice that could have taken up a place along Duke of Gloucester Street. It was a pretty pastiche, with heavy chimneys of the William and Mary College/Nelson House variety seeming to serve the grease pit as well as the office, and with cross-panel doors like those at Tuckahoe in Goochland County expanded to garagelike width. The craftsmanship was equal to Moorehead's design. The Flemish bond brickwork was as perfectly resolved as that of the town's contemporary reconstructions, with excellent rubbed and gauged work punctuating its edges. Windows were finished with paneled reveals, and the office walls were sheathed with beaded boards. Restroom signs hung from genuine wrought-iron brackets, and most of the hardware was bought from Colonial Williamsburg's Craft House.

The station was unceremoniously cleared around 1974 for the far less carefully detailed Hospitality House hotel. (Photograph: Virginia Department of Historic Resources)

EAC

BIBLIOGRAPHICAL NOTES

Frequently Cited Sources

Brownell et al., *Making Virginia Architecture*
Charles E. Brownell, Calder Loth, William M. S. Rasmussen, and Richard Guy Wilson, *The Making of Virginia Architecture* (Charlottesville, 1992).

Bucklen and Bucklen, *County Courthouses*
Mary Kegley Bucklen and Larrie L. Bucklen, *County Courthouses of Virginia: Old and New* (Charleston, W.Va., ca. 1988).

Chambers, *Lynchburg*
S. Allen Chambers, Jr., *Lynchburg: An Architectural History* (Charlottesville, 1981).

Forman, *The Virginia Eastern Shore*
Henry Chandlee Forman, *The Virginia Eastern Shore and Its British Origins: History, Gardens & Antiquities* (Easton, Md., 1975).

Lancaster, *Virginia Homes and Churches*
Robert A. Lancaster, Jr., *Historic Virginia Homes and Churches* (Philadelphia, 1915).

Lane, *Architecture of Virginia*
Mills Lane, *Architecture of the Old South: Virginia* (Savannah, Ga., 1996).

Lay, *Jefferson Country*
K. Edward Lay, *The Architecture of Jefferson Country: Charlottesville and Albemarle County, Virginia* (Charlottesville, 2000).

Lyle and Simpson, *Lexington*
Royster Lyle, Jr., and Pamela Hemenway Simpson, *The Architecture of Historic Lexington* (Charlottesville, 1977).

Miller, *Antebellum Orange*
Ann L. Miller, *Antebellum Orange: The Pre–Civil War Homes, Public Buildings, and Historic Sites of Orange County, Virginia* (Orange, Va., 1988).

O'Dell, *Architecture of Henrico*
Jeffrey M. O'Dell, *Inventory of Early Architecture and Historic Sites, County of Henrico, Virginia* (rev. ed., Richmond, 1978).

O'Dell, *Chesterfield County*
Jeffrey M. O'Dell, *Chesterfield County: Early Architecture and Historic Sites* (Chesterfield, Va., 1983).

Peters and Peters, *Courthouses*
John O. and Margaret T. Peters, *Virginia's Historic Courthouses* (Charlottesville, 1995).

Scott, *Houses of Richmond*
Mary Wingfield Scott, *Houses of Old Richmond* (New York, 1941).

Scott, *Richmond Neighborhoods*
Mary Wingfield Scott, *Old Richmond Neighborhoods* (Richmond, 1950).

VMHB
The Virginia Magazine of History and Biography

Waterman, *Mansions of Virginia*
Thomas Tileston Waterman, *The Mansions of Virginia, 1706–1776* (Chapel Hill, N.C., 1946).

Wells and Dalton, *Virginia Architects*
John E. Wells and Robert E. Dalton, *The Virginia Architects, 1835–1955: A Biographical Dictionary* (Richmond, 1997).

Whitelaw, *Virginia's Eastern Shore*
Ralph T. Whitelaw, *Virginia's Eastern Shore: A History of Northampton and Accomack Counties* (Camden, Maine, 1989).

Introduction

1. Thomas Jefferson, *Notes on the State of Virginia*, ed. William Peden (Chapel Hill, N.C., 1955), 152.

2. Carl Lounsbury of the Colonial Williamsburg Foundation has proven that the reconstruction was flawed. The entrance porches on the major (west and east) façades were not on balance with the surrounding windows, as the reconstructed building indicates; the semicircular apses actually eliminated a potential south bay, throwing off the symmetry. See Lounsbury, "Beaux-Arts Ideals and Colonial Reality: The Reconstruction of Williamsburg's Capitol, 1928–1934," *Journal of the Society of Architectural Historians* 49 (December 1990), 373–89.
3. Information courtesy of K. Edward Lay.
4. Information courtesy of S. Allen Chambers, Jr.
5. Information courtesy of Mary Ruffin Hanbury.
6. Information courtesy of Stephanie Jacobe.
7. Information courtesy of Pamela Hemenway Simpson.

Chapter I – Lost Domestic Architecture

ADAMS–VAN LEW HOUSE, 2311 East Grace Street, Richmond
Scott, *Houses of Richmond*, 68–74; Elizabeth Louisa Van Lew, *Album, 1845–1897*, Mss5:5 V3257:1, Virginia Historical Society.

AMBLER HOUSE, Jamestown
Brownell et al., *Making Virginia Architecture*, 20; Daniel D. Reiff, *Small Georgian Houses in England and Virginia* (Cranbury, N.J., 1986), 234–35.

BARBOURSVILLE, Barboursville, Orange County
James Barbour to Thomas Jefferson, 29 March 1817, Barbour Family Papers, Alderman Library, University of Virginia; Miller, *Antebellum Orange*, 68–69; Lane, *Architecture of Virginia*, 108–9.

BARN ELMS, Hartfield vicinity, Middlesex County
Louise Gray, *Historic Buildings in Middlesex County, Virginia, 1650–1875* (Charlotte, N.C., 1978), 101–4; Gilbert Chinard, ed., *A Huguenot Exile in Virginia* (New York, 1934), 119–20.

BATHURST, Essex County
Historic American Buildings Survey, VA-129.

BELLE FARM, Gloucester County
Edward A. Chappell, "Belle Farm: A Brief Assessment," unpublished report, Colonial Williamsburg Foundation, 1991; Edward A. Chappell, "Belle Farm," in *Making Virginia Architecture*, by Brownell et al., 208–9; Marcus Whiffen, *Eighteenth-Century Houses of Williamsburg* (Williamsburg, Va., 1984), 42–44.

BELVIDERE, in block bounded by Pine, China, Belvidere, and Spring Streets, Oregon Hill, Richmond
B. H. Latrobe, *Latrobe's View of America, 1795–1820*, Edward C. Carter II et al., eds. (New Haven, Conn., 1985), esp. 72–73, 120–21, also 26, 70–71, 144–45; William Byrd I, William Byrd II, and William Byrd III, *The Correspondence of the Three William Byrds of Westover, Virginia, 1684–1776*, Marion Tinling, ed. (Charlottesville, 1977), esp. 2:603–14, 622–26, 700–702; B. H. Latrobe, *The Virginia Journals of Benjamin Henry Latrobe, 1795–1798*, Edward C. Carter II et al., eds., 2 vols. (New Haven, Conn., 1977), 1:91, 133, and pl. 11, and 2:340–41; B. H. Latrobe, *The Papers of Benjamin Henry Latrobe*, Thomas E. Jeffrey, ed. (Clifton, N.J., 1976), microfiche, 159/B8–B9, 248/A2–A3; Scott, *Richmond Neighborhoods*, 179, 205, 213, 216; Edward L. Ryan, "Note on 'Belvidere,'" *VMHB* 40 (1931), 139–45; map of the city of Richmond accompanying Moses Ellyson, *Richmond Directory and Business Advertiser for 1856* (Richmond, 1856); *Richmond Daily Dispatch*, 6 February 1854; Charles S. Morgan, *Plan of Richmond (Henrico County) Manchester & Springhill, Virginia* (n.p., 1848); County of Henrico, Deed Book 15, 274 (plat accompanying Benjamin J. Harris and Sarah Harris to Samuel P. Parsons, 20 June 1817); County of Henrico, Deed Book 11, 202–3 (Margaret Harvie to Benjamin J. Harris, 17 December 1814); B. H. Latrobe, Sketchbook 1, 33 (view of Washington's Island) and 36 (view of Richmond), and Sketchbook 2, 29–30 (Belvidere from the southwest) and 43 (Belvidere from the northwest), Maryland Historical Society, Baltimore, Md.; B. H. Latrobe, "An Essay on Landscape," MS, 2 vols., 1798–99, 1:24–25 (with remnant of a lost Washington's Island landscape), Library of Virginia; Mutual Assurance Society of Virginia, policies n. 50 (1796), n. 1109 and n. 87 (1806), n. 1799 (1815), and n. 4550 (1822), Library of Virginia; Henry Lee and Anne Hill Carter Lee, deed of sale of "Belvidere" to Bushrod Washington, 21 June 1795, Edmund Jennings Lee Papers, Mss1 L5113 a53, Virginia Historical Society; Rev. Andrew Burnaby, *Travels through the Middle Settlements in North-America. In the Years 1759 and With Observations upon the State of the Colonies*, 2nd ed. (London, 1775), 13.

BELVOIR, Fort Belvoir, Fairfax County
Virginia Gazette, 2 June 1774, printed by Purdie and Dixon; "Inventory of the Furniture of the Several Rooms at Belvoir" and "Account of Sales at Belvoir," Virginia Historical Society; William M. S. Rasmussen and Robert S. Tilton, *George Washington: The Man behind the Myths* (Charlottesville and London, 1999), 20–27.

BEWDLEY, on the Rappahannock River, Lancaster County
Richmond Times-Dispatch, 11 December 1932; Lancaster, *Virginia Homes and Churches*, 312–13.

BLACK HEATH, Midlothian vicinity, Chesterfield County
O'Dell, *Chesterfield County*, 288–90.

BOSCOBEL, Fredericksburg vicinity, Stafford County
Richard Beale Davis, ed., *William Fitzhugh and His Chesapeake World, 1676–1701* (Chapel Hill, N.C., 1963), 3–55, 60–61, 201–8, 373–75; George Harrison Sanford King, *Register of Saint Paul's Parish, 1715–1798* (Fredericksburg, 1960); *Register of Overwharton Parish, Stafford County, Virginia, 1723–1758* (Fredericksburg, 1961); *King George County, Virginia, Will Book A-1, 1721–1752 and Miscellaneous Notes* (Fredericksburg, 1978); Jerrilyn Eby, *They Called Stafford Home* (Bowie, Md., 1997), 231–34; Lancaster, *Virginia Homes and Churches*, 351–54.

BOTT, MILES, HOUSE, 216 Cowardin Avenue, Richmond
Historic American Buildings Survey, VA-119; Scott, *Houses of Richmond*, 62–65; David L. Pulliam, "The Old House," *Saturday News Supplement*, 1 December 1900.

BOWERS, WILLIAM H., HOUSE, southwest corner of Sycamore and Bank Streets, Petersburg
Virginia Department of Historic Resources archives file, 123-53; *South Side Daily Democrat*, 1857; City of Petersburg, Deed Book 8, 88 (1927); Deed Book 8, 104 (1828); Deed Book 12, 49 (1841), Deed Book 42, 483 (1881), Land Tax Books, 1026–31; Mutual Assurance Society of Virginia, policy r. 15, v. 101, n. 10560 (1837), Library of Virginia.

BOYCE-MACFARLANE HOUSE, corner of Fifth and Leigh Streets, Richmond
Mutual Assurance Society of Virginia, policies n. 282 (1798) and n. 885 (1807), Library of Virginia; Sanborn Fire Insurance Map, 1895, Library of Virginia; Scott, *Houses of Richmond*, 54–56; Scott, *Richmond Neighborhoods*, 243–44; Karri L. Jurgens, "The Hancock-Wirt-Caskie House (1808–9): Its History and Context as a Richmond 'Octagonal' House" (master's thesis, Virginia Commonwealth University, 2000).

BROCK FARM QUARTERS, state route 615, Nimo vicinity, Virginia Beach
Historic American Buildings Survey, VA-400; Sadie Scott Kellam and V. Hope Kellam, *Old Houses of Princess Anne, Virginia* (Portsmouth, 1931), 146–9; Carl R. Lounsbury, ed., *An Illustrated Glossary of Early Southern Architecture & Landscape* (New York, 1994), 278–9.

BUENA VISTA (NOZECTHOS), Henrico County
O'Dell, *Architecture of Henrico*, 119.

BULL HILL (MITCHELLS), Mansion Drive, Hopewell
Francis Earl Lutz, *The Prince George–Hopewell Story* (Richmond, 1957), 24, 250; Virginia Department of Historic Resources archives file, 116-04; interview with Junius R. Fishburne, Jr., former owner of the house built on the site of Bull Hill, 9 June 2000.

CABELL, DR. JOHN J., HOUSE, Main Street between Fifth and Sixth Streets, Lynchburg
Chambers, *Lynchburg*, 33–37.

CAMERON LODGE, Gordonsville vicinity, Orange County
"Cameron Lodge," file, Orange County Historical Society; Ann Miller, unpublished research.

CARR, DANIEL F., HOUSE, West Main Street, Charlottesville
Lay, *Jefferson Country*, 105–6.

CASERTA, Eastville vicinity, Northampton County
Whitelaw, *Virginia's Eastern Shore*, 304; Virginia Department of Historic Resources archives file, 134-09.

CASTALIA, Cismont vicinity, Albemarle County
Virginia Department of Historic Resources archives file, 02-152; Edward C. Mead, *Historic Homes of the Southwest Mountains* (Philadelphia, 1899), 139–52; Roy Wheeler, *Historic Virginia* (Charlottesville, 1948), 187–92.

CEDAR HALL, Hampton
Roberta Nicholls, "Cedar Hall: The Grandeur That Was Home," *Daily Press*, 2 May 1976.

CHATSWORTH, Tree Hill vicinity, Henrico County
Marquis de Chastellux, *Travels in North America*, trans. Howard C. Rice, Jr. (Chapel Hill, N.C., 1963), 2:426–27; Gerald S. Cowden, "The Randolphs of Turkey Island: A Prosopography of the First Generations, 1650–1806" (Ph.D. dissertation, College of William and Mary, 1977); J. F. D. Smyth, *A Tour in the United States of America* (London, 1784), 1:28; John Wayles to Messrs. Farrell and James, 9 July 1769, American Loyalist Claims, Public Records Office, T 79/30, Colonial Williamsburg, cited in Cowden, 193; O'Dell, *Architecture of Henrico*, 36.

CHERRY GROVE, Eastville vicinity, Northampton County
Whitelaw, *Virginia's Eastern Shore*, 225; Forman, *The Virginia Eastern Shore*, 95–96.

CHESTNUT GROVE, on the Pamunkey River, courthouse vicinity, New Kent County
Malcolm Hart Harris, *Old New Kent County: Some Accounts of the Planters, Plantations, and Places in New Kent County* (West Point, Va., 1977), 1:82–86, 256–57; Virginius C. Hall, Jr., *Portraits in the Collection of the Virginia Historical Society* (Charlottesville, 1981), 66.

CLEVE, near Dogue, King George County
Frank Conger Baldwin, "Early Architecture of the Rappahannock Valley: II, Cleve Manor," *Journal of the American Institute of Architects* (June 1915), 234–40; Lancaster, *Virginia Homes and Churches*, 346–47; Lane, *Architecture of Virginia*, 50; Barbara Burlison Mooney, "'True Worth Is Highly Shown in Living Well': Architectural Patronage in Eighteenth-Century Virginia" (Ph.D. dissertation, University of Illinois at Champaign-Urbana, 1991), 550–71; Daniel D. Reiff, *Small Georgian Houses in England and Virginia* (Cranbury, N.J., 1986), 273–74; Waterman, *Mansions of Virginia*, 178–83.

CLIFTON (BENJAMIN J. HARRIS HOUSE), Old Fourteenth Street at the former Apricot Alley, Richmond
Karri L. Jurgens, "The Hancock-Wirt-Caskie House (1808–9): Its History and Context as a Richmond 'Octagonal' House" (master's thesis, Virginia Commonwealth University, 2000); Drew St. J. Carneal, *Richmond's Fan District* (Richmond, 1996), chap. 4; Charles Pool and Dulaney Ward, "Jacob House," National Register of Historic Places nomination (draft, not submitted, 1995), photocopy, Special Collections and Archives, James Branch Cabell Library, Virginia Commonwealth University; Jeffrey A. Cohen and Charles E. Brownell, *The Architectural Drawings of Benjamin Henry Latrobe*, 2 vols. (New Haven, Conn., 1994), 1:55, 291–303; Brownell et al., *Making Virginia Architecture*, 276–77; Rosalie Stier Calvert, *Mistress of Riversdale: The Plantation Letters of Rosalie Stier Calvert, 1795–1821*, Margaret Law Callcott, ed. (Baltimore, 1991); Talbot Hamlin, *Benjamin Henry Latrobe* (New York, 1955), 103, 105, 115; Scott, *Richmond Neighborhoods*, 120–22; Constance Cary Harrison, *Recollections Grave and Gay* (New York, 1911), 67–68; Edwin G. Booth, *In War Time: Two Years in the Confederacy and Two Years North* (Philadelphia, 1885), n.p.; Charles M. Wallace (attrib.), "A Glimpse of the Past—Old Homes in Richmond," *Richmond Dispatch*, 26 July 1885; Samuel Mordecai, *Virginia, Especially Richmond, in By-Gone Days* (Richmond, 1946 reprint of 1860 2nd ed.), n. 51, 57, 61, 321, 328; Mutual Assurance Society of Virginia, policies n. 1086 (1818), n. 4549 (1822), n. 5402 (1825), n. 7483 (1829), n. 10033 (1837), n. 11256 (1843), n. 15747 (1851), and n. 19244 (1858).

COLROSS, Oronoco Street, between Fayette and Henry Streets, Alexandria
Ethelyn Cox, *Historic Alexandria, Virginia, Street by Street: A Survey of Existing Early Buildings* (Alexandria, 1976), 99.

CONRAD HOUSE, 12 North Cameron Street, Winchester
Virginia Department of Historic Resources archives file, 138-05.

CORBIN HALL (CHINCOTEAGUE FARM), Horntown vicinity, Accomack County
Forman, *The Virginia Eastern Shore*, 289–94; Virginia Department of Historic Resources archives file, 01-07.

COROTOMAN, Weems vicinity, Lancaster County
Waterman, *Mansions of Virginia*, 110; Carter L. Hudgins, "Patrician Culture, Public Ritual and Political Authority in Virginia, 1680–1740" (Ph.D. dissertation, College of William and Mary, 1984), 48, 56.

CUNNINGHAM-ARCHER HOUSE, 101 North Sixth Street, Richmond
Scott, *Houses of Richmond*, 118–21.

DOVER, Sabot vicinity, Goochland County
Cece Bullard, *Goochland Yesterday and Today: A Pictorial History* (Virginia Beach, 1974), 60–62.

DREWRY'S MANSION, below Manchester, Richmond
Benjamin B. Weisiger III, *Old Manchester and Its Environs, 1769–1910* (Richmond, 1993), 90; O'Dell, *Chesterfield County*, 270–71.

DRYSDALE GLEBE, Newtown vicinity, King and Queen County
Virginia Cox, "The Glebes of Drysdale Parish," *King and Queen Historical Society Bulletin* 14 (1963), 5–6; Historic American Buildings Survey, VA-398.

DUNLOP-BRYDON-TENNANT HOUSE, southeast corner of Adams and Washington Streets, Petersburg
City of Petersburg, Deed Book 4, 258 (1814); Will Book 3, 315 (will of David Dunlop Brydon, 1841); Land Tax Books, 1878–1881, 1885, 1890; Mutual Assurance Society of Virginia, policies r. 10, v. 77, n. 3302 (1822); r. 12, v. 86, n. 5805 (1829); r. 15, v. 101, n. 10475 (1837); r. 18, v. 112, n. 13697 (1844); r. 20, v. 123, n. 16968 (1851); r. 2, v. 184, n. 20409 (1858), Library of Virginia.

DUNLORA, Charlottesville vicinity, Albemarle County
Bryan Clark Green, "In the Wake of Thomas Jefferson: The Architectural Education and Career of Thomas R. Blackburn, Architect in Antebellum Virginia" (Ph.D. dissertation, University of Virginia, forthcoming); Lay, *Jefferson Country*, 125–26.

EAST HILL (BOLLINGBROOK), on Bolling's Hill between Jefferson and Madison Streets, and between Bank and Franklin Streets, Petersburg
Edward A. Wyatt, *Along Petersburg Streets* (Richmond, 1943), 24–25; Mutual Assurance Society of Virginia, policies r. 6, v. 52, n. 472 (1815); r. 12, n. 5751 (1829); r. 18, v. 112, n. 13656 (1844); r. 20, v. 123, n. 16924 (1851); and r. 22, v. 134?, n. 20384 (1858), Library of Virginia; Petersburg Land Tax Books, 1852–1856, 1860.

EASTWOOD, London Bridge vicinity, Virginia Beach
Charles Royster, *The Fabulous History of the Dismal Swamp Company: A Story of George Washington's Times* (New York, 1999), 227–28; Historic American Buildings Survey, VA-242; Sadie Scott Kellam and V. Hope Kellam, *Old Houses of Princess Anne, Virginia* (Portsmouth, 1931), 64.

EASTWOOD, Manakin-Sabot vicinity, Goochland County
Cece Bullard, *Goochland Yesterday and Today: A Pictorial History* (Virginia Beach, 1974), 62–68.

EDGEHILL, Shadwell vicinity, Albemarle County
Drawing N0006/K170, Coolidge Collection, Massachusetts Historical Society; William Howard Adams, ed., *The Eye of Thomas Jefferson* (Washington, D.C., 1967), 282; Lay, *Jefferson Country*, 118–19, 132; Bryan Clark Green, "In the Wake of Thomas Jefferson: The Architectural Education and Career of Thomas R. Blackburn, Architect in Antebellum Virginia" (Ph.D. dissertation, University of Virginia, forthcoming); E. C. Mead, *Historic Homes of the Southwest Mountains* (Philadelphia, 1899), 65–74; Fiske Kimball, *Thomas Jefferson, Architect* (New York, 1968 reprint of 1916 ed.), 173.

ENNISCORTHY BARN, Keene vicinity, Albemarle County
Elizabeth Langhorne, K. Edward Lay, and William D. Rieley, *A Virginia Family and Its Plantation Houses* (Charlottesville, 1987), 107; Lay, *Jefferson Country*, 64, 76–77.

EXETER, Leesburg vicinity, Loudon County
Virginia Department of Historic Resources archives file, 53-77.

FAIRFIELD, White Marsh vicinity, Gloucester County
Carter's Creek plat, no. 240, September 1847, Surveyors Book No.1 (1817–52), Gloucester County courthouse; Edward A. Chappell, Virginia Historic Landmarks Commission, "Fairfield Site," National Register of Historic Places nomination, February 1973; Lancaster, *Virginia Homes and Churches*, 225–30; *Richmond Times-Dispatch*, 12 November 1911; Thomas Tileston Waterman and John A. Barrows, *Domestic Colonial Architecture of Tidewater Virginia* (New York, 1932), 30–35; Waterman, *Mansions of Virginia*, 25–27; Paul Baker Touart, *Somerset: An Architectural History* (Annapolis, Md., 1990), 50, 53, 88, 198–99; H. Chandlee Forman, *Tidewater Maryland Architecture and Gardens* (New York, 1956), 23–25, 43; Gilbert Chinard, ed., *A Huguenot Exile in Virginia* (New York, 1934), 119–20.

FORBES, WHITMELL S., HOUSE, 3401 Monument Avenue (entire block), Richmond
Sarah Shields Driggs, Richard Guy Wilson, and Robert P. Winthrop, *Richmond's Monument Avenue* (Chapel Hill, N.C., forthcoming 2001).

FORT RHODES, Luray vicinity, Page County
Edward A. Chappell, "Acculturation in the Shenandoah Valley: Rhenish Houses of the Massanutten Settlement," *Proceedings of the American Philosophical Society* 124 (February 1980), 55–89; Edward Chappell, "Germans and Swiss," in *America's Architectural Roots*, ed. Dell Upton (Washington, D.C., 1986), 68–73; Harry M. Strickler, *A Short History of Page County, Virginia* (Richmond, 1952); Margaret T. Peters and Dell Upton, Virginia Historic Landmarks Commission, "Fort Rodes," National Register of Historic Places nomination, 1977.

FOUR MILE TREE PLANTATION, OVERSEER'S HOUSE, Surry County
Philip St. George Cocke, Letterbook, 1848, University of Virginia Library, Special Collections Department, Cocke Papers, No. 640 etc., Box 189; Cary Charles Cocke to

William Old, Letterbook, 8 August 1838, University of Virginia Library, Special Collections Department, Cocke Papers, No. 640 etc., Box 189; Philip St. George Cocke to William Maxwell, Letterbook, 1 May 1845, University of Virginia Library, Special Collections Department, Cocke Papers, No. 640 etc., Box 189.

FREEMAN, SAMUEL, HOUSE (DE SAUSSURE HOUSE), 316 East Main Street, Richmond
Historic American Buildings Survey, VA-114; Scott, *Houses of Richmond*, 197.

GALT, MARY, HOUSE, 1011 St. James Street, Richmond
Gregg D. Kimball, "African-Virginians and the Vernacular Building Tradition in Richmond City, 1790–1860," in *Perspectives in Vernacular Architecture, IV*, ed. Thomas Carter and Bernard L. Herman (Columbia, Mo., 1991), 121–29; John Maddox, *The Richmond Directory, Register, and Almanac for the Year 1819* (Richmond, 1819), 50, 55; W. L. Montague, *The Richmond Directory and Business Advertiser for 1852* (Baltimore, 1852), 139–49; Scott, *Richmond Neighborhoods*, 296–98.

GARST LOG HOUSE, off Garst Cabin Road at intersection with Grandin Road Extension, Roanoke County
Deedie Kagey, *When Past Is Prologue: A History of Roanoke County* (Roanoke, l988), 51; "Garst Log Cabin Meeting Topic," *Roanoke World-News*, 7 December l973, 12 et seq.

GERMANNA, northeastern Orange County
Miller, *Antebellum Orange*, 154; W. W. Scott, *History of Orange County* (Richmond, 1907), 87–92.

THE GLEBE, vicinity of Saluda and Urbanna, Middlesex County
Louise Gray, *Historic Buildings in Middlesex County, Virginia, 1650–1875* (Charlotte, N.C., 1978), 8–11.

GREEN SPRING HOUSE, near the junction of Virginia state routes 5 and 614, Colonial National Historical Park, James City County
Virginia Department of Historic Resources archives file, 47-06 (Green Spring Archaeological Site) and 47-82 (Governor's Land Archaeological District); Michael Symes, under "Crinkle-crankle wall," in *A Glossary of Garden History*, 2nd ed. (Princes Risborough, England, 2000); Allan Greenberg, *George Washington, Architect* (New York, 1999), 40–41, n. 158, 69; Calder Loth, ed., *The Virginia Landmarks Register*, 4th ed. (Charlottesville, 1999), 240; Warren M. Billings, under "Berkeley, Sir William," in the *Dictionary of Virginia Biography*, John T. Kneebone and others, eds., 1 vol. to date (Richmond, 1998–); Ivor Noël Hume, "Ghosts at Green Spring," *Colonial Williamsburg* 18 (spring 1996), 24–32; Warren M. Billings, "Sir William Berkeley and the Diversification of the Virginia Economy," *VMHB* 104 (autumn 1996), 433–54; Warren M. Billings, "Imagining Green Spring House," *Virginia Cavalcade* 44 (autumn 1994), 84–95; Jeffrey A. Cohen and Charles E. Brownell, *The Architectural Drawings of Benjamin Henry Latrobe*, 2 vols. (New Haven, Conn., 1994), 1:80–82, 112–114, 145; Carl R. Lounsbury, ed., *An Illustrated Glossary of Early Southern Architecture & Landscape* (New York, 1994), under "arcade," "balcony," "colonnade," "covered way," "gallery," "passage," "piazza," "porch," "portico," and "veranda"; Brownell et al., *Making Virginia Architecture*, 1, 3, 5, 6, 8, 19; Jay Edwards, "The Complex Origins of the American Domestic Piazza-Veranda-Gallery," *Material Culture* 21 (summer 1989), 2–58; Jean O'Neill, under "Serpentine, crinkle-crankle, or ribbon wall," in *The Oxford Companion to Gardens*, ed. Sir Geoffrey Jellicoe et al. (Oxford, 1986); Edward C. Carter II et al., eds., *Latrobe's View of America, 1795–1820* (New Haven, Conn., 1985), 100–102; Richard L. Perry, "The Front Porch as Stage and Symbol in the Deep South," *Journal of American Culture* 8 (summer 1985), 13–18; O'Neill, "Walls in Half-Circles and Serpentine Walls," *Garden History* 8 (winter 1980), 69–76; J. Paul Hudson, "Green Spring Plantation," *The Iron Worker* 34 (winter 1970), 2–12; Louis R. Caywood, "Green Spring Plantation," *VMHB* 65 (January 1957), 67–83; Caywood, *Excavations at Green Spring Plantation* (Yorktown, 1955).

GREENWAY COURT, White Post vicinity, Clarke County
John Pendleton Kennedy, cited in *Annals of Clarke County Virginia: Volume 1, Old Homes, Families, etc.*, Stuart E. Brown (Berryville, Va., 1983); Josiah Look Dickinson, *The Fairfax Proprietary: The Northern Neck, the Fairfax Manors and Beginnings of Warren County in Virginia* (Front Royal, Va., 1959), 36–52l; John Wayland, *Historic Homes of Northern Virginia and the Eastern Panhandle of West Virginia* (Staunton, Va., 1937), 90–93.

GROVE HILL, Fincastle vicinity, Botetourt County
Frances J. Niederer, "Grove Hill, Virginia, Home of Gen. James Breckenridge," *Daughters of the American Revolution Magazine* (November 1961), 629–30; Niederer, *The Town of Fincastle, Virginia* (Charlottesville, 1965), 17–20; Mutual Assurance Society of Virginia, policies n. 2319 (1804) and n. 1134 (1806).

HARVIE-GAMBLE HOUSE (THE WHITE HOUSE, GRAY CASTLE), Gamble's Hill, Richmond
Karri L. Jurgens, "The Hancock-Wirt-Caskie House (1808–9): Its History and Context as a Richmond 'Octagonal' House" (master's thesis, Virginia Commonwealth University, 2000); Anya Jabour, "Quite a Woman of Business: Elizabeth Washington Gamble

Wirt, 1784–1857," *Virginia Cavalcade* 49 (spring 2000), 64–75; Drew St. J. Carneal, *Richmond's Fan District* (Richmond, 1996), 30–31; Jeffrey A. Cohen and Charles E. Brownell, *The Architectural Drawings of Benjamin Henry Latrobe*, 2 vols. (New Haven, Conn., 1994), 1:155–60; Edward F. Zimmer and Pamela J. Scott, "Alexander Parris, B. Henry Latrobe, and the John Wickham House in Richmond, Virginia," *Journal of the Society of Architectural Historians* 41 (October 1982), 202–11; Talbot Hamlin, *Benjamin Henry Latrobe* (New York, 1955), 99–101, 103–5; Scott, *Richmond Neighborhoods*, 90, 92, 98, 186–88, 213; Sally Nelson Robins, "'Gray Castle' or 'The Gamble House,'" *Historic Homes of Richmond, Richmond News Illustrated Saturday Magazine* (8 September 1900), 12–14; Thomas M. Ladd, "Cabell's Square, Gamble's Hill," survey, May 1852, "Houses—Richmond: Gamble," vertical file, Valentine Museum; Mutual Assurance Society of Virginia, policy n. 635 (1802), Library of Virginia.

HAWFIELD, Orange vicinity, Orange County
W. W. Scott, *A History of Orange County, Virginia* (Richmond, 1907), 205; "Hawfield" file, Orange County Historical Society; Ann Miller, unpublished research.

HAYES-McCANCE HOUSE, 801 East Leigh Street, Richmond
Scott, *Houses of Richmond*, 138–41; Lancaster, *Virginia Homes and Churches*, 141–42.

HOBSON-NOLTING HOUSE, 409 East Main Street, Richmond
Historic American Buildings Survey, VA-160; "Hobson-Nolting House," vertical file, Valentine Museum; Scott, *Houses of Richmond*, 248–53.

HOUSE OFF GREEN SPRING (CENTERVILLE) ROAD, Toano vicinity, James City County
Harold R. Shurtleff, *The Log Cabin Myth* (Cambridge, Mass., 1939); Henry Glassie, "The Types of the Southern Mountain Cabin," in *The Study of American Folklore*, Jan H. Brunvand, 3rd ed. (New York, 1986), 529–62.

HOWERTON-WELLS HOUSE, Rocky Run vicinity, Dinwiddie County
John G. Zehmer, unpublished research.

JAMES-DUNLOP HOUSE, Hinton (Friend) Street, in the block bounded by Hinton, Davis (Folly), Washington, and Market Streets, Petersburg
Dulaney Ward, Jr., unpublished research.

KINLOCH, Loretto vicinity, Essex County
Baylor Family Papers, Mss1 B3445e FA2, Virginia Historical Society; James B. Slaughter, *Settlers, Southerners, Americans: The History of Essex County, Virginia, 1608–1984* (Tappahannock, Va., 1985), 105; Lane, *Architecture of Virginia*, 192–93; Kimberly L. Rorrer, "Antiquity, the Middle Ages, and the Virginia Work of Robert Cary Long (1810–1849)," in *The Styles of Virginia Architecture*, abstracts of the Fourth Annual Architectural History Symposium, ed. Charles E. Brownell (Richmond, 1996), 13–14.

LABURNUM, Brook Road, Richmond
Anne Ferris, "Joseph Bryan's Lost Laburnum, Richmond, Virginia, 1884–1906," in *The Architecture of Virginia, New Findings from Virginia Commonwealth University: The Second Annual Architectural History Symposium* (Richmond, 1994), 24–25; *Richmond-Dispatch*, 29 July 1885.

LEADBEATER HOUSE, 414 North Washington Street, Alexandria
Historic American Buildings Survey, VA-457.

THE LODGE (ELK HILL, RED LODGE), Genito Road and Route 609, Amelia County
Muriel B. Rogers, "John Hartwell Cocke (1780–1866) and Philip St. George Cocke (1809–1861), Virginia Architectural Patrons" (Ph.D. dissertation, Virginia Commonwealth University, forthcoming); Brent Tarter, under "Archer, William Segar," in *The Dictionary of Virginia Biography*, ed. John T. Kneebone et al., 1 vol. to date (Richmond, 1998–); Rogers, "John Hartwell Cocke's Bremo Recess: The Romantic Colonial Revival Comes to Ante-Bellum Virginia," *The Bulletin: The Publication of the Fluvanna County Historical Society* 61 (spring 1996), i–iii, 1–40; Rogers, "John Hartwell Cocke's Bremo Recess: Tudor-Stuart Architecture and the Romantic Colonial Revival in Ante-Bellum Virginia" (master's thesis, Virginia Commonwealth University, 1994); Brownell et al., *Making Virginia Architecture*, 276–77; Jane B. Davies, "Works and Projects," in *Alexander Jackson Davis, American Architect*, ed. Amelia Peck (New York, 1992), 114; Roger Hale Newton, *Town & Davis, Architects: Pioneers in American Revivalist Architecture* (New York, 1942), 299; Alexander J. Davis, Journal, 120, A. J. Davis Collection, vol. 1, Metropolitan Museum of Art, New York.

LOG HOUSE, New River vicinity, Giles County
Carl R. Lounsbury, ed., *An Illustrated Glossary of Early Southern Architecture and Landscape* (New York, 1994), 216–17.

LONGWOOD, East Main Street, Salem
Virginia Department of Historic Resources archives file, 129-20.

LUDLAM-ANDERSON HOUSE, 113 West Franklin Street, Richmond
Times and Compiler, 31 October 1844; Scott, *Houses of Richmond*, 230–44; Karri L. Jurgens, "F. C. Gravely and the Ludlam-Anderson House (ca. 1844): The Resurrection of a Virginia Architect and a Richmond Greek Revival Villa," in *Architecture and the Decorative Arts: New Findings from Virginia Commonwealth University*, abstracts of the Fifth Annual Architectural History Symposium, ed. Charles Brownell and Sharon Hill (Richmond, 1997), 7–11; Asher Benjamin, *The Architect, or Complete Builder's Guide* (Boston, 1845), pl. 15; *Tredegar Company Records*, Business Records, IV, Journals, Library of Virginia; *Tredegar Company Records*, Estate Ledger, November 1892; Franklin Fire Insurance Company, Policy No. 9526, Historical Society of Pennsylvania; Jurgens, "The Impact of Palladio's Basilican Church Designs in Britain and North America," in *The Classical Tradition: From Andrea Palladio to John Russell Pope*, abstracts of the Sixth Annual Architectural History Symposium, ed. Charles Brownell (Richmond, 1998), 7–9.

MALVERN HILL, Varina vicinity, Henrico County
O'Dell, *Architecture of Henrico*, 106–8; Lancaster, *Virginia Homes and Churches*, 104–5.

MANNSFIELD, east of Fredericksburg, Spotsylvania County
Isaac Weld, *Travels through the States of North America* (London, 1800), 1:146; Waterman, *Mansions of Virginia*, 264–69.

MAPLEWOOD (VILLA NOUVA), Dolley Madison Boulevard near Capital Beltway interchange, Fairfax County
Diane N. Rafuse, *Maplewood* (Fairfax County History Commission, 1970); Virginia Department of Historic Resources archives file, 29-47.

MASSIE, ROBERT WITHERS, HOUSE, west corner of Federal and Tenth Streets, Lynchburg
Chambers, *Lynchburg*, 349–52.

MATTISSIPPI (STURGIS HOUSE), Occohannock Creek, Northampton County
Whitelaw, *Virginia's Eastern Shore*, 528–31; Historic American Buildings Survey, VA-547; Forman, *The Virginia Eastern Shore*, 65–70.

McRAE, ALEXANDER, HOUSE, 311 North Ninth Street, Richmond
Scott, *Houses of Richmond*, 75–78, 54–56; City of Richmond, Land Tax Records 1801–1815, Library of Virginia; Mutual Assurance Society of Virginia, policies n. 2219 (1804), n. 285 (1805), n. 184 (1808), n. 213 (1809), n. 1162 (1813), n. 1217 (1814), Library of Virginia; "McRae House," vertical file, Valentine Museum; *Richmond Enquirer*, 7 November 1820; Karri L. Jurgens, "The Hancock-Wirt-Caskie House (1808–9): Its History and Context as a Richmond 'Octagonal' House" (master's thesis, Virginia Commonwealth University, 2000).

MENOKIN, Warsaw vicinity, Richmond County
Tayloe Family Papers (account book of 1708–1778, Mss1 T2118b1), Virginia Historical Society; Elizabeth Brand Monroe, "William Buckland in the Northern Neck" (master's thesis, University of Virginia, 1975), 53–58; Waterman and Barrows, *Domestic Colonial Architecture of Tidewater Virginia* (New York, 1932), 151–52; Waterman, *Mansions of Virginia*, 309–10.

MERCHENT HOUSE, Dumfries, Prince William County
Historic American Buildings Survey, VA-91.

MOLDAVIA (ALLAN HOUSE), in block bounded by Fifth, Main, Sixth, and Cary Streets, Richmond
"Moldavia," vertical file, Valentine Museum; "Moldavia," vertical file, Edgar Allan Poe Museum, Richmond; Karri L. Jurgens, "The Hancock-Wirt-Caskie House (1808–9): Its History and Context as a Richmond 'Octagonal' House" (master's thesis, Virginia Commonwealth University, 2000); Lay, *Jefferson Country*, 103, passim on Oldham; William L. Beiswanger, "Jefferson's Sources from Antiquity in the Design of Monticello," *The Magazine Antiques* 144 (July 1993), 58–69; Gregg D. Kimball, "African-Virginians and the Vernacular Building Tradition in Richmond City, 1790–1860," in *Perspectives in Vernacular Architecture, IV*, ed. Thomas Carter and Bernard L. Herman (Columbia, Mo., 1991), 121–29; Scott, *Houses of Richmond*, 46–49 passim; Louise Allan Mayo, "The Allan House," *Historic Homes of Richmond, Richmond News Illustrated Saturday Magazine* (28 July 1900), 12–13; "The Tabernacle Site: Builders' Prices 100 Years Ago—Did Poe Ever Live at the 'Allan House'?" *Richmond Dispatch*, 18 March 1894; Thomas H. Ellis to George E. Woodberry, 28 May 1884, published as "The Homes of Poe at Richmond" in *The Life of Edgar Allan Poe, Personal and Literary, with His Chief Correspondence with Men of Letters*, by George E. Woodberry, 2 vols. (Boston, 1909), 2:359–65; Samuel Mordecai, *Virginia, Especially Richmond, in By-Gone Days* (Richmond, 1946 reprint of 1860 2nd ed.), 128–32; Mutual Assurance Society of Virginia, policies n. 1500 (1820), n. 4510 (1822), n. 6727 (1829), n. 9488 (before 1834), n. 12536 (1844), n. 2715 (1851), n. 17576 (1853), and n. 19216 (1958), Library of Virginia; City of Richmond, Book 2, 273–94 (Last Will and Testament of Joseph Gallego, 1818); Jefferson to James Oldham, 19 January 1805, in *Jefferson, Papers, 1606–1889*, 65 reels of microfilm made from the originals in the Thomas Jefferson Papers, Library of Congress, Washington, D.C., 1974, reel 32 (both Jefferson quotations); *Vir-*

ginia Gazette, 9 and 16 February 1802 and 24 March 1804; City of Richmond, Deed Book 2, 491–92, 493–96, 579–81 (contract between the Randolphs and Winston, 30 May 1798); Deed Book 3, 291–2; Deed Book 4, 45–47, Library of Virginia.

MONROE, JAMES, BIRTHPLACE, Colonial Beach vicinity, Westmoreland County
Virginia Department of Historic Resources archives file, 96-46.

MORATTICO HALL, southern Richmond County, at the confluence of Lancaster Creek (formerly Morattico Creek) and the Rappahannock River
Russell P. Bernabo, "Henry Francis duPont's Interior Design Aesthetic and Winterthur's Flock Room" (master's thesis, University of Delaware, 1989); Richmond County Land and Probate Records, Warsaw, Va.; Waterman, Mansions of Virginia, 62–67; manuscripts, Winterthur Museum Library.

MORRISON HOUSE, West Main and Liberty Streets, Harrisonburg
Virginia Department of Historic Resources archives file, 115-06.

MOUNT ATHOS, Kelly vicinity, Campbell County
Virginia Department of Historic Resources archives file, 15-19.

MOUNT ATHOS, Somerset vicinity, Orange County
George F. Barber, Modern Dwellings, 5th ed. (Knoxville, Tenn., 1905), 216; "Mount Athos," file, Orange County Historical Society; Ann Miller, unpublished research; Wells and Dalton, Virginia Architects, 1, 255.

MOUNT ERIN (FARM HILL, CAMERON CASTLE), east side of Adams Street between Apollo and Cupid Streets, Petersburg
Dulaney Ward, Jr., unpublished research.

MOUNT SAN ANGELO, Route 29, Sweet Briar, Amherst County
Virginia Department of Historic Resources archives file, 5-27; Amherst New Era-Progress, 26 July 1979; Amherst New Era-Progress, 5 June 1980.

MOUNT SHARON, Orange vicinity
Ann Miller, unpublished research; Wells and Dalton, Virginia Architects, 242; W. W. Scott, A History of Orange County, Virginia (Richmond, 1907), 209–10.

MOUNT VERNON BARN, Mount Vernon vicinity, Fairfax County
John C. Fitzpatrick, ed., The Writings of George Washington (Washington, D.C., 1931–40), 32:292–96, 33:295–97; William M. S. Rasmussen and Robert S. Tilton, George Washington: The Man behind the Myths (Charlottesville and London, 1999), 237–39.

MOUNT WARREN, Warren, Albemarle County
Lay, Jefferson Country, 58–59.

MURRELL, JOHN WILLIAM, HOUSE, Second and Harrison Streets, Lynchburg
Chambers, Lynchburg, 192–95.

NOMINI HALL, near Montross, Westmoreland County
Louis Morton, Robert Carter of Nomini Hall (Williamsburg, 1945); Waterman, Mansions of Virginia, 136–42; papers of Robert Carter III, Virginia Historical Society. Two versions of the sketch of Nomini Hall are known.

NYDRIE, Keene vicinity, Albemarle County
Lay, Jefferson Country, 230.

OLD STONE FORT, Middle Marsh Brook, Middletown vicinity, Frederick County
Historic American Buildings Survey, VA-210; Edward A. Chappell, "Acculturation in the Shenandoah Valley: Rhenish Houses of the Massanutten Settlement," Proceedings of the American Philosophical Society 124 (February 1980), 55–89; Edward A. Chappell, "Germans and Swiss," in America's Architectural Roots, ed. Dell Upton (Washington, D.C., 1986), 68–73.

OSSIAN HALL, Annandale vicinity, Fairfax County
Eleanor Lee Templeman, "Ossian Hall," Historical Society of Fairfax County, Virginia Bulletin 7 (1960–61), 38–45; Constance M. Greiff, Lost America: From the Atlantic to the Mississippi (Princeton, N.J., 1974), 8.

PECKATONE, on the Potomac River, Sandy Point vicinity, Westmoreland County
Waterman, Mansions of Virginia, 192–95; Elizabeth Dos Passos, "Peckatone, Then and Now," Northern Neck of Virginia Historical Magazine 23 (1973), 2427–36.

PENDLETON HOUSE (EDMUNDSBURY), Bowling Green vicinity, Caroline County
Mary Tod Haley, Caroline County: A Pictorial History (Norfolk, 1985), 15; Marshall Wingfield, A History of Caroline County Virginia (Richmond, 1924), 199–204.

PRATT'S CASTLE, 324 South Fourth Street, Richmond
Julian Cavalier, American Castles (Cranbury, N.J., 1973), 115–23; Scott, Houses of Richmond, 286–87.

RAVENSWORTH, Springfield, Fairfax County
Eleanor Lee Templeman, "Ravensworth," Historical Society of Fairfax County, Virginia Bulletin 7 (1960–61), 46–49; Salie Nelson, "Aftermath," The Taylor-Trotwood Magazine (January 1909), 323–31.

RED HILL, Brookneal vicinity, Charlotte County
Virginia Department of Historic Resources archives file, 19-29.

RINGFIELD, Yorktown vicinity, York County
Charles E. Hatch, Jr., Ringfield Plantation (National Park Service Office of History and Historic Architecture, 1970).

ROANOKE, Randolph vicinity, Charlotte County
Henry Howe, Historical Collections of Virginia (Charleston, S.C., 1845), 223–28.

ROCKLANDS, Gordonsville vicinity, Orange County
"At Rocklands," in The Old Virginia Gentleman and Other Sketches, by George W. Bagby (Richmond, 1938), 221–22; "Rocklands," file, Orange County Historical Society; Ann Miller, unpublished research; William H. B. Thomas, Gordonsville, Virginia: Historic Crossroads Town (Verona, Va., 1971), 88–89; Wells and Dalton, Virginia Architects, 471.

ROLLESTON, Virginia Beach (formerly Princess Anne County)
Virginia Beach Public Library, The Beach: A History of Virginia Beach, Va (Virginia Beach, 1996), 64–67, 131–32; Stephen Mansfield, Princess Anne County and Virginia Beach: A Pictorial History (Norfolk, 1989), 20, 65–67.

ROSE HALL, 625 Ohio Street, Waynesboro
Curtis L. Bowman, Sr., Waynesboro Days of Yore (Waynesboro, 1991), 1:139–40; Virginia Department of Historic Resources archives file, 136-6.

ROSELAND MANOR, Strawberry Banks, Hampton
Virginia Department of Historic Resources archives file, 114-03; Wells and Dalton, Virginia Architects, 103.

ROSEWELL, White Marsh vicinity, Gloucester County
Edward A. Chappell, "Rosewell's Architecture Reevaluated," in Discovering Rosewell: An Historical, Architectural, and Archaeological Overview, ed. Rachel Most (Gloucester, Va., 1994), 9–44; Daniel D. Reiff, Small Georgian Houses in England and Virginia: Origins and Development through the 1750s (London and Toronto, 1986), 288–94; William Byrd II, The London Diary (1717–1721) and Other Writings, ed. Louis B. Wright and Marion Tinling (New York, 1958), 505–6; Bennie Brown, Jr., "Rosewell: An Architectural Study of an Eighteenth-Century Virginia Plantation" (master's thesis, University of Georgia, 1973); Betty Crowe Leviner, "The Pages of Rosewell" and "Rosewell Revisited," Journal of Early Southern Decorative Arts XIII (May 1987), 1–43 and XIX (November 1993), 1–45; Waterman and Barrows, Domestic Colonial Architecture of Tidewater Virginia (New York, 1932), 94–95; Mutual Assurance Society of Virginia, policy n. 701 (21 June 1802); Francis Norton Mason, John Norton, et al., Merchants of London and Virginia (Richmond, 1937), 199; "Who Ruined Rosewell?" Glo-Quips, Magazine of Gloucester 5.4 (26 February 1964); US Congress, The Congressional Record 80, pt. 4 (16 March 1936), 3790 and 80, pt. 9 (1 June 1936), 9228. The brickwork at Rosewell made allowance for connectors to be bonded into the side walls.

SABOT HILL, Sabot vicinity, Goochland County
Cece Bullard, Goochland Yesterday and Today: A Pictorial History (Virginia Beach, 1974), 60–65; Hélène Barret Agee, Facets of Goochland (Virginia) History (Richmond, 1962), 167.

SALISBURY, site of present Salisbury Country Club, Chesterfield County
O'Dell, Chesterfield County, 287–88; Lancaster, Virginia Homes and Churches, 162–64.

SEA VIEW, Locustville vicinity, Accomack County
Whitelaw, Virginia's Eastern Shore, 884–85; Virginia Department of Historic Resources archives file, 01-77.

SHELTON-BURTON HOUSE, 723 Main Street, Danville
Art Work of Lynchburg and Danville, Virginia (Chicago, 1903), n.p.; Edward Pollock, Illustrated Sketchbook of Danville, Virginia: Its Manufactures and Commerce (Danville, 1976), 156, 182; Wells and Dalton, Virginia Architects, 470; Philip Alexander Bruce, History of Virginia (Chicago, 1924), 6:291–92; Thomas K. Stahl, A History of the First Presbyterian Church, Danville, Virginia: 1826–1976 (Greensboro, N.C., and Danville, 1976), 46–47.

SPRING HILL (PRISON HILL), Tabb Street between Market and Union Streets, Petersburg
City of Petersburg, Will Book 1, 382 (1804); Book 2, 182 (1822); Land Tax Books,

1797–1802, 1805–1812, 1814–1818, 1820; Mutual Assurance Society of Virginia, policies r. 6, v. 52, n. 494 (1815); r. 10, v. 77, n. 3396 (1822); r. 12, v. 86, n. 5902 (1829); r. 15, v. 102, n. 10655 (1837); r. 18, n. 13901 (1844); r. 20, v. 123, n. 17193 (1851); r. 23, v. 135, n. 20687 (1858), Library of Virginia.

TAR BAY, Hopewell vicinity, Prince George County
Edward A. Wyatt IV, *Plantation Houses around Petersburg* (Petersburg, 1955), 5; Virginia Department of Historic Resources archives file, 74-13.

TEBBS HOUSE, Dumfries, Prince William County
Waterman, *Mansions of Virginia*, 230–35.

TEDINGTON, Sandy Point, Charles City County
"Lightfoot Family," *William and Mary Quarterly* 3, ser. 1 (1894), 104–11; Edith Tunis Sale, *Interiors of Virginia Houses of Colonial Times* (Richmond, 1927), 463–71.

TOWLES POINT, Bertrand vicinity, juncture of Rappahannock and Corotoman Rivers, Lancaster County
Lancaster, *Virginia Homes and Churches*, 315–16; "Towles Family," *VMHB* 8 (1900), 320–21, 428–29 and 9 (1901), 198–200, 324–26, 433–35; Historic American Buildings Survey, VA-62; Forman, *The Virginia Eastern Shore*, 75–78, 103.

UNIDENTIFIED HOUSE, Gloucester County

THE UNION, Palmyra vicinity, Fluvanna County
Fiske Kimball, *Thomas Jefferson, Architect* (New York, 1968 reprint of 1916 ed.), 198–99; K231q, K231r, Coolidge Collection, Massachusetts Historical Society; Bryan Clark Green, "In the Wake of Thomas Jefferson: The Architectural Education and Career of Thomas R. Blackburn, Architect in Antebellum Virginia" (Ph.D. dissertation, University of Virginia, forthcoming); Joseph Martin, *A New and Comprehensive Gazetteer of Virginia and the District of Columbia* (Charlottesville, 1836), 176; Virginia Department of Historic Resources archives file, 192-13.

VARNUM-MAHONE HOUSE, 42 South Market Street, Petersburg
Edward A. Wyatt, *Along Petersburg Streets* (Richmond, 1943), 30–31; City of Petersburg, Deed Book 10, 124 (1835), 245 (1837); Deed Book 14, 15 (1843); Deed Book 15, 234 (1845); Deed Book 35, 373 (1873); Land Tax Books, 1837–1840, 1843, 1850, 1873–75; Nelson Morehouse Blake, *William Mahone of Virginia: Soldier and Political Insurgent* (Richmond, 1935); A. M., *The City of Petersburg: The Book of Its Chamber of Commerce* (Petersburg, 1894), 51–53.

VIEWMONT (SECOND) (FRY HOUSE), Carter's Bridge vicinity, Albemarle County
Lay, *Jefferson Country*, 47–48; Edgar Woods, *Albemarle County in Virginia* (Harrisonburg, Va., 1972 reprint of 1900 ed.), 197–98, 356–57; Mary Rawlings, *Antebellum Albemarle* (Charlottesville, 1974), 13.

WESTBROOK, Westbrook Avenue, Richmond
O'Dell, *Architecture of Henrico*, 210–11; Andrew Morrison, ed., *The City on the James: Richmond, Virginia, The Chamber of Commerce Book* (Richmond, 1893), 58.

WEST HILL, on Bolling's Hill just west of Adams Street and north of Tabb Street, Petersburg
Edward A. Wyatt, *Along Petersburg Streets* (Richmond, 1943), 27; Mutual Assurance Society of Virginia, policies r. 3, v. 30, n. 2175 (1804); r. 8, v. 64, n. 698 (1805); r. 9, v. 69, n. 1549 (1815); r. 10, v. 76, n. 3235 (1822); r. 12, v. 85, n. 5714 (1829); r. 15, v. 101, n. 10459 (1837); r. 18, v. 112, n. 13666 (1844); r. 20, v. 123, n. 16913 (1851); r. 22, v. 134, n. 20374 (1858), Library of Virginia.

THE WESTMORELAND CLUB (GRAY-STANARD HOUSE), 601 East Grace Street, Richmond
Scott, *Houses of Richmond*, 198–201; Lancaster, *Virginia Homes and Churches*, 149–50.

WHITE HOUSE (SECOND), on the Pamunkey River, New Kent County
Malcolm Hart Harris, *Old New Kent County: Some Accounts of the Planters, Plantations, and Places in New Kent County* (West Point, Va., 1977), 1:118–25; William M. S. Rasmussen and Robert S. Tilton, *George Washington: The Man behind the Myths* (Charlottesville and London, 1999), 81–86; inventory of the Daniel Parke Custis estate, April 1759, Virginia Historical Society.

WHITLOCK-GRAHAM HOUSE, 201 West Franklin Street, Richmond
William B. O'Neal, *Architecture in Virginia* (Richmond, 1968), 45–46; Robert P. Winthrop, *Architecture in Downtown Richmond* (Richmond, 1982), 149.

WILLIAMSON HOUSE, Virginia Military Institute, Lexington
Lyle and Simpson, *Lexington*, 223–25, 279–80.

WITHROW HOUSE, Main Street, Waynesboro
Virginia Department of Historic Resources archives file, 136-11; Curtis L. Bowman, *Waynesboro Days of Yore* (Waynesboro, 1991), 1:131.

YORK COUNTY POOR FARM, DAIRY, Grafton vicinity, York County
Historic American Buildings Survey, VA-100; Carl R. Lounsbury, ed., *An Illustrated Glossary of Early Southern Architecture and Landscape* (New York, 1994), 109.

Chapter II – Lost Civic Architecture

ACCOMACK COUNTY COURTHOUSE, Accomac
William H. Gaines, Jr., "Courthouses of Virginia's Eastern Shore," *Virginia Cavalcade* 24 (1964), 20–27; Bucklen and Bucklen, *County Courthouses*, 1; L. Floyd Nock III, *Drummondtown, "A One Horse Town": Accomac Court House, Virginia* (Verona, Va., 1976), 11.

THE ALAMO, HAMPDEN-SYDNEY COLLEGE, Prince Edward County
Virginia Department of Historic Resources archives file, 73-13.

ALEXANDRIA COURTHOUSE, Columbus between Queen and Princess Streets, Alexandria
Brownell et al., *Making Virginia Architecture*, 260–61.

ALEXANDRIA POST OFFICE AND CUSTOMHOUSE, southwest corner of Prince and South St. Asaph Streets, Alexandria
Lowell Klock, "Ammi B. Young, Supervising Architect of the Treasury, and His 1858 Alexandria Post Office and Customhouse," *The Alexandria Chronicle* 2 (summer 1994), 1–10; Pamela Scott and Antoinette J. Lee, *Buildings of the District of Columbia* (New York, 1993), 35, 155–56, 403–4.

ALLEGHANY COUNTY COURTHOUSE, Covington
Bucklen and Bucklen, *County Courthouses*, 5–6; William H. Gaines, Jr., "Courthouses of Alleghany County," *Virginia Cavalcade* 22 (1972), 4–9.

AMELIA COUNTY COURTHOUSE, Amelia
Bucklen and Bucklen, *County Courthouses*, 6–7; William H. Gaines, Jr., "Courthouses of Amelia and Dinwiddie Counties," *Virginia Cavalcade* 18 (1969), 17–28; Kathleen H. Hadfield, ed., *Historical Notes on Amelia County, Virginia* (Amelia, Va., 1982), 8–9, 65, 177, 470–71.

ANATOMICAL THEATRE, UNIVERSITY OF VIRGINIA, McCormick Road opposite Hotel A, Charlottesville
William B. O'Neal, *Pictorial History of the University of Virginia* (Charlottesville, 1968).

ANNEX (NEW HALL), UNIVERSITY OF VIRGINIA, Charlottesville
Richard Guy Wilson and Sara M. Butler, *The Campus Guide: University of Virginia* (Princeton, N.J., 1999); John Hammond Moore, "That 'Commodious' Annex to Jefferson's Rotunda," *Virginia Cavalcade* 29 (autumn 1979), 114–23.

APPOMATTOX COUNTY COURTHOUSE, Appomattox National Battlefield Park
"Appomattox Court House National Historical Park," National Register of Historic Places registration form (1971); Department of Historic Resources archives file, 6-33; Peters and Peters, *Courthouses* (1995), 90–91.

ARLINGTON COUNTY COURTHOUSE, Arlington
Bucklen and Bucklen, *County Courthouses*, 3–4; communication from James M. Palmer, archivist, Arlington County Historical Society, 21 September 2000.

ARMORY, CITY OFFICE, AND MARKET BUILDING, City Hall Avenue between Brewer and Monticello Streets, Norfolk
Carroll Walker, *Carroll Walker's Norfolk: A Tercentennial Pictorial History* (Norfolk, 1981); Bynum Shaw, "Medieval Look and Pigeons Removed," *Virginian Pilot*, 30 October 1949; Louisa Venable Kyle, "Passing of the City Market Recalls Times When Other Markets Filled a Like Purpose," *Virginian Pilot and Portsmouth Star*, 14 August 1955; Donna L. Koch, "The City Market," *Virginian Pilot*, 6 November 1996.

AUGUSTA COUNTY COURTHOUSE, northeast corner of South Augusta and East Johnson Streets, Staunton
"Augusta County Courthouse," National Register of Historic Places nomination, 1982; Bryan Clark Green, "In the Wake of Thomas Jefferson: The Architectural Education and Career of Thomas R. Blackburn, Architect in Antebellum Virginia" (Ph.D. dissertation, University of Virginia, forthcoming); Joseph Martin, *A New and Comprehensive Gazetteer of Virginia and the District of Columbia* (Charlottesville, 1836), 319; William T. Frazier, "T. J. Collins: A Local Virginia Architect and His Practice at the Turn of the Century" (master's thesis, University of Virginia, 1976); George Mays, "Courthouse Records Wide Scope," *The Staunton Leader*, 2 July 1976; Bucklen and Bucklen, *County Courthouses*, 8–10; Peters and Peters, *Courthouses*, 172–74.

BEDFORD COUNTY COURTHOUSE, New London
Bucklen and Bucklen, *County Courthouses*, 12–13; William H. Gaines, Jr., "Courthouses of Bedford and Charlotte Counties," *Virginia Cavalcade* 21 (1971), 4–13.

BEDFORD COUNTY COURTHOUSE, Main Street, Bedford
Bucklen and Bucklen, *County Courthouses*, 12–13; William H. Gaines, Jr., "Courthouses of Bedford and Charlotte Counties," *Virginia Cavalcade* 21 (1971), 4–13.

BIGGERS SCHOOL, Fifth and Clay Streets, Lynchburg
Chambers, *Lynchburg*, 258–60.

BUCKINGHAM COUNTY COURTHOUSE, Buckingham Court House
Charles Yancey to Thomas Jefferson, 12 July 1821, and Jefferson to Yancey, 23 July 1821, Jefferson Papers, Library of Congress, ser. 2, vol. 90, nos. 4 and 25; Joseph Martin, ed., *A New and Comprehensive Gazetteer of Virginia and the District of Columbia* (Charlottesville, 1836), 150 (identifies the Charlotte County courthouse as by Jefferson); J. C. Carrington, *Charlotte County, Virginia* (Richmond, 1907), 21; R. F. Hutcheson, *Charlotte County, Virginia: Historic Sketch of the Charlotte Court House* (Richmond, 1928), 14; William H. Gaines, Jr., "Courthouses of Bedford and Charlotte Counties," *Virginia Cavalcade* 24 (1971), 5–13; "Specifications for the Goochland County Courthouse," Cocke Family Papers, Alderman Library, University of Virginia, Box 182.

THE CAGE, Seventeenth Street Market, Seventeenth and Main Streets, Richmond
Bryan Clark Green, "The Structure of Civic Exchange: Market Houses in Early Virginia," in *Shaping Community: Perspectives in Vernacular Architecture, VI*, ed. Elizabeth Collins Cromley and Carter L. Hudgins (Columbia, Mo., 1997), 189–203; John Cook Wyllie, ed., "'Observations Made During a Short Residence in Virginia': In a Letter from Thomas H. Palmer, May 30, 1814," *VMHB* 76 (October 1968), 395; Samuel Mordecai, *Virginia, Especially Richmond, in By-Gone Days* (Richmond, 1946 reprint of 1860 2nd ed.), 23.

CHESAPEAKE FEMALE COLLEGE (later, SOLDIERS' HOME), Hampton
Chester D. Bradley, M.D., "From Croton Oil to Isotopes: One Hundred Years of Medicine at Hampton Veterans Administration Center," unpublished manuscript, City of Hampton's Historical Collections; Thomas Belvin, "Hampton Veterans Center Celebrates Centennial of Care," *Daily Press*, 4 November 1979; "Plot of Kecoughtan, VA, Veterans Administration Center, Kecoughtan, VA," 1956, sheet 4 of 4; *Southern Branch National Home for Disabled Volunteer Soldiers: Souvenir and Illustrated History* (Washington, D.C., 1915).

CHESTERFIELD COUNTY COURTHOUSE, Route 10, Chesterfield
O'Dell, *Chesterfield County*, 373–75; Virginia Department of Historic Resources archives file, 20-227, copy of 1804 court order for addition.

CLAY, HENRY, STATUE, PAVILION FOR, Capitol Square, Richmond
W. W. Scott and W. G. Stanard, *The Capitol of Virginia and of the Confederate States: Being a Descriptive and Historical Catalog of the Pubic Square and Buildings, and of the Statuary, Paintings and Curios Therein* (Richmond, 1894), 21–22, 32; Mary Wingfield Scott and Louise F. Catterall, *Virginia's Capitol Square: Its Buildings & Its Monuments* (Richmond, 1957), 29; Elizabeth R. Varon, "'The Ladies Are Whigs': Lucy Barbour, Henry Clay, and Nineteenth-Century Virginia Politics," *Virginia Cavalcade* 42 (1992), 73–83.

CLIFTON FORGE YMCA, Ridgeway Street, Clifton Forge, Alleghany County
Horton P. Beirne, ed., *Historical Sketches by Gay Arritt* (Covington, Va., 1982), 49.

COVERED BRIDGES
"An Album for the Nostalgic, Covered Bridges in Virginia," *Virginia Cavalcade* 1 (1951), 17–19.

CULPEPER COUNTY COURTHOUSE, Davis Street, Culpeper
Eugene M. Scheel, *Culpeper: A Virginia County's History through 1920* (Culpeper, 1982), 88; Crimora Waite, "Culpeper County Courthouse," unpublished report in Virginia Department of Historic Resources archives file, 204-20.

DANVILLE COURTHOUSE, 505 Patton Street, Danville
Art Work of Lynchburg and Danville, Virginia (Chicago, 1903), n.p.; George W. Dame et al., *Historical Sketch of Roman Eagle Lodge* (Danville, 1939), 28; Delos D. Hughes, correspondence with the author, August 1999; Brownell et al., *Making Virginia Architecture*, 292; Calder Loth, ed., *The Virginia Landmarks Register*, 4th ed. (Charlottesville, 1999), 434–35; Peters and Peters, *Courthouses*, 218; Mary Cahill and Gary Grant, *Victorian Danville* (Danville, 1996), 91–93.

DANVILLE MILITARY INSTITUTE, southwest corner of Kemper Road at South Main Street, Danville
Art Work of Lynchburg and Danville, Virginia (Chicago, 1903), n.p.; Jane Gray Hagan, *The Story of Danville* (New York, 1950), 80–83; Adrian O'Connor, "DCC Origins in Military College's 'Castle on the Hill,'" *Danville Register & Bee*, 2 October 1992; O'Connor, "DTI, VPI-D Share Campus, Then Give Way to College," *Danville Register & Bee*, 3 October 1992; Wells and Dalton, *Virginia Architects*, 223, 311.

EASTERN LUNATIC ASYLUM, bounded by Francis, Nassau, Henry, and Court Streets, Williamsburg
John M. Galt, *Report of the Directors [of Eastern Lunatic Asylum] to the Legislature* (1857); Shomer S. Zwelling, *Quest for a Cure: The Public Hospital in Williamsburg, 1773–1885* (Williamsburg, 1985); Blanton McLean, "Eastern Asylum and the Third Revolution in Psychiatry: Dr. John Galt's Advanced Therapeutic Community, 1841–1862," in *Williamsburg, Virginia: A City before the State, 1699–1999*, ed. Robert P. Maccubin (Williamsburg, 2000), 80–94; Marcus Whiffen, *The Public Buildings of Williamsburg, Colonial Capital of Virginia* (Williamsburg, 1958), 161–66; Jane Carson, *We Were There: Descriptions of Williamsburg, 1699–1859* (Williamsburg, 1965), 61,104–5; Wells and Dalton, *Virginia Architects*, 471.

EQUESTRIAN FOUNTAIN, intersection of Hull Street and Cowardin Avenue, Richmond
Benjamin B. Weisiger III, *Old Manchester and Its Environs, 1769–1910* (Richmond, 1993), 25; W. Hugh Goodwyn et al., *A Time to Remember: A Pictorial History of Chesterfield County, Virginia, 1860 to 1960* (Chesterfield County, 1993), 85.

THE FLETCHER SCHOOL, rural Greene County
William A. Link, "'Rough Times'; Rural Education in Late-Nineteenth-Century Virginia," *Virginia Cavalcade* 37 (1987), 16–27.

FRANKLIN COUNTY COURTHOUSE, Rocky Mount
John S. and Emily J. Salmon, *Franklin County, Virginia, 1786–1986: A Bicentennial History* (Rocky Mount, Va., 1993), 89–91.

GATEKEEPER'S LODGE, UNIVERSITY OF VIRGINIA, Charlottesville
Richard Guy Wilson and Sara M. Butler, *The Campus Guide: University of Virginia* (Princeton, N.J., 1999); William B. O'Neal, *Pictorial History of the University of Virginia* (Charlottesville, 1968), 62.

GENERAL HOSPITAL #43, Hampton
Chester D. Bradley, M.D., "From Croton Oil to Isotopes: One Hundred Years of Medicine at Hampton Veterans Administration Center," unpublished manuscript, City of Hampton's Historical Collections; Thomas Belvin, "Hampton Veterans Center Celebrates Centennial of Care," *Daily Press*, 4 November 1979; "Plot of Kecoughtan, VA, Veterans Administration Center, Kecoughtan, VA," 1956, sheet 4 of 4; *Southern Branch National Home for Disabled Volunteer Soldiers: Souvenir and Illustrated History* (Washington, D.C., 1915).

GORDONSVILLE FEMALE INSTITUTE, Baker Street, Gordonsville, Orange County
William H. B. Thomas, *Gordonsville, Virginia: Historic Crossroads Town* (Verona, Va., 1971), 77–80.

HAYES HALL, VIRGINIA COLLEGE AND VIRGINIA SEMINARY, DeWitt Street, Lynchburg
Calder Loth, ed., *Virginia Landmarks of Black History* (Charlottesville, 1995), 179–80; Virginia Department of Historic Resources archives file, 118-59.

HENRICO COUNTY COURTHOUSE, Twenty-second and Main Streets, Richmond
Mutual Assurance Society of Virginia, policies n. 3560 (1825), n. 7107 (1829); O'Dell, *Architecture of Henrico*, 53–54; Scott, *Richmond Neighborhoods*, 64–65.

THE LEXINGTON ARSENAL, Valley Road, Lexington
Lyle and Simpson, *Lexington*, 211–12; Francis H. Smith, *Virginia Military Institute* (Lynchburg, 1912), 51–52, 65.

LIBBY PRISON, 2001 East Cary Street, Richmond
W. Asbury Christian, *Richmond: Her Past and Present* (Richmond, 1912), 22, 237, 301, 407; *Libby Prison War Museum* (Chicago, 1889); David D. Ryan, *Cornbread and Maggots—Cloak and Dagger: Union Prisoners and Spies in Civil War Richmond* (Richmond, 1994), 64–65; Scott, *Richmond Neighborhoods*, 82–84.

LIBERTY HALL, WASHINGTON AND LEE UNIVERSITY, Lexington
Lyle and Simpson, *Lexington*, 12–13, 145–47, 177–78.

LOUISA COUNTY COURTHOUSE, Louisa
Bucklen and Bucklen, *County Courthouses*, 60; Porter C. Wright, "Contract for Constructing the 1818 Courthouse," *Louisa County Historical Society Magazine* 3 (1971), 68–71.

LYNCHBURG COLLEGE (FIRST), in block bounded by Wise, Tenth, Floyd, and Eleventh Streets, Lynchburg
Chambers, *Lynchburg*, 142–47; Lyle and Simpson, *Lexington*, 228–29.

LYNCHBURG FEMALE ORPHAN ASYLUM, Memorial Avenue, Lynchburg
Chambers, *Lynchburg*, 226–28.

LYNCHBURG MARKET, Ninth Street, between Church and Main Streets, Lynchburg
Bryan Clark Green, "The Structure of Civic Exchange: Market Houses in Early Virginia," in *Shaping Community: Perspectives in Vernacular Architecture, VI*, ed. Elizabeth Collins Cromley and Carter L. Hudgins (Columbia, Mo., 1997), 189–203; Chambers, *Lynchburg*, 41–43.

MARGARET ACADEMY, Cheriton vicinity, Accomack County
Whitelaw, *Virginia's Eastern Shore*, 730–35, 932–33; Lancaster, *Virginia Homes and Churches*, 493–94.

MONTGOMERY COUNTY COURTHOUSE, Christiansburg
Bucklen and Bucklen, *County Courthouses*, 65–67; Charles W. Crush, *The Montgomery County Story, 1776–1957* (Christiansburg, Va., 1957), 162–63.

NORTHAMPTON COUNTY COURTHOUSE, Eastville
Forman, *The Virginia Eastern Shore*, 147; William H. Gaines, Jr., "Courthouses of Virginia's Eastern Shore," *Virginia Cavalcade* 24 (1964), 20–27; Whitelaw, *Virginia's Eastern Shore*, 147.

PRINCE EDWARD COUNTY COURTHOUSE, Worsham
William H. Gaines, Jr., "Courthouses of Prince Edward and Nottoway Counties," *Virginia Cavalcade* 20 (1970), 40–47.

PRINCE EDWARD COUNTY COURTHOUSE, Farmville
Charles Edward Burrell, *A History of Prince Edward County, Virginia, from Formation in 1753 to Present* (Richmond, 1922), 40–42; William H. Gaines, Jr., "Courthouses of Prince Edward and Nottoway Counties," *Virginia Cavalcade* 20 (1970), 40–47.

RANDOLPH-MACON ACADEMY, Front Royal
Virginia Department of Historic Resources archives file, 112-08.

RICHMOND CITY HALL, facing Broad, Capitol, and Eleventh Streets, Richmond
"The City Hall," *Richmond Dispatch*, 7 February 1874; drawing of Richmond City Hall by Robert Mills, Library of Virginia; Selden Richardson, "Robert Mills's City Hall for Richmond, 1816–1818," *Arris, Journal of the Southeast Chapter, Society of Architectural Historians* 10 (1999).

RICHMOND COLLEGE, MAIN BUILDING, in the former block bounded by Ryland, Franklin, Lombardy, and Broad Streets, Richmond
Brownell et al., *Making Virginia Architecture*, 286; Claire Millhiser Rosenbaum, *A Gem of a College: The History of Westhampton College, 1914–1989* (Richmond, 1989), 9–10; Wells and Dalton, *Virginia Architects*, 247.

RICHMOND FEMALE INSTITUTE, Tenth Street between Marshall and Clay Streets, Richmond
Brownell et al., *Making Virginia Architecture*, 286–87; Richmond Female Institute, *Catalog of the Richmond Female Institute, Richmond, Virginia* (Richmond, 1855), 5, 7.

ROANOKE COUNTY COURTHOUSE, Main Street, Salem
Bucklen and Bucklen, *County Courthouses*, 86–87; Jim Fulghum, "Roanoke County Courthouse," unpublished manuscript in Virginia Department of Historic Resources archives file, 129-8.

ROCKINGHAM COUNTY COURTHOUSE, Harrisonburg
I. L. Terrell, "Courthouses of Rockingham County," *Virginia Cavalcade* 23 (1973), 42–47; John W. Wayland, *Historic Harrisonburg* (Staunton, Va., 1949, 1973), 31–42; Bucklen and Bucklen, *County Courthouses*, 88–90.

ROTUNDA, UNIVERSITY OF VIRGINIA, Charlottesville
Richard Guy Wilson and Sara M. Butler, *The Campus Guide: University of Virginia* (Princeton, N.J., 1999); William B. O'Neal, *Pictorial History of the University of Virginia* (Charlottesville, 1968); Richard Guy Wilson, *"Arise and Build!" A Centennial Commemoration of the 1895 Fire* (Charlottesville, 1995); Richard Guy Wilson, ed., *Thomas Jefferson's Academical Village: The Creation of an Architectural Masterpiece* (Charlottesville, 1993), 55–57, 64–65.

SEABOARD MARKET AND ARMORY, corner of County and South Streets, Portsmouth
Wells and Dalton, *Virginia Architects*, 75–76, 344–50; Robert W. Wentz, *Portsmouth: A Pictorial History* (Virginia Beach, 1975), 13, 20–21.

SEVENTEENTH STREET MARKET (NEW MARKET), Seventeenth and Main Streets, Richmond
Bryan Clark Green, "The Structure of Civic Exchange: Market Houses in Early Virginia," in *Shaping Community: Perspectives in Vernacular Architecture, VI*, ed. Elizabeth Collins Cromley and Carter L. Hudgins (Columbia, Mo., 1997), 189–203; Scott, *Richmond Neighborhoods*, 64, 67.

SMYTH COUNTY COURTHOUSE, Marion
Sally Harris, "Courthouses of Smyth County," *Virginia Cavalcade* 30 (1980), 30–37; Goodridge Wilson, *Smyth County History and Traditions* (Kingsport, Tenn., 1932), 82–83.

SPRINGWOOD TRUSS BRIDGE, Springwood, Botetourt County
Virginia Department of Historic Resources archives file, 111-03.

SURRY COUNTY COURTHOUSE, Route 10, Surry
William H. Gaines, Jr., "Courthouses of Surry and Sussex Counties," *Virginia Cavalcade* 19 (1969), 42–47; "Surry County Courthouse Complex," National Register of Historic Places Inventory Form (1986).

TEMPERANCE HALL, UNIVERSITY OF VIRGINIA, Main Street, Charlottesville
Lay, *Jefferson Country*, 101; William B. O'Neal, *Pictorial History of the University of Virginia* (Charlottesville, 1976), 60.

TOBACCO EXCHANGE, Shockoe Slip at Thirteenth Street, Richmond
Eugene Ferslew, *The Second Annual Directory for the City of Richmond to Which Is Added a Business Directory for 1860* (Richmond, 1860), 37; *The [Richmond] State*, 5 September 1877; Joseph Clarke Robert, "Rise of the Tobacco Warehouse Auction System in Virginia," *Agricultural History* VII (October 1933), 171–82; *The Richmond News Leader*, 29 September 1955, 16 July 1955; James K. Sanford, *A Century of Commerce, 1867–1967* (Richmond, 1967), 20.

UNITED STATES POST OFFICE, Church Avenue at First Street, Roanoke
Brownell et al., *Making Virginia Architecture*, 89, 318.

US POST OFFICE AND FEDERAL BUILDING, 530 Main Street, Danville
Art Work of Lynchburg and Danville, Virginia (Chicago, 1903), n.p.; Edward Pollock, *Illustrated Sketchbook of Danville, Virginia: Its Manufactures and Commerce* (Danville, 1976), 72, 74–75; Brownell et al., *Making Virginia Architecture*, 99; Jane Gray Hagan, *The Story of Danville* (New York, 1950), 35–36; Peters and Peters, *Courthouses*, 218–19; J. Daniel Pezzoni, "Downtown Danville Historic District," National Register of Historic Places Inventory nomination form (1993), 4, 38–39; Wells and Dalton, *Virginia Architects*, 197–98; *Danville Register*, 17 March 1937, 4.

VIRGINIA HALL, VIRGINIA STATE UNIVERSITY, Ettrick, Chesterfield County
O'Dell, *Chesterfield County*, 56–57.

VIRGINIA MANUFACTORY OF ARMS/RICHMOND ARMORY, southern terminus of Seventh Street at the James River, Richmond
Elizabeth J. Barnett, "The Architecture of John Clarke (1766–1844), Richmond Industrialist and Amateur Architect" (master's thesis, Virginia Commonwealth University, forthcoming); Giles Cromwell, *The Virginia Manufactory of Arms* (Charlottesville, 1976), 24–30.

VIRGINIA MUSEUM (FIRST), Twelfth Street between Bank and G (now Grace) Streets, Richmond
R. Lewis Wright, "James Warrell, Artist and Entrepreneur," *Virginia Cavalcade* 22 (winter 1973), 9; *Richmond Commercial Register*, 6 June 1816; James Warrell to Charles Bird King, 15 July 1816, Virginia Historical Society; *Richmond Compiler*, 21 January 1820; Mutual Assurance Society of Virginia, policy r. 6, v. 55, Virginia Department of Historic Resources.

VIRGINIA STATE PENITENTIARY, Belvidere and Spring Streets, Richmond
Elizabeth J. Barnett, "The Architecture of John Clarke (1766–1844), Richmond Industrialist and Amateur Architect" (master's thesis, Virginia Commonwealth University, forthcoming); Stephanie Jacobe, "Albert L. West (1825–1892), Richmond Architect" (working title, master's thesis, Virginia Commonwealth University, forthcoming); Tom H. Ray, "Marion J. Dimmock (1842–1908), 'Dean of Richmond Architects'" (working title, master's thesis, Virginia Commonwealth University, forthcoming); Jeffrey A. Cohen and Charles E. Brownell, *The Architectural Drawings of Benjamin Henry Latrobe*, 2 vols. (New Haven, Conn., 1994), esp. 1:98–112; Richard Silverman, "Latrobe's Design for the Virginia Penitentiary" (master's thesis, University of Virginia, 1992); Brownell et al., *Making Virginia Architecture*, 71–73, 228–31; Harnsberger and Associates, "Virginia State Penitentiary," measured drawings, Ashley Robbins and Maria Isabel Beas, delineators, November 1991, Commonwealth Architects, Richmond; Talbot Hamlin, *Benjamin Henry Latrobe* (New York, 1955), esp. 120–26.

THE WASHINGTON LANCASTERIAN (FREE) SCHOOL, Washington Street, Alexandria
William M. S. Rasmussen and Robert S. Tilton, *George Washington: The Man Behind the Myths* (Charlottesville, 1999), 280; George Washington, Last Will and Testament, 9 July 1799, in *The Writings of George Washington*, ed. John C. Fitzpatrick, 37 vols. (Washington, D.C., 1931–40), 37:275–94; Washington to the trustees of the Alexandria Academy, 17 December 1785, in *The Papers of George Washington, Confederation Series*, ed. W. W. Abbot, 6 vols. (Charlottesville, 1993–97), 3:463–64; Ethelyn Cox, *Historic Alexandria, Virginia, Street by Street* (Alexandria, 1976), 182.

WILLIAMSBURG–JAMES CITY COURTHOUSE, Francis Street at South England Street, Williamsburg
"James City County Court House & Jail," drawings by Joseph E. Kenny and Singleton P. Moorehead, reviewed by Thomas Mott Shaw, 1931, Special Collections, John D. Rockefeller Library, Colonial Williamsburg Foundation; "East Flanking Building, Courthouse Group," drawings by Foster Townsend, Milton Grigg, and J. D., reviewed by Walter Macomber, 1931; "West Flanking Building, Courthouse Group," drawings by Grigg and Finlay Ferguson, Jr., checked by Macomber, 1931, both Department of Architecture and Engineering Files, Colonial Williamsburg Foundation; courthouse correspondence, Colonial Williamsburg Foundation Archives.

Chapter III – Lost Religious Architecture

AETZ CHAYIM SYNAGOGUE, 728 Wilson Street, Danville
Mary Cahill and Gary Grant, *Victorian Danville* (Danville, 1996), 102–4.

ALL SAINTS EPISCOPAL CHURCH (FIRST), Madison Street between Franklin and Grace Streets, Richmond
The [Richmond] State, 2 December 1887, 4; *Richmond News Leader*, 19 October 1935; All Saints Episcopal Church, *All Saints Church, Richmond, Virginia, from Christmas 1888 to Christmas 1903* (Richmond, 1904).

ALL SAINTS EPISCOPAL CHURCH (SECOND), 300 West Franklin Street, Richmond
Jennie Hughes, *All Saints Episcopal Church, Richmond, Virginia, 1888–1958* (Richmond, 1960), 1–3; All Saints Episcopal Church, *All Saints Church, Richmond, Virginia, from Christmas 1888 to Christmas 1903* (Richmond, 1904); All Saints Church (Protestant Episcopal), Henrico County, Va., Records, 1883–1983, Virginia Historical Society; John Montague Massengale and Robert A. M. Stern, *New York 1900: Metropolitan Architecture and Urbanism, 1890–1915* (New York, 1983), 113–16; Dalton and Wells, *Virginia Architects*, 20, 76–77; William H. Gaines, *A History of Grace and Holy Trinity Episcopal Church, 1858–1987* (Richmond, 1987), 15–19; Rachel M. Bradshaw, "Tiffany Windows in Richmond and Petersburg, Virginia" (master's thesis, Virginia Commonwealth University, 1997), 92–122.

BAPTIST CHURCH, East Nelson Street, Lexington
Lyle and Simpson, *Lexington*, 43–44.

BETH AHABAH SYNAGOGUE, Eleventh Street between Marshall and Clay Streets, Richmond
Minute Book of Congregation Beth Ahabah's Board of Managers Meetings, 1865–1880, Beth Ahabah Museum and Archives, 392, 419–20; Herbert T. Ezekiel and Gaston Lichtenstein, *The History of the Jews of Richmond* (Richmond, 1917), 258–72.

BETH SHALOME SYNAGOGUE, Mayo Street (east side) north of Franklin Street, Richmond
Minutes of Congregation Beth Shalome's Board of Managers, Beth Ahabah Museum and Archives, 59–63; "Re-opening of the Portuguese Synagogue," *Daily Dispatch*, 24 March 1866; "Local Matters, Interesting Service at Beth Shalom on Saturday," *Daily Dispatch*, 12 January 1874; Herbert T. Ezekiel and Gaston Lichtenstein, *The History of the Jews of Richmond* (Richmond, 1917), 236–57; Louis Ginsberg, *The Jews of Richmond* (Petersburg, 1969), 24–25.

BROAD STREET METHODIST CHURCH, 1000 East Broad Street, Richmond
Samuel Sloan, *City and Suburban Architecture* (New York, 1976), 89–91; Edward Leigh Pell, ed., *A Hundred Years of Richmond Methodism: The Story As Told at the Centennial Celebration of 1899* (Richmond, 1899); "Broad Street Methodist Church," vertical file, Valentine Museum; Stephanie Jacobe, "Albert L. West (1825–1892), Richmond Architect" (working title, master's thesis, Virginia Commonwealth University, forthcoming).

CHRIST EPISCOPAL CHURCH, block bounded by East Jefferson, Water Street, Second Street, NW, and First Street, Charlottesville
Lay, *Jefferson Country*, 160.

CHRIST EPISCOPAL CHURCH, East Freemason Street at Cumberland Street, Norfolk
Virginia Department of Historic Resources archives file, 122-04.

COURT STREET METHODIST CHURCH, Court and Seventh Streets, Lynchburg
Chambers, *Lynchburg*, 158–61.

EASTERN SHORE CHAPEL, London Bridge vicinity, Virginia Beach
Henry Irving Brock, *Colonial Churches in Virginia* (Richmond, 1930), 70; James Scott Rawlings, *Virginia's Colonial Churches* (Richmond, 1963), 15; Virginia Department of Historic Resources archives file, 134-09.

FIRST AFRICAN BAPTIST CHURCH, corner of College and Broad Streets, Richmond
"An Old Landmark," *Harper's Weekly*, 27 June 1874, 545; *Richmond Daily Dispatch*, 16 August 1876.

FIRST BAPTIST CHURCH, northeast corner of East Jefferson and Second Streets, Charlottesville
Lay, *Jefferson Country*, 207–8.

FIRST BAPTIST CHURCH, 407 North Jefferson Street, NW, Roanoke
Virginia Department of Historic Resources archives file, 128-37.

FIRST CHRISTIAN CHURCH, Main and Fifth Streets, Lynchburg
Chambers, *Lynchburg*, 383–85.

FIRST PRESBYTERIAN CHURCH, Tenth and Capitol Streets (dismantled and reconstructed 1884–85 at Grace and Madison Streets), Richmond
Dalton and Wells, *Virginia Architects*, 165–66; First Presbyterian Church Minutes, Morton W. Smith Library, Union Theological Seminary, Richmond; *The Presbyterian Magazine* (September 1853), 425–28; *Richmond Daily Dispatch*, 17 October 1853, 1.

GRACE STREET PRESBYTERIAN CHURCH, northwest corner of Grace and Fourth Streets, Richmond
Jack Abernathy, *Living Monument: The Story of Grace Covenant Presbyterian Church, 1790–1990* (Richmond, 1990), 7–8, 15; *Richmond Dispatch*, 8 August 1881 and 9 September 1881; *Richmond Times-Dispatch*, 28 September 1906.

HIGH STREET PRESBYTERIAN CHURCH, south side of High Street between Market and Davis Streets, Petersburg
History of Second Presbyterian Church, microfilm of W. S. Simpson scrapbook, Alderman Library, copy at McKenney Library, Petersburg.

MAPSICO EPISCOPAL CHURCH, Charles City vicinity, Charles City County
Telephone interview with Harrison R. Tyler, 18 September 2000; notes on Mapsico Church supplied by Sherry B. Tyler, Charles City Center for Local History, Charles City.

NORFOLK PRESBYTERIAN CHURCH, Catherine (now Bank) and Charlotte Streets
George D. Armstrong, *The Early History of the First Presbyterian Church of Norfolk* (manuscript, n.d.); Rev. Ellis O'Neal and William C. Wooldridge, *First Presbyterian Church Norfolk* (manuscript, 1996).

PACE MEMORIAL METHODIST CHURCH, 700 West Franklin Street, Richmond
Emily Gallup, ed., *Pace Memorial Methodist Church* (Richmond, 1977), n.p.; Pace Memorial Methodist Church, *Inside Your Church and Mine: Pace Memorial Methodist Church South* (n.p., 1934), 2–3; Donald Traser, "We Dedicate This Church—With a Hymn," *The Hymn* 46 (January 1995), 23–26; "Pace Memorial Methodist Church," vertical file, Valentine Museum.

PAYNE'S CHURCH, Ox Road, Fairfax County
Minutes of the Vestry of Truro Parish, Virginia 1732–1785 (Lorton, Va., 1974), 95–97; Rev. J. Nelson Barry, "Trinity Parish, Charles County, Maryland," *Maryland Historical Magazine* 1 (December 1906), 324–30; Waterman, *Mansions of Virginia*, 243–339; research files, Museum of Early Southern Decorative Arts, Winston- Salem, NC.

POPLAR GROVE CHURCH, Poplar Grove National Cemetery, off Vaughan Road south of Flank Road, Dinwiddie County
Olsen, "Poplar Grove National Cemetery History," 1954, on file at the Petersburg National Battlefield.

SECOND BAPTIST CHURCH, Main and Sixth Streets, Richmond
John S. Moore, *The History of Second Baptist Church, Richmond, Virginia 1820–1995* (Richmond, 1998), 34–35, 66, 72.

ST. ANDREW'S EPISCOPAL CHURCH, corner of Laurel and Beverley Streets, Oregon Hill, Richmond
William N. Glenn, *St. Andrew's Episcopal Church and Its Environs* (Richmond,1978); *Richmond News Leader*, 12 January 1949.

ST. JAMES'S EPISCOPAL CHURCH, Fifth and Marshall Streets, Richmond
Minor T. Weisiger, Donald R. Traser, and E. Randolph Trice, *Not Hearers Only: A History of St. James's Episcopal Church, Richmond, Virginia, 1835–1985* (Richmond, 1986), 5–16; Wells and Dalton, *Virginia Architects*; Scott, *Richmond Neighborhoods*, 226–29; *[Richmond] Daily Dispatch*, 13 November 1878.

ST. PAUL'S EPISCOPAL CHURCH, Seventh and Church Streets, Lynchburg
Chambers, *Lynchburg*, 161–67.

TABB STREET PRESBYTERIAN CHURCH, Tabb Street, Petersburg
Dulaney Ward, Jr., unpublished research.

ZION BAPTIST CHURCH, Crossroads, Albemarle County
Lay, *Jefferson Country*, 239.

Chapter IV – Lost Commercial Architecture

ALEXANDRIA SLAVE PENS (FRANKLIN AND ARMFIELD OFFICE), 1300
block of Duke Street, Alexandria
Alexandria Phenix Gazette, 12 December 1828; Calder Loth, ed., *Virginia Landmarks of
Black History* (Charlottesville, 1995), 70–81; Virginia Department of Historic Resources archives file, 100-105.

THE ALLEGHANY HOTEL, Goshen, Rockbridge County
Royster Lyle, Jr., "Rockbridge County's Boom Hotels," *Virginia Cavalcade* 20 (winter
1971), 4–13. For the Hotel Altemonte, see Brownell et al., *Making Virginia Architecture*, 314–15.

AMERICAN SAVINGS BANK, 116 Campbell Avenue West, Roanoke
George S. Jack and E. B. Jacobs, *History of Roanoke County; History of Roanoke City and
History of the Norfolk and Western Railway Company* (Roanoke, 1912), 133.

ATLANTIC HOTEL, Main, Granby, and Randolph Streets, Norfolk
Broadside, Virginia Historical Society; Betsy L. Fahlman, Beth N. Rossheim, David W.
Steadman, and Peter Stewart, *A Tricentennial Celebration: Norfolk 1682–1982* (Norfolk,
1982), 117–18.

BALTIMORE & OHIO RAILROAD/SOUTHERN RAILWAY DEPOT, Woodstock
Donald R. Traser, *Virginia Railway Depots* (Richmond, 1998), 20.

BOLLINGBROOK HOTEL (IMPERIAL HOTEL, STRATFORD HOTEL), north-
east corner of Bollingbrook and Second Streets, Petersburg
Edward Pollock, *Historical and Industrial Guide to Petersburg* (Petersburg, 1884); Edward A. Wyatt, *Along Petersburg Streets* (Richmond, 1943), 14; Edward A. Wyatt IV and
James G. Scott, *Petersburg's Story* (Richmond, 1960); *South Side Daily Democrat*, 1857;
Petersburg Daily Index, 1868–71; *Petersburg Daily Appeal*, 1872–73; *Petersburg Index &
Appeal*, 1874–75; *Rural Messenger*, 1875; City of Petersburg, Deed Book 8, 174, 175,
187 (1828); Land Tax Books, 1829; Mutual Assurance Society of Virginia, policies n.
3681 (1829); r. 10, v. 101, n. 10460 (1837); r. 18, v. 112, n. 13671 (1844); r. 20, v.
123, n. 16928 (1851), Library of Virginia.

BOLLINGBROOK STREET THEATRE ([THIRD] PETERSBURG THEATRE),
northeast corner of Bollingbrook and Phoenix Streets, Petersburg
C. A. Bingham, *Busby: The Regency Architect of Brighton & Hove* (1991); Wyatt, *Along
Petersburg Streets* (Richmond, 1943), 12–13; Wyatt and Scott, *Petersburg's Story* (Richmond, 1960); *South Side Daily Democrat*, 1854, 1855; *Petersburg Daily Express*, 1859,
1865; *The Press*, 1860, *Petersburg Index*, 1867; City of Petersburg, Deed Book 9, 105
(1832); Deed Book 10, 503 (1838); Deed Book 11, 430 (1840); Deed Book 13, 300
(1843); Deed Book 18, 387 (1850); Deed Book 20, 107 (1853); Deed Book 22, 534
(1855) and 536 (1855); Deed Book 25, 552 (1860); Deed Book 30, 70 (1867); Land
Tax Books, 1829–1835, 1850–1857, 1859, 1861.

BRANCH BANK OF THE UNITED STATES, Granby Street at College Place, Norfolk
Kenneth Hafertepe, "Banking Houses in the United States: The First Generation,
1781–1811," *Winterthur Portfolio* 35 (spring 2000), 1–52; Thomas C. Parramore with
Peter C. Stewart and Tommy L. Bogger, *Norfolk: The First Four Centuries*
(Charlottesville, 1994), 137; T. Harry Gatton, *Banking in Virginia* (Richmond, 1993),
1, 9; Jeffrey A. Cohen in *Drawing toward Building: Philadelphia Architectural Graphics,
1732–1986*, by James F. O'Gorman et al. (Philadelphia, 1986), 43–44 and nos. 6, 20–
21; Carroll Walker, *Norfolk: A Pictorial History from the "Those Were the Days" Collection*, ed. Linda G. Fates (Virginia Beach, 1975), 143; Louisa Venable Kyle, *Tidewater
Virginia in Years Gone By: A Pictorial History* (Norfolk, 1964), n.p.; Andrew Morrison,
ed., *Pictures in Maritime Dixie: Norfolk, Va., Port and City. The Chamber of Commerce
Book* (Norfolk, 1893), 50; B. Henry Latrobe to William Loughton Smith, 21 March
1804, in *The Correspondence and Miscellaneous Papers of Benjamin Henry Latrobe*, ed.
John C. Van Horne and others, 3 vols. (New Haven, Conn., 1984–88), 1:458–60;
Frederick Graff Papers, 76x138.2a-2i, Joseph Downs Collection of Manuscripts and
Printed Ephemera, Winterthur Library.

BYRD MILL, Louisa vicinity, Louisa County
William B. O'Neal, *Architecture in Virginia: An Official Guide to Four Centuries of
Building in the Old Dominion* (Richmond, 1968), 157; "Gristmill in Louisa Destroyed
by Fire," *Richmond Times-Dispatch*, 27 December 1968.

CASINO, Rivermont Park, Lynchburg
Chambers, *Lynchburg*, 395–96.

CENTURY THEATRE, southeast corner of Sycamore and Bank Streets, Petersburg
City of Petersburg, Deed Book 88, 268–69 (1916); Deed Book 91, 461 (1917); Deed
Book 95, 300 (1919); Deed Book 105, 381 (1923); Deed Book 112, 378 (1926); Deed
Book 117, 210 (1928); Deed Book 131, 419 (1936); Deed Book 134, 100 (1937);
Deed Book 304, 651 (1970); Land Tax Books, 1918–19.

CHAMBER OF COMMERCE BUILDING, Ninth and Main Streets, Richmond
American Architect and Building News, 27 June 1891; *The Manufacturer's Record*, 22
April 1892, 41; 1 July 1892, 45; *The [Richmond] State*, 4 September 1891, 4; 29 December 1893, 1; *Richmond Dispatch*, 29 December 1893; *Report of the Chamber of Commerce of Richmond, Virginia, 1891–1893* (Richmond, 1893); Edmond H. Brill, *History
of the Richmond Chamber of Commerce* (Richmond, 1967).

THE COLONNADE BUILDING AND WARM SPRINGS HOTEL, Warm Springs,
Bath County
Stan Cohen, *The Homestead and Warm Springs Valley, Virginia* (Charleston, W.Va.,
1984), 49–58; Marshall W. Fishwick, *Springlore in Virginia* (Bowling Green, Ohio,
1978), 138–39; James C. Kelly and William M. S. Rasmussen, *The Virginia Landscape:
A Cultural History* (Charlottesville, 2000), 63–64.

CONOCO SERVICE STATION, Richmond Road at Scotland Street, Williamsburg
"Service Station, Williamsburg, Virginia," drawings by R. H. Berglund, Continental Oil
Company, Engineering Department, 25 August 1939 and 22 September 1939, eleva-
tions by Singleton P. Moorehead, undated, copies in Special Collections, John D.
Rockefeller Library, Colonial Williamsburg Foundation; Conoco/Colonial
Williamsburg Foundation correspondence, 1939–40, "Architectural Requests," Colonial
Williamsburg Foundation Archives; Paul Buchanan, discussion with Edward A.
Chappell, 23 April 1980.

CRAWFORD HOUSE HOTEL, 450 Crawford Street, Portsmouth
Virginia Department of Historic Resources archives file, 124–26.

THE DEHART HOTEL, Lexington
Stuart Moore, "Greater Lexington—1890," *Rockbridge Historical Society Proceedings* 5
(1961), 70–79; Royster Lyle, Jr., "Rockbridge County's Boom Hotels," *Virginia Cavalcade* 20 (1971), 4–13.

DUNLOP MILLS, Manchester district, Richmond
Thomas S. Berry, "The Rise of Flour Milling in Richmond," *VMHB* 78 (1970), 387–
408; James K. Sanford, ed., *Richmond: Her Triumphs, Tragedies & Growth* (Richmond,
1975), 19–21; Virginius Dabney, *Richmond: The Story of a City* (Garden City, N.Y.,
1976), 62–63, 204, 352.

EARLY RETAIL STORES
Ann Smart Martin, "Commercial Space as Consumption Arena: Retail Stores in Early
Virginia," in *People, Power, Places: Perspectives in Vernacular Architecture, VIII*, ed. Sally
McMurry and Annmarie Adams (Knoxville, Tenn., 2000), 201–18.

EXCHANGE BANK, 1104 East Main Street, Richmond
Isaiah Rogers's journal, typescript copy, Valentine Museum; Scott, *Richmond Neighbor-
hoods*, 136; Charles Houston, "Declared Surplus: Historic Columns Fall on Evil Days,"
Richmond News Leader, 19 March 1959, in "Exchange Bank," file, Valentine Museum.

EXCHANGE HOTEL, southeast corner of Franklin and Fourteenth Streets, Richmond
Richmond Whig, 2 July 1841; Mutual Assurance Society of Virginia, policy n. 19579, v.
137, microfilm, Library of Virginia; "The Hotel's History: Reminiscences of the Old
Exchange Which Has Just Been Closed," *Richmond Dispatch*, 22 March 1896, in "Ex-
change Hotel," file, Valentine Museum; W. Asbury Christian, *Richmond: Her Past and
Present* (Richmond, 1912), 143–45, 152, 165, 197; Charles Dickens, *American Notes*
(New York, n.d.), 129–30; Scott, *Richmond Neighborhoods*, 129; Lane, *Architecture of
Virginia*, 183–84.

FAUQUIER WHITE SULPHUR SPRINGS HOTEL, on the Rappahannock River,
Warrenton and Opal vicinity, Fauquier County
Richmond Enquirer, 3 July 1835, 1; Frederick William Franck, "The Virginia Legislature
at the Fauquier Springs in 1849," *VMHB* 58 (1950), 67–83; Eugene M. Scheel, *The
Guide to Fauquier: A Survey of the Architecture and History of a Virginia County*
(Warrenton, Va., 1976), 11; James C. Kelly and William M. S. Rasmussen, *The Virginia
Landscape: A Cultural History* (Charlottesville, 2000), 61–62; Samuel Mordecai, *Descrip-
tion of the Album of Virginia* (Richmond, 1980 reprint of 1857 ed.), 29.

FIRST NATIONAL BANK, 503–7 King Street, Alexandria
Historic American Buildings Survey, VA-672; *Alexandria Gazette*, 15 April 1908.

FORD'S HOTEL (POWHATAN HOUSE), 1101 East Broad Street, Richmond
W. Asbury Christian, *Richmond, Her Past and Present*, (Richmond, 1912), 145, 160,
174; Robert Beverley Munford, Jr., *Richmond Homes and Memories* (Richmond, 1936),
115–16, 184.

FOREST LODGE, Mountain Road at the Richmond, Fredericksburg & Potomac track crossing, Glen Allen, Henrico County
Edwin J. Slipek, Jr., *Changing Landscape: Glen Allen, Mountain Road to Edge City, Glen Allen* (Glen Allen, 1999), 18–19.

THE GABLES HOTEL (formerly THE ELKTON), Elkton, Rockingham County
Larry R. Huffman, "There's a Small Hotel," *Harrisonburg Rockingham Historical Society Newsletter* 18 (winter 1996), n.p.

GALLEGO MILLS, Twelfth Street between Cary and Canal Streets (at the former James River and Kanawha Canal Turning Basin), Richmond
Thomas S. Berry, "The Rise of Flour Milling in Richmond," *VMHB* 78 (1970), 387–408; Samuel Mordecai, *Virginia, Especially Richmond, in By-Gone Days* (Richmond, 1946 reprint of 1860 2nd ed.), 328–30; James K. Sanford, ed., *Richmond, Her Triumphs, Tragedies & Growth* (Richmond, 1975), 19–21; Virginius Dabney, *Richmond: The Story of a City* (Garden City, N.Y., 1976), 62–63, 204, 352.

GOLDEN BALL TAVERN (RICHARD HANSON HOUSE), southeast corner of Old and Market Streets, Petersburg
Dulaney Ward, Jr., unpublished research.

GORDON INN (GORDON'S TAVERN), at the intersection of Routes 15, 33, and 231, Gordonsville, Orange County
Miller, *Antebellum Orange*, 41–42; William H. B. Thomas, *Gordonsville, Virginia: Historic Crossroads Town* (Verona, Va., 1971), 3–9; "Gordonsville Tavern," file, Orange County Historical Society.

GRAND PAVILION, YORKTOWN CENTENNIAL EXHIBITION, Yorktown
Brownell et al., *Making Virginia Architecture*, 310; Paul Rouse, "Yorktown Centennial Celebration: 1881 Extravaganza," *Virginia Cavalcade* 24 (autumn 1974), 80–87; *Report of the Commissioner for Vermont, upon the Yorktown Centennial Celebration* (Rutland, Vt., 1880), 1–13.

HALL, for the GRAND FOUNTAIN, UNITED ORDER OF TRUE REFORMERS, Fulton neighborhood, Richmond
Bryan Clark Green, "Daniel J. Farrar, Sr.," in *Biographical Dictionary of African American Architects, 1865–1945*, ed. Dreck Wilson (New York, forthcoming 2002); "D. J. Farrar," *[Richmond] Daily Planet*, 9 February 1895; "Prominent Builder and Contractor Is Laid to Rest," *[Richmond] Daily Planet*, 17 March 1923; obituary, *[Chicago] Defender*, 17 March 1923; Wells and Dalton, *Virginia Architects*, 137; W. P. Burrell and D. E. Johnson, *Twenty-Five Years History of the Grand Fountain of the United Order of True Reformers, 1881–1905* (Richmond, 1909), 30, 37, 97, 203; D. Webster Davis, *The Life and Public Services of William Washington Browne: Founder of the Grand Fountain U. O. of True Reformers and Organizer of the First Distinctive Negro Bank in America* (Philadelphia, 1910), 111–20; Peter J. Rachleff, *Black Labor in the South: Richmond, Virginia, 1865–1890* (Philadelphia, 1984), 154, 164; Luther Porter Jackson, *Negro Office Holders in Virginia, 1865–1895* (Norfolk, 1945), 57, 83.

HAXALL MILLS, southern terminus of Twelfth and Thirteenth Streets and part of what is now Browns Island, Richmond
Thomas S. Berry, "The Rise of Flour Milling in Richmond," *VMHB* 78 (1970), 387–498; Samuel Mordecai, *Virginia, Especially Richmond, in By-Gone Days* (Richmond, 1946 reprint of 1860 2nd ed.), 328–30; James K. Sanford, ed., *Richmond, Her Triumphs, Tragedies & Growth* (Richmond, 1975), 19–21; Virginius Dabney, *Richmond: The Story of a City* (Garden City, N.Y., 1976), 62–63, 204, 224, 248; Alexander Gardner, *Gardner's Photographic Sketch Book of the War* (Washington, D.C., 1866), n.p.

HOMESTEAD (FIRST), Hot Springs, Bath County
Samuel Mordecai, *Description of the Album of Virginia* (Richmond, 1980 reprint of 1857 ed.), 30; Stan Cohen, *The Homestead and Warm Springs Valley, Virginia* (Charleston, W.Va., 1984), 9–48; Marshall W. Fishwick, *Springlore in Virginia* (Bowling Green, Ohio, 1978), 128–49.

HOTEL CHAMBERLIN, Old Point Comfort, Hampton
Van Hawkins, *Hampton/Newport News: A Pictorial History* (Virginia Beach, 1975), 24–29; Winifred R. MacIntosh, "The Hotels of Old Point Comfort: A Material Culture Study" (master's thesis, College of William and Mary, 1990).

INTERMONT HOTEL, area of Fudge, Prospect, Highland, and Monroe Streets, Covington, Alleghany County
Horton P. Beirne, ed., *Historical Sketches by Gay Arritt* (Covington, Va., 1982), 104–8.

IRON FRONT BUILDING, west side of Sycamore Street just south of Tabb Street, Petersburg
Edward Pollock, *Historical and Industrial Guide to Petersburg* (1884), 49; *The [Petersburg] Press*, 10 February 1860, 12 April 1860; *[Petersburg] Daily Express*, 16 September 1859; City of Petersburg, Deed Book 25, 551 (1860); Deed Book 26, 543 (1862); Deed Book 26, 491 (1861); Deed Book 27, 334 (1863); Land Tax Books, 1859–64.

IRON GATE HOTEL, Iron Gate, Alleghany County
Horton P. Beirne, ed., *Historical Sketches by Gay Arritt* (Covington, Va., 1982), 54–55; communication from Mrs. Calvin P. Wright, Alleghany Historical Society, 29 September 2000.

JEFFERSON HOTEL, Court Square, Charlottesville
Lay, *Jefferson Country*, 170–72.

KENT, PAINE AND COMPANY HEADQUARTERS, Main Street between Eleventh and Twelfth Streets, Richmond
Mutual Assurance Society of Virginia, policies r. 14, v. 93; r. 22, v. 132, Library of Virginia; Samuel Mordecai, *Richmond in By-Gone Days* (Richmond, 1946 reprint of 1860 2nd ed.), 58.

LARKIN COMPANY PAVILION, JAMESTOWN TERCENTENNIAL EXPOSITION, Norfolk
Brownell et al., *Making Virginia Architecture*, 100; Richard Guy Wilson and Joseph Dye Lahendro, "Larkin Company Jamestown Exhibition Pavilion," *Frank Lloyd Wright Newsletter* 3 (1980), 9; Paul V. Turner, "Frank Lloyd Wright's Other Larkin Building," *Journal of the Society of Architectural Historians* 39 (1980), 394–96; Yukio Futagawa, ed., *Frank Lloyd Wright Monograph* (Toyko, 1987), 46; *The Official Blue Book of the Jamestown Ter-Centennial Exposition* (Norfolk, 1907), 505, 585.

LAW BUILDING, 807 Main Street, Lynchburg
Chambers, *Lynchburg*, 309–12.

MARSHALL HOUSE HOTEL, King and Pitt Streets, Alexandria
William Francis Smith and T. Michael Miller, *A Seaport Saga: Portrait of Old Alexandria, Virginia* (Norfolk, 1989), 85; *Alexandria Gazette*, 25 February 1873.

MECKLENBURG HOTEL AND SANITORIUM, Chase City, Mecklenburg County
Gerald Tate Gilliam, "The Mecklenburg Hotel in Chase City," *The Southsider* 17, no. 2 (1998), 28–30; Jeffrey St. John, *Landmarks 1765–1990: A Brief History of Mecklenburg County, Virginia* (Boydton, Va., 1990), 78–81.

MONTGOMERY WHITE SULPHUR SPRINGS, Blacksburg vicinity, Montgomery County
Samuel Mordecai, *Description of the Album of Virginia* (Richmond, 1980 reprint of 1857 ed.), 13; Dorothy H. Bodell, *Montgomery White Sulphur Springs: A History of the Resort, Hospital, Cemeteries, Markers, and Monument* (Blacksburg, Va., 1993); Marshall W. Fishwick, *Springlore in Virginia* (Bowling Green, Ohio, 1978), 225–37.

MONTICELLO HOTEL, Granby Street and City Hall Avenue, Norfolk
Betsy L. Fahlman, Beth N. Rossheim, David W. Steadman, and Peter Stewart, *A Tricentennial Celebration: Norfolk 1682–1982* (Norfolk, 1982), 117–18.

MOSS TOBACCO FACTORY, Clarksville, Mecklenburg County
Virginia Department of Historic Resources archives file, 192-13.

THE MOZART ACADEMY OF MUSIC, North Eighth Street between Franklin and Grace Streets, Richmond
Fifty Years in Richmond: 1898–1948 (Richmond, 1948), 19; Robert Beverley Munford, *Richmond Homes and Memories* (Richmond, 1936), 75; Robert P. Winthrop, *Architecture in Downtown Richmond* (Richmond, 1982), 18.

NEGRO BUILDING, JAMESTOWN TERCENTENNIAL EXPOSITION, Norfolk
Brownell et al., *Making Virginia Architecture*, 93; *The Official Blue Book of the Jamestown Ter-Centennial Exposition* (Norfolk, 1907), 675–78; Giles B. Jackson and D. Webster Davis, *The Industrial History of the Negro Race in the United States* (Richmond, 1908), 176.

OLD STONE WINDMILL, Winter Harbor, Mathews County
Mathews County Panorama: A Pictorial History of Mathews County, Virginia, 1791–1941 (Mathews County, Va., 1983), 83–84; *History and Progress, Mathews County, Virginia* (Mathews County, Va., 1982), 5–6; *The Miller in Eighteenth-Century Virginia* (Williamsburg, 1973), 9, 11; Forman, *The Virginia Eastern Shore*, 55, 70.

PEACOCK BALLROOM, SEASIDE PARK, Thirtieth to Thirty-third Streets, Virginia Beach
Virginia Beach Public Library, *The Beach: A History of Virginia Beach, Va.* (Virginia Beach, 1996); Joseph W. Dunn, Jr., and Barbara S. Lyle, *Virginia Beach: Wish You Were Here* (Norfolk, 1983).

PETERSBURG ACADEMY OF MUSIC, northeast corner of West Bank Street and St. Paul's Alley, Petersburg
Program of the Fifth Annual Music Festival; City of Petersburg, Deed Book 31, 319 (1868); Deed Book 34, 58–59 (1871); Deed Book 37, 539 (1876); Deed Book 48, 98 (1886); Deed Book 49, 302 (1887) and 685 (1888); Deed Book 55, 558 (1893); Deed

Book 59, 354 (1896) and 394 (1896); Land Tax Books, 1869–1872, 1874, 1876–1881, 1885–1888.

PETERSBURG LIBRARY HALL, Sycamore and Bollingbrook Streets, Petersburg
Dulaney Ward, Jr., unpublished research.

PRATT'S VIRGINIA SKY-LIGHT DAGUERREAN GALLERY, 145 East Main Street, Richmond
Elliot & Nye's Virginia Directory and Business Register for 1852 (Richmond, 1852), 54; Scott, *Richmond Neighborhoods*, 280; William A. Pratt [grandson of William Pratt], *History of Virginia: Virginia Biography* (Chicago and New York, 1924), 6:94–95.

PRINCESS ANNE HOTEL, Twenty-fourth Street and Oceanfront, Virginia Beach
Joseph W. Dunn, Jr., and Barbara S. Lyle, *Virginia Beach: Wish You Were Here* (Norfolk, 1983), 73–76.

PROVIDENCE FORGE MILL, Providence Forge, New Kent County
Historic American Buildings Survey, VA-110; Carl R. Lounsbury, ed., *An Illustrated Glossary of Early Southern Architecture and Landscape* (New York, 1994), 231.

RICHMOND & DANVILLE RAILROAD (LATER SOUTHERN RAILWAY) DE-POT, Leesburg
Donald R. Traser, *Virginia Railway Depots* (Richmond, 1998), 193; *The State*, 26 February 1881.

RIVERSIDE COTTON MILLS, MILL #6, in the block between the Main and Worsham Street bridges, along US Route 58 and the Dan River, Danville
Thomas Hargrove et al., "Dan River Basin Cultural Resources Study," submitted to the US Army Corps of Engineers, Wilmington District, by Archaeological Research Consultants, Inc. (Chapel Hill, N.C., 1981), 36–37, 58; Robert Sidney Smith, *Mill on the Dan: A History of Dan River Mills, 1882–1950* (Durham, N.C., 1960), 18–19.

THE ROCKBRIDGE HOTEL, Glasgow, Rockbridge County
Royster Lyle, Jr., "Rockbridge County's Boom Hotels," *Virginia Cavalcade* 20 (1971), 4–13.

ROGERS SHOP, Covington
Bucklen and Bucklen, *County Courthouses*, 5–6; William H. Gaines, Jr., "Courthouses of Alleghany County," *Virginia Cavalcade* 22 (1972), 4–9; Oren F. Morton, *A Centennial History of Alleghany County, Virginia* (Dayton, Va., 1923), 44.

ROMAN EAGLE MASONIC LODGE, southeast corner of Main Street at South Union, Danville
Art Work of Lynchburg and Danville, Virginia (Chicago, 1903), n.p.; Daniel Pezzoni, "Downtown Danville Historic District," National Register of Historic Places Inventory nomination form (1993), 3, 57; George W. Dame et al., *Historical Sketch of Roman Eagle Lodge* (Danville, 1939), 43, 126–30, 297–99; Jane Gray Hagan, *The Story of Danville* (New York, 1950), 121; Wells and Dalton, *Virginia Architects*, 294, 296.

SOUTHERN LITERARY MESSENGER BUILDING, 1501 East Main Street, Richmond
Virginius Dabney, *Richmond: The Story of a City* (Garden City, N.Y., 1976), 278–79; Scott, *Houses of Richmond*, 7–11.

SPENCER'S HOTEL (later THE COLONIAL INN), Duke of Gloucester and Queen Streets, Williamsburg Historic American Buildings Survey, VA-356; Parke Rouse, Jr., *Cows on the Campus: Williamsburg in Bygone Days* (Richmond, 1973), 74–76.

ST. LUKE PENNY SAVINGS BANK, southeast corner of Marshall and First Streets, Richmond
Thomas Tyler Potterfield, Jr., "Professor Charles T. Russell, 1875–1942: Virginia's Pioneer African-American Architect," unpublished research; C. T. Russell, "Experience Practical and Professional," "Charles T. Russell," unpublished essay in student file, Hampton University Archives.

TAVERNS
Historic American Buildings Survey, VA-312; Lay, *Jefferson Country*, 168–69; Carl R. Lounsbury, ed., *An Illustrated Glossary of Early Southern Architecture and Landscape* (New York, 1994), 369; William Francis Smith and T. Michael Miller, *A Seaport Saga: Portrait of Old Alexandria, Virginia* (Norfolk, 1989), 42.

TERMINAL STATION, Main Street, Norfolk
Donald R. Traser, *Virginia Railway Depots* (Richmond, 1998), 180–81.

TRUE REFORMERS HALL, 604 North Second Street, Richmond
W. P. Burrell and D. E. Johnson, *Twenty-Five Years History of the Grand Fountain of the United Order of True Reformers, 1881–1905* (Richmond, 1909), 30, 37, 97, 203; D. Webster Davis, *The Life and Public Services of William Washington Browne: Founder of*

the Grand Fountain U. O. of True Reformers and Organizer of the First Distinctive Negro Bank in America (Philadelphia, 1910), 117–20; David M. Fahey, *The Black Lodge in White America: "True Reformer" Browne and His Economic Strategy* (Dayton, Ohio, 1994), 1–5; Wells and Dalton, *Virginia Architects*, 33.

UNION HOTEL, Main and Nineteenth Streets, Richmond
Sarah Shields Driggs, "Otis Manson and Neoclassicism in Central Virginia" (master's thesis, University of Virginia, 1988), 28–36; Lane, *Architecture of Virginia*, 158, 200–201.

UNION STATION, Jefferson Street between Eighth and Ninth Streets, Lynchburg
Chambers, *Lynchburg*, 309–10.

WESTOVER HOTEL (later WESTOVER HALL, LYNCHBURG COLLEGE), West Lynchburg
Chambers, *Lynchburg*, 295–302.